OCR PSYCHOLOGY

for A Level & AS

Revision Guide

Cara Flanagan

Jock McGinty

Illuminate Publishing

Acknowledgements

The authors would like to express their appreciation to all of those people who have made this book possible and supported us during the long hours of work.

Number 1 is Rick Jackman, our publisher, who has been unswervingly enthusiastic and understanding, and is always a joy to work with. He has been supported at Illuminate Publishing by Clare Jackman and Peter Burton.

Our second big thanks goes to Nic Watson who has edited this book with great thoroughness, as always doing a superb job and with such passion. Another joy to work with.

Finally, our thanks to our design team. The original design comes from the meister artist Nigel Harriss who produced the beautiful plans for our spreads. Subsequently Stephanie White (Kamae Design) has implemented this design with enormous care and patience in order to fit everything onto each page.

And, of course, thank you to all the teachers and students reading this book.

The authors

Cara Flanagan writes, speaks and organises - she has written many books for A Level Psychology, and she speaks at and organises student conferences. She is senior editor of *Psychology Review*. In a previous life she was a teacher probably for more years than you have been alive and also an examiner for an equally long time. Her spare time (what there is of it) involves her husband and children (now adults), walking and pubs.

Jock McGinty is Head of Psychology and Head of Sixth Form at Watford Grammar School for Boys. He has taught Psychology for over 20 years and is a senior A Level examiner. He is currently Chair of the Association for the Teaching of Psychology. Away from psychology Jock spends his time dreaming of hitting golf balls and skiing.

Published in 2022 by Illuminate Publishing Limited, an imprint of Hodder Education, an Hachette UK Company, Carmelite House, 50 Victoria Embankment, London EC4Y 0DZ

Orders: Please visit www.illuminatepublishing.com or email sales@illuminatepublishing.com

British Library Cataloguing in Publication Data

A catalogue record for this book is available from the British Library.

ISBN 978-1-913963-24-8

Printed in the UK by Ashford Colour Press Ltd.

04.22

The publisher's policy is to use papers that are natural, renewable and recyclable products made from wood grown in sustainable forests. The logging and manufacturing processes are expected to conform to the environmental regulations of the country of origin.

Every effort has been made to contact copyright holders of material produced in this book. If notified, the publisher will be pleased to rectify any errors or omissions at the earliest opportunity.

Editor: Nic Watson

Design: Nigel Harriss

Layout: Stephanie White (Kamae Design)

Contents

 For a free download of suggested answers to the Exam-style questions visit www.illuminatepublishing.com/ocrpsych

The exam papers

Research methods

Component 1 (AS and AL)

- AS = 75 marks   AL = 90 marks
- AS = $1\frac{1}{2}$ hours   AL = 2 hours
- AS = 50% of total   AL = 30% of total

Psychological themes through core studies

Component 2 (AS and AL)

- AS = 75 marks   AL = 105 marks
- AS = $1\frac{1}{2}$ hours   AL = 2 hours
- AS = 50% of total   AL = 35% of total

Applied psychology

Component 3 (AL only)

- 105 marks
- 2 hours
- 35% of total A level

Exam-style question examples

The exam-style question examples throughout this book should help you identify many of the different ways that questions will be asked in the exam. Go to www.illuminatepublishing.com/ocrpsych for a free download of suggested answers.

The AOs indicate what skill is being assessed in any exam question. In some questions a mixture of skills are assessed.

Assessment objectives (AO)

Your exam answers are assessed in terms of three assessment objectives:

AO1 Demonstrate knowledge and understanding of scientific ideas, processes, techniques and procedures.

AO2 Apply knowledge and understanding of scientific ideas, processes, techniques and procedures.

AO3 Analyse, interpret and evaluate scientific information, ideas and evidence.

How do you know which AO?

The command word in a question tells you which skill to use.

The list below explains the most commonly used command words.

AO1 command words	Identify	Name, select or recognise.	The command word tells you what to do, but the number of marks is equally important. As a general rule write one point for each mark available (one point is sometimes just one sentence, or one line in the exam booklet. But sometimes one word is enough and at other times you need more than one sentence/line for a point).
	Give	Produce an answer from a given source or memory.	
	Define / What is meant by	Give the meaning of.	
	Outline	Concentrate on the main points of the topic.	
	Describe	Give a detailed account of your knowledge and understanding.	
	Explain	Describe, giving reasons and causes.	
	Justify	Give reasons for a view or idea.	
	Suggest	Provide advice based on the information supplied in the source or question.	
AO2 command words	Use ... to explain	Provide the main points from a source or topic, and then give reasons and causes.	
AO3 command words	Evaluate	Give an opinion by exploring the strengths and weaknesses.	
	Analyse	Separate information into components and identify their characteristics. Discuss the strengths and weaknesses of a topic or argument and make reasoned comments.	
	Compare	Show the similarities and differences between two or more topics.	
	Assess	Make an informed judgement.	
	Discuss	Explore a topic by describing it (AO1) and looking at the strengths and weaknesses.	

The front page

The front page of the exam paper contains the following information:

INSTRUCTIONS

- Use black ink.
- Answer **all** the questions.
- Write your answer to each question in the space provided. If additional space is required, use the lined page(s) at the end of this booklet. The question number(s) must be clearly shown.

INFORMATION

- The total mark for this paper is XXX.
- The marks for each question are shown in brackets [ ].
- Quality of extended responses will be assessed in questions marked with an asterisk (*).
- This document consists of XXX pages.

Component 1 Research methods also states:

You must have:

- A scientific or graphical calculator.

Some of the content varies, e.g. Component 3 wouldn't say 'Answer **all** the questions'.

'Quality of extended responses'

The mark schemes for questions worth 10 or more marks credit your ability to construct and develop a sustained and coherent line of reasoning in your answer.

- *'Sustained' means you do it repeatedly using different arguments (not just once or twice).*

- *'Coherent' means your arguments stick together.*

You can improve the quality of your response by using connecting words or phrases (e.g. 'similarly' and 'despite the previous argument').

The examiner

There isn't just one examiner - there are thousands of examiners. They are all experienced teachers of psychology who sit at home and usually mark your exam papers online.

Components 1 and 2

For Components 1 and 2 your answers are clipped, i.e. they are electronically cut up and sent to examiners to be marked. This means that the examiner only sees one particular answer at a time. Therefore, if you write in the margins or continue an answer somewhere else, the examiner won't see this. The papers are checked for writing in the margins, but it's better to be safe.

This online system of marking is very fair because it means that, for Components 1 and 2, different questions are marked by different examiners so you can't be penalised by one slightly harsher examiner.

In addition, the fact that the marking is done online means senior examiners can regularly check the marking.

Component 3

For Component 3, one examiner marks your whole paper, and a senior examiner checks a sample of the examiner's work.

Don't forget to take your calculator into the Research methods exam!

Make it easier for the examiner

Examiners want to give you marks, honestly. But you have to 'play the game':

- **Don't write too much or too little** Write an appropriate amount for the marks available. You have just over a minute per mark. A useful rule is to write about 20-25 words per mark which allows you important thinking time as well.

- **Short-answer questions** If a question is worth 3 marks, write three sentences, each of which should be worth 1 mark.

- **Long-answer questions** Set your response out clearly ... but what does 'clearly' mean? For example, use sentence starters to signpost your answer to the examiner, such as, 'A strength of the social area is ...', 'This is a weakness because ...', 'An example of this is ...', 'This suggests that...'.

Also, clarity is improved in long answers by using lots of paragraphs, so the examiner can see each point you are making.

Make the examiner's life as easy as possible and get them on your side!

Component 1 (AS and A Level)
Research methods (H167/01 and H567/01)

Exam section	Type of question	Example question	Advice
Section A: Multiple choice questions 20 marks	1-mark multiple choice AO1 AO2 AO3	In Casey *et al.*'s second experiment, what sampling technique was used? **A** opportunity **B** self-selected **C** snowball **D** random　　　　　　[1]	Start by reading the question and thinking what the answer might be. Now look at the answers and dismiss any answers you are certain are wrong. Narrowing down the possibilities will help you be certain.
Section B: Research design and response 35 marks This section (and Section C) begins with a 'novel source' – a description of some research that will be new to you. The themes for questions will be the planning and design of research, the evaluation of research and improvements to research.	Short-answer AO1	Write an appropriate research aim for this study.　　　　　[2] Write a one-tailed alternative hypothesis for this study.　　[3]	For 3 marks, include three elements, e.g. (1) state both conditions of the IV, (2) state how the DV is operationalised, (3) make sure the hypothesis is directional.
	Short-answer AO3	Describe **one** weakness of using the correlation technique in this study.　　　　　　　　　[3] Give **one** strength of using time sampling in this study.　　[3]	To structure evaluation points use PEC (or PEEC, see page 11). So, for 3 marks: (P) state your critical POINT. (E) provide context with EXAMPLES from the study. (C) draw a CONCLUSION explaining what the criticism means.
	Improving research AO3	Explain how you could reduce the possibility of social desirability bias in this study.　　　　[4]	For 2 marks, explain the concept (e.g. social desirability bias) and for 2 marks give examples from the study to support your explanation.
	'Design a study' question AO2 *Note:* *In the AL exam there are four bullet points (RFs).* *In the AS exam there are only three bullet points (RFs) and 12 marks.*	Explain how you would use self-report to investigate study habits. Justify your decisions as part of your explanation. You must refer to: ● the sample ● your questionnaire ● open and closed questions ● semantic differential rating scale questions. You should use your own experience of practical activities to inform your response.　　　　[15 for AL]	Ensure you address all required features (RFs). Each RF requires you to do four things: 1. Provide a detailed account of how you would carry out the study for the RF. 2. Provide a reason why you would use the RF. 3. Put the RF in context. 4. Make explicit reference to your own experiences doing practical work for the RF.
Section C: Data analysis and interpretation 35 marks Analyse and interpret novel data or a piece of hypothetical research using descriptive and/or inferential statistics.	Short-answer AO1	Identify **two** findings from the data presented in this graph.　　[4]	Only use data that is given in the novel source.
	Short-answer AO3	Outline **one** strength of the data collected in this study.　　[3] Write **one** conclusion based on your calculation of the mean.　[3]	Make sure you refer to the context of the study when a question includes the phrase 'in this study'.

Exam section	Type of question	Example question	Advice
Section A: Core studies 35 marks	Short-answer AO1	Outline the sample in Grant *et al.*'s study. **[2]**	It is important to provide details. In this question you could include the number of participants, gender, age, occupation.
	Short-answer AO2	Explain why Chaney *et al.*'s study can be placed in the developmental area. **[3]**	You must show knowledge of the area of psychology and give a reason why this links to the core study (using a result or conclusion from the study).
Section B: Areas, perspectives and debates 35 marks One parted question relating the core studies to areas, perspectives and debates. *Long-answer questions = questions worth 10 or more marks.*	Short-answer AO3	Suggest **one** weakness of the type of data collected in Grant *et al.*'s study. **[3]**	Use PEC (see facing page).
	Comparison questions AO1 AO3	Compare the individual differences area with the behaviourist perspective. Support your answer with examples from relevant core studies. **[6]** Outline **one** similarity and **one** difference between the cognitive area and the psychodynamic perspective. Support your answer with examples from relevant core studies. **[8]**	The best way to structure your answer to a compare (or similarity/difference) question is to make two points (either similarities or differences) between the named areas and/or perspectives. For each point: • Identify the similarity/difference. • Explain or elaborate the similarity/difference. • Then support each similarity/difference with relevant evidence from two appropriate core studies highlighting how they are similar/different.
	Long-answer discuss/evaluate question AO3	Evaluate the extent to which psychological research can be considered scientific. Use examples from the biological area to support your answer. **[10 AS or AL]** Discuss the free will/determinism debate in psychology. Use examples from appropriate research to support your answer. **[12 AS] or [15 AL]**	• For a 10-mark question, make three points and use PEC to structure each evaluation point. • For either a 12- or 15-mark question, three points is perfectly adequate. • The examples (E) in each critical point may be specified in the exam question. For example, in the 10-mark question on the left the examples must come from the biological area.
Section C: Practical applications 35 marks Requires learners to analyse and interpret novel data or a piece of hypothetical research using descriptive and/or inferential statistics.	Short-answer AO2	[Stem for this question might be a newspaper or magazine article or a blog or diary entry.] Identify **two** psychological issues raised by the article. Support your answer with evidence from the article. **[6]** Write **one** conclusion based on your calculation of the mean in this study. **[3]**	For each issue: 1. Identify the issue. 2. Explain the issue. 3. Provide specific detail from the article that supports the link between your issue and the article.

Component 3 (A Level only)
Applied psychology (H167/03 and H567/03)

Exam section	Type of question	Example question	Advice
Section A: Issues in mental health 35 marks	Short-answer AO1	Outline how Szasz (2011) defends his view that there is no such thing as mental illness. **[4]**	Identify two reasons and, for each one, give an explanation.
	Short-answer AO2	Describe a biological treatment for **one** specific disorder. **[5]** Explain how a biological treatment can contribute to the success of the economy and society. **[4]**	Two aspects to your answer: • Provide a detailed description (e.g. of one biological treatment). • Place that description in the context of the question (e.g. one specific and named disorder).
	Short-answer AO1 AO3	Discuss social sensitivity in the Gottesman *et al.* (2010) study. **[6]** Discuss **one** strength and **one** weakness of a non-biological treatment of one specific disorder. **[5]**	It is best to do just two evaluation points (too many points means not enough time for explanation). For each evaluation point, follow PEC (see facing page).
	Long- answer AO1 AO3	To what extent do medical model explanations support the nature side of the nature/nurture debate? **[10]**	'To what extent' requires you to make an informed judgement using key research to support your answer. Consider alternative points of view.
Section B: Options **70 marks** Questions on the Applied options. In each option there is one parted question containing three longer answer questions (parts a, b and c). Choose **two** options and answer **all** parts of the question in the options you have chosen: • Option 1 - Child psychology (35 marks) • Option 2 - Criminal psychology (35 marks) • Option 3 - Environmental psychology (35 marks) • Option 4 - Sport and exercise psychology (35 marks)	Part (a) questions AO1 AO2	Option 1 example: Using the key research by Johnson and Young (2002), explain how television advertising can affect children. **[10]** Option 4 example: Outline the key research by Kroll and Crenshaw (1970) and use it to explain personality in sport. **[10]**	Two aspects to your answer: • Detailed summary of the study, for 5 marks. • Application, for 5 marks. Note: You should write more for the detailed summary because of the requirement for detail.
	Part (b) questions AO1 AO3	Option 2 example: Discuss methodological issues in relation to the collection and processing of forensic evidence. **[15]** Option 3 example: Evaluate the validity of research into territory and personal space in the workplace. **[15]**	Three aspects to your answer: • 2 marks for outlining the debate/issue named. • About 10 marks for three evaluation points (PEC), elaborated using the key research. • About 3 marks for making comparisons between the key research and the background research.
	Part (c) questions AO2	Option 3 example: [Stem] Ajaz lives next door to a family with children learning to play brass musical instruments. [Question] Outline **one** strategy Ajaz could use to cope with the stress he feels when hearing the brass instruments. **[10]**	• Your answer must contain a detailed description of an application. • At the same time, you must focus on applying this description to the stem. To do this keep including words/phrases from the stem.

Create revision cards

For the **description** part of your revision card:	Consider revising for questions on the social area, e.g. Outline the principles of the social area = 2 marks.
	For 2 marks, you need two points + elaboration for each.
	• Record a 'trigger' word in the left-hand column of each row.
	• Record about 20 words in the right-hand column of each row (making 40 words which is about right for 2 marks).

Trigger	Description
others	The social area is about understanding people's interactions with **others** and the effect of **other** people on our behaviour, whether they are present or not.
ethics	The social area has a duty to consider **ethics** because social investigations often try to influence participants' behaviour without the participants knowing.

For the **evaluation** part:	For each evaluation point, you need to be able to prepare the elaboration using the PEC rule (see pages 6 and 11).
	• Record a trigger word in the left-hand column.
	• Add an example and/or explanation, and a conclusion at the end.
	• A well-elaborated evaluation point should be about 60 words.

Trigger		Description
P	students	In the Bocchiaro *et al.* study the sample were all **students** which is a limitation.
E	protesting	For example, students are probably more likely to be proactive in **protesting** about unfair practices than older adults. This would mean that they may be more likely to be willing to be disobedient and blow the whistle.
C	bias	Therefore, this creates a sampling **bias** because the sample distorts the results.

Practise

Rehearse the content.	Cover up the right-hand column and try to recall what is there using the trigger phrase.
Rehearse the trigger phrases.	When you are sitting on the bus or doing any mindless task, see if you can remember all the trigger phrases for one topic.
Practise writing timed answers.	1. Write down trigger words before you start (= thinking time).
	2. Give yourself $1\frac{1}{2}$ minutes per mark of writing time – set a timer when you start.

Don't learn too much.

If you attempt to learn too much you will just try to squeeze it into the exam and you don't have time.

Focus on fewer points and make sure you can explain them in detail and can apply them – that is where the marks are.

Being world class means practising world class!

Reward

Don't forget to give yourself a reward for practising hard!

On this spread, we look at the skills you require to succeed in the exam - having the expertise to describe (AO1), apply (AO2) and/or evaluate (AO3) your knowledge of psychological concepts, theories and research.

Expert description (AO1) DETAIL

To produce top-class description you need to understand the concept of *detail*. The term 'detail' refers to specific pieces of information. You don't have to write lots. In fact, you should write less but include *specific bits* of information, e.g. specialist terms, researchers' names, percentages etc. that provide detailed meaning. For example:

- This is good → Chaney *et al.* (2004) showed how adherence to medical regimes can be changed using a Funhaler. (16 words)
- This isn't good → One study looked at how children coped better with their medical problems using a different method. (16 words)

The first example is more detailed than the first though they are both the same length.

An expert AO1 exam answer also needs to be accurate and have clarity.	**What is accuracy?** *Accuracy* refers to being correct. You are not necessarily penalised for inaccuracy but you should avoid muddled or confused answers. **What is clarity?** One useful way to ensure *clarity* is to always try to explain what you have just written so the examiner understands what you mean. State your point and then give an example to clarify what you mean.

Expert application (AO2) EXPLICIT

Applying core studies to a theme or area

A good way to do this is to use specific terminology from studies, themes or areas - in this way, you provide *explicit* context. For example:

[Question] Explain why Casey *et al.*'s (2011) study is placed in the biological area. [2]

- This is good → Casey *et al.* links to the biological area as they look at parts of the brain. They showed how reward centres (e.g. ventral striatum) linked to impulse control and delay of gratification. (32 words)
- This isn't good → Casey *et al.* links to the biological area because it involved understanding the brain. They looked at how people are high and low delayers and how it helps them control their behaviour. (32 words)

Applying research methods

Research methods questions often begin with a 'stem' followed by questions that end 'in this study', indicating that you must apply your knowledge to the study. For example:

[Stem] A psychologist wanted to use the observation method to investigate the behaviour of young people in coffee shops.

[Question] Outline how the psychologist could use event sampling in this study. [2]

- This is good → Event sampling could be used by drawing up a list of behavioural categories we might expect to see in a coffee shop and counting every time the young people show each behaviour (e.g. drinking coffee) in a specified time period. (40 words)
- This isn't good → Event sampling in this study could involve drawing up a detailed list of various categories that would be relevant and then two researchers would count every time each behaviour occurs in a specified time period. Using two people ensures accuracy. (40 words)

The study was an experiment.

There were 45 participants.

A strength is the sample was representative.

A weakness is there were ethical issues.

List-like exam answers are bad. It's actually quite easy to list lots of points, but providing detail and explaining the points is the challenge.

'But I wrote loads'

Just because you have written loads in an exam answer doesn't mean you will get high marks.

Students who write a long answer often end up with a low grade overall because ...

- *Long essays tend to ramble and much of what is there is not relevant to the question.*
- *Long lists of studies and lists of evaluation points don't get high marks because they lack the detail and elaboration required for high marks.*
- *Long essays are often very descriptive and there are never more than 5 marks for description.*
- *Spending too much time on one question means less time available for other questions.*

Where's the detail?

Introduction

Expert evaluation (AO3) EFFECTIVE

Top-class AO3 needs elaboration to make the point effective. Use PEC or PEEC. For example:

Give **one** strength of the Simons and Chabris study into inattentional blindness. **[2]**

1. **Beginner level**: State your **POINT (P)**: One limitation is ... This theory is supported by ... One strength is ....

2. **Intermediate level**: Add some context/**EXAMPLE (E)**:
   - This is good → One strength is there was a high control of variables because they all used the same videos that were the same length. (22 words)
   - This isn't good → One strength is that there was a high control of variables because of the way they designed their study to be controlled. (22 words)

   The second example is generic - it could be used as a strength for any study.

   Context is king.

3. **Higher level**: Add further **EXPLANATION (E)** to make the point thorough:
   - One strength ... videos that were the same length. This prevents extraneous variables affecting the independent variable. (This adds 8 words)

4. **Finish** with a **CONCLUSION (C)**, e.g. 'This shows/means that ...':
   - ... This means that the study will have higher internal validity. (This adds 10 words, total = 40 words)

If you find higher level difficult, then just do intermediate. In a 15-mark Applied psychology essay (extended response), there are 13 marks for AO3: four intermediate-level evaluations (PEC) should be sufficient or three higher-level (PEEC) evaluations.

Whatever you do, AVOID a list of beginner-level criticisms with no context.

Understanding generic mark descriptors

The descriptors in the table below show the basic principles of how all exam answers are marked. Check the OCR website for the latest mark schemes.

For example, for a good mark your task is to understand what you have to do to produce *detailed* description (see facing page), *explicit* application (see facing page) and *effective* evaluation (see above).

Descriptor	AO1 Knowledge and understanding	AO2 Application	AO3 Analysis, interpretation and/or evaluation
Good	Good, relevant, accurate, *detailed*.	*Explicit*, accurate, relevant.	Mainly relevant, valid and *effective* conclusions, highly skilled argument.
Reasonable	Reasonable, generally accurate, lacking some *detail*.	Partially *explicit*, accurate, relevant.	Partially relevant, valid and *effective* conclusions, reasonable argument.
Limited	Limited, lacking *detail*.	May be related to general topic area rather than specific question.	Analysis etc. may be related to the question, some valid conclusions.
Basic	Basic, partially relevant, no *detail*.	Lacking in focus.	Analysis etc. not related to the question, basic conclusions.

Context is king.

Good evaluation points must have **CONTEXT** *(e.g. evidence) to be effective. They also should be well-elaborated/ explained.*

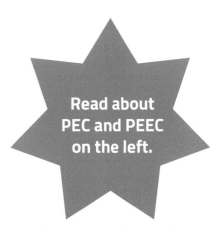

Read about PEC and PEEC on the left.

On the next two spreads we use the mark scheme on the left to assess some student answers, to show you what goes on in examiners' minds when they are marking.

Understanding marking
Short-answer questions

Question from Component 1: Outline what is meant by a semi-structured interview. [2] Answer: *A semi-structured interview involves a researcher putting questions to a participant in real time. A key feature of this is that some questions are prepared already by the interviewer and others are made up during the interview depending on the participant's responses.* (42 words)	**Examiner comments** 2 out of 2 AO1 marks A relevant, accurate and detailed outline because it explains what an interview is and how a semi-structured interview is different from other types of interview (questions are a mix of being predetermined and arising spontaneously during the interview).
Question from Component 1: Write an alternative one-tailed correlational hypothesis for this study. [3] Answer: *When a person measures their character strengths using a questionnaire and their psychology test percentage at the end of term, both variables will go up.* (25 words)	1 out of 3 AO2 marks An alternative hypothesis is stated but the wording is unclear. There is reference to both variables, but only one is operationalised. There is 1 mark for stating a positive/negative correlation and there would have been a further 2 marks if both variables were fully operationalised. We have said you should write about 20-25 words per mark (page 5) but some questions don't require as much. Even a fully operationalised hypothesis would not need 60 words. There are no 'one size fits all' rules.
Question from Component 2: Describe the sampling technique in Milgram's study. [2] Answer: *Milgram used a sample of people in his study who responded to a newspaper advert asking for people to take part in a study about memory and learning. They were told they would be paid $4 for taking part, which was a lot of money then.* (46 words)	1 out of 2 AO1 marks An accurate answer but lacking detail. The sample has been described but not named (i.e. 'self-selected sampling') - an important detail. Other details have been included (e.g. how much they were paid) but those details are not relevant here.
Question from Component 2: Describe one difference between Kohlberg's study on moral development and Lee *et al.*'s study on truth-telling. [3] Answer: *One difference between the two studies is the research design. For example, in his study, Kohlberg uses a longitudinal design which meant that he carried it out over a long period of time (the study lasted for 12 years). Lee et al. also conducted a study about moral development. Their research design measured truth-telling using a 7-point scale with Chinese and Canadian children and found that being in a Chinese culture affects moral development.* (74 words)	2 out of 3 AO3 marks The evaluation is reasonable, generally accurate but lacking some detail. A difference has been identified (type of research design). Context related to research design has been provided in reasonable detail from the Kohlberg study. However, the detail from the Lee *et al.* study is not relevant - there are details about the sample and how truth-telling was measured but these are not relevant details. You must compare like with like, in this case the point is that Lee *et al.* did a cross-sectional study - they tested participants at different ages but did it at one point in time. It's like saying the difference between oranges and apples is that oranges are juicy but apples cost a lot.
Question from Component 3: Outline a biological treatment of one specific disorder. [5] Answer: *Electroconvulsive therapy (ECT) is a biological treatment for depression. It involves electrodes being placed on a patient's head and passing an electric current through the patient's brain. The current causes a seizure that can last for about a minute. The patient cannot feel anything during the procedure. The patient usually undergoes a few ECT sessions so that any treatment lasts for a good period of time.* *ECT is used because it works quickly and effectively and so this is a strength but a weakness is that it causes side effects.* (90 words)	2 out of 5 AO2 marks Application of knowledge is basic - the disorder has been named but beyond that there is no attempt to apply the treatment to the disorder itself. The first paragraph contains a detailed description of how ECT works. This description is worth some credit, but the question requires candidates to show *how* ECT is used to treat one disorder. For example, a candidate might write that the blood flow to the areas of the brain linked to depression (e.g. limbic system) is stimulated by the ECT activity. As often as possible you should link your knowledge to the specific disorder. The second paragraph offers evaluation which is not relevant to this question and not creditworthy.

Question from Component 2 (AO1+AO3): Discuss the strengths and weaknesses of the biological area. Use examples from appropriate core studies to support your answer. [12]

Answer: *A strength of the biological area is that it uses specialist scientific equipment that can be used to measure behaviour very precisely. This is a strength because it produces quantitative data that is objective, for example in the study by Casey et al., high- and low-delayer participants' brains were scanned during the tasks using fMRI scans to relate delay of gratification to activity in certain brain structures such as the right inferior frontal cortex. This means that research into the biological area is likely to be valid as it provides an accurate representation of people's brains while they are resisting impulses.*

Another strength of the biological area is that it supports the nature side of the nature/nurture debate in psychology. The nature argument focuses on innate explanations for behaviour such as genes and our physiology and biological psychology presents the brain and body as determined by genes. This provides a counterargument to the nurture side of the nature/nurture debate. The nurture argument on the other hand tries to explain our behaviour through learning from experiences and the environment around us.

A weakness is that the biological area is known for taking a very reductionist approach. Reductionism is where complex behaviours are broken down into more simple explanations. The focus of biological psychology is on biological and physical processes, for example in Sperry's study on split brains, he suggests that lateralisation of function is reduced solely to differences in brain structure rather than other factors such as experience. This suggests that the biological area provides a limited explanation of human behaviour and this means that it supports the reductionist side of the reductionism/holism debate. (275 words)

Examiner comments

10 out of 12 marks (an A* answer)

Paragraph 1: The value of using objective scientific equipment (fMRI scans) is a relevant point. The use of the scans is then explained, ending with a conclusion about why this is a strength. The example uses specific terminology (detail) from the core study. This paragraph fits the descriptors for 'good' (see levels mark scheme below).

Paragraph 2: Partially relevant, but there is no example provided from a core study to support the nature argument, e.g. Sperry and regions of the brain could be used. On the other hand there is a reasonable argument explaining how the biological area supports the nature position. This paragraph fits the descriptors for 'reasonable'.

Paragraph 3: Good and relevant knowledge is presented and the example is accurate and detailed. Analysis of the point of criticism is relevant with effective conclusions. This paragraph fits the descriptors for 'good'.

Overall, there is analysis of the topic by describing it and looking at the strengths and weaknesses. Knowledge and understanding is good, relevant and detailed. Analysis is partially relevant with reasonable arguments.

How to mark

The overall mark is determined by selecting the descriptors (in the table on the right) that best represent what the student has written.

STEP 1 AO1

Overall, what descriptor on the right best describes the AO1 content of this answer? Is it 'Good, relevant, accurate, detailed' or 'Reasonable, generally accurate, lacking some detail'?

We feel it is 'Good, relevant, accurate, detailed' but there are elements of the row below. So, we placed our tick in the middle of the first row.

STEP 2 AO3

Do the same for the analysis in this answer – identify the best fit descriptor and then decide where in the box to place your tick.

We placed it near the top of the second row.

STEP 3 The final mark

On balance the mark for this answer would be at the bottom of the first row, i.e. 10 marks.

The levels mark scheme

Level of response	AO1 Knowledge and understanding		AO3 Analysis, interpretation and/or evaluation	
Good 10-12 marks	Good, relevant, accurate, *detailed*.	✓	Mainly relevant, valid and *effective* conclusions, highly skilled argument.	
Reasonable 7-9 marks	Reasonable, generally accurate, lacking some *detail*.		Partially relevant, valid and *effective* conclusions, reasonable argument.	✓
Limited 4-6 marks	Limited, lacking *detail*.		Analysis etc. may be related to the question, some valid conclusions.	
Basic 1-3 marks	Basic, partially relevant, no *detail*.		Analysis etc. not related to the question, basic conclusions.	

Check the OCR website for the latest mark schemes as these do change. Mark schemes also vary slightly from one question to another.

Understanding marking

Long-answer questions

Question from Component 2 (AO1+ AO3): Discuss ethical considerations in relation to the individual differences area. Use examples from relevant core studies to support your answer. [12]

Answer: *One ethical consideration that is relevant is that of informed consent. This means that participants in a study know what is going on so they can decide if they want to participate. So for instance, Freud should have asked Little Hans if he was happy to be involved in his study, but because Hans was only 5, Freud decided to ask his dad instead. Hans's dad made an actual diary of everything that happened in Hans's family life, for example when his sister was born. This is different from Baron-Cohen's study because the participants knew that the study was about reading emotions from people's eyes and they agreed to take part. This was a quasi-experiment with 3 groups that answered a questionnaire about whether people could tell what other people were thinking in magazine photographs. So, I think that the ethics of studies into the area of individual differences is good. However, participants from Baron-Cohen's study might have found it difficult to understand what the study was really about.*

Another ethical point is that of protection from harm which means that participants are not harmed physically or psychologically. This also means that psychologists can't always judge this before a study begins. Little Hans did not come to any physical harm as he only answered his dad's questions. Also, in Baron-Cohen, the participants might have found it difficult to find a job if it was discovered that they scored badly on the test. This is because people find it hard to tell what others are thinking.

Protection from harm also means that participants are not upset when they are carrying out the tasks given to them by psychologists. The reasons why psychologists don't want to upset participants is that they want to be able to use them again in future research. (302 words)

Examiner comments

5 out of 12 marks (probably a Grade D)

Paragraph 1: A relevant point (informed consent) is discussed. However, the example from Freud is not wholly correct - Hans's father presented the case to Freud thus tacitly supplying informed consent. Since Hans was very young, informed consent from him might not be regarded as necessary. The example from Baron-Cohen *et al.*'s study is not made relevant - there is brief reference to informed consent ('the participants knew that the study was about ...') but the remaining information is irrelevant. Overall knowledge and understanding lacks some detail (i.e. 'limited'). Analysis, in the form of conclusions, is mainly 'basic' (e.g. 'ethics of studies into the area of individual differences is good'). The first paragraph fits the descriptors for 'limited'.

Paragraph 2: A relevant point about protection from harm is highlighted, but the example from Freud lacks detail. Analysis is evidenced (e.g. 'Also, in Baron-Cohen ...') but this would be described as 'basic'. This paragraph, overall, fits the descriptors for 'limited'.

Paragraph 3: Knowledge and understanding are basic and only partially relevant, and no analysis is present.

How to mark

STEP 1 AO1

We feel the AO1 is best described as 'limited, lacking detail'. The first paragraph is at the high end of 'limited' but the other two are 'limited/basic'. Therefore, our tick is in the middle of the third row.

STEP 2 AO3

We feel the AO3 is best described as 'basic' (analysis not related to the question), though there are also elements of the row above (analysis that may be related to the question with some valid conclusions). Therefore, our tick is in the bottom of the third row.

STEP 3 The final mark

On balance the mark for this answer would be in the middle of the third row, i.e. 5 marks.

The levels mark scheme

Level of response	AO1 Knowledge and understanding		AO3 Analysis, interpretation and/or evaluation	
Good 10-12 marks	Good, relevant, accurate, *detailed*.		Mainly relevant, valid and *effective* conclusions, highly skilled argument.	
Reasonable 7-9 marks	Reasonable, generally accurate, lacking some *detail*.		Partially relevant, valid and *effective* conclusions, reasonable argument.	
Limited 4-6 marks	Limited, lacking *detail*.	✓	Analysis etc. may be related to the question, some valid conclusions.	✓
Basic 1-3 marks	Basic, partially relevant, no *detail*.		Analysis etc. not related to the question, basic conclusions.	

Check the OCR website for the latest mark schemes as these do change.
Mark schemes also vary slightly from one question to another.

Question from Component 1 (AO1+ AO3): Psychologists want to investigate whether students living in cities do better at school than those in rural communities. Explain how you would use the experimental method to conduct this research. Justify your decisions as part of your explanation.

In your answer, the required features that you must refer to are:

- the sampling technique
- the type of experimental design
- at least one control of variables
- type of data collected.

You should use your own experience of practical activities to inform your response. **[15]**

Answer: *In the study on whether students living in cities do better at school than those in rural communities, I would use self-selected sampling which would mean students would be motivated to take part and less likely to drop out. This would be done by placing an advert with my contact details on a noticeboard asking for students to respond. When I carried out an investigation, I used a self-selected sample by putting up an advert in the sixth form centre asking for students to meet me at lunchtime to take part in my study into the effect of time on how sixth formers remember playing cards. This meant they were selecting themselves to take part.*

I would use an independent measures design for my investigation. This is because I will be using groups of students from two different schools. This means that it avoids participants guessing the aims of the experiment and I can compare the differences in their school performance, e.g. AS or A Level results. I used an independent measures experimental design in my own research into the effect of time on how sixth formers in my school remember playing cards.

One control of variables I could use with students living in cities or rural communities would be to make sure that I only used the exam results from students who study OCR Psychology. This is also good because it means they will sit the exams at the same time under exam conditions.

I could collect quantitative data from students living in cities and those in rural communities as it allows for statistical analyses to be carried out so that I can draw conclusions. When I used quantitative data in my own research, I used an opportunity sample to gather participants from my school and collected people's opinions. (300 words)

Examiner comments

7 out of 15 marks (probably a Grade C)

Paragraph 1: The first RF is addressed in context (students in cities/rural communities). Description of how to carry out the sampling is accurate and there is appropriate justification for its use. There is explicit reference to own practical work. This paragraph fits the descriptors for 'good'.

Paragraph 2: RF is not addressed in context, there is some appropriate justification for the design, and some reference to own practical work. A 'reasonable' paragraph.

Paragraph 3: RF is addressed in context. There is weak justification of control of variables and no reference to own practical work. Overall, this is 'basic'.

Paragraph 4: RF is addressed in context, there is an attempt at justification for quantitative data, and weak reference to own practical work (no aims or procedure). Overall, this is 'limited'.

How to mark

STEP 1 Required features

The RFs are a mixture of all the rows and three are in context. We placed our tick in the middle of the second row.

STEP 2 Justification

Again, we have a mixture of all four rows, so we placed our tick at the bottom of the second row.

STEP 3 Own practical work

There is one explicit link to own practical work and one that is 'some mention' and one that is 'weak', so the tick is at the top of the third row.

STEP 4 The final mark

On balance the mark for this answer would be at the bottom of the second row (7 marks). One more RF in context would have made a difference.

The levels mark scheme

Level of response	Required features (RFs)		Justification of decisions		Reference to own practical work	
Good 12–15 marks	4 RFs in context, accurate, detailed.		Appropriate justification.		Explicit, clear aims and procedures.	
Reasonable 8–11 marks	3 RFs in context, reasonably accurate, detailed.	✓	Some appropriate justification.	✓	Some mention of aim or procedures.	
Limited 4–7 marks	2 RFs in context, limited.		Attempt to justify.		An attempt.	✓
Basic 1–3 marks	1 RF, very brief.		Weak or none.		Weak or none.	

Note: The criteria in this table are not provided by OCR. The mark scheme for this type of question is complex so we have developed our own grid for marking.

Populations and samples

50%

Your mark on Component 01 (Research methods) is worth 50% of your final mark for AS.

For A level students Component 01 accounts for 30% of the final mark.

This means you could forget the rest of this book and just focus on this one chapter - and pass the AS exam. For AL you do need to know a bit more than Research methods, but not much!

The Component 1 Research methods exam is divided into three sections:

Section A is multiple choice, and includes questions that refer to the research methodology in individual core studies. See page 6 for an example.

Section B and C questions will refer to a scenario. We have included lots of these types of questions throughout this chapter.

Revision booster

Note that Section B and C questions say '*in this study*' (see below). This means that you have to include an example from the scenario to put your answer in context. There will be a mark for it, so don't miss out.

Exam-style question examples

Component 1 Section B:

Psychologists want to investigate the impact of eating chocolate on the dreams of university students.

1. Explain how a psychologist could select an opportunity sample of participants in this study. **[3]**

2. Explain how a researcher could increase the generalisability of the findings of this study. **[3]**

3. Explain **one** strength of using opportunity sampling in this study. **[3]**

4. Explain **one** weakness of using opportunity sampling in this study. **[3]**

Sampling issues

Target population and sample	The *target population* is the group of people psychologists are interested in when conducting a particular area of research, e.g. adolescents in the UK. Psychologists select a small group of participants (called a *sample*) from the target population.
Generalisability	Researchers hope to generalise from their sample to the target population. For example, if a researcher wants to investigate the dreams of adolescents in the UK, then a sample of UK adolescents will be recruited and the results from this sample will be used to make statements that apply to all UK adolescents. The principle of generalisability is very important as researchers want to draw conclusions about a target population based on the research they conduct with a small sample.
Representativeness	Such generalisations only make sense if the sample is representative of the target population. The aim of all sampling techniques is to produce a representative sample.
How many participants should be in a sample?	The number of participants in any study varies enormously. Questionnaires are easy to distribute to hundreds if not thousands of people. Participant numbers in experiments are usually much smaller, e.g. 25 participants may be sufficient (Coolican 1996). Small samples can still be representative and may have advantages over very large samples that can obscure important individual differences.

The **sample** is drawn from a **target population** (the group of people the researcher is interested in).

Target population

This is a sample of the target population - the participants in the study.

Sampling techniques

Opportunity sampling	The sample is produced by selecting people who are most easily available at the time of the study.
	How? Ask people walking past you in your common room at school, i.e. select those who are available.
	➕ Easiest technique because you just use the first participants you can find.
	➖ Inevitably biased because the sample is drawn from a small part of the target population.
Random sampling	The sample is produced by using a random technique. Such techniques mean that every member of the target population has an equal chance of being selected.
	How? Place all names of the target population in a hat and draw out the required number.
	➕ Unbiased because all members of the target population have an equal chance of selection. (Note that a researcher may end up with a biased sample because not all of the identified participants agree to participate.)
	➖ Takes more time and effort than other methods because you need to obtain a list of all the members of your target population, then identify the sample and then contact the people identified and ask if they will take part.
Self-selected sampling	The sample is produced by asking for volunteers.
	How? Advertise in a newspaper or on a noticeboard.
	➕ A way to find willing participants – researchers need committed participants for time-consuming studies.
	➕ Participants are less likely to drop out as they volunteered.
	➖ Sample is biased because volunteer participants are more highly motivated and/or with extra time on their hands than the population in general (= volunteer bias).
Snowball sampling	The sample is produced using referrals from initial participants to generate additional participants.
	How? Current participants recruit further participants from among people they know. Thus the sample group appears to grow like a snowball.
	➕ Enables a researcher to locate groups of people who are difficult to access, such as people who go bowling or people addicted to drugs (once you have one person you can then ask them to recommend a friend).
	➖ The sample is not likely to be a good cross-section of the population because it is made up of friends of friends.

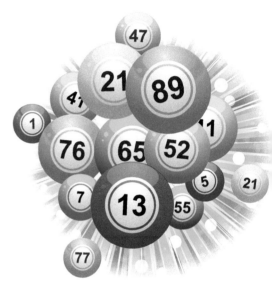

Randomness in a lottery draw means the numbers 1, 2, 3 and 4 are just as likely to come up as 7, 13, 21 and 89.

Exam-style question examples

Component 1 Section B:

A psychologist is investigating the impact of watching TV comedy on the mental health of care home residents.

1. Outline how the psychologist could gather participants in this study using random sampling. [2]

2. Describe how self-selected sampling could be used to obtain a sample in this study. [3]

3. Give **one** strength of using random sampling in this study. [3]

4. Outline **one** weakness of using self-selected sampling in this study. [3]

Sampling bias is a methodological issue and is discussed on page 96.

Self-report

Do people love it or hate it? You can find out by asking them using a questionnaire or an interview.

Quantitative and qualitative data is explained on page 31.

Revision booster

The term Likert scale is often used incorrectly by students to describe all rating scales. A Likert scale is just one specific type of rating scale that focuses on answers ranging from one extreme attitude to another.

Exam-style question examples

Component 1 Section B:

Lots of children travel home from school on the bus. Researchers want to investigate how the children occupy themselves on the journey using the self-report method.

1. Briefly outline how open questions could be used in this study. **[2]**

2. Explain how a rating scale could be used in this study. **[2]**

3. Explain **one** strength of using a questionnaire in this study. **[6]**

4. Give **one** weakness of using a questionnaire in this study. **[3]**

Self-report	The term *self-report* refers to any data collection method that involves asking people to report their thoughts, feelings or behaviour. This data can be collected by: • **Questionnaire** People are given a fixed, predetermined set of questions (i.e. structured). Respondents may record their own answers. • **Interview** When questions are delivered in real time it is called an interview. 'Real time' means that the respondent answers each question out loud as it is presented by an interviewer. Questions may be fixed (structured) or may develop through the course of the interview (unstructured). See facing page.

Designing self-reports

Closed question	Has a fixed number of possible answers. Closed questions provide quantitative data, i.e. answers that can be counted.
	✚ Easy to analyse because data is in numbers (quantitative data) and can be easily summarised using averages (measures of central tendency) as well as simple graphs. This generally makes it easier to draw conclusions.
	▭ May not permit people to express their precise feelings, so data collected may be low in validity.
	▭ Tends not to uncover new insights.
Open question	Respondents are invited to provide their own answers. Open questions tend to produce qualitative data.
	✚ Provides rich details of how people behave as they express what they actually think, rather than being restricted by preconceived categories. This increases the validity of the data collected.
	▭ More difficult to detect patterns and draw conclusions because there are likely to be a wide range of respondents' answers.
Rating scale	Respondents are asked to give an assessment of their views using a scale, e.g. from 1 to 5 where 5 represents very positive and 1 represents very negative.
	✚ Reasonably objective way to represent attitudes related to the topic being researched.
	✚ Produces quantitative data which is easy to analyse or represent in graphs.
	▭ Respondents may avoid ends of scales and go for the 'middle of the road', thus answers do not represent true feelings, i.e. lack validity.

Questionnaires

➕ Can be easily repeated so that data can be collected from large numbers of people relatively cheaply and quickly.

➕ Respondents may feel more willing to reveal personal information in a questionnaire than in an interview.

➖ The sample may be biased because only certain kinds of people fill in questionnaires, e.g. literate individuals willing to spend time filling them in.

Interviews

Structured interview	Predetermined questions delivered by an interviewer who does not probe beyond the answers received but may answer questions from the person being interviewed (e.g. asking for further explanation).
	➕ Can be easily repeated.
	➕ Easier to analyse than unstructured interviews because answers are more predictable.
	➖ The interviewer's expectations may influence the answers the interviewee gives (called *researcher/interviewer bias*).
Semi-structured interview	Some questions are predetermined but also new questions are developed as the interview proceeds.
	➕ More detailed information can be obtained from each respondent than in a structured interview because subsequent questions are specially shaped to the participant.
	➕ Can access information that may not be revealed by predetermined questions.
	➖ More affected by interviewer bias than structured interviews because the interviewer is developing questions on the spot and may be prone to issues such as inadvertently asking leading questions.
Unstructured interview	No questions are decided in advance. Strengths and weaknesses are the same as for semi-structured interviews.

Comparing questionnaires and interviews

Questionnaires

Can be given out to lots of people and therefore produce a large amount of data.

People may feel more willing to reveal confidential information because the presence of an interviewer may make them feel evaluated.

Interviews

Numbers of participants are restricted because interviews take time and employing interviewers is expensive.

People may reveal more information because a skilled interviewer can encourage more thoughtful responses.

Perhaps one of the best ways to find out what young people think of climate goals is to ask for their views using a semi-structured interview. The interviewer can then develop their questions depending on the answers given.

Revision booster

Self-report methods can be used in an experiment as a way to measure a DV. Or a non-experimental study may just focus on the answers given in a questionnaire/interview.

Some students are confused by 'self-report' and think it refers to peer review or report writing.

Exam-style question examples

Component 1 Section B:

A butcher has started selling a new brand of sausage that has proven to be very popular. A consumer psychologist decides to conduct a study to find out more from the butcher as to why it is so popular.

1. Briefly outline how a semi-structured interview could be used in this study. **[2]**

2. Explain how a psychologist might use a structured interview in this study. **[2]**

3. Explain **one** strength of using an interview in this study. **[3]**

4. Give **one** weakness of using an interview in this study. **[3]**

For a measure of behaviour to be reliable, each participant must be tested in exactly the same way.

Revision booster

Students frequently forget that simply comparing results is not enough to ensure inter-rater reliability.

There has to be high agreement between the compared results.

Exam-style question examples

Component 1 Section B:

Psychology students interviewed children to find out their views on the posters of healthy food displayed in their school canteen. The students asked the children various questions about whether the posters encouraged them to eat more healthy food.

1. Describe how the students could make the research method used in this study reliable. **[3]**

2. Explain how the psychology students could check the inter-rater reliability of the data collected during the interviews in this study. **[3]**

3. Explain **one** strength of using a standardised procedure to ensure reliability in this study. **[3]**

4. Explain **one** way in which children's answers to the interview questions in this study may lack reliability. **[3]**

Reliability of self-report

The term *reliability* refers to consistency.

A self-report method is considered reliable if it can be repeated and the same or similar results are found.

The reliability of a person's answers may be affected by, for example:

- Changes in circumstances – a person may be less willing to answer fully if questioned in the evening when they are tired. Therefore, such conditions must be kept constant each time people are tested.
- Ambiguous questions – people interpret these differently, so there won't be consistency between people because they are answering different questions.

Assessing the reliability of an interview	**Inter-rater reliability** The consistency between two different interviewers. This can be checked by comparing the results from two or more interviewers who questioned the same person. The answers given should be the same if the interview is reliable.
Assessing the reliability of a test or questionnaire	**External reliability** A measure of whether something varies from one time to another, i.e. is consistent over time. **Test-retest** The same psychological test is given to the same people on two occasions to see if the same result is obtained.
	Internal reliability A measure of whether something is consistent within itself. **Split-half method** Test items are split into two halves and the scores on both halves compared. Scores should be similar if the test is reliable.

Reliable, but not valid Not reliable, not valid Reliable and valid

Being reliable is being consistent (above left and above right). Being valid is being on target, in relation to what you are aiming to do (above right).

Psychological tests

Psychologists measure psychological variables (e.g. personality) using psychological tests. Such tests are similar to self-report techniques. On psychological tests the questions are usually called 'test items'.

Researchers have to develop ways to ensure that the data they collect is both meaningful (valid) and consistent (reliable).

Validity of self-report

The term *validity* refers to the 'trueness' of data collected. This can be affected by the following issues:

- **Ambiguity** If a person doesn't understand a question on a questionnaire, they will give a meaningless answer, which reduces the validity of the data collected.
- **Social desirability bias** People often prefer to provide answers that makes them 'look better'.
- **Leading questions** People give the answer desired by the researcher if the form of the question 'suggests' the 'correct' answer.

External validity	The extent to which results from a test or questionnaire or interview can be generalised beyond the particular study.
	Population validity The extent to which results can be generalised to other groups of people besides the participants who took part in the study.
	Ecological validity The ability to generalise a result beyond the particular setting to other settings, e.g. whether responses to questions on a topic actually represent the target behaviour.
Internal validity	Whether a test/questionnaire/interview does assess what it intended to assess.
	Researcher bias An interviewer has expectations and beliefs which may be unconsciously communicated to participants through, for example, tone of voice or phrasing of a question. Researcher bias may also be demonstrated in a test or questionnaire, e.g. the researcher might write a leading question.
	Face validity Whether the items on a test/questionnaire/interview look like they are assessing what the researcher intended to assess, e.g. on a questionnaire about aggression, questions should be related to aggression.
Construct validity	Whether a test/questionnaire/interview assesses the underlying concept(s) or construct(s), e.g. a questionnaire on obedience is assessed by considering various theoretical views about obedience (i.e. the underlying constructs) and the extent to which they have been represented by the questionnaire.
Concurrent validity	This can be established by comparing performance on a new test/questionnaire/interview with a previously validated one on the same topic. If the new measure produces a similar outcome to the older one then this demonstrates concurrent validity.
Criterion validity	The extent that test scores can predict a future behaviour or attitude, e.g. an IQ test score would have high criterion validity if it was positively related to GCSE performance.

Using pilot studies (a small preliminary study to test the procedures) can help improve the internal reliability and validity of questionnaires as researchers can reword or rescale any questions that participants find confusing.

Revision booster

Students often get the concepts of reliability and validity confused so it is important you can understand the difference between the two concepts. Think 'consistency' and 'trueness'.

Exam-style question examples

Component 1 Section B:

A group of psychologists wish to survey the attitudes of lorry drivers towards long working days. They use a questionnaire to find out about the views of the lorry drivers.

1. Outline how the psychologists could ensure face validity of the questionnaire used in this study. [2]

2. Explain how social desirability bias might impact on the validity of the findings in this study. [2]

3. Explain **one** strength of ensuring criterion validity in this study. [3]

4. Explain **one** way in which researcher bias may affect the validity of responses to a questionnaire. [3]

Reliability and validity are methodological issues and are discussed on pages 95-96.

Revision booster

Students very often get confused between sampling techniques to identify participants for a study (e.g. opportunity sampling covered on page 17) and sampling techniques to collect observational data (event and time sampling, covered on this page).

An observational study may use both kinds of sampling techniques to identify participants and then to collect observational data.

Coding frames let researchers record specific behaviours within a behaviour category.

Exam-style question examples

Component 1 Section B:

Lots of students use coaches to travel around Europe on holiday. Researchers want to investigate how the students occupy themselves on the journey using an observational method.

1. Outline what behavioural categories the researchers could use in this study. [2]

2. Explain how the researchers could use event sampling to collect observations in this study. [3]

3. Describe **one** strength of using time sampling in this study. [3]

4. Explain **one** weakness of using a structured observation in this study. [3]

Making observations

Structured observational techniques

Observational research aims to be objective and rigorous. For this reason, it is necessary to use systematic procedures.

➕ What people say they do is often different from what they actually do, so observations give a different take on behaviour than other research methods (such as self-report).

➖ Observers may 'see' what they expect to see (observer bias), reducing the validity of observations.

➖ Observations cannot provide information about what people think or feel.

Designing observations

Behavioural categories

Objective methods to separate the continuous stream of action into components.

Categories are arranged as a list, each with a code.

The whole thing is called a *coding frame*.

➕ Enables systematic observations to be made so important information is not overlooked.

➖ Categories may not cover all possibilities, so some behaviours are not recorded (low validity).

➖ Poorly designed coding frames reduce reliability (and validity).

Event and time sampling

Note that there are structured observation techniques and structured observation environments.

Event sampling Involves drawing up a list of behavioural categories and counting every time each behaviour occurs in a specified time period.

Time sampling Involves recording behavioural categories at regular intervals, e.g. every 5 seconds.

➕ Both event and time sampling make observing behaviour manageable because they avoid having to record everything.

➕ Event sampling is useful when behaviour to-be-recorded only happens occasionally.

➕ Time sampling allows for tracking of time-related changes in behaviour.

➖ Observer may miss some observations if too many things happen at once, reducing validity.

➖ Observations may not be representative.

➖ Time sampling may decrease validity because some behaviours/events are missed if they happen outside the observation interval.

Types of observation

Controlled observation

Some variables are changed (manipulated) by the researcher, e.g. in a laboratory. May involve unstructured techniques.

✛ Controlled environment allows focus (e.g. children playing with toys), increases validity.	▭ Environment may feel unnatural so participants' behaviour may not be 'normal', reduces validity.

Naturalistic observation

Environment unstructured. May use structured techniques.

✛ A realistic picture of natural, spontaneous behaviour, increases ecological validity.	▭ Participants may know they are being observed which alters their behaviour (demand characteristics), reduces validity.

Structured observation

A system (e.g. behavioural categories) is used to restrict and organise the collection of information.

✛ Improves inter-rater reliability as observations are more consistent.	▭ Observers may 'see' or 'hear' what they expect (researcher/observer bias), reduces validity.

Unstructured observation

Observer records all relevant behaviour but has no system.

✛ Useful when behaviour to-be-studied is largely unpredictable.	▭ Behaviours recorded are those that are most obvious, but may not be the most relevant.
✛ Used as a pilot study.	

Non-participant observation

Observer is not a participant in the behaviour being observed.

✛ Increased objectivity due to psychological and physical distance, increases validity.	▭ Observer may misinterpret communications within the group, reduces validity.

Participant observation

Observer is a participant in the behaviour being observed.

✛ Likely to provide special insights into behaviour.	▭ Objectivity reduced (observer bias).
✛ Able to monitor and record behaviour in closer detail.	▭ May be difficult to record behaviour unobtrusively.

Covert observation

Observations made without a participant's knowledge.

✛ Participants behave more naturally, increases validity.	▭ Ethical issues about observing people without permission.

Overt observation

Participant is aware of being observed.

✛ Avoids lack of informed consent.	▭ Participants may alter their behaviour due to observer effect.

Reliability and validity in observations

If observations are reliable we should collect the same data if two people record observations of the same data (inter-rater reliability). This is calculated by correlating the scores of one observer with the scores of another.

If observations are valid then observers should not be influenced by their expectations of what they may see (observer bias).

Exam-style question examples

Component 1 Section B:

A primary school head teacher wants to find out if students are correctly using the new recycling bins at her school, e.g. putting plastics in the red plastics bin and paper in the blue paper bin.

1. Outline how a researcher could use an unstructured observation in this study. **[2]**

2. Explain how a researcher could carry out a covert observation in this study. **[3]**

3. Explain **one** strength of using a non-participant observation in this study. **[3]**

4. Explain **one** weakness of using a naturalistic observation in this study. **[3]**

Recording what you see (or hear) isn't that easy.

Experiments

The key feature of all kinds of experiment is that there is an IV (cause) and a DV (effect).

Revision booster

Remember that research questions don't really differ from research aims – but if an exam question asks you to give a research question it must have a question mark (i.e. it is a question).

Research aim: To investigate whether sunshine causes people to be in a better mood.

Research question: Does sunshine put people in a better mood?

And both are different from hypotheses.

Exam-style question examples

Component 1 Section B:

Psychology students want to carry out an experiment to investigate the effect of time on the number of playing cards that can be recalled.

1. Identify the independent variable in this study. **[2]**

2. Explain how students could operationalise the dependent variable in this study. **[3]**

3. Write a one-tailed alternative hypothesis for this study. **[3]**

4. Explain how a two-tailed hypothesis for this study would be different from a one-tailed hypothesis. **[3]**

Experiment	A research method which demonstrates causal relationships. All experiments have an IV and a DV.	
	Loftus and Palmer's study is an experiment.	
Variables	**Independent variable** (IV) Directly manipulated by the experimenter in order to observe the effect of this variation on the DV.	In Loftus and Palmer's experiment, the IV was the verb used to describe the impact of the accident.
		In this experiment there were five levels of the IV but there are usually two.
	Dependent variable (DV) Measured to assess the effects of the IV.	In Loftus and Palmer's experiment, the DV was the estimated speed the car was travelling at.

Designing experiments

Operationalisation	Variables must be operationalised, i.e. defined in a way that they can easily be tested.	If I want to investigate whether people are happier on a sunny day, I need to operationalise 'happier' (e.g. measure on a rating scale).
Hypothesis Also called the **alternative hypothesis** Abbreviated as H_1	A hypothesis is a precise and testable statement about the world. It is about people (or animals) not participants.	
	An experimental hypothesis states the relationship between the IV and DV.	People are in a better mood on a sunny day.
	It must include all levels of the IV.	People are in a better mood on a sunny day *than on a day when it isn't sunny.*
	It should be precise and testable and operationalised.	People *rate themselves as happier on a five-point mood scale* when it is sunny than on a day when it isn't sunny.
Direction of hypothesis	**One-tailed (directional)** The hypothesis states the direction of the difference.	People rate themselves as *happier* on a five-point mood scale …
	Two-tailed (non-directional) The hypothesis just states there is a difference.	People rate themselves *differently* on a five-point mood scale …
Null hypothesis Abbreviated as H_0	A statement of no difference.	*There is no difference* in the way people rate themselves on a five-point mood scale …

Experimental design

Researchers need to decide whether to have one group of participants who do both levels of the IV or have more than one group of participants.

Repeated measures	Each participant takes part in every condition under test. Each condition represents one level of the IV. There may also be a control condition.
	➕ Good control of participant variables because the same person is tested across conditions.
	➕ Fewer participants needed than with independent measures.
	➖ Order effects are produced, e.g. practice or boredom effects.
	➖ Participants may guess the purpose of the experiment because they do both conditions, potentially making the aims obvious.
	Dealing with weaknesses Order effects can be controlled by presenting each experimental condition first or last in equal measure (e.g. ABBA). This is called *counterbalancing*.
Independent measures	There are two (or more) experimental groups, each representing one level of the IV and/or acting as a control group. Participants are allocated (randomly or otherwise) to one of these groups.
	➕ Avoids order effects because each participant is tested once.
	➕ Avoids participants guessing the aims of the experiment.
	➖ There is no control of participant variables.
	➖ Needs more participants than with a repeated measures design.
	Dealing with weaknesses Use random allocation of participants to conditions, so participant variables should not cluster in one group.
Matched pairs design	Participants who are similar on key variables (e.g. memory ability, age) are paired. One member of the pair is placed in Group A and the other in Group B.
	➕ Acts as a control for participant variables because of the matching (like repeated measures).
	➕ Avoids order effects because it is like independent measures.
	➖ Very time-consuming to match participants on key variables.
	➖ May not control all participant variables because you can only match on variables known to be relevant, but it could be that other variables are important.
	Dealing with weaknesses Start with a large group of participants to ensure you can obtain matched participants on key variables.
Control groups/ conditions	Control groups/conditions act as a baseline to see what answer participants give if they are not exposed to any condition in an experiment. For example, in Loftus and Palmer's second experiment the control group were not asked a question about the speed of the cars.

Are people in a better mood on a sunny day?
- IV is sunny day
- DV is score on mood rating scale

Repeated measures

Condition A
Sunny day

Condition B
Cloudy day

The same people take part in condition A and B.

Independent measures

Group A
Sunny day

Group B
Cloudy day

Group A has 10 people and group B has 8 people - the groups don't have to be equal.

Whilst we may expect people in the repeated measures design to be in a better mood on a sunny day, they may become bored of sitting in the sun and become grumpy (an example of the boredom effect which then acts as an extraneous variable - see page 26).

Revision booster

Remember the strengths of a repeated measures design are the weaknesses of an independent measures design, and vice versa.

Exam-style question examples

Component 1 Section B:

Psychologists want to investigate if there is a difference in reading skills between A Level Maths students and A Level English students.

1. Outline how an independent measures design could be used in this study. **[2]**

2. Describe how a control group could be used in this study. **[2]**

3. Explain **one** strength of using an independent measures design in this study. **[3]**

4. Explain **one** weakness of using a matched pairs design in this study. **[3]**

Experiments (continued)

Demand characteristics

People seek cues about how to behave, e.g. most people sit relatively quietly watching a football game at home, but at a football ground they are more likely to chant and jump up and down.

These different situations 'demand' different behaviours.

Revision booster

Students often get confused about how to describe experiments that also use another method. For example, Bandura *et al.* is an experiment but also uses observation as a technique to measure the DV. Baron-Cohen *et al.* is an experiment but uses self-report to measure the DV.

Remember that if there is an IV and a DV, the study is an experiment.

Exam-style question examples

Component 1 Section B:

An experiment is conducted to investigate whether students living in cities do better at school than those living in rural communities.

1. Outline **two** extraneous variables that should be controlled in this study. [2]

2. Explain how researcher bias may impact the findings in this study. [3]

3. Describe **one** way a psychologist could deal with possible demand characteristics in this study. [2]

4. Explain **one** way a psychologist could deal with possible researcher effects in this study. [2]

Validity Refers to whether the data collected from an experiment (or any kind of study) genuinely represents people's everyday behaviour (see page 21).

Internal validity In an experiment, refers to whether changes in the DV are due to the IV, otherwise the researcher is not testing what they intended to test.

External validity In an experiment, refers to the extent to which research results can be generalised to other people and settings.

Internal validity

Demand characteristics	Cues in an experimental situation that communicate to participants what is expected of them. This may unconsciously affect a participant's behaviour.	If a participant is given a memory test in the morning and one in the afternoon, they may guess the aim (to assess the effects of time of day) and try to perform the same each time.
	Dealing with it Use independent measures to avoid cues from doing the same task twice.	
Extraneous variable	Any variable other than the IV that might potentially affect the DV and thereby confound the results. This includes both participant and situational variables.	Ethnicity is a participant variable (a characteristic of the participant). Weather is a situational variable (a feature of the environment).
	Dealing with it Variables are held constant (e.g. participants are all the same ethnicity) or researchers randomly allocate participants across conditions.	
Researcher bias	A researcher's expectations may encourage certain behaviours in participants. The result is that the researcher's expectations are fulfilled.	An experimenter might unconsciously encourage group A participants more than group B, which would explain why participants in group A do better on that task.
	Dealing with it The person who designs a study should not be the person who conducts it.	
Researcher effects	Anything that the researcher does that has an effect on a participant's performance, other than what was intended.	Direct effects, e.g. encouraging certain responses. Indirect effects, e.g. the way the results are analysed.
	Dealing with it Use peer review to ensure high standards in research design.	

External validity

Ecological validity	The ability to generalise a research effect beyond the particular research setting to other settings.	Many studies use tasks that do not represent everyday activities, e.g. film clips used by Loftus and Palmer to study eyewitness accounts of a car accident.

Dealing with it Conduct research in everyday settings (low control, i.e. low internal validity) and compare to studies which are highly controlled but lack ecological validity.

Population validity	The extent to which a study's results can be generalised to groups of people besides the participants.	A study with only student participants (e.g. Loftus and Palmer) would not generalise to the wider population as students are young and intelligent, and therefore may have better memories.

Dealing with it Use a wider target population and don't use opportunity sampling.

Types of experiment

Laboratory experiment	Experiment conducted in a very controlled environment.

➕ High level of control is possible, so extraneous variables can be minimised (increasing internal validity).

➕ Can be easily replicated as the environment has been mostly controlled (increasing internal validity).

➖ Artificial situation where participants may not behave naturally, so low ecological validity.

➖ Demand characteristics and researcher bias/effects may reduce validity.

Field experiment	Experiment conducted in everyday surroundings.

➕ Less contrived, usually higher ecological validity.

➕ Participants usually unaware of being studied, no demand characteristics or researcher bias (increasing internal validity).

➖ Less control of extraneous variables (reducing internal validity).

➖ Ethical issues, because participants generally are not aware of being studied and cannot give consent.

Quasi-experiment	Experimenter does not manipulate the IV.

➕ Allows research where an IV can't be manipulated for ethical or practical reasons.

➕ Enables psychologists to study 'real' issues, e.g. autism.

➖ No causal relationships as IV not directly manipulated.

➖ Less control of extraneous variables (low internal validity).

Marionettes are puppets that are controlled and manipulated. When an experimenter 'manipulates the IV' they are causing a deliberate change.

A study that is low in internal validity will lack external validity as there is no value in generalising meaningless results.

Exam-style question examples

Component 1 Section B:

Psychologists advertised for university students to help them in a study. The volunteers came to the psychology laboratory. Some of them were given written instructions about the task whereas others were given the instructions verbally.

1. Outline how a psychologist could improve the population validity in this study. **[3]**

2. Describe **two** variables the researchers should control in this study. **[2]**

3. Outline **one** strength of conducting this study as a laboratory experiment. **[3]**

4. Outline **one** weakness of conducting this study as a laboratory experiment. **[3]**

Correlation

Revision booster

Never use the word 'association' in a hypothesis. It is 'relationship' for a correlation, 'difference' for an experiment.

A **correlation coefficient** *measures the strength of a correlation. +1 is a perfect positive correlation and -1 is a perfect negative correlation.*

+.80 or -.80 is a strong correlation

+.50 or -.50 is moderate

+.20 or -.20 is weak

The inferential statistic Spearman's rho produces the correlation coefficient (see page 36).

It's great when relationships are positive but it's not always the case.

Exam-style question examples

Component 1 Section B:

A teacher found there was a relationship between his students' 'strength of character' scores and their marks on a psychology test.

1. Identify the co-variables in this study. **[2]**

2. Describe a positive correlation in this study. **[2]**

3. Outline **one** strength of using a correlational analysis in this study. **[3]**

4. Outline **one** weakness of using a correlational analysis in this study. **[3]**

Correlational analysis

A correlation (or correlational analysis) is a way of measuring the *relationship* between two variables instead of looking at the *difference* as we do in an experiment.

➕ A way to represent the degree to which two continuous variables are related.

➕ Strong correlations can lead to further study as there may be a causal link.

➖ Cannot show a cause-and-effect relationship.

➖ There may be intervening variables that explain why the co-variables are linked.

Scatter diagram

A graph showing the correlation between co-variables. Each dot = a pair of scores.

For each individual, a score for each co-variable is obtained, e.g. age and beauty.

Positive correlation

The correlation coefficient for the data on the right is +.80

The two variables increase together.

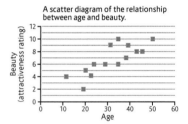

Negative correlation

The correlation coefficient for the data on the right is -.50

As one variable increases the other one decreases.

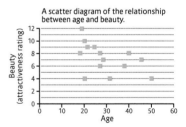

No correlation

The correlation coefficient for the data on the right is -.20

No correlation means that the two variables are not related in any way.

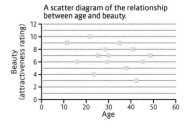

BPS code of ethics and conduct

Respect Includes informed consent, confidentiality, privacy and right to withdraw.
Competence Includes awareness of professional ethics and making ethical decisions.
Responsibility Includes protection from harm and debriefing.
Integrity Includes honesty (avoiding deception) and addressing misconduct.

Ways of dealing with ethical issues

Debriefing A post-research interview that aims to restore participants to the state they were in at the start of the study.

Ethics committee Looks at all possible ethical issues and at how researchers plan to deal with these and then give permission for the research to proceed.

Presumptive consent A method of dealing with lack of informed consent or deception by asking another group of people whether they would take part. The researcher then *presumes* the actual participants would feel the same.

Ethics involves balancing the costs to the participants involved in research with the benefits to society. Some of the most well-known research is seen as having ethical concerns, e.g. Milgram.

Anonymity and confidentiality	Participants' right to protect personal data by withholding their name (anonymity) or keeping data safe (confidentiality).	
	Data Protection Act makes confidentiality a legal right.	... But some details of a study may lead to an individual's identification.
Deception	Participant is not told the true research aims of a study and/or not told what they will be required to do.	
	Prevents truly informed consent.	... But knowing aims would spoil the study.
		Deception can be relatively harmless and/or reduced by debriefing.
Informed consent	Participants are given comprehensive information concerning the nature and purpose of a study and their role in it.	
	Participants need this information to decide whether to participate.	... But not all can give informed consent, e.g. children.
		Providing informed consent can reveal the aim of a study.
Privacy	A person's right to control the information about themselves.	
	It is acceptable to be observed in a public place.	... But, if participants know they are being observed, this affects their behaviour.
Right to withdraw	Participants should be told that they can stop participating in a study if they are uncomfortable.	
	Participants should be protected from harm.	... But their loss may bias the study's results.
Protection from harm	Participants should not experience negative physical effects (e.g. physical injury), nor negative psychological effects (e.g. lowered self-esteem or embarrassment).	
	Participants should be in the same 'state' they were in at the beginning.	... But researchers may not be able to estimate harm before conducting a study.

Revision booster

Students often make the mistake of regarding ethical issues as always being negative. Researchers whose research adheres to the BPS code of ethics are acting in a positive way towards their participants.

Exam-style question examples

Component 1 Section B:

Researchers want to investigate people's attitudes towards recycling in their local community using a questionnaire.

1. Outline how the BPS ethical issues of respect are relevant in this study. **[3]**

2. Explain how the researchers could use the principle of presumptive consent in this study. **[3]**

3. Explain how the researchers could deal with the BPS ethical issue of responsibility in this study. **[3]**

4. Outline how the researchers should deal with ethical issues before they start conducting this study. **[2]**

Chapter 1 Research methods

Dealing with data
Descriptive statistics

Do not feel afraid - Statistics Hero is here to help: The only tricky task is calculating the variance or standard deviation (SD):

1. *Know the formula for the variance.*
2. *Get the order right when calculating.*
3. *SD is the square root of the variance.*
4. *Be prepared to calculate the answer or to just describe what you would do.*

How to calculate the variance

1. *Calculate the mean ($\bar{x}$) for the data set.*
2. *Calculate the difference between each number (x) and the mean: $x - \bar{x}$*
3. *Square the result for each data item: $(x - \bar{x})^2$*
4. *Add up the differences squared: $\Sigma(x - \bar{x})^2$*
5. *Divide by the number of values (n) minus 1*

   The formula: $\dfrac{\Sigma(x - \bar{x})^2}{n - 1}$

Exam-style question examples

Component 1 Section C:

Psychology students investigated the effects of time of day on recall. 25 people memorised and recalled a list of words in the morning and 25 did the same task in the afternoon.

1. Outline how the students could find the means of each data set in this study. **[2]**

2. Describe how the students could find the range of the data in this study. **[2]**

3. Give **one** strength of using the median of the data in this study as a measure of central tendency. **[3]**

4. Give **one** weakness of calculating the standard deviation for the data in this study as a measure of dispersion. **[3]**

In order to make sense of raw data from research, it needs to be described or summarised in some way.

This is called *descriptive statistics*.

Measures of central tendency (averages)

Mean — **How?** Add up all the numbers and divide by the number of numbers.

➕ 'Sensitive' because the values of all the data are reflected in the final calculation.

➖ Can't be used with nominal data.

➖ Can be unrepresentative of the numbers if there are extreme values.

Median — **How?** Place all values in order from smallest to largest. Select the middle value. If there are two middle values calculate the mean of these two values.

➕ Not affected by extreme scores.

➖ Not as 'sensitive' as the mean because not all values are represented.

Mode — **How?** Identify the group or groups which is/are most frequent.

➕ Useful when the data is in categories (nominal data).

➖ Not a useful way of describing data when there are several modes.

Measures of dispersion (the spread of the data)

Range — **How?** Arrange data from highest to lowest. Subtract lowest from highest.

➕ Easy to calculate.

➖ Affected by extreme values.

➖ Fails to take account of the distribution of the numbers around the mean.

Variance and standard deviation — **How?** Each number is subtracted from the mean, ignoring plus or minus values. The result is then squared for each data item. The resultant differences squared are added up and a mean value is calculated (see above left).

The standard deviation is the square root of the variance.

➕ A precise measure of dispersion as all the exact values are taken into account.

➕ It is not difficult to calculate if you have a calculator.

➖ May hide some of the characteristics of the data set (e.g. extreme values).

Types of data

Quantitative data Deals with numbers and is data that can be measured. Psychologists develop measures of psychological variables so they can look at averages and differences between groups.

Qualitative data Deals with descriptions and is data that is observed not measured. Psychologists examine behaviour through the messages people produce about their attitudes, beliefs, fears and emotions.

Raw data	Data before it has been processed in any way. Researchers put raw data into a table and then process it using various processing methods (discussed on the facing page).
Quantitative data	Data that is numerical, i.e. quantities.
	➕ Easier to analyse because data is in numbers which can be summarised using descriptive statistics. This generally makes it easier to draw conclusions.
	➖ Oversimplifies reality and human experience because it suggests that there are simple answers.
Qualitative data	Data that is in words or pictures, non-numerical.
	➕ Represents the true complexities of human behaviour.
	➕ Provides rich details because participants are given a free range to express themselves, increasing validity.
	➖ More difficult to detect patterns and draw conclusions because of the large variety of information collected.
Primary data	Data collected by a researcher specifically for the study currently being undertaken.
	➕ Data collection can be designed so it fits the aims and hypothesis of the study.
	➖ Very lengthy and expensive process because designing a study takes a lot of time, as does recruiting participants and then conducting the study.
Secondary data	Information that was collected for a purpose other than the current one, e.g. government statistics.
	➕ Simpler to use someone else's data and cheaper because it doesn't have to be collected.
	➕ Data may have been subjected to statistical testing and thus it is known whether it is significant.
	➖ The data may not exactly fit the needs of the study.

Remember that you MUST take a calculator into the Research methods exam.

A scientific or graphical calculator is best – in case you want to check a standard deviation!

Social media provides a lot of raw data, e.g. the number of likes for different products. These can be processed by companies to find out the target audience for their product.

Revision booster

An exam question might ask you to explain whether you would use the mean or median with a particular data set, and also ask you to explain your answer.

To answer this, check whether the data set has extreme values (outliers), in which case it is better to use the median.

The same advice applies to questions that ask whether the range or standard deviation is best. Range is more affected by extreme values.

Exam-style question examples

Component 1 Section C:

Using the question scenario on the facing page:

1. Describe the type of data collected in this study. [2]

2. Outline how qualitative data could have been collected in this study. [3]

3. Give **one** strength of the data collected in this study. [3]

4. Give **one** weakness of the data collected in this study. [3]

For bar charts, a space is left between each column to show the lack of continuity in the data.

Revision booster

You may be asked to sketch a graph in the exam – make sure you label the axes (with units) and give the graph a title. Clear labels mean more marks.

If you are asked to draw a pie chart, include your calculations on the size of each slice of the 'pie' as there may well be marks for this too.

Exam-style question examples

Component 1 Section C:

A psychologist has collected data about 40 people's favourite flavour of ice cream. She found that 20 people liked mint choc chip, 7 people liked strawberry, 3 people liked vanilla and 10 people liked pistachio best.

1. Outline how the data in this study could be presented in a pie chart. **[3]**

2. Explain how a frequency table could be used to record the data in this study. **[2]**

3. Explain why a bar chart is suitable to use in presenting data in this study. **[2]**

4. Explain why a pie chart is suitable to use in presenting data in this study. **[3]**

Tables and graphs

Raw data table	A table is a means of arranging raw data in rows and columns.

Frequency table — A table displaying a record of how often an event occurred.

Frequency table showing the answers given by 50 people asked to name their favourite colour.

Colour	Frequency	Total
Red	ЖЖ ЖЖ ЖЖ	15
Yellow	ЖЖ ЖЖ	10
Blue	ЖЖ IIII	9
Green	IIII	4
Purple	ЖЖ ЖЖ II	12

Bar chart — In a bar chart the height of each bar represents the frequency of each item.

Bar charts are especially suitable for nominal data (see bottom of facing page).

Graph A Bar chart to show favourite colour.

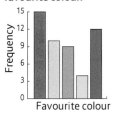

Histogram — A histogram is similar to a bar chart except it allows for continuous data and the area within the bars must be proportional to the frequencies represented. This means that the vertical axis (frequency) must start at zero. In addition, the horizontal axis must be continuous. There should be no gaps between the bars.

Graph B Histogram with line graph superimposed to show the ages of people who attended a concert.

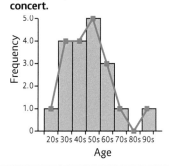

Line graph — A line graph, like a histogram, has continuous data on the *x*-axis. There is a dot to mark the top of each bar and each dot is connected by a line (see blue line on graph B).

Pie chart — A pie chart represents frequency data. Each slice of the 'pie' represents the proportion (or fraction) of the total.

Graph C shows the frequency data for favourite colours (above). The total was 50 so, for each slice, we divide the frequency by 50 and multiply by 360 (degrees in a circle) = degrees of the pie slice.

Graph C Pie chart to show favourite colour.

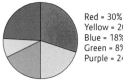

Red = 30%
Yellow = 20%
Blue = 18%
Green = 8%
Purple = 24%

Scatter diagram — A graph to display correlation data (see examples on page 28).

Data distributions

When we plot frequency data, the *y*-axis usually represents frequency and the *x*-axis is the item of interest, as in a histogram. When plotting this data we can see an overall pattern of the data, especially with a large data set. This pattern is called a distribution.

Normal distribution curves	Nomal distributions occur when variables are distributed so that most of the scores are clustered around the mean, median and mode.	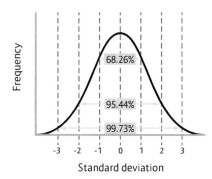 *The percentage of people in each part of the normal distribution curve is shown above.*

Skewed distribution curves	In a skewed distribution the mean, median and mode are not the same. In a positive skew most of the scores are bunched towards the left. The mode is to the left of the mean because the mean is affected by the extreme scores tailing off to the right. In a negative skew most of the scores are bunched to the right.	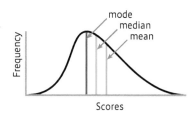 *Positive skew (tail is right, in a positive direction, mode to left).* 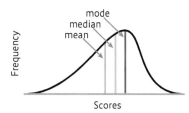 *Negative skew (tail is left, in a negative direction, mode to right).*

Levels of measurement

Nominal data	Data is in separate categories, such as grouping 50 people according to their height: tall, medium and short.
Ordinal data	Data is ordered in some way, for example asking your 50 people to line up in order of size. The 'difference' between each person is not the same.
Interval data	Data is measured using units of equal intervals, such as measuring everyone's height in centimetres.

Even though the Tower of Pisa is skewed to the left, it doesn't look very positive.

Exam-style question examples

Component 1 Section C:

In a research study, participants were asked to state the time of day they typically went to sleep.

1. Explain why the data in this study would be classed as interval level data. **[2]**

2. Explain why the data in this study will show a negative skew. **[3]**

3. Explain **one** strength of using interval data rather than ordinal data in psychological research. **[2]**

4. Explain **one** strength of plotting data in this study. **[3]**

Inferential statistics

Inferential testing is a topic that worries many students but, to be honest, once questions are diced up, the exam demands are small.

This spread and the next spread will cover what you need to know on the inferential tests that are required for the exam.

Note that the observed value is sometimes called the 'calculated value' because it has to be calculated.

Exam-style question examples

Component 1 Section C:

A psychology teacher planned a lesson on inferential statistics. He wanted students to understand the terms psychologists use when carrying out their analysis.

1. Explain what students understood by the term 'probability' from the lesson. **[2]**

2. Explain what students understood by the term 'significance' from the lesson. **[2]**

3. Outline what students understood by the term 'significance level' from the lesson. **[2]**

4. Outline what the teacher meant when he used the term 'Type 1 error' in the lesson. **[3]**

Key concepts

Probability (p)	A measure of the likelihood that an event may occur.
	Probability is given as a number between 0 and 1 (where 0 indicates impossibility and 1 indicates certainty).
Inferential test (sometimes called 'inferential statistical test')	Procedures (based on probability) for drawing logical conclusions (inferences) about the target population from which samples are drawn.
	Inferential tests are classed as parametric or non-parametric. The criteria for parametric inferential tests are that the data must be: (1) interval, (2) drawn from a population with a normal distribution, (3) from groups with similar variances.
Observed value	Researchers collect data and use an inferential test to produce an observed value.
Critical value	A statistically determined value which represents the likelihood of an event happening.
	The observed value is compared with critical values found in a table of critical values. This allows a researcher to decide whether to accept or reject the null hypothesis.
Significance	A statistical term indicating that the research results are sufficiently strong to enable a researcher to reject the null hypothesis under test and accept the alternative hypothesis.
Significance level	The level of probability at which it has been agreed to reject the null hypothesis. Psychologists usually use a probability of 0.05 (5%).

Type 1 and Type 2 errors

Type 1 error occurs when a researcher rejects a null hypothesis that is true (false positive). For example, in a criminal court case the defendant is found guilty when actually they were not guilty.	An optimistic error, too lenient (likely when using $p < 0.10$)
Type 2 error occurs when a researcher accepts a null hypothesis that was not true (false negative). For example, a defendant is found not guilty when actually they were guilty.	A pessimistic error, too stringent (likely when using $p < 0.01$)

Using inferential tests

You need to be familiar with FIVE inferential tests (listed in the orange boxes).

In the exam, you may be asked to:

1. Select the most appropriate inferential test to use for different data (below).

2. Explain why you selected a particular test (below).

3. Substitute values into a test formula, calculate the test statistic (page 36).

4. Look at critical value tables, compare them to observed values and write a statement of significance (page 37).

Don't bury your head in the sand about which test to choose - use the decision tree below.

A decision tree to identify the right test to use

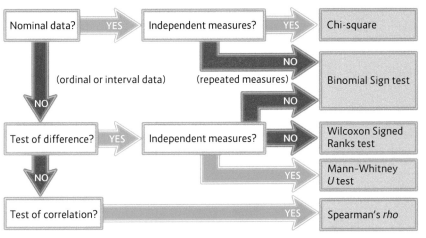

Chi-square	Nominal, independent measures, difference or correlation
Binomial Sign test	Nominal/ordinal/interval, repeated measures, difference
Wilcoxon Signed Ranks test	Ordinal/interval, repeated measures, difference
Mann-Whitney *U* test	Ordinal/interval, independent measures, difference
Spearman's *rho*	Ordinal/interval, independent measures, correlation

Note: *nominal, ordinal* and *interval* are explained on page 33.

Examples of how to select the right test

Scenario 1 Researchers wanted to analyse the data from five groups of students. Each group was given a different verb and asked to estimate the speed of a car after watching short videos of car crashes.

- Nominal data? No, the data collected is speed estimates (*interval level*).
- Test of difference? Yes.
- Independent measures? Yes, looking at five groups of students.

Therefore, the researchers should use a Mann-Whitney *U* test.

Scenario 2 Psychologists wanted to find out if there was a difference in personality dimensions, e.g. extraversion and agreeableness, between obedient participants, disobedient participants and whistle-blowers.

- Nominal data? Yes, the data collected is personality dimensions.
- Independent measures? Yes, looking at groups of participants.

Therefore, the researchers should use a Chi-square test.

Scenario 3 Psychologists looked at the relationship between volume of the hippocampus and years spent driving a taxi.

- Nominal data? No, it is interval data.
- Test of difference? No, looking at a relationship between the co-variables.

Therefore, the researchers should use a Spearman's *rho* test.

Exam-style question examples

Component 1 Section C:

Use the decision tree above to:

1. Identify the appropriate inferential test to use to analyse the data from a group of men looking to see if their hair growth is longer (in millimetres) after using a hair growth product than before. Give reasons for your answer. **[3]**

2. Identify the appropriate inferential test to use to analyse the data obtained when investigating the difference in psychology test scores between men and women students. Give reasons for your answer. **[3]**

3. Explain why researchers would use the Spearman's *rho* test to analyse data investigating the relationship between age and attractiveness ratings. **[3]**

Bright idea - focus on the demands of the exam. The revision boosters will help.

Revision booster

You may be asked to:

1. **Describe the steps to be taken to calculate any of the five named inferential tests.**

2. **Substitute values in a formula and calculate the statistic – this only applies to the three tests with formulae and you will be given the formula in the exam.**

Exam-style question examples

Component 1 Section C:

1. A Binomial Sign test was used to analyse data to see if blood pressure is lower after a stress management programme than before it.

   Describe how to calculate an observed *S* value in a Binomial Sign test for this study. **[3]**

2. A Mann-Whitney *U* test was used to analyse the difference in reaction time between two groups.

   Using the formula provided calculate the value of *U* for the data provided below.

   R = 87.5 and N = 10

   $$U = R - \frac{[N(N+1)]}{2}$$ **[4]**

Calculate observed values

Binomial Sign test (symbol is *S*)	**Place raw data in table** Data for group A in column 1 and group B in column 2. **Work out signs** Record a plus (+) in column 3 if the number in column 1 is bigger than the number in column 2. Otherwise, record a minus (–) or a zero (0) if equal. **Find observed value of *S*** Count the number of pluses and minuses. Select the smaller value.
Wilcoxon Signed Ranks test (symbol is *T*) *N* is the number of participants.	**Place raw data in table** As above. **Find differences** Calculate the difference between each pair of scores. Omit zero differences from the ranking and reduce *N* accordingly. **Rank the differences** Rank from low to high, ignoring signs. **Find observed value of *T*** Add ranks for all positive differences and ranks for all negative differences. *T* is the total that is smaller.
Mann-Whitney *U* test (symbol is *U*)	**Place raw data in table** Data for condition A in column 1 and condition B in column 2. **Rank data** Rank all data items from both conditions jointly. Add up ranks for each column: total for column 1 is R_1 and for column 2 is R_2. **Find observed value of *U*** Select smaller value (R_1 or R_2) to use, e.g. smallest R = 121.5, *N* = 14. $$U = R - \frac{[N(N+1)]}{2} = 121.5 - \frac{(14 \times 15)}{2} = 16.5$$
Spearman's *rho* (symbol is *rho*)	**Place raw data in table** Data for co-variable A in column 1 and co-variable B in column 2. **Rank each co-variable** Rank A and B separately, from low to high. **Calculate the difference (d) between the ranks** For co-variable A and B. Square the differences, and add them up (Σd^2). **Find observed value of *rho*** e.g. $\Sigma d^2 = 261$, *N* = 10 $$rho = 1 - \frac{6 \Sigma d^2}{N(N^2-1)} = 1 - \frac{6 \times 261}{10(100-1)} = 1 - \frac{1566}{990} = -0.58$$
Chi-square (symbol is χ^2)	**Contingency table** Place observed values (O) in contingency table, e.g. 2 × 2 contingency table has two rows and two columns (plus totals for each row/column). **Find observed value of χ^2** The formula for each cell is $(E-O)^2 / E$ and then all values are added up to calculate χ^2. To calculate E (expected frequency), evenly distribute sample in the contingency table. E is the same for every cell.

Chapter 1 Research methods

Component 1

Using critical value tables

To find out if the observed (calculated) value is significant we compare it with critical values found in critical value tables for each test.

To find the critical value we use:

- The number of data values (N).*
- The kind of hypothesis (one-tailed or two-tailed).
- The desired level of significance, usually 0.05 as this is a good compromise between being too stringent (0.01 level) or too lenient (0.10 level) and making a Type 1 or 2 error.

* For Chi-square calculate degrees of freedom (instead of N), the formula is: (number of rows - 1) × (number of columns - 1) in a contingency table.

Inferential tests give the probability that a particular set of data did not occur by chance. The level of significance that psychologists tend to use is 0.05. This means that there is a 0.05 or 5% probability that the result would have occurred by chance.

Worked example

Binomial Sign test

If the observed (calculated) value is not significant, we accept the null hypothesis and reject the alternative hypothesis.

However, if the observed value is significant then we reject the null hypothesis and accept the alternative hypothesis.

Table of critical values of S

Level of significance for a one-tailed test	0.05	0.01
Level of significance for a two-tailed test	0.10	0.02
N		
5	0	
6	0	0
7	0	0
8	1	0
9	1	1
10	1	1
11	2	1
12	2	2
13	3	2
14	3	2
15	3	3
20	5	5
25	7	7
30	10	9

Observed value of S must be EQUAL TO or LESS THAN the critical value in this table for significance to be shown.

Statement of significance

If our observed value is 5 with 12 participants, we conclude:

The observed value (5) is greater than the critical value (2) (N = 12, one-tailed hypothesis, 0.05 level of significance). Therefore, the result is not significant.

The null hypothesis is accepted that there is no difference in blood pressure before and after the stress management training programme.

We reject the null hypothesis (and accept the alternative hypothesis) at the 5% level:

- If our observed value is 2 with 12 participants.
- If our observed value is 5 with 20 participants.

We reject the null hypothesis at the 1% level:

- If our observed value is 2 with 12 participants but if the hypothesis was two-tailed it would be the 2% level.

Greater or less than

Use the Rule of R to compare observed and critical values.

For inferential tests containing the letter R, the observed value must be **equal to or gReateR than** the critical value:

- SpeaRman's
- Chi-squaRe

For all other tests, the observed value must be **equal to or less than** the critical value:

- Binomial Sign test
- Wilcoxon
- Mann-Whitney

How to remember which is which

Mr and Mrs Wilcoxon are married and do everything together (repeated measures). Mr Mann and Ms Whitney are just friends (independent measures).

How science works

The only way to disprove a theory that all swans are white, is to seek disproof (falsification) and find a black swan.

Peer review

Peer review is the assessment of scientific work by fellow academics who are experts in the same field. Its purpose is to help decide what research should be funded, to share research results with the academic community and to assess university departments in terms of quality.

Reviewing is usually done anonymously so reviewers can be honest and objective.

Exam-style question examples

Component 1 Section C:

A psychology student created revision cards to help him recall information for his exam.

1. Describe what the student could write on the card to help him understand the term 'falsification'. **[2]**

2. Outline what the student could write on the card to help him understand the term 'objectivity'. **[2]**

Scientific method

In order to test the truth of the observations a scientist makes, they follow a series of well-defined steps called the *scientific method*.

1. Make observations	Observation: People from the north of the UK are funnier than people from the south.
2. Produce a testable hypothesis	A testable hypothesis is one that is operationalised, i.e. all variables are described in terms of how they can be measured. Operationalised hypothesis: UK participants who live north of Manchester (latitude 53°N) are rated as funnier when they tell a predetermined set of jokes than people who live south of that latitude.
3. Design a study to test hypothesis	This could be an experiment, observation, self-report or correlation. Design: Experiment, participants could be selected randomly from phonebooks in the north and south. Each participant must read out five preselected jokes to an independent panel who rate how funny the jokes were.
4. Draw conclusions	For example, 'These results suggest that people ...'.

Nature and principles of scientific enquiry

Cause and effect	Experimental research demonstrates a causal relationship by deliberately manipulating an independent variable and observing its effect on a dependent variable.
Control	Refers to the extent to which any variable is held constant or regulated by a researcher.
Falsification	The attempt to prove something wrong.
Induction and deduction	Induction: reasoning from particular to general, starting with making observations, testing them and proposing theories. Deduction: reasoning from general to particular, starting with a theory and looking for confirmation.
Objectivity	Being uninfluenced by personal opinions, being free of bias. The opposite is subjectivity.
Quantifiable measurements	Recording behaviour in numbers – this makes subsequent analysis and interpretation easier.
Replicability	If a result from a research study is true (valid) then it should be possible to obtain the same result if the study is repeated.
Standardisation	Ensuring that all procedures are the same for every participant so their performances are comparable.

Report writing

The sections and subsections of the report in a journal follow the structure below. We have followed a similar structure when reporting the core studies in this book.

Abstract	A summary of the study covering the aims, hypothesis, method (including procedures), results and conclusions. Usually about 150–200 words.
Introduction	A review of previous research, the focus of which should lead logically to the aims, so the reader is convinced of the reasons for this particular research.
Method	The overall method, e.g. laboratory experiment. The method section of the report includes details of the design, sample and materials/apparatus.
Design	The particular variation of the method, e.g. repeated measures or covert observation.
Sample	Information about how many participants took part, details of age, gender and any other important characteristics.
Materials/ apparatus	Brief details of any psychological tests, questionnaires, equipment or other materials used.
Procedure	A step-by-step account of what the researchers did, detailed enough to enable other researchers to replicate the study exactly. Ethical issues may be mentioned.
Results	This section contains what the researcher found, which includes descriptive statistics and inferential statistics.
Discussion	This section may include: • A summary of the results. • A consideration of the relationship to previous research. • Comments on possible methodological problems that arose and improvements suggested. • Implications for psychological theory and possible real-world applications. • Suggestions for future research.
References	The Harvard system of referencing, for example: Milgram, S. (1963) Behavioural study of obedience. *Journal of Abnormal and Social Psychology*, *67*, (4), 371–378. [Author surname, initial(s), date of publication, title of article, title of journal, volume, (issue), page numbers]
Appendices	Contains examples of materials (e.g. questionnaire, standardised instructions), raw data, calculations.

And one more thing ... the specification for Research methods also says:

Learners should understand how society makes decisions about scientific issues and how psychology contributes to the success of the economy and society.

We have included some pointers throughout this revision guide.

Abstracts appear at the beginning of a research report, but are only written once the research report has been completed.

Revision booster

Recall the structure of your favourite core study to help you to remember what information should appear in each section of a psychology research report.

Exam-style question examples

Component 1 Section C:

A university psychology lecturer wants to write some guidelines on how to structure a research report for her first-year students.

1. Outline the information the lecturer should include in her guidelines for the 'abstract' in a research report. **[2]**

2. Describe how the lecturer would explain the purpose of the introduction section of a research report. **[2]**

3. Outline what information the lecturer would recommend is included in the discussion section of a research report. **[2]**

4. Describe what information the lecturer would suggest is included in the appendices section of a research report. **[2]**

The social area

Obedience is an indispensable part of social life. In order for people to live in communities, some system of authority is required.

Good answers always include the use of the specialist terms for the topic, e.g. tyranny, whistle-blowing, diffusion of responsibility.

Revision booster

Pay attention to the difference between the situational perspective and the social area.

The situational perspective (in the individual/situational debate) concerns the effect of the situation (physical and social) on our behaviour (in contrast with the effect of individual factors, e.g. biological).

The social area is only concerned with the effect of other people on our behaviour – so it is just one component of situational influences.

Key concepts	**Social interaction** Social psychology aims to understand people in the context of their interactions with others. An early example of the social area is Triplett's (1897) experimental work. He showed that competition with others improved performance, e.g. racing cyclists achieved better times on a circuit when they had someone pacing them.
	Social influence The social area has a special duty to consider ethics because psychologists investigating social influence attempt to influence participants' behaviour without the participants knowing. However, such influences are common in everyday life (e.g. teachers and health professionals), so social influence research isn't always unethical.
Everyday applications	**Prevention of mindless obedience** For example, in the emergency services and the prison service.
	Encouraging resistance to tyranny For example, soldiers should resist blindly following orders.
	Encouraging altruistic behaviour For example, encouraging people to consider the cost and benefits of helping.
Similarities	Social psychology is similar to developmental psychology as they share methods and approaches to the study of people, e.g. both build models of social behaviour, and both focus on the whole person, their cognition, emotion and behaviour.
Differences	Social psychology is different from biological psychology and cognitive psychology because social behaviour is affected by culture whereas our biological and cognitive behaviour is more universal.
	Social behaviour varies across cultures (it is ethnocentric), e.g. Milgram's study was conducted in America (an individualist culture) but his findings about obedience may not apply to collectivist cultures.
Evaluation	✚ **Control of variables** Is often high, e.g. Bocchiaro *et al.* controlled the behaviour and script of the experimenter, which meant valid conclusions could be drawn about responses to authority.
	✚ **Provides insights** Into behaviour and helps us understand how we are influenced by others, e.g. Milgram's study shows how people are surprisingly obedient.
	➖ **Uncontrolled extraneous variables** Can affect findings, e.g. Piliavin *et al.*'s study took place on the New York subway where many factors may influence helping behaviours, such as how much attention the passengers paid to the confederates.
	➖ **Research can take place in unrealistic settings** For example, Bocchiaro *et al.*'s study was conducted in a university laboratory where participants knew their behaviour was being studied, creating demand characteristics.

Links between the area and the perspectives/debates

The social area is compared to the other four areas on page 97.

The perspectives, and debates are explained on pages 90-94.

Behaviourist perspective Social behaviours (such as obedience) may be learned through reinforcement. For example, individuals may learn that obedience is rewarded by observing the behaviour of others who act as role models.

Psychodynamic perspective Authoritarian personality explains obedience in terms of a punitive parent who creates hostility in the child. This hostility is displaced on to weaker people and creates an exaggerated respect for authority.

Nature/nurture Levine *et al.*'s study suggests that helping behaviour may be an outcome of nurture rather than nature. As helping varies so much from culture to culture, perhaps it is more likely to be learned than to be a fundamental feature of human nature.

Free will/determinism Behaviour is determined by social roles and influence of other people. For example, Milgram's study of obedience suggests that the participants' obedience was caused by the 'prods' given by the experimenter rather than their spontaneous choice.

Individual/situational Arousal in the Piliavin *et al.* cost-reward model is influenced by situational factors, e.g. the proximity to an emergency situation. Situational factors in Levine *et al.*'s study are understood in a broad sense to include wider cultural and socioeconomic factors.

You need to be ready for questions on all eight debates. We have covered three here - you can read about the others on pages 91-94.

It's great when the effect we have on other people is a positive one - let's do this more often!

Revision booster

Make sure you know the key themes for each pair of studies. For example, both Milgram and Bocchiaro *et al.* are linked to the theme of *responses to people in authority*. This will help you to contextualise your short-answer responses.

Links between the area and the core studies

Core study 1 Milgram on *Obedience*	Participants' obedience was influenced by the presence of a legitimate authority figure in a prestigious location, dressed in a laboratory coat. This shows how other people influence our behaviour.
Core study 2 Bocchiaro *et al.* on *Disobedience*	Participants showed higher levels of obedience and lower levels of whistle-blowing than predicted. This suggests that disobedience, as well as obedience, can be attributed to situational factors rather than dispositional ones.
Core study 3 Piliavin *et al.* on the *Subway Samaritan*	In this study there was a high rate of helping which can be explained by the fact that participants believed the costs of not helping were high and the costs of helping were low. This was presumably because of the social situation, i.e. a closed subway carriage with a clear emergency.
Core study 4 Levine *et al.* on *Cross-cultural altruism*	Helping behaviour varied from one city to another and was related to economic productivity. This shows that helping behaviour is influenced by culture, which is a situational factor.

Exam-style question examples

Component 2 Section A:

1. Outline how Bocchiaro *et al.*'s study relates to the theme of responses to people in authority. **[3]**

2. Explain how Bocchiaro *et al.*'s research links to the social area. **[3]**

Component 2 Section B:

1. Outline **two** principles or concepts of the social area of psychology. **[4]**

2. Explain why the results of research into social psychology are ethnocentric. **[3]**

3. a) Outline **one** weakness of research into the social area. **[3]**
   b) Outline **one** strength of research into the social area. **[3]**

4. Outline **two** everyday applications of research into the social area. **[4]**

5. Describe how the social area supports the nurture side of the nature/nurture debate. **[2]**

Social core study 1 (classic)
Milgram (1963) on *Obedience*

Background

Research into obedience
Milgram wondered if German obedience in World War II was dispositional, and wanted to pilot a procedure to assess obedience.

Aims
To investigate:

- The process of obedience.
- The power of a legitimate authority, even when a command requires destructive behaviour.

Method

Design
Controlled observation (in a laboratory), using self-report. Milgram called it an experiment but it was not really an experiment because there was no independent variable.

Sample
40 American men aged 20-50, recruited via a newspaper advert. The men had varied occupational and educational backgrounds but there were no high school or college students. Participants were paid $4 plus 50c for transport.

Materials/apparatus
Shock generator with 30 switches, labelled from 15 to 450 volts, in increments of 15 volts. Labels described voltage intensity, e.g. 'strong shock'.

Procedure

1. Study took place at Yale University.
2. Participants were told the study was about punishment and learning, and were told they would be paid $4.50.
3. Naïve volunteer participant introduced to other 'participant', a confederate (Mr Wallace). Drew (rigged) lots for role of teacher (T) and learner (L). Real participant always played the teacher.
4. L was strapped to electrodes in one room, T in other room with experimenter (E).
5. T and L were advised shocks would be painful but there would be no tissue damage. T given 45-volt test shock to show shocks were real.
6. T read the questions to L who was strapped in chair in a separate room, answering using a four-way panel.
7. If T expressed a desire to stop delivering shocks, then E had a set of statements ('prods') to deliver, e.g. 'The experiment requires that you continue'.
8. When the shock level reached 300 volts, L had been instructed to pound on the wall. This pounding on the wall was repeated again at 315 volts and after that L stopped responding.

Results

Quantitative

1. All 40 participants (100%) continued giving shocks up to 300 volts.
2. Five participants (12.5%) stopped at this critical point of 300 volts.
3. Nine more participants stopped between 315 and 375 volts.
4. Obedience: 26 out of 40 participants (65%) continued to the end (450 volts) and were considered obedient.
5. Disobedience: 14 out of 40 participants were disobedient.

Qualitative

6. Many participants showed signs of nervousness: sweating, trembling, stuttering, biting their lips and groaning.
7. Uncontrollable seizures were observed for three participants.
8. Participants' comments showed their distress, e.g. '*He's banging in there. I'm gonna chicken out. I'd like to continue, but... I'm sorry I can't do that to a man*'.

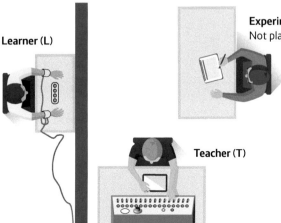

Learner (L)

Experimenter (E)
Not played by Milgram

A diagram of the room set-up showing the experimenter and teacher in one room, and learner in a separate room. The shock generator is in front of the teacher.

Teacher (T)

Conclusions

People are surprisingly obedient to authority.

The study demonstrated the power of the situation in obedient behaviour, rather than disposition (the 'Germans are different' hypothesis).

A significant number of participants were disobedient.

Links between the core study and the methodological issues

Research method and techniques

 Study conducted in a controlled laboratory environment, which means that potential extraneous variables (e.g. shock levels) can be controlled. This increases internal validity.

⊖ Participants were aware their behaviour was being studied because they were brought into the laboratory. This creates demand characteristics so participants might realise the study is about obedience and try to be more obedient.

Validity

⊖ Participants may not have believed they were delivering real shocks, which threatens the meaningfulness of the results.

⊖ Milgram believed that his results showed that people were very obedient. However, Haslam *et al.* (2014) showed that participants only continued for the first three prods. All participants who were given prod 4 ('You have no other choice, you must go on') disobeyed. This challenges the conclusion about obedience because, when participants were told they must blindly obey, they did not.

Sampling bias

⊕ Sample included men from a range of occupations and educational backgrounds, so it was likely to be representative of the target population.

⊖ There may be gender differences which limit the generalisability of the results. Milgram subsequently conducted the same study with women and found similar levels of obedience.

Ethical considerations

⊕ Despite being distressed by the experience, participants were debriefed and many felt very positive about the study.

⊖ Debriefing was delayed for up to a year, so Milgram failed in a duty of care.

⊖ Deception was used as participants were told the study was about learning and the electric shocks were real. This means participants were deprived of the right to give informed consent. This is important because they were exposed to psychological harm.

Ethnocentrism

⊖ A feature of the sample is that only Americans were involved.

America is an individualist culture which is characterised by people being more concerned with individual gains than the 'common good'. This might have made participants more obedient.

Members of collectivist cultures might be more concerned with the learner's suffering and less likely to obey an authority figure.

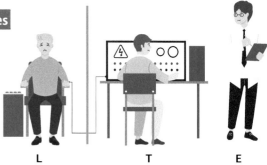

L   T   E

The learner was strapped into an 'electric chair apparatus' and given 'shocks' if he made a mistake on the learning task.

Revision booster

When revising try to remember five key pieces of terminology from each core study, e.g. for Milgram you may choose 'authority figure', 'prods', 'obedience', 'shocks' and 'seizures'. Using these words or phrases helps you to be concise and precise in short-answer questions – demonstrating good use of terminology.

Exam-style question examples

Component 2 Section A:

1. Outline the aims of Milgram's study. [2]

2. Describe the sample in Milgram's study. [2]

3. Outline **one** of the 'prods' used by Milgram in his study. [2]

4. Outline **two** procedures that made participants think Milgram's study was real. [4]

5. Outline **two** quantitative results from Milgram's study. [2]

6. Outline **one** strength of the quantitative data from Milgram's study. [3]

7. Describe a strength of the sampling method used by Milgram. [3]

8. Outline **one** ethical consideration from the Milgram study. [2]

How psychology contributes to the success of the economy and society …
It helps to find ways to explain our relationships with people in authority, and how to make these positive.

Social core study 2 (contemporary)
Bocchiaro *et al.* (2012) on *Disobedience*

Background

Disobedience and unjust authority

In Milgram's study participants were required to obey an unjust authority. What happens when people are offered the option to take personal action against unjust authority (i.e. disobey)?

Aims

To investigate:

- How people deal with unethical/unjust requests.
- Differences between how people think they will behave and how they actually behave.
- Personality characteristics of people who obey/disobey/whistle-blow.

Method

Design

Controlled observation (in a laboratory). The 'experimental paradigm' was a hypothetical unethical study on sensory deprivation to see whether participants would obey a request to write a statement to a fellow student and/or blow the whistle by filling in a form about the ethics of the proposed study.

Sample

Self-selected sample of 149 Dutch university students (96 women and 53 men), paid €7 or given course credit.

Two further groups of participants used to predict obedience behaviour: 92 students in pilot tests and 138 'comparison' students.

Materials/apparatus

A research committee ethics form for participants to complete and post anonymously - this would constitute whistle-blowing.

Personality tests: HEXACO-PI-R, Decomposed Games Measure.

Procedure

1. Eight pilot tests were conducted to check how believable the study was, and to gain ethical approval.
2. The 'comparison' group of participants was asked to predict how they would behave if they were a participant in the study and how other participants would behave.
3. The experimenter discussed a future research project with each participant, in a laboratory at the University of Amsterdam.
4. The experimenter asked each participant:
   - To give names of other students to take part in an unethical study.
   - To write an enthusiastic statement encouraging fellow students to take part and not mention the negative effects of sensory deprivation.
   - To fill in the University Research Committee ethical approval form.
5. Participants wrote statements in a second room and were given an opportunity to fill in a form to express concern about the ethics of the proposed study.
6. Participants completed the two psychological tests.
7. Entire session lasted about 40 minutes.
8. All participants were debriefed.

Results

1. 'Comparison' group thought they would be unlikely to obey (3.6% said they would obey) but thought others would be more likely to obey (18.8%).
2. 76.5% of the 'real' participants obeyed.
3. 64.5% of the 'comparison' group thought that they were most likely to blow the whistle compared to 31.9% who thought they would disobey.
4. The opposite was true for real participants, 9.4% of the 'real' participants blew the whistle and 14.1% disobeyed.
5. 14 participants were whistle-blowers (9.4%). Of these, five blew the whistle and also disobeyed, and nine blew the whistle but obeyed.
6. There were no significant differences between those who obeyed or disobeyed (and blew the whistle) in terms of gender, religious affiliation, the six key personality traits or social orientation. Whistle-blowers tended to have more 'faith' than other participants.

Bocchiaro et al.'s research paradigm looked at traumatic effects of sensory deprivation but only 9.4% of participants 'blew the whistle' because they thought it was unethical.

Conclusions

What people believe they will do is quite different from what they actually do.

This belief that they are 'better than average' may make them blind to social pressures and thus more vulnerable to them.

Situational rather than dispositional factors may offer a better explanation for disobedience.

Links between the core study and the methodological issues

Research method and techniques

⊕ The procedure was standardised, e.g. the paradigm used and the timings and locations were the same for all participants. Therefore, uncontrolled factors were minimised.

⊕ Obedience was tested in an ethical manner.

⊖ Participants may have been alert to the contrived situation and guessed the aims of the study, creating demand characteristics. However, the researchers reported that the participants did appear to believe the cover story.

Validity and reliability

⊕ The personality tests used have good validity and reliability.

- HEXACO-PI-R test: high levels of self-observer agreement (validity) and of internal consistency (reliability).
- Decomposed Games Measure: criterion validity of behaviour in social situations and good test-retest reliability.

Sampling bias

⊕ The sample included both men and women. Therefore, the final analysis could consider whether gender differences might explain the observed behaviour.

⊖ The sample were all university students with fewer responsibilities than older adults. Students might be more proactive in protesting about unfair practices. Such participants may be more likely to be disobedient and blow the whistle than the general population.

Types of data

⊕ Quantitative data provided assessments of levels of obedience and personality traits, e.g. knowing each participant's score on the personality test. This makes it easy to analyse results.

⊖ However, quantitative measures might oversimplify complex behaviours and personality traits.

⊕ Qualitative data was provided in the comments made by participants during the study and during debriefing.

Ethical considerations

⊕ Participants gave informed consent as they knew what was involved. Even though they did not know the true aims, participants had the right to withdraw and were debriefed.

⊖ Participants were deceived about the premise for the unethical study and the requirements for recruiting.

Ethnocentrism

⊖ The experimenter belonged to the same ethnic group as the participants (all Dutch and all members of the university), so participants may have responded in a more positive way towards him. There may have been less obedience if the experimenter was felt to be an 'outsider'.

Whistle-blowers are protected by law and should not be treated unfairly or lose their job if they 'blow the whistle'.

Know the BPS code of ethics and conduct for research in psychology (see page 29), and make sure you can explain how it is applied to the core studies in the social area, e.g. the ethical principle of 'respect' is demonstrated in the informed consent that was gained by Bocchiaro et al.

Exam-style question examples

Component 2 Section A:

1. Outline the aims of the Bocchiaro *et al.* study. **[2]**

2. Identify the research design used in the Bocchiaro *et al.* study. **[2]**

3. Describe the sample used in the Bocchiaro *et al.* study. **[2]**

4. Identify the **two** personality tests participants completed in the Bocchiaro *et al.* study. **[2]**

5. In the Bocchiaro *et al.* study, what instructions were the participants given for writing the statement to their fellow students? **[4]**

6. Outline a strength of the procedure used by Bocchiaro *et al.* **[3]**

7. Give **one** strength of the quantitative data in the Bocchiaro *et al.* study. **[4]**

8. Outline **one** piece of evidence to show how the Bocchiaro *et al.* study can be considered ethical. **[2]**

Social core study 3 (classic)
Piliavin *et al.* (1969) on the *Subway Samaritan*

> * The term 'race' was used by Piliavin *et al.* to refer to the colour of the victim's skin. We have chosen to use 'ethnicity' in our descriptions.

Background

Bystander behaviour and diffusion of responsibility

Bystanders in an emergency situation often do not offer help. This is described as *bystander behaviour*. In a large group each person feels less responsibility and this may explain bystander behaviour.

Aims

To investigate the effects of four independent variables (see right) on helping behaviour in a real-life setting.

Method

Design

Field experiment, independent measures design, using observational techniques. It is also a snapshot study.

IVs: Type of victim (drunk or cane), ethnicity* (black or white), gender of helpers (men or women), presence of model, group size.

DVs: Time it took for help to be offered and number of people who offered help.

Sample

Opportunity sample of 4,450 passengers on the New York subway, weekdays 11 am to 3 pm from 15 April to 26 June 1968. 60% of passengers were men.

Materials/apparatus

Each trial involved the 'victim' carrying either a black cane or a liquor bottle wrapped in brown paper, standing next to a pole in the middle of the carriage.

Procedure

1. 103 trials of one ride on the New York subway lasting $7\frac{1}{2}$ minutes. On each trial four students boarded using different doors.

2. The victim stood next to the pole in the centre of the critical area. After 70 seconds, the victim collapsed and remained on the floor until he received help or until the train stopped and the model helped him up.

3. On 38 trials the victim smelled of liquor and carried a liquor bottle (drunk condition). On 65 trials, the victim appeared sober and carried a black cane (cane condition).

4. The model was in the critical or the adjacent area, and either helped early (70 seconds after initial collapse) or late (150 seconds later).

5. The observers sat outside the critical area.

6. Observer 1 noted (a) ethnicity, gender and location (EGL) of people in the critical area, (b) number of people in the car, (c) number of people who helped, (d) EGL of people who helped.

7. Observer 2 noted (a) EGL of people in the adjacent area, (b) how long it took for the first person to help after the victim collapsed and/or after the model appeared.

8. Both observers recorded comments spontaneously made by nearby passengers.

Cost–reward matrix

	Helping	Not helping
Costs	Effort Harm Embarrassment	Disapproval Blame Guilt
Rewards	Praise from others and self	Continuation of other activities

Results

Type of victim (drunk or cane)

1. A person using a cane is more likely to receive help than one who appears drunk.

2. Help is more quickly forthcoming for a person with a cane than a 'drunk' victim.

3. The median latency for cane trials was 5 seconds.

Ethnicity and gender of helpers

4. The black victim received help less quickly than white victims.

5. A slight 'same-ethnicity effect' was found in the drunk condition.

6. 90% of first helpers were men, whereas only 60% of passengers were men.

Presence of model

7. The model intervening early (after 70 seconds) had slightly more effect than the late model (150 seconds).

Group size

8. 'Diffusion of responsibility' was not found in this study. Helping was greater in seven-person groups than three-person groups.

Comments from passengers

9. For example, 'It's for men to help him' or 'You feel so bad when you don't know what to do'.

Conclusions

A cost–reward model (see left) can predict when help will be forthcoming in an emergency situation where escape is not possible:

- The emergency situation creates heightened arousal. The decision to help is motivated by a selfish desire to rid oneself of this unpleasant emotional state.

- Action will depend on whether the rewards of helping are greater than the costs of not helping.

Links between the core study and the methodological issues

Research method and techniques

➕ The study was conducted in the natural environment of the New York subway where people were unaware of being studied, reducing demand characteristics.

➖ Extraneous variables are difficult to control in a field experiment (on the subway train). Factors other than the independent variables may have influenced the likelihood of helping, e.g. people may have been stressed by the urban environment.

Reliability

➕ Standardised procedures were used, e.g. the victim was always dressed identically. (However, there were no checks of whether the teams followed these procedures.)

➖ The reliability of the observations may be low as only one person made each set of observations.

Sampling bias

➕ A very large sample collected over a period of several months containing a wide cross-section of people, and generalisable to the target population.

➖ Despite having a large sample, participants had characteristics that make them unrepresentative, e.g. living in or visiting a city and probably accustomed to being faced with emergency situations.

Types of data

➕ Most data was quantitative, which is useful for comparing speed and frequency of helping in different trials.

➕ Qualitative data was comments from people sitting in the carriage e.g. 'It's for men to help him'. Such comments help us understand reasons for not helping.

Ethical considerations

➖ Informed consent can't be obtained in a field experiment. This is particularly important in this study due to the risk of psychological harm from seeing someone collapse, especially for those participants who did not offer help and may have felt bad afterwards.

➖ Participants may have been upset by what they witnessed and there was no debriefing, so participants may have been left wondering if the victim was OK.

Ethnocentrism

➖ The results may be specific to some cultures and not others. America is an individualist culture which is characterised by people being more concerned with individual gains than the 'common good'.

In contrast, people living in a collectivist culture might show greater willingness to help in an emergency situation and greater concern about the costs of not helping.

Piliavin et al.'s study explains helping behaviour in situations where escape is not possible and where bystanders are face-to-face with a victim.

Revision booster

Always aim to explain your point in the context of the study – just saying the study is/isn't valid or is/isn't reliable will not be enough. You need to be able to contextualise your point by using the phrase 'such as', e.g. Piliavin *et al.*'s procedure is reliable as they used standardised procedures *such as* the victim participated in both cane and drunk trials.

Exam-style question examples

Component 2 Section A:

1. Outline what you understand by the term 'bystander behaviour'. **[2]**

2. Identify **one** independent variable in Piliavin *et al.*'s study. **[2]**

3. Describe the appearance of the victim and the materials used in the drunk condition of Piliavin *et al.*'s study. **[2]**

4. Outline the details recorded by the observers in Piliavin *et al.*'s study. **[2]**

5. Suggest **one** weakness in the way the observers recorded the data in Piliavin *et al.*'s study. **[2]**

6. Give **one** strength of how Piliavin *et al.* reduced the sampling bias in their study. **[3]**

7. Explain why Piliavin *et al.*'s study may be considered ethnocentric. **[3]**

8. Explain **two** ways Piliavin *et al.*'s study can be considered unethical. **[4]**

The exam questions above are just representative examples. Read the guidance for Component 2 exam questions on page 7.

Social core study 4 (contemporary)
Levine *et al.* (2001) on *Cross-cultural altruism*

Background

Research on helping behaviour
Research has looked at whether people are more helpful in some environments than others, e.g. urban versus rural communities or large versus smaller cities.

Aims
To investigate:

- Culturally meaningful characteristics of helping.
- Cultural differences in helping.
- Community characteristics associated with helping strangers: economic, cultural and cognitive.

Method

Design
Quasi-experiment, independent measures design, cross-cultural.

Community variables were measured in the following ways:

- Population size - United Nations Demographic Yearbook.
- Economic productivity - Purchasing power parity (PPP).
- Cultural values - Six experts rated individualism-collectivism.
- Pace of life - Walking speed between two markers.

Sample
Largest city in 23 countries, testing average of 50 people in each city. Selection criteria: over 17, not physically disabled, not very old or carrying heavy objects.

Materials/apparatus
In different scenarios researchers needed a pen, a set of magazines, a leg brace, or some dark glasses and a white cane.

Procedure

1. Data collected in cities on summer weekdays.
2. Applied selection criteria (see above) to approaching pedestrians.
3. Participants were the second pedestrian to cross an imaginary line on pavement.

Three measures of helping behaviour

4. Dropped pen: Experimenter (E) accidentally dropped pen 10 feet from solitary participant/pedestrian (P).

   424 Ps were approached, classed as 'helping' if P told E that E dropped a pen or if P returned the pen.

5. Hurt leg: E walked with limp and wore a leg brace, dropped and tried to pick up magazines.

   493 Ps were approached, classed as 'helping' if P offered to pick up magazines or picked them up.

6. Helping blind person across street: E had dark glasses and white cane, waiting to cross road.

   281 Ps were approached, classed as 'helping' if P told E that light was green or helped E cross.

Results

1. Some consistency across measures of helping, e.g. between dropped pen and blind person scores, and between hurt leg and dropped pen scores.
2. There were no gender differences.
3. Standard score calculated for each country/city for each measure of helping, e.g. Brazil = 1.66.

Relationship of community variables to helping

4. *Economic productivity* A significant negative correlation between economic productivity (PPP) and overall helping ($p < 0.15$) (cities with lower economic productivity were more helpful).
5. *Pace of life* A positive correlation, not significant, between walking speed and overall helping (people in faster cities were less likely to offer help).
6. *Cultural values* Individualist countries were slightly less helpful.
7. *Population size* No correlation with helpfulness.
8. *Simpatia cultures* (Brazil, Costa Rica, El Salvador, Mexico and Spain) Significantly more helpful than non-simpatia ($p < 0.02$).

People may be more sympathetic and helpful from a 'simpatia' culture e.g. Costa Rica.

Conclusions

The data provides some support for the view that big cities do have a 'personality' and some cities may have more of a 'helping personality' than others.

To gain further understanding a multitude of variables need to be tracked.

The results challenge a biological view of altruism as they indicate that cultural variables may be significant.

Links between the core study and the methodological issues

Research method and techniques

⊕ Each of the three measures (dropped pen, hurt leg, helping a blind person) could be clearly operationalised and standardised so that it was clear that a person needed help and whether or not help had been given.

⊖ The study was only looking at one kind of (rather superficial) helpfulness - an everyday favour. Results could not be generalised to the kind of altruism that would enhance survival.

⊖ The 'pace of life' measure was crude, e.g. observing how quickly people walked in each country.

Validity

⊕ Study took place in a natural environment where pedestrians were walking, therefore it captured real helping behaviour.

⊖ However, extraneous variables were not well-controlled, e.g. different experimenter was used in each location, so individual characteristics may explain different helping rates.

Reliability

⊕ Different helping measures were scripted and standardised. Experimenters were trained for consistency.

⊖ However, the experimenter was a different person in each country, so may have performed each scenario slightly differently.

Sampling bias

⊕ Several cultures are compared, so more useful conclusions can be drawn about cultural differences in helping.

⊕ Areas in each city were chosen so they were comparable.

⊖ Sample of 23 countries considered by the researchers to be small, with many cultures not included - most were from individualist cultures.

⊖ A small sample also makes it more difficult to detect trends in behaviour.

Types of data

⊕ Quantitative data provided a simple figure, e.g. Costa Rica (1.52) and USA (-1.74) to compare helpfulness in different cultures.

⊖ Gained no insight into why people helped or did not help. This could have been gathered through a debrief after the participant/pedestrian had passed the experimenter.

Ethical considerations

⊖ As this quasi-experiment was conducted in the field, informed consent was not possible.

⊕ However, this matters less when amount of distress is minimal (as in this study), although mild distress may have been experienced.

The fast pace of life of a city means people may experience sensory overload (Milgram 1970) and therefore screen out behaviours such as noticing a blind person needing help to cross the street.

Ethnocentrism is a tricky concept - it is not the same as sampling bias. Ethnocentrism refers to the bias in seeing things from the point of view of a particular social group, whereas sampling bias is a systematic error created by using participants who do not fully represent the population.

Exam-style question examples

Component 2 Section A:

1. Describe the aims of the Levine *et al.* study. **[2]**

2. Outline the community variables measured in the Levine *et al.* study. **[4]**

3. Describe the sample in the Levine *et al.* study. **[2]**

4. From the Levine *et al.* study, outline the procedure for the 'dropped pen' measure of helping behaviour. **[3]**

5. From the Levine *et al.* study, describe the results in relation to '*simpatia*' and '*non-simpatia*' cultures. **[3]**

6. Give **one** strength of the type of data collected by Levine *et al.* **[3]**

7. Outline **two** weaknesses of the sample used by Levine *et al.* in their study. **[4]**

8. In what way might the Levine *et al.* study lack reliability? **[2]**

Methodological issues are discussed in Chapter 1 and also on pages 95-96.

Cognitive psychology is the dominant approach in modern psychology.

Good answers always include the use of the specialist terms for the topic, e.g. computer metaphor, information processing, mechanistic, attention.

The method of loci

This is a method used by memory experts, based on contextual cues. You imagine walking around a well-known building or street and place items in particular places, such as the letters CBT are put in a dish of spaghetti in your fridge. The more bizarre the image the better. Then, when trying to recall a list of items, you repeat your mental journey. Have a look at some examples on YouTube.

It seems our memories have evolved to remember contextual links – you will have experienced this, for example when you eat something unusual you may recall the last time you ate the same thing.

Key concepts	**The computer metaphor** The human mind is studied by comparing it to the processes of machines and information-processing models of cognition. These models are based on computer processes, e.g. input, processing, output.
	Experimentation Wundt set up the first psychology laboratory in Germany in 1879. The laboratory researched topics such as sensory processes and perception and also looked at reaction time, learning, attention and emotion.
	Nowadays, participants in cognitive research may be asked to respond to small changes on a computer screen. The studies mainly deal with abstract tasks in unreal situations.
Everyday applications	**Artificial intelligence** Research in cognitive psychology can be applied to making intelligent machines, e.g. robots.
	Cognitive behaviour therapy (CBT) People are taught to think (cognitive) differently about their mental health problems (e.g. depression) and put this into practice (behavioural). CBT is the most commonly used psychological treatment for a range of mental health problems.
	Mnemonics These are instructional strategies designed to help students improve their memory of important information, based on psychological understanding of how memory works. For example, contextual cues trigger recall and are used in many memory techniques (e.g. method of loci, see left).
Similarities	Cognitive psychology is most connected to biological psychology and the behaviourist perspective because of the use of controlled experiments in laboratory conditions.
Differences	Cognitive psychology differs from the behaviourist perspective because it considers what is going on inside the brain rather than just studying behaviour.
Evaluation	⊕ **Experimental research** Cognitive psychology lends itself to experiments as single variables can be isolated and tested, e.g. the verb in Loftus and Palmer's study. Identifying single variables enables cause-and-effect conclusions to be made.
	⊕ **Control of variables** Creates high internal validity, e.g. Grant *et al.*'s procedures were standardised, enabling easy replication to confirm the results.
	⊖ **Lacks mundane realism** As the tasks used to test mental abilities are often contrived, e.g. Loftus and Palmer's participants estimated speed from film slides (which lack emotional involvement).
	⊖ **Mechanistic explanations** Human thinking is represented in terms of how a machine might behave rather than a human, e.g. Grant *et al.* saw context as a trigger for memory (machine-like).

Links between the area and the perspectives/debates

The cognitive area is compared to the other four areas on page 97.

The perspectives and debates are explained on pages 90-94.

Behaviourist perspective Cognitive concepts (e.g. attention) can be explained via operant conditioning. A reward may increase the likelihood of people paying attention to unexpected objects, such as the gorilla or woman with an umbrella in Simons and Chabris' study.

Psychodynamic perspective Things we are not aware of may still influence our behaviour. Moray showed how affective cues (e.g. our name) can break the attentional block and move into our consciousness.

Individual/situational There is support for situational explanations as behaviour is affected by cues in the situation, e.g. leading questions affected memory in Loftus and Palmer's study.

Usefulness Research has important real-world applications, e.g. Loftus and Palmer's conclusions suggest that some convictions are based on unsound eyewitness testimony.

Psychology as a science Both Simons and Chabris and Moray illustrate how we can investigate internal mental processes in scientific and controlled ways, e.g. Simons and Chabris used videos that were the same length and the unexpected images had the same duration.

Processing information involves thinking, but don't try to multi-task as your brain can only focus on one thing at a time.

Revision booster

Using terminology from the principles and concepts of the cognitive area (e.g. 'information processing') makes your answers specific to the area and not simply specific to a core study. You can always add examples from core studies (e.g. Loftus and Palmer) to support your answer to a question on the cognitive area.

The debates on the left are examples of how you might link the area to the debates. All eight debates are explained on pages 91-94.

Links between the area and the core studies

Core study 1 Loftus and Palmer on *Eyewitness testimony*	Loftus and Palmer's study shows us that the input-process-output computer metaphor can be used to explain how eyewitness testimony of an event can be affected by leading questions that lead to a reconstructed memory, e.g. participants see the videos of car crashes, the verb reconstructs their memory and this affects their output (their speed estimate).
Core study 2 Grant *et al.* on *Context-dependent memory*	Grant *et al.*'s study looks at internal mental processes. In particular they showed how the recall of memories can be linked to environment context-dependency (EC) effects, such that recall is improved when the context of learning matches the context of recall.
Core study 3 Moray on *Auditory attention*	Attention is the first link in a chain of cognitive processes such as perception and memory. So Moray's study has a theoretical benefit in helping us to understand our wider cognitive systems. His research helped us to understand better how the attentional system processes reject certain messages.
Core study 4 Simons and Chabris on *Visual inattention*	Simons and Chabris' study has helped show how some external factors (such as task difficulty) can influence cognitive processes (such as inattentional blindness - by making inattentional blindness more or less likely to occur).

Exam-style question examples

Component 2 Section A:

1. In Loftus and Palmer's research, describe how a computer metaphor can be used to explain eyewitness testimony. [3]

2. Explain how Moray's research is linked to the cognitive area. [3]

Component 2 Section B:

1. Outline **two** principles of the cognitive area. [2]

2. Explain why reliability tends to be high in research into the cognitive area. [4]

3. a) Outline **one** weakness of research into the cognitive area. [3]
   b) Outline **one** strength of research into the cognitive area. [3]

4. Outline **two** everyday applications of research into the cognitive area. [4]

5. Describe how the cognitive area supports psychology as a science. [2]

Cognitive core study 1 (classic)

Loftus and Palmer (1974) on *Eyewitness testimony*

Background

Research into memory

Memory does not simply record what happens.

Certain questions/statements lead a person to give a particular answer. Such statements are called *leading questions*.

Aims

- Experiment 1: To test the effect of leading questions on recall.
- Experiment 2: To see if a leading question changes a person's subsequent memory of the event.

Method

Design

Laboratory experiments, independent measures design. Experiment 1 was a snapshot study (one time frame), repeated measures. Experiment 2 was longitudinal, over one week.

IV: Experiment 1 and 2 = the verb (e.g. 'smashed').

DV: Experiment 1 = estimate of speed.

Experiment 2 = whether participants said they saw broken glass.

Sample

Experiment 1: 45 US college students, in five groups.

Experiment 2: 150 US college students, in three groups.

Materials/apparatus

Experiment 1: Seven brief film clips of car accidents plus questionnaire.

Experiment 2: One-minute film of a four-second multiple car accident.

Procedure

Experiment 1

1. Participants were asked to describe the accident and answer questions, including one critical question: *How fast were the cars going when they* [insert verb] *each other?*
2. There were five different verb conditions: hit, contacted, smashed, bumped, collided.
3. Participants were asked (on the questionnaire) to estimate the car's speed in miles per hour (mph).

Experiment 2

4. Part 1: Participants were asked to describe the accident and answered questions about the film, including critical question.
5. Three groups of participants:
   - Experimental group 1: The verb was 'smashed'.
   - Experimental group 2: The verb was 'hit'.
   - Control group (group 3): There was no question.
6. Part 2: Participants returned to the lab a week later.
7. They were asked further questions about the film clips, e.g. *'Did you see any broken glass?'*. (There was not any broken glass in any of the film clips.)

Results

Experiment 1

1. Mean speed estimates were faster for the 'smashed' group (40.5 mph) than the 'contacted' group (31.8 mph).
2. Mean speed estimates for the others were: collided 39.3 mph, bumped 38.1 mph and hit 34.0 mph.
3. Participants were poor at estimating speed. Actual speeds in four clips were: 20, 30, 30 and 40 mph – but participants' mean estimates were between 36 and 40 mph.

Experiment 2

4. Mean speed estimates were faster for those who heard the verb 'smashed' (10.46 mph) than those with the verb 'hit' (8.0 mph).
5. More participants who heard the verb 'smashed' reported seeing broken glass (16 out of 50 participants) than other participants.
6. Seven (out of 50) participants with the verb 'hit' and six (out of 50) in the control group reported seeing broken glass.
7. Overall, most participants correctly reported seeing no broken glass (121 out of 150).

Conclusions

Experiment 1: The way a question is asked can influence the answer given.

Experiment 2: Such questions influence the memory that is stored rather than just biasing a person's response.

Two types of information make up our memory of a complex event: (1) information from our perception of the event and (2) the information we receive after the event.

Even if someone thinks they remember the crash in detail, it does not mean that it actually happened in that way.

Links between the core study and the methodological issues

Research method and techniques

➕ Laboratory conditions mean extraneous variables can be controlled, so high internal validity, e.g. in 'real life', estimates of speed might be affected by where a person is standing. In a laboratory we can ensure that each participant witnesses the accident from the same position.

➖ Watching films is not the same as watching a real accident, so participants lack emotional involvement. Foster *et al.* (1994) found that people in real accidents are likely to remember more.

➖ The study involved a task that people are not good at - estimating the speed of a moving vehicle.

Reliability

➕ Quantitative data is relatively straightforward to assess the reliability of the measurements that are made. Could ask the same participants to repeat the task a second time and would expect to get the same speed estimates each time.

Sampling bias

➕ Opportunity sample of US students on degree courses that were easy for researchers to obtain.

➖ Students have unique characteristics (e.g. more intelligent and have better memories than the average person) so might be less likely to be affected by leading questions. This research may underestimate the effect of leading questions.

Types of data

➕ Quantitative data - the estimates of speed and number of YES or NO answers. Such data produces simple conclusions but fairly superficial.

➕ Qualitative data - following each film the participants received a questionnaire asking them to 'give an account of the accident you have just seen', providing greater detail.

Ethical considerations

➖ Fully informed consent not obtained from participants. If participants were aware of the aims, they would have been aware that the questions were 'leading' and been more careful in the responses they gave.

➕ Deception was relatively mild (no psychological harm) and helped collect important data about the inaccuracy of eyewitness testimony.

Ethnocentrism

➖ America is an individualist culture, which might affect the willingness of people to be influenced by leading questions.

People from collectivist cultures may be more influenced by what other people say as they value the links within a group more than individual needs.

Be able to link each core study to its area. In this case the core study (Loftus and Palmer) is linked to the cognitive area because the study explains behaviour in terms of internal mental processes - the memory of what speed a car was travelling at is altered by information in our minds (leading questions).

Ambiguous details, such as shirt colour, are more difficult to remember, especially if a participant is given misleading information (leading questions).

Exam-style question examples

Component 2 Section A:

1. Outline the aim of the second Loftus and Palmer experiment. **[2]**

2. Outline the experimental design used in Loftus and Palmer's first experiment. **[2]**

3. Identify the independent variable in Loftus and Palmer's second experiment. **[2]**

4. Identify **two** of the verbs used in Loftus and Palmer's first experiment. **[2]**

5. Outline **two** types of information that make up our memory of a complex event. **[4]**

6. Explain why the findings from Loftus and Palmer's study can be seen to be high in reliability. **[2]**

7. Give **one** strength of the research method used by Loftus and Palmer. **[4]**

8. Give a strength of the sampling technique used by Loftus and Palmer. **[3]**

How psychology contributes to the success of the economy and society ... Loftus and Palmer's research can help make our communities safer by understanding the effect of leading questions on jury verdicts.

Cognitive core study 2 (contemporary)
Grant *et al.* (1998) on *Context-dependent memory*

Background

Research into environmental context

The environmental context-dependency (EC) effect refers to cues that may trigger you to remember something, e.g. if you revisit a place you have been before you may suddenly recall events that happened when you were last there. The place (environment) acts as a cue to recall.

Aims

To look at EC effects with different types of material, specifically the effects of noise.

Method

Design

Laboratory experiment, independent measures design with four conditions:

	Test in silence	Test with background noise
Read in silence	Condition 1	Condition 2
Read with background noise	Condition 3	Condition 4

IV 1: Whether reading and test were matching or not (conditions 1 and 4).

IV 2: Effects of studying in noisy versus silent conditions (conditions 1 and 2 versus 3 and 4).

DV: Number of items correctly recalled on a short-answer and multiple-choice test.

Sample

Opportunity sample of 39 American participants, 17 women and 22 men, aged 17 to 56 years.

Materials/apparatus

A passage on psychoimmunology, a 'noisy' tape created by recording students in a cafeteria, headphones, test of recall with 10 short-answer questions and 16 multiple-choice questions.

Procedure

1. Each experimenter had standardised instructions to read aloud.

2. Participants read the article once (they could highlight important parts of the text) and were told they would be given short-answer and multiple-choice tests on their comprehension.

3. All participants wore headphones while they read, and heard moderately loud noise or silence but were told to ignore the noise.

4. The time taken to read the passage was recorded by the experimenters.

5. A break of about two minutes followed participants' reading to minimise simple recall of information from short-term memory.

6. Participants were tested on their recall wearing headphones and were told beforehand that the background would be noisy or silent.

7. Short-answer test was given first and then multiple-choice test.

8. Participants were debriefed at the end. Altogether the entire procedure lasted about 30 minutes.

Results

1. Participants in all experimental conditions spent roughly an equal amount of time reading the article.

2. Participants performed better on multiple-choice tests than short-answer tests, i.e. better on the test of recognition than the test of recall.

3. The lowest score on the multiple-choice test was 79% whereas the highest score on the short-answer recall test was 67%.

4. Participants got higher test scores on the two matching conditions, i.e. the noisy study–noisy test and silent study–silent test conditions (see graph below left).

5. There was a significant EC effect for both kinds of test as shown by inferential statistics.

6. Time taken to read the article was not significantly different between the noisy and silent reading conditions.

7. Noise did not have a negative effect on studying. Overall the students who studied in the noisy conditions did slightly better on the final tests than those studying in silent conditions.

Conclusions

Environmental context-dependency (EC) effects occur for meaningful material.

Both recognition and recall are affected by EC effects.

Background noise does not appear to have a detrimental effect on studying.

Mean % recall on both tests for all four groups.

Legend: Matching conditions / Non-matching conditions

Silent-silent: 81%
Noisy-noisy: 79%
Silent-noisy: 67%
Noisy-silent: 70%

Links between the core study and the methodological issues

Research method and techniques

⊕ The task had mundane realism - reading an article and trying to recall information was similar to what students typically do, so the results of the study can be generalised to the everyday life of students.

⊖ Participants were tested in somewhat varying conditions, so extraneous variables (e.g. other distractions in the room where they studied or were tested) may have affected final test score.

Validity

⊖ Smith (1982) suggests that EC effects probably do not affect exam learning. Most students study in more than one environment and so multiple learning environments make information context-*independent*, reducing the validity of these results.

⊖ This study lacks ecological validity as EC effects are largely eliminated when meaningful associations are created between the pieces of information learned.

Sampling bias

⊕ Participants were students and friends of the experimenters. This is an appropriate sample to use when studying EC dependency effects on recall of meaningful material.

⊖ Students are not always motivated in research, so some of them may not have tried very hard on the tests they were given.

Type of data

⊕ Quantitative data only - the final comparison involved using test scores. This makes it easy to analyse the data.

Ethical considerations

⊕ Informed consent gained as participants knew the experiment was a class project and it was voluntary.

⊕ Participants debriefed afterwards and data kept confidential.

⊖ Protection from harm had to be considered as participants may feel they did not do very well on the test and this could cause a loss of confidence in their academic abilities.

Ethnocentrism

⊖ The participants were American and thus exposed to a culture that tends to focus on learning in a classroom.

Other cultures may spend more time learning in natural contexts where EC effects may be different.

Grant et al.'s research is potentially of considerable importance to students when studying. This means that a student sample was appropriate.

Revision booster

Linking the study to the theme is an important skill that shows understanding. Grant *et al.* showed how the recall of memories can be linked to EC effects, such that recall is improved when the context of learning matches the context of recall.

Exam-style question examples

Component 2 Section A:

1. Describe the aim of the Grant *et al.* study. **[2]**

2. Identify the dependent variables in the Grant *et al.* study. **[2]**

3. Outline the materials used in the Grant *et al.* study. **[2]**

4. Describe the sample used in the Grant *et al.* study. **[2]**

5. Outline **two** results from the Grant *et al.* study. **[4]**

6. Describe a weakness of the sample used by Grant *et al.* **[3]**

7. Explain **one** strength of the task used in the Grant *et al.* study. **[3]**

8. Outline **one** ethical consideration in Grant *et al.*'s study. **[2]**

Cognitive core study 3 (classic)
Moray (1959) on *Auditory attention*

Background

Shadowing

Shadowing involves the listener paying attention to one message (shadowed) but not the other message (rejected).

Cherry (1953) tested this 'selective attention' and found no recall of the 'rejected' message.

Aims

- Experiment 1: To test Cherry's results more rigorously.
- Experiment 2: To see if some messages can break through the attentional block.
- Experiment 3: To see if expectations affect message processing to the rejected ear.

Method

Design

Laboratory experiment: Experiments 1 and 2 repeated measures design, experiment 3 independent measures design.

Experiment 1 IV: Message played to shadowed or rejected ear.
DV: Number of words recalled in rejected message.

Experiment 2 IV: Effect of affective* or non-affective messages [*contained person's name].
DV: Number of affective instructions responded to.

Experiment 3 IV 1: Whether digits were inserted into one or two messages.
IV 2: Whether participants were told they would be asked questions about shadowed message or told to remember digits.
DV: Number of digits correctly remembered.

Sample

Men and women, undergraduates or research workers. Experiment 1 = participant number unknown, experiment 2 = 12 participants, experiment 3 = 14 participants.

Materials/apparatus

Two tape recorders, prose passage and word lists, avometer.

Procedure

1. Four passages played for shadow practice.

Experiment 1

2. Passage presented to shadowed ear and list of words presented 35 times to rejected ear.

3. Rejected message tested using free recall, then a recognition test of similar words as a control.

Experiment 2

4. Participants shadowed ten passages to right ear while another passage played to rejected left ear.

5. Shadowed right ear received instructions to create an expectation or 'set' for further messages.

6. Rejected left ear heard affective messages (with participant's name) or non-affective messages.

Experiment 3

7. Participants shadow one message in each ear.

8. Digits inserted towards the end of both messages, one message or neither message.

9. Group 1 asked questions about shadowed content, group 2 told to remember all digits.

Results

Experiment 1

1. Mean of 4.9 words (out of 7) recognised from shadowed message.

2. Mean of 1.9 words (out of 7) recognised from rejected message.

3. Mean of 2.6 words (out of 7) recognised from the control list.

Experiment 2

4. 20 out of 39 affective messages responded to by rejected ear compared to 4 out of 36 non-affective messages.

5. This difference is significant ($p < 0.01$).

6. There was some effect of expectation or 'set' but not significant – mean frequency of hearing affective message with a pre-passage warning was 0.8 whereas it was 0.33 with no warning.

Experiment 3

7. No significant difference between the number of digits recalled by either group, i.e. warning to remember all the digits or not.

Conclusions

Experiment 1 showed that the content of the rejected message is blocked, supporting Cherry.

Experiment 2 showed that an affective message breaks through the attentional barrier.

Experiment 3 showed neutral material was not important enough to break the barrier even when warned.

A dichotic message is when two messages are played, one to each ear. This illustration shows a dogchotic message.

Links between the core study and the methodological issues

Research method and techniques	⊕ Laboratory conditions mean extraneous variables are controlled, e.g. incoming messages in headphones were identical and sound levels were kept constant.
	⊖ Laboratory conditions mean participants are often aware of being studied so respond to demand characteristics, e.g. they may realise that they should attend especially to the shadowed message. In everyday life people may divide their attention.
Validity	⊖ Listening to sounds through headphones and being asked to block out or shadow what is heard is extremely artificial.
	⊕ However, everyday experiences would tend to confirm that we do tune out other conversations and sounds. Therefore, the ecological validity of the study is sound.
Reliability	⊕ Moray's procedures were highly standardised, e.g. the way each passage of prose and the word list was presented was the same for every participant. This means that the research could be replicated to check for reliability of results into auditory attention.
Sampling bias	⊕ The sample was easily accessible as Moray used undergraduates or researchers he worked with. This opportunity sample saved him time and money on obtaining participants.
	⊖ The sample is unrepresentative as students and researchers are likely to have high cognitive ability and may perform better on attentional tasks, reducing population validity.
Type of data	⊕ Quantitative data, e.g. mean number of words counted for shadowed and rejected ear. This makes it easy to compare the two conditions, and use inferential tests to determine significance.
Ethical considerations	⊕ Participants were not fully informed of the aims of the study or that in experiment 3 they would be tested on recall of information. This may be seen as a mild yet acceptable use of deception.
Ethnocentrism	⊖ People in individualist cultures may be more accustomed to selective attention. Whereas people in collectivist cultures may be more likely to pay attention to everything around them as they are more focused on group behaviour rather than individuals. There is evidence that children from individualist cultures learn skills related to focused attention more easily than children from collectivist cultures (Kuwabara and Smith 2012).

When writing evaluations you should always:

- *State the point and then explain it.*
- *Contextualise your answers by using specific details from the study to back up the point you are making.*
- *Comment on what you conclude.*

Coffee and a mobile, this lack of attention could be dangerous when crossing the road.

Exam-style question examples

Component 2 Section A:

1. Outline **two** of the aims from Moray's study. [2]

2. Explain the term 'shadowing' from Moray's study. [2]

3. Describe a control used in Moray's first experiment. [2]

4. Describe the results from Moray's third experiment. [2]

5. Identify the **two** independent variables in Moray's third experiment. [2]

6. Give **one** strength of using a repeated measures design in Moray's study. [3]

7. Outline **one** way in which Moray's procedure can be seen to be reliable. [4]

8. Describe **one** weakness of the sample used by Moray. [3]

Cognitive core study 4 (contemporary)
Simons and Chabris (1999) on *Visual inattention*

Background

Visual attention and inattentional blindness

Visual attention (selective looking) refers to the fact that, even though the eye records all visual experience, we do not pay attention to everything.

Change blindness = failing to notice large changes from one view to the next.

Inattentional blindness = failing to notice an unexpected object if attention is diverted.

Aims

To investigate factors affecting visual detection rates:

- Visual similarity of unexpected and attended object.
- Task difficulty.
- Superimposed or live version of a display.
- Nature of the unusual event.

Method

Design

Laboratory experiment, independent measures design with 16 conditions.

IV 1: Unexpected event was an umbrella woman or gorilla.

IV 2: Film was transparent or opaque.

IV 3: Task was easy or hard.

IV 4: Observer followed black or white team.

DV: Percentage of observers noticing unexpected event.

Sample

Self-selected sample of 228 mainly American undergraduates. Final analysis included 192 observers (36 were ruled out as they knew about inattentional blindness already).

Materials/apparatus

Four videotapes of two teams of three players (dressed in black or white) throwing a basketball, lasting 75 secs. After 44–48 secs an unexpected event lasting 5 secs occurred, e.g. person holding umbrella or wearing a gorilla costume walked from left to right.

Procedure

1. Participants took part in only one condition and were tested individually.

2. Participants watched black or white team.

3. Participants counted silently the number of passes (easy) or number of bounce and aerial passes (hard) made by the attended team.

4. Participants wrote down their count scores.

5. Participants were asked surprise questions about the unexpected event, e.g. *Did you notice anything unusual on the video? Did you notice anything other than the six players? Did you see anyone else? Did you see a gorilla/woman carrying an umbrella walk across the screen?*

6. Participants who said 'yes' were asked for details.

7. Participants who said they knew of inattentional blindness were discarded.

8. Participants gave informed consent and were debriefed.

Results

1. The key result is that 54% of participants noticed the unexpected event, 46% did not notice it.

Results for the four IVs

2. Umbrella woman was noticed more than the gorilla (65% vs. 44%, $p < 0.004$).

3. Unexpected event was noticed more in opaque than transparent condition (67% vs. 42%, $p < 0.001$).

4. Unexpected event was noticed more in the easy rather than hard condition (64% vs. 45%, $p < 0.009$).

5. In gorilla condition, participants watching the black team noticed it more than white team (58% vs. 27%, $p < 0.002$).

6. In umbrella condition there was little difference between black and white teams (62% vs. 69%, $p < 0.519$).

Other results

7. The standard deviations of the hard and easy conditions were 6.77 and 2.71 showing the hard condition was more difficult.

8. Inaccurate counting was not a factor (no significant correlation between noticing and poor counting, $r = .15$).

Pay attention – you would not want to miss this gorilla!

Conclusions

People are less likely to notice unexpected events if they are visually dissimilar to attended events.

An unexpected object can be undetected even when it passes through the area of attentional focus in the eye (fovea).

This shows there is no conscious perception without attention.

Links between the core study and the methodological issues

Research method and techniques

➕ Laboratory conditions enable high control over extraneous variables, e.g. all the videos were the same length (75 secs). This means that the experimental conditions were carefully standardised.

➖ Laboratory experiments may create demand characteristics. However, one factor that was controlled was excluding data from observers who knew of inattentional blindness (as this would have affected their behaviour).

Validity

➖ It is often not the laboratory setting that lowers validity but the task. Simons and Chabris' task of watching a filmed event is rather contrived.

➕ However, researchers overcome such issues by conducting further, possibly less controlled research in more natural settings or with more natural tasks.

Reliability

➕ Highly standardised procedures were used, e.g. the same four questions were asked of observers about the unexpected event. The researchers found that observers answered consistently across all questions. This suggests that reliability was high.

Sampling bias

➕ The final sample for analysis of 192 observers can be considered large. This can be seen as representative of the main target population (university undergraduates).

➖ University undergraduates may have higher cognitive abilities and perform better on attention tasks, so the sample may not be representative of everyone. Additionally, as they were self-selected they may have tried harder on the tasks than other people.

Type of data

➕ Quantitative data – the percentages of observers noticing the unexpected event in the 16 conditions. This makes it easier, for example, to compare the umbrella woman with the gorilla condition (65% vs. 44%). This also allows inferential statistics to determine if the results are meaningful, e.g. umbrella woman versus gorilla was highly significant at $p < 0.004$.

Ethical considerations

➕ Observers gave informed consent and were debriefed afterwards including having the tape replayed if they wished.

Ethnocentrism

➖ We might not expect the brain processes involved in attention to be affected by culture but research suggests otherwise. Children from individualist cultures learn to interpret two-dimensional films (similar to those used in this study) as three-dimensional, but this is not true for children from collectivist cultures (Hudson 1960). This suggests that Simons and Chabris' results may only be relevant to certain cultures.

Magicians have relied for centuries on our failure to notice changes when we are not paying attention.

Exam-style question examples

Component 2 Section A:

1. Explain the term 'change blindness' from Simons and Chabris' study. [2]

2. Identify **two** of the factors Simons and Chabris investigated that may affect visual detection rates. [2]

3. Identify the dependent variable in Simons and Chabris' study. [2]

4. Describe the results from the study by Simons and Chabris. [4]

5. Outline **two** conclusions from the study by Simons and Chabris. [4]

6. Describe **one** strength of the research method used in the Simons and Chabris study. [4]

7. Give **one** weakness of using a laboratory experiment in Simons and Chabris' study. [3]

8. Describe **one** weakness of the sample used by Simons and Chabris. [2]

Revision booster

It is important to explain your point in the context of the study – just saying 'Simons and Chabris used controls' will not be enough. You can ensure you contextualise by using the phrase 'for example' or 'such as': Simons and Chabris used controls *such as* all the videos were the same length in order to standardise experimental conditions.

The developmental area

The main focus of developmental psychology is on children because it is in the first few years of life that we can observe the most dramatic changes. However, psychologists study development across the life span.

Good answers always include the use of the specialist terms for the topic, e.g. lifespan, predetermined stages, maturation, nature/nurture, genetics, environment.

Revision booster

Know the different positions of the nature/nurture debate and make sure you can explain in detail how each developmental core study relates to both nature and nurture.

Top band exam answers require you to justify *how* research supports these concepts, so you should be able to elaborate your points and also refer to the interaction between nature and nurture.

Key concepts	**Nature/nature** This debate looks at the relative importance of genetics (nature) over experience (nurture). Some behaviours have a strong genetic component, e.g. children crawling and walking. But some characteristics we share with our parents may be due to being brought up by them (nurture) rather than sharing their genes (nature).
	Stages If development involves the emergence of new strategies and skills at different times, it is useful to talk about stages of development. You can use informal stages (e.g. the 'terrible twos') or more formal ideas (e.g. Freud's stages of psychosexual development). A stage approach helps us to see the sequence of development that occurs in many children.
Everyday applications	**Improving the lives of young children** For example, reducing asthma attacks in young children by increasing their use of a spacer device (the Funhaler in Chaney *et al.*'s study).
	Improving parenting Bandura *et al.* showed that aggression is learned from role models. This highlights the importance of parents being non-aggressive and demonstrating positive behaviours towards their children, e.g. good health routines.
	Reducing exposure to violence Bandura *et al.* showed that viewing aggressive behaviour may increase imitation of such behaviour. This suggests the need for regulation of what is shown on television.
Similarities	Developmental psychology shares much of its approach and methods with social psychology, e.g. looking at the development of aggression.
	It also uses some techniques from cognitive psychology to investigate how children develop their cognitive processes, e.g. Kohlberg's study of how thinking develops.
Differences	Other areas of psychology pay less attention to how behaviour changes over time, e.g. cognitive studies tend to use snapshot studies to focus on the individual characteristics and cognitive processes.
Evaluation	⊕ **Interaction between nature and nurture** Demonstrated in developmental studies, e.g. Bandura *et al.* showed aggression can be learned by observing role models and suggested that such learning would interact with innate tendencies to be more aggressive.
	⊕ **Demand characteristics** Are less likely to affect results because children are often the participants, e.g. Chaney *et al.* on use of Funhaler.
	⊖ **Ethical issues** Conducting research with children who are unable to give their own consent, e.g. photographs of the participants in Bandura *et al.*'s study continue to circulate without their direct consent.
	⊖ **Attrition** Longitudinal research is not always easy because participants drop out over time leaving a biased sample. This might have happened in Chaney *et al.*'s study if it had continued.

Links between the area and the perspectives/debates

The developmental area is compared to the other four areas on page 97.

The perspectives and debates are explained on pages 90–94.

Behaviourist perspective Both Bandura *et al.* and Chaney *et al.* show how behaviour is learned, e.g. Chaney *et al.* showed how enjoyment of using a Funhaler acted as direct reinforcement.

Psychodynamic perspective The concept of identification is used to explain social learning in Bandura *et al.*'s study as boys identified more with the same-gender model.

Nature/nurture Bandura *et al.* ask the question whether children are born to be aggressive or whether they learn to be aggressive through imitation (nurture).

Free will/determinism Kohlberg argued that moral thinking is determined mostly by innate processes that unfold throughout maturation. Lee *et al.* suggest social and cultural factors determine how moral development progresses.

Individual/situational There is support for situational explanations as children's behaviour is affected by external influences, e.g. exposure to and use of Funhaler in Chaney *et al.*'s study.

Usefulness Bandura *et al.*'s study helps to reduce aggression in children and Chaney *et al.*'s research has obvious usefulness in reducing asthma attacks in children.

There may be a question on any of the eight debates. We only have room for four.

Viewers in the UK watch a regular diet of violence and murder. Bandura et al.*'s study suggests that this may be imitated by some people in their everyday lives.*

Revision booster

Students often give strengths and weaknesses of *studies* when asked to evaluate *areas*. When answering questions about areas, the focus should be on strengths and weaknesses of the *area*, using examples from *studies* to support the point.

Links between the area and the core studies

Core study 1 Bandura *et al.* on *Aggression*	Bandura *et al.*'s study shows us that people learn new behaviours they have observed from the environment (e.g. aggression towards a Bobo doll from a role model) and they then generalise these behaviours to other situations. This changes their development.
Core study 2 Chaney *et al.* on *Funhaler*	Chaney *et al.* look at how children can learn to increase compliance to a medical regime for asthma using the external influence of a Funhaler. This supports the nurture position in the nature/nurture debate, suggesting that nurture is an important influence on development.
Core study 3 Kohlberg on *Moral development*	Kohlberg's theory of moral development consists of three levels, each divided into two stages. For example, children in the preconventional level pass through the stages of punishment and instrumental orientations before moving on to the conventional level. This progression is determined by nature, suggesting that nature is an important influence on development.
Core study 4 Lee *et al.* on *Truth telling*	Lee *et al.* highlight age-related changes in truth telling, suggesting that continued exposure to the Chinese cultural emphasis on modesty has an impact on moral development. For example, Chinese children in prosocial situations rated truth telling less positively than Canadian children do. This suggests that nurture is an important influence on development.

Exam-style question examples

Component 2 Section A:

1. Describe how Chaney *et al.*'s research relates to external influences on children's behaviour. **[3]**

2. Explain how Lee *et al.*'s research is linked to the developmental area. **[3]**

Component 2 Section B:

1. Outline **two** principles of the developmental area. **[2]**

2. Outline ethical issues in research into the developmental area. **[4]**

3. a) Outline **one** weakness of research into the developmental area. **[3]**
   b) Outline **one** strength of research into the developmental area. **[3]**

4. Outline **two** everyday applications of research into the developmental area. **[4]**

5. Describe how the developmental area supports determinism. **[2]**

Developmental core study 1 (classic)

Bandura *et al.* (1961) on *Aggression*

Background

Learning theory

The behaviourist perspective suggests behaviour is learned directly through classical and operant conditioning.

Social learning theory

Bandura suggested that learning also occurs with indirect rewards. His social learning theory proposed that people observe 'role models' and imitate their behaviour.

Aims

To investigate whether:

- Children will imitate specific acts of aggression and behave more aggressively generally.
- Participants are more likely to imitate same-gender models and boys more likely than girls to imitate aggression.

Method

Design

Laboratory experiment, matched participants design (based on aggressiveness), using observational techniques.

IV: Aggressive or non-aggressive model, gender of model and gender of child.

DV: Imitation of aggressive acts observed in the experimental room.

Sample

Opportunity sample. Children from a university nursery school in Stanford, California. 36 boys and 36 girls, aged between 37 and 69 months (mean age 52 months).

Materials/apparatus

The children and model played with various toys including a Bobo doll, which is an inflatable doll about five feet tall.

Procedure

Phase 1: Modelling

1. Children played in an experimental room, watching a model play with toys including a Bobo doll.

2. Children placed in:
   - Experimental group 1 (aggressive group): Observed an aggressive model who sat on Bobo, punched it, said 'Pow', etc.
   - Experimental group 2 (non-aggressive group): Observed a non-aggressive model.
   - Control group: No model present.

3. Experimental groups subdivided into four: boys and girls observed the same- and opposite-gender model.

Phase 2: Aggression arousal

4. Children taken to another room and played with attractive toys.

5. This play was stopped so children would feel frustrated.

Phase 3: Tested for delayed imitation

6. Children taken to third room and were observed playing with toys, including the Bobo doll.

7. Children observed through one-way mirror.

8. Observations recorded as imitative aggression (e.g. sitting on Bobo), partially imitative (e.g. using mallet on other toys), and non-imitative (e.g. squeezing Bobo).

Results

Imitation of aggression

1. *Complete imitation* Children in the aggressive group imitated models' physical and verbal behaviours (e.g. saying 'Pow'), both aggressive and non-aggressive behaviours.

2. Children in the non-aggressive and control groups displayed very few aggressive behaviours.

3. *Partial imitation* Children in the aggressive group imitated models' behaviours.

4. *Non-imitative aggression* The aggressive group displayed more non-imitative aggression than the non-aggressive group.

5. *Non-aggressive behaviour* Children in the non-aggressive group played non-aggressively with dolls more than children in other groups.

Gender effects

6. Same-gender imitation for boys but not for girls.

7. Men models had a greater influence than women models.

8. Boys imitated more physical aggression than girls.

Girls imitated less physical aggression than boys, perhaps because it is seen as less appropriate for girls to behave aggressively.

Conclusions

People will produce new behaviours that they have observed and generalise these behaviours to other situations.

The study also shows that men are more likely to be modelled, possibly because of their perceived higher status (at the time of this study).

Links between the core study and the methodological issues

Research method and techniques

➕ The manipulation of IVs allowed conclusions about causal effects, e.g. watching a model's behaviour causes imitation of aggression.

➕ Laboratory conditions mean extraneous variables can be well-controlled, e.g. matching participants on aggressiveness (see right). Therefore, there was high internal validity.

➖ Children were aware their behaviour was being studied. This may lead to demand characteristics - the Bobo doll 'invited' children to behave aggressively.

➖ Observational techniques were used to measure imitation of aggression, these may be affected by observer bias.

Validity

➕ Aggressive behaviour towards an inflatable doll might not be representative of everyday life as people may be quite willing to hit a doll but not a person.

➖ This is a snapshot study looking at short-term effects of observing aggression - modelling effects may wear off. This reduces the validity of the study because we cannot generalise results to extended time periods.

Sampling bias

➕ Participants were children, which allowed Bandura *et al.* to show how easily youngsters imitate models.

➖ Children are more impressionable than adults and may be more likely to be influenced by the behaviour of an aggressive model, which makes it difficult to generalise the results to adults.

Types of data

➕ Quantitative data - counting the number of aggressive behaviours displayed.

➕ Qualitative data - recording the kinds of imitation that were made.

Ethical considerations

➕ Parental informed consent is regarded as acceptable but children should have a say.

➖ The intervention aimed to increase the children's aggressiveness (lack of protection from psychological harm). There was no attempt to reduce their aggressiveness after the study.

➖ Behaviour was observed covertly, so children should have been debriefed at the end of the study.

Ethnocentrism

➖ Participants were from a middle-class American nursery school who may be less exposed to aggressive models in everyday lives than children who live in more violent areas of America.

Children in a less violent society than America might be less willing to imitate antisocial behaviour.

Aggressiveness ratings of the children were used to ensure that each group contained equally aggressive children. Aggressiveness was judged by the children's teachers and one of the experimenters. They rated the children on 5-point rating scales for physical aggression, verbal aggression, aggression towards inanimate objects and aggressive inhibition.

Revision booster

Where do students go wrong on exam questions related to Bandura *et al.*?

Students sometimes forget the following details: there is a non-aggressive model and a no-model condition, children were tested one at a time, there are three IVs and the observations used three behavioural categories.

Exam-style question examples

Component 2 Section A:

1. Outline the aims of Bandura *et al.*'s study. **[2]**

2. Describe the sample in the Bandura *et al.* study. **[2]**

3. Identify the dependent variable in the Bandura *et al.* study. **[2]**

4. Outline the modelling phase in Bandura *et al.*'s procedure. **[4]**

5. Outline **two** results regarding imitation of aggression in Bandura *et al.*'s study. **[4]**

6. Outline what you understand by the term 'social learning theory' with reference to Bandura *et al.*'s study. **[2]**

7. Outline **one** weakness of the research method used in the Bandura *et al.* study. **[3]**

8. Evaluate the ethics of the study by Bandura *et al.* **[4]**

9. Give a strength of the data collected in the Bandura *et al.* study. **[3]**

Don't forget to read the exam advice on pages 4-15.

Developmental core study 2 (contemporary)
Chaney *et al.* (2004) *on Funhaler*

Background

Asthma
Asthma is potentially a dangerous condition treated using medication via an inhaler.

Non-compliance
'Non-compliance' describes patients who do not follow medical advice. This may happen if parents (or other caregivers) do not ensure compliance or children find inhalers unpleasant.

Aims
To conduct a pilot study to see whether a 'Funhaler' would increase medical compliance in young children with asthma.

Method

Design
Field experiment, repeated measures design using self-report to collect data.

IV: Child using conventional asthma spacer device or Funhaler.

DV: Data on use of spacer and on attitudes collected from parents.

Sample
Opportunity sample, 32 children attending clinics within 51 km radius in Australia and their parents. Children aged between 1.5 and 6 years, mean age 3.2 years. Average duration of asthma was 2.2 years. There were 22 boys and 10 girls.

Materials/apparatus
New spacer designed for children (the Funhaler). Looks like a brightly coloured toy with a spinning disk and whistle activated by child's breathing pattern.

Two matched questionnaires of mainly Yes/No questions and fixed-choice questions given before and after children used the Funhaler. The questionnaires measured attitudes to the use of an inhaler and compliance to the medication.

Procedure

1. Parents of children with asthma contacted and study explained to them.

2. Informed consent obtained from parents before being interviewed.

3. One parent interviewed using questionnaire 1.

4. The one parent was asked about their attitude and their child's attitude to the existing conventional spacer (CS).

5. Children were given a Funhaler to use under adult supervision for two weeks in place of their current device.

6. Funhaler use assessed by phoning parents once, at random, during the study. Asked about use on previous day.

7. Parents were visited by the researcher at the end of the two weeks and questionnaire 2 was given to the parent who responded on the first occasion.

8. The one parent was asked about their attitude and their child's attitude to the Funhaler.

Results

1. *Adherence* 81% of children used the Funhaler compared to 59% using CS.

2. *Technique of medication* 80% of the children took four or more breaths using the Funhaler compared to 50% breathing similarly using a CS.

3. *Improvement in children* Of the 15 children who took fewer than four breaths using a CS, 11 improved with Funhaler.

4. *Success in medication* 22/30 (73%) of parents claimed they were always successful in medicating their child using the Funhaler compared to 3/30 (10%) with a CS.

5. *Improvement in parents* 19 parents who were unsuccessful medicating their child with a CS became always successful when switching to the Funhaler.

6. *Children's positive attitudes* For example, 68% experienced pleasure with the Funhaler compared to 10% with a CS.

7. *Children's negative attitudes* For example, Funhaler aroused more suspicion in children (10%) than a CS (0%).

8. *Parents' positive attitudes* For example, 61% were completely happy with the Funhaler compared to 10% completely happy with a CS.

Conclusions

The Funhaler is useful in improving compliance rates for spacer use in young children, thus reducing asthma attacks.

More research is needed to investigate whether the positive results of this study are maintained over longer term use.

Possibly one reason young children resist using an inhaler (such as the one on the left) is because it is designed for an adult, e.g. it is hard to press down on the top.

Links between the core study and the methodological issues

Research method and techniques

➕ An experimental method was used, meaning causal conclusions can be drawn about effects of a conventional spacer versus the Funhaler on compliance rates and attitudes towards the spacer device.

➕ Repeated measures design controls for the effect of participant variables, e.g. some children may have more severe asthma or be naturally more compliant. This increases the validity of results.

➖ Social desirability bias (see right) may be shown by parents in self-reports as they may have provided more positive views about the Funhaler because they knew the aims of the study.

➖ Repeated measures design raises problems of order effects because the Funhaler device was always used second. This may reduce the validity of the results.

Validity

➖ The trials were short-term, lasting only two weeks. The positive attitudes expressed by parents may be related to the novelty of the device. Over a longer period (e.g. six months) use of the Funhaler by parents and children may have less positive attitudes.

➖ Additionally, attempts to assess Funhaler use were very limited – parents were asked only once during the two-week period about Funhaler use. This questions the results' validity.

Reliability

➖ The questionnaires may lack reliability, e.g. parents may have interpreted terms such as 'mild' or 'strong' differently when assessing their child's dislike of the inhaler.

Sampling bias

➖ The opportunity sample was easy to obtain but not representative of the general population. The sample came from area of 51 km radius that may have unique characteristics, e.g. more willing to try a new device.

➖ There may have been a recruitment effect, e.g. parents who agreed to take part had more compliant children because those parents with more difficult children declined, leaving a more positive group of families.

Type of data

➕ Quantitative data – parents were asked either Yes/No questions or questions with a fixed range of answers.

➖ Forced-choice questions such as 'always use spacer' versus 'do not always use spacer' means that finer detail was lost.

Ethical considerations

➖ Informed consent was obtained from parents but children might later object to having been used in a trial of a new medical device.

➖ Psychological harm may be caused as children may feel embarrassed about using a spacer device.

➖ One of the researchers was a shareholder in the company selling the Funhaler.

The parents in Chaney et al.'s study may not have given accurate responses to the questionnaires. For example, they may have wanted to present a positive impression (social desirability bias) of their family and say, 'Yes, of course I administered the medicine'.

Revision booster

You may be asked to link the study to the theme. The Chaney *et al.* study highlights external influences on children's behaviour as it shows how the characteristics of the Funhaler (e.g. the colours, spinning disk and whistle) increased the levels of compliance to the medical regime.

Exam-style question examples

Component 2 Section A:

1. Outline the aims of the Chaney *et al.* study. **[2]**

2. Explain the experimental design used in the Chaney *et al.* study. **[3]**

3. Identify the independent variable in the Chaney *et al.* study. **[2]**

4. Describe the Funhaler apparatus used by Chaney *et al.* in their study. **[2]**

5. Describe the sample used by Chaney *et al.* **[2]**

6. Outline **two** strengths of the design used in the Chaney *et al.* study. **[4]**

7. Give **one** weakness of the validity of the procedure used by Chaney *et al.* **[3]**

8. Describe a weakness of the type of data collected in the Chaney *et al.* study. **[2]**

How psychology contributes to the success of the economy and society ... This core study improves health care for children.

Developmental core study 3 (classic)
Kohlberg (1968) on *Moral development*

Background

Theory of moral development

Kohlberg believed children's thinking about moral decisions changes as they age, as a consequence of maturation. He identified three levels of development: preconventional, conventional, postconventional. Each level has two stages and can be assessed using moral dilemmas.

Aims

Kohlberg sought further support for his theory, with a particular focus on whether everyone went through Stage 5.

Method

Design

Longitudinal and cross-cultural study, using two quasi-experiments.

American longitudinal study IV: Age   DV: Stage of development

Cross-cultural sample   IV: Culture DV: Stage of development

Sample

American longitudinal study: 75 American boys from Chicago, 10–16 years old at start and 22–28 years at end. Boys from lower and higher socio-economic families, and a spread of religious backgrounds.

Cross-cultural sample: Boys from Great Britain*, Canada*, Mexico and Turkey, plus boys from two villages - Atayal (Malaysian aboriginal) and Taiwanese [*results not included here].

Materials/apparatus

Moral dilemmas related to 25 moral concepts, e.g. 'the value of a human life'.

Procedure

American longitudinal study

1. Boys assessed at either 10, 13 or 16 years old, then retested every three or four years until age 24.

2. Boys' level of moral development assessed by moral dilemmas, e.g. the Heinz dilemma.

3. Boys asked open questions about the dilemmas.

4. Questions were adjusted depending on the previous answer.

5. The oral interview took about 45 minutes and covered nine dilemmas.

Cross-cultural sample

6. Boys from two rural villages in Malaysia and Taiwan were tested.

7. Boys were asked about a story involving the theft of food.

8. Boys from two isolated villages in Yucatán (Mexico) and Turkey were also tested.

Results

American longitudinal study

1. Responses on the moral issue of 'value of human life' from two boys were analysed. For example, Tommy (aged 10) mixed up value of a life with property a person owned = Stage 1 reasoning, Richard (aged 24) argued for absolute values of justice = Stage 6 reasoning.

2. Both boys showed progression of moral reasoning, though Tommy's was slower despite being a bright boy (IQ 120).

Across cultures

3. At age 10, Stage 1 reasoning is the most common in all countries.

4. At age 16, in the USA, the order was reversed with Stage 5 being the most common followed by 4, 3, 2, 1, 6.

5. Similar results were found in Mexico and Taiwan but development was slower, with Stage 3 being the most common at age 16.

6. Villages in Yucatán and Turkey showed steady progress but Stage 1 was the most common.

7. Stage 6 was rarely found in any culture.

8. Middle-class children were more advanced than lower-class children.

The semi-structured interviews allowed follow-up questions based on participants' previous answers, producing detailed information about moral development.

Conclusions

Moral reasoning develops with age in a fixed and invariant sequence of stages.

Similar in all countries but at different rates.

Middle-class children move through the sequence faster and further than lower-class children.

Links between the core study and the methodological issues

Research method and techniques

✛ Longitudinal designs mean that participant variables are controlled, e.g. so that aspects of participants' personality would not affect differences in the development of moral reasoning between boys.

⊟ In longitudinal studies, participants often drop out over time (*attrition*), e.g. Kohlberg's original sample was 84 boys but nine boys had dropped out by the time results were analysed. This may bias the sample.

Validity

✛ Kohlberg's aim was to assess moral reasoning not moral behaviour so he was testing what he intended to, showing high internal validity.

⊟ However, what people *believe* about right and wrong does not predict what they actually *do*, thus Kohlberg's study is low in ecological validity.

⊟ Additionally, the moral dilemmas were hypothetical scenarios and may have made little sense to young boys, which lowers the validity.

Reliability

✛ Kohlberg produced a complex system to turn qualitative data into quantitative data to make the classification of moral development reliable. This provided good inter-rater reliability and good test-retest reliability.

Sampling bias

⊟ Kohlberg's research is biased towards men/boys (i.e. androcentric). The dilemmas were written by a man (Kohlberg), based on a principle of justice favoured by men, and tested on a sample of men/boys only. Thus, Kohlberg's study provides evidence for only one kind of moral reasoning.

⊟ Gilligan (1982) argued that Kohlberg's focus on justice overlooked the ethic of care upon which many women and some men make their moral judgements.

Types of data

✛ Quantitative data - each participant was represented by a number indicating their stage of development, e.g. Richard (aged 16) saw life as important for all humans but dependent on someone else's authority (God) = Stage 4 reasoning.

✛ Qualitative data - boys were asked to provide reasons why they made such a decision.

Ethical considerations

✛ It is assumed that the boys and their parents gave the initial informed consent and that there was no deception - it was clear to them what the task was.

✛ The interview itself was unlikely to be stressful, as shown by the fact that the majority of participants returned to be interviewed several times.

Ethnocentrism

✛ The cross-cultural part of Kohlberg's study means the focus was not solely on American culture and that his ideas were universal. Testing of the Atayal and Taiwanese boys involved an interpreter to help him make unbiased judgements. He also reframed the moral dilemma he used so it would make better sense in that culture.

'The man who understands justice is more likely to practise it' - a quote from Kohlberg supported by his own research, as he found that youths who understood justice acted more justly.

Revision booster

Students often get muddled between the longitudinal study of boys and the cross-sectional/cross-cultural study. So, make sure you know the differences and can clearly explain them.

Exam-style question examples

Component 2 Section A:

1. Outline Kohlberg's **three** levels of moral development. [2]

2. Describe the design used by Kohlberg. [2]

3. Identify the independent variable in Kohlberg's American longitudinal study. [2]

4. Describe the cross-cultural sample used by Kohlberg. [2]

5. Outline how Kohlberg assessed moral development in his American longitudinal study. [4]

6. Give **one** strength of the research method used in the Kohlberg study. [3]

7. Describe a weakness of the sample used in the Kohlberg study. [2]

8. Outline **two** strengths of the type of data collected by Kohlberg. [4]

How psychology contributes to the success of the economy and society ...
Understanding stages of moral development is important for understanding why people behave as they do.

Developmental core study 4 (contemporary)
Lee *et al.* (1997) on *Truth telling*

Background

Moral judgements of lying
Young children find it hard to use intention when making moral judgements about 'naughtiness', e.g. judging if lying is good or bad in particular situations.

Aims
To compare children from an individualist (Canadian) and a collectivist (Chinese) culture, expecting:

- In prosocial situations, Chinese children would rate truth telling less positively and lie telling less negatively than Canadian children.
- This difference to increase with age.
- No difference in antisocial situations.

Method

Design
Laboratory and quasi-experiments.

IV 1: Social and physical story (independent measures/laboratory experiment).

IV 2: Prosocial and antisocial story (repeated measures/laboratory experiment).

IV 3: Age 7, 9 and 11 years (cross-sectional/quasi-experiment).

IV 4: Chinese and Canadian children (cross-cultural/quasi-experiment).

DV: Rated story character's deed and what the character said, on a 7-point scale (3 = very very good, –3 = very very naughty).

Sample
120 Chinese children, mean ages 7.5, 9.4 and 11.3 years, 20 boys and 20 girls in each age group.

108 Canadian children, mean ages 7.4, 9.6 and 11.5 years.

Materials/apparatus
Four types of story: (1) Prosocial + truth telling, (2) Prosocial + lie telling, (3) Antisocial + truth telling, (4) Antisocial + lie telling.

Procedure

1. Participants were randomly assigned to the social or physical story condition.
2. Each child was tested individually.
3. 7-point rating scale was explained.
4. Four stories (social or physical):
   - 'Deed' section was read to the child.
   - Question 1: *Is what the child did good or naughty?*
   - Answer given verbally/nonverbally or both, on the rating chart.
   - Second section of story was read.
   - Question 2: *Is what the child said to his teacher naughty or good?*
   - Answer given verbally/nonverbally or both, on the rating chart.
5. Each time the stories were read, the order of the stories was alternated. The order of 'naughty' or 'good' was also changed.

Young children find it difficult to consider a person's intention when deciding whether someone is lying or not.

Results

1. No significant differences were found between boys or girls, or for changed order of the stories.
2. The planned analysis was 2 × 2 × 3 design. This is 2 (culture: Canadian and Chinese) × 2 (story: physical and social) × 3 (age: 7, 9 and 11).
3. Prosocial + truth telling
   - No significant difference for question 2.
   - Significant interaction between age and culture. Chinese children's prosocial/truth telling ratings became *less* positive as they got older.
4. Prosocial + lie telling
   - No significant difference for question 2.
   - Significant interaction between age and culture. All children's prosocial/lie telling ratings became *more* positive as they got older, especially the Chinese children.
5. Antisocial + truth telling
   - All children rated truth telling positively.
6. Antisocial + lie telling
   - Significant interaction between age and culture. All children's antisocial/lie telling ratings became *less* positive as they got older.
   - Significant difference between the social and physical story condition for 7-year-old children.

Conclusions

There were age-related changes, suggesting that continued exposure to the Chinese cultural emphasis on modesty has an impact on moral development.

This shows that, although cognitive factors may be important, cultural factors also matter in moral development.

Links between the core study and the methodological issues

Research method and techniques

✛ The study tested a range of variables, e.g. gender was manipulated across conditions and the researchers were able to show that this was not related to the children's moral judgements.

✛ Culture (individualist versus collectivist) was varied across conditions so comparisons could be made.

⊟ Cultural conditions were not manipulated by the researcher which means we cannot conclude that culture *caused* the observed differences, e.g. Lee *et al.* didn't manipulate how children were socialised at school.

⊟ Moral judgements were based on the way that the children reacted to stories, which may not reflect everyday moral judgements.

Validity and reliability

✛ The procedures were very simple and easy to standardise, which made the method of assessing moral judgements reliable.

✛ This also meant that results can be checked by someone else as the procedures are replicable, which then supports the validity of the results.

Sampling bias

✛ The sample size was large. Even the individual experimental conditions (e.g. 7-year-old Canadian girls given social stories) had at least eight participants. Having a larger sample makes the results more generalisable.

⊟ The samples were not representative of all communities as all the children came from urban rather than rural backgrounds.

⊟ Little information was available regarding the participants' sociocultural background, so educational background of parents or other factors are significant extraneous variables.

Type of data

✛ Quantitative data – children gave a rating between +3 and -3 (7-point scale) for how good or naughty they thought the child in the story was. For each story a mean value was calculated for each cultural and age group.

Ethical considerations

✛ We can presume that the children's parents provided informed consent and there was a debrief.

✛ Parents and children would have the right to withdraw if the children felt distressed during questioning.

Ethnocentrism

⊟ Lee *et al.* considered the effects of different cultural practices on moral judgements between individualist and collectivist cultures. However, differences between groups of children could be due to socialisation practices in primary school.

People living in urban environments may be more advanced in their moral development than those in more rural situations because they experience more frequent interpersonal issues and dilemmas.

Revision booster

You may be asked to link a core study to its appropriate area of psychology. First, look at the principles of the area, e.g. one principle of the developmental area is that people go through changes during their lives. Second, use evidence from the core study to support these principles, e.g. Lee *et al.* showed there were age-related changes in truth telling due to exposure to the Chinese culture.

Exam-style question examples

Component 2 Section A:

1. Outline how the dependent variable was measured in Lee *et al.*'s study. **[3]**

2. Describe the sample used by Lee *et al.* **[3]**

3. Describe the **four** types of story used by Lee *et al.* **[4]**

4. Outline **two** aims of the Lee *et al.* study. **[4]**

5. Describe question 1 in the Lee *et al.* study. **[2]**

6. Describe **one** strength of the research method used in the Lee *et al.* study. **[4]**

7. Give a weakness of the sample used in the Lee *et al.* study. **[3]**

8. Describe **one** strength of the ethical considerations in the Lee *et al.* study. **[2]**

The exam questions above are just representative examples. Read the guidance for Component 2 exam questions on page 7.

The biological area

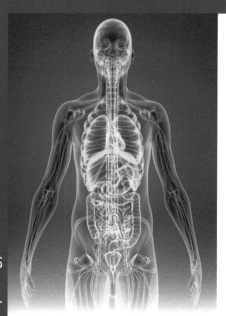

Biological psychology explores human behaviour and experience by looking at people as if they are biological machines.

Good answers always include the use of the specialist terms for the topic, e.g. localisation, neurons, hormones, genes, biological processes, scientific.

Biological and physiological factors

The terms 'biological' and 'physiological' refer to more or less the same thing though, strictly speaking, there is a subtle difference. Physiology is a branch of biology that is concerned with bodily processes (neurotransmitters, hormones, muscles etc). Physiology = 'of the body'. Biology includes physiological processes but additionally looks at genetic factors.

Revision booster

Use retrieval practice – the act of pulling information 'out' from your mind dramatically improves learning.

Tests and quizzes are good methods to promote retrieval. Write your own test on the biological area and swap your test with others.

Key concepts	**Biological machines** A machine metaphor can be applied to the brain, i.e. it can be regarded as a machine where the collection of chemicals and cells produce the reflective, thinking, feeling organism that is aware of itself and able to act and make choices.
	Localisation of function The machine model also conceptualises the brain as a set of components. Researchers have mapped the brain, identifying components of the brain that are responsible for particular tasks, e.g. language.
Everyday applications	**Giving advice to people with brain damage** Casey *et al.* showed that the frontal lobes are important in decision-making. These lobes are also linked to aggressive behaviour.
	Use of drugs to alter undesirable behaviour Depression can be reduced by boosting levels of serotonin using drugs such as SSRIs.
	Psychosurgery Aggression and anxiety have been reduced using lobotomies (severing frontal brain connections). Such operations are based on understanding the link between parts of the brain and aggression/anxiety (i.e. understanding localisation).
Similarities	Biological psychology is connected with cognitive psychology in the form of cognitive neuroscience, where the cognitive processes are explained in terms of the neural mechanisms.
Differences	Unlike social and developmental psychology, biological psychology uses the techniques of the traditional sciences to examine and catalogue the brain.
Evaluation	⊕ **Specialist scientific equipment** Can measure behaviour precisely and objectively, e.g. Casey *et al.* used fMRI scans to relate delay of gratification to activity in certain brain structures (e.g. right inferior frontal cortex).
	⊕ **Nature perspective** Biological psychology presents the brain and body as determined by genes. This provides a counterargument to the nurture side of the nature/nurture debate, e.g. Sperry explains how our brains are hardwired as the left hemisphere in most people governs language.
	⊖ **Small samples** For example, Sperry's study included only 11 patients who had 'split-brains', which reduces validity because there were unique characteristics of the sample used.
	⊖ **Reductionist approach** The focus of biological psychology is on biological/physical processes, e.g. Casey *et al.* suggest that delay of gratification is reduced solely to differences in brain reactivity rather than other factors, such as experience.

Links between the area and the perspectives/debates

The biological area is compared to the other four areas on page 97.

The perspectives and debates are explained on pages 90-94.

Behaviourist perspective Delay of gratification can be explained in terms of operant conditioning - that people can learn to resist temptation if rewarded. Brain centres identified in Casey *et al.* (ventral striatum) are known as reward centres, therefore the reason for poor impulse control is poor response to rewards.

Psychodynamic perspective Poor impulse control is explained by the psychodynamic perspective in terms of a personality dominated by the id and lacking control by the superego.

Nature/nurture Sperry's patients learned to overcome the restrictions of their brain operation in everyday life.

Free will/determinism Biological core studies provide support for determinist explanations. Sperry's study shows how brain connections determine the way that we interact with the world. An intact brain integrates information received by each hemisphere but the split brain cannot do this.

Psychology as a science Biological studies rely on controlled methods of investigation, e.g. Blakemore and Cooper used either vertical or horizontal environments to rear the kittens.

Links between the area and the core studies

Core study 1
Sperry on
Split brains

Sperry's study shows us that different regions of the brain explain lateralisation of function. For example, the right hemisphere is 'silent' as it cannot respond verbally but It can respond with some emotion, e.g. giggling.

Core study 2
Casey *et al.* on
Delay of gratification

Casey *et al.* look at parts of the brain. In particular, they showed how reward centres (e.g. ventral striatum) could be linked to impulse control and delay of gratification.

Core study 3
Blakemore and
Cooper on
Early visual experience

Blakemore and Cooper conclude that the visual cortex may adjust itself as it matures in response to visual experience. This 'plasticity' was demonstrated by the changes in brain cells from their innate orientation to the orientation related to their experience.

Core study 4
Maguire *et al.* on
Taxi drivers

Maguire *et al.*'s research indicates one brain structure (the hippocampus) is related to spatial memory (navigational skills). The correlation between the size of parts of the hippocampus and experience in taxi drivers confirmed the role of nurture in the development of a biological system.

You need to be ready for questions on all eight debates.

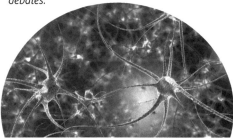

Brain plasticity involves the nervous system changing its structure and function in response to internal and external stimuli.

Revision booster

To show how the studies link to the area, you can use the concepts and principles of the area as a framework.

Then add examples from a core study.

For example, state that the biological area explains how regions of the brain affect behaviour. Then amplify this by explaining that the study by Casey *et al.* shows that low delayers had more activity than high delayers in the ventral striatum, an area of the brain involved in delay of gratification and impulse control.

Exam-style question examples

Component 2 Section A:

1. In Casey *et al.*'s research, describe how regions of the brain explain delay of gratification. **[3]**

2. Explain how Maguire *et al.*'s research is linked to the biological area. **[3]**

Component 2 Section B:

1. Outline **two** principles of the biological area. **[2]**

2. Explain why reliability tends to be high in research into the biological area. **[4]**

3. a) Outline **one** weakness of research into the biological area. **[3]**
   b) Outline **one** strength of research into the biological area. **[3]**

4. Outline **two** everyday applications of research into the biological area. **[4]**

5. Describe how the biological area supports the nature side of the nature/nurture debate. **[2]**

Biological core study 1 (classic)
Sperry (1968) on *Split brains*

Background

Hemispheres of the brain
The brain has two hemispheres (left and right, LH and RH) joined by the corpus callosum.

Hemisphere deconnection (split-brain) involves cutting the connections between the LH and RH.

Aims
To investigate:

- The psychological effects of hemispheric deconnection in patients with severe epilepsy.
- How the LH and RH work in individuals with an intact brain.

Method

Design
Controlled observation and a snapshot study, series of clinical case studies. This is also a quasi-experiment, independent groups design.

IV: Presence or absence of split brain.

DV: Participant's performance on various visual and tactile tasks.

Sample
Opportunity sample of 11 patients who had a split-brain operation following severe epileptic seizures. Patients were referred to the White Memorial Centre in Los Angeles, USA.

Materials/apparatus
A tachistoscope - a device that displays visual stimuli that are back-projected onto a screen. Objects for tactile tasks, e.g. keys.

Procedure

1. Participants were seated in front of a screen and asked to focus on a cross in the middle of the screen. One eye was covered.

2. Images were flashed on the screen each for 0.1 second so that the eye only had time to process the image in the visual field where it was placed.

3. The tasks test how the LH and RH respond to input from left visual field (LVF) and right visual field (RVF), and left and right hand.

Tasks used to test abilities

4. *Visual and verbal task* Participants were shown one image to the LVF and a different image to the RVF. Asked to say or write what they saw.

5. *Visual* Material shown to one visual field only.

6. *Visual and tactile task* Participants were asked to select an object from below the screen to match what they saw.

7. *Dual processing tactile task* Two objects were placed simultaneously, one in each hand, and then hidden in a pile of objects. Each hand was required to recognise the objects.

8. *Everyday life* Participants interviewed about everyday effects.

Results

1. *Visual and verbal task* Display $ sign to LVF and ? sign to RVF: participant reported seeing the ? sign and can draw $ sign with left hand.

2. *One visual field only*:
   - *RVF only* Participant described visual material in speech and writing as normal.
   - *LVF only* Participant reported nothing or saw flash of light on left.
   - *LVF only* Participant selected similar objects with left hand, e.g. watch and clock.
   - Picture of a pretty woman to LVF only - participant giggled but said he saw nothing.

3. *Visual and tactile task* When an object was placed in the left hand, participants made wild guesses and were unaware they were holding anything.

4. *Dual processing tactile task* Participant's right (or left) hand selected an object but each hand ignored the other hand's objects.

5. *Everyday life* Participants were able to watch TV or read books with no complaints, and their intellect and personality were unchanged. But they reported short-term memory deficits and difficulties with concentration.

Sperry used a tachistoscope (projector) to display images to only one visual field. This allowed him to isolate the function of each hemisphere.

Conclusions

Functions are lateralised in the brain.

The RH is 'silent' as it cannot respond verbally. It can respond with some emotion (e.g. giggling).

In a sense we all have two minds in one body.

Links between the core study and the methodological issues

Research method and techniques

✛ The use of objective tests to measure the patients' capabilities provides an unbiased means of assessing the effects of the operation, so high internal validity. For example, showing $ and ? signs to different visual fields to see which could be described verbally.

⊖ The study is a quasi-experiment so certain confounding variables can't be controlled, e.g. differences in patients' behaviour in tests, compared to participants with an 'intact' brain, could be due to their epilepsy rather than their split brain.

Reliability

✛ Participants were tested on a variety of tasks, carried out the same way each time.

✛ Results were consistent, e.g. LH always responded only to information presented to RVF, so tasks have some degree of reliability.

Sampling bias

✛ Using participants with a split brain provided an opportunity to study one aspect of brain function that would not be possible in an 'intact' brain.

⊖ Capabilities of epileptic patients may have been affected by their epileptic seizures, not the split-brain operation, so results should be generalised with caution.

⊖ Also sample size of 11 was relatively small, individual differences (e.g. handedness) may have affected the results.

Type of data

✛ Primary, qualitative data, e.g. how a patient responded to a symbol displayed to RVF. Data specifically focused on aims of study and gave rich, in-depth detail about the effects of the split-brain operation.

Ethical considerations

⊖ Participants with a split brain may have found it difficult to give informed consent due to trauma of surgery or epilepsy.

⊖ Repeated testing and realisation of effects of brain operation may have caused psychological harm.

Ethnocentrism

⊖ The split-brain operations described in this study were conducted in America and possibly reflect an American (and European) concern with the measurement of behaviour and the identification of localised components of the brain as a means of understanding behaviour.

It is possible to understand behaviour without this reductionist approach and instead focus on how the whole system functions.

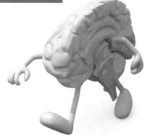

Sperry showed that each hemisphere has different functions - one more emotional than the other.

A common public image of psychologists is of therapists and 'psychobabblers' who appear on daytime television. However, do not forget that psychology is a science that involves testing hypotheses, e.g. objectively comparing the effects of the presence or absence of a split brain in Sperry's study. Always emphasise the science in your exam answers.

Exam-style question examples

Component 2 Section A:

1. In the study by Sperry, outline what is meant by 'split brain'. [2]

2. What technique did Sperry use to present information to only one hemisphere? [2]

3. Outline **two** tests used by Sperry on participants who had undergone a split-brain operation. [2]

4. From Sperry's study outline evidence that indicates that language is processed in the left hemisphere of the brain. [3]

5. In Sperry's study, describe how participants with a split brain responded to visual material presented to their right visual field (RVF). [2]

6. Give **one** strength of the research method used by Sperry. [4]

7. Outline **one** strength of the type of data collected in the study by Sperry. [2]

8. Describe **one** weakness of the sample used in the Sperry study. [3]

Methodological issues are discussed in Chapter 1 and also on pages 95-96.

Biological core study 2 (contemporary)
Casey *et al.* (2011) on *Delay of gratification*

Background

The marshmallow test

Mischel (1972) investigated the ability to defer gratification (resist temptation) by asking children to wait before eating a treat.

Aims

To investigate:

- Whether the ability to delay is a consistent personality trait.
- Whether this ability can be linked to differences in the way the brain behaves when resisting temptation.

Method

Design

Longitudinal study conducted over 40 years. The present part of the study involved two quasi-experiments, independent measures design.

IV: In both experiments, whether participants were high delayers or low delayers (established by initial test of delayed gratification when aged 4-6 years old).

DV: Experiment 1 - reaction time and accuracy on certain go/nogo tasks.

DV: Experiment 2 - activity in areas of the brain associated with cognitive control.

Sample

Experiment 1: 59 participants, 32 high delayers (20 women, 12 men, mean age 44.6 years) and 27 low delayers (16 women, 11 men, mean age 44.3 years).

Experiment 2: 27 of the participants in experiment 1. One excluded due to poor performance, leaving 26 participants.

Materials/apparatus

Neutral and emotional faces from NimStim set of facial characteristics. Laptop in experiment 1 and fMRI scanner in experiment 2.

Procedure

Experiment 1

1. Participants tested on laptops in own homes.
2. Participants were given go/nogo task (photo of a man's/woman's face). Had to press a button on any trial where photo matched the target (= go) and not press if photo did not match the target (= nogo).
3. Participants told to respond as quickly and accurately as possible.
4. Photographs shown for 500 milliseconds with one second interval between photographs.
5. 160 trials presented per run in pseudorandomised order (120 go, 40 nogo).
6. Participant had two 'runs' - a hot version of faces with emotional expressions (fearful or happy) and a cool run with neutral faces.

Experiment 2

7. Only the hot version was run with 70 go and 26 nogo trials for each expression (fearful and happy).
8. An fMRI brain scan was used to assess brain activity during this task.

Results

Experiment 1

1. Participants who were high delayers as children were better at impulse control as adults.
2. No significant difference between high and low delayers in reaction time or accuracy (on go trials).
3. On nogo trials low delayers performed less well than the high delayers on hot trials.
4. Low delayers were especially poor on the happy nogo trials.

Experiment 2

5. Low delayers committed more false alarms than high delayers on the nogo trials.
6. Three main effects, greater activation of:
   - Right inferior frontal cortex with correctly inhibited response on a nogo trial.
   - Primary motor cortex with correct response on a go trial.
   - Left cerebellum with correct response on a go trial.
7. On nogo trials low delayers had (a) reduced activity in right inferior frontal cortex, and (b) more activity in ventral striatum when shown a happy face.

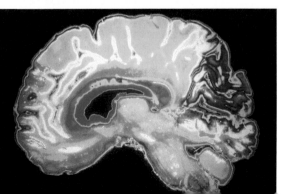

fMRI scans allow brain areas (e.g. right inferior frontal cortex) to be assessed during go/nogo tasks.

Conclusions

Adults who could delay gratification as children continue to be able to delay as adults.

Differences are apparent at both behavioural and neural levels.

There are important implications for cognitive control, for example, related to addiction.

Links between the core study and the methodological issues

Research method and techniques	⊕ A quasi-experiment permits the study of behaviour that cannot be manipulated, e.g. ability to delay gratification.
	⊕ This research is useful because low delayers are prone to undesirable physical and mental health problems so teaching better impulse control can help improve lives.
	⊖ Participants are not randomly allocated to conditions in quasi-experiments so there may be extraneous variables, such as personality differences. For example, people who have more difficulty paying attention may find it difficult to delay gratification.
	⊖ In a longitudinal study some participants drop out (called *attrition*) which biases the sample. For example, the low delayers remaining in experiment 2 may be more aggressive, which would act as an extraneous variable.
Reliability	⊖ The reliability of fMRI scans is not as good as some believe. A review by Bennett and Miller (2010) suggested that consistency between measurements can be as low as 30%, e.g. because of poor equipment. No reliability data was provided in this core study.
Sampling bias	⊕ The sample in this study was large – this was possible because Casey *et al.* could draw on participants from the 1972 study (children who went to the Bing Nursery at Stanford University).
	⊖ The study is relevant to certain cultural groups and not others as an American (individualist) bias may overemphasise the importance of delay of gratification, which may be less important in collectivist groups.
Type of data	⊕ Quantitative data – experiment 1 measured reaction times and the number and percentage of false alarms. Experiment 2 used information about brain activity and volume from fMRI scans.
Ethical considerations	⊕ Both experiments had institutional review board approval, and all participants provided consent.
	⊖ Low delayers may have experienced loss of self-esteem (psychological harm) as it is regarded as desirable to be able to control one's impulses.
	⊖ Use of fMRI may cause physical harm as it is an unpleasant experience (noisy and claustrophobic) and difficult for participant to withdraw once scanning has started.
Ethnocentrism	⊖ The self-control investigated has a very individualist orientation, e.g. focuses on the individual's needs to control impulses for better performance.
	Collectivist societies may focus on how impulse control benefits group needs as a whole.

Revision booster

When asked to make comparisons between studies you should always use points of methodology, such as looking at the type of data used. Sperry collected primary, qualitative data (e.g. how a patient responded to a symbol displayed to their RVF) whereas Casey *et al.* collected quantitative data (e.g. as reaction times and the number and percentage of false alarms).

Casey et al.*'s research is important in understanding why some people are more prone to addiction. This suggests that addiction might be improved by helping to improve impulse control.*

Exam-style question examples

Component 2 Section A:

1. Describe the aims of the Casey *et al.* study. **[2]**

2. Identify **one** dependent variable in experiment 1 of Casey *et al.*'s study. **[2]**

3. Describe the sample in Casey *et al.*'s first experiment. **[2]**

4. Describe the go/nogo tasks in Casey *et al.*'s first experiment. **[3]**

5. Outline **two** results from Casey *et al.*'s second experiment. **[2]**

6. Describe **two** weaknesses of the research method used by Casey *et al.* **[3]**

7. Describe **one** weakness of the sample used in Casey *et al.*'s study. **[2]**

8. Outline an ethical consideration of the Casey *et al.* study. **[3]**

Biological core study 3 (classic)
Blakemore and Cooper (1970) on *Early visual experience*

Background

The visual cortex and plasticity

Hubel and Wiesel (1959) found that columns of cells in visual cortex respond to one particular orientation of a line, e.g. 45°.

Hirsch and Spinelli exposed cats' eyes to only vertical or only horizontal stripes and found that each cell in the visual cortex only responded to one of these orientations. This shows that the visual cortex is 'plastic'.

Aims

To investigate:

- Physiological and behavioural effects of restricted early visual experience on development of the visual cortex.
- Whether brain plasticity occurs due to nurture rather than nature.

Method

Design

Laboratory experiment, independent measures design.

IV: Kittens' early experience was a horizontal or vertical environment.

DVs: (1) Behavioural, (2) neurophysiological differences between cats.

Sample

Two newborn kittens at the beginning of the study, five months old during the behavioural tests and $7\frac{1}{2}$ months old for neurological tests.

Materials/apparatus

A special cylinder was constructed with no corners or edges (see illustration on facing page).

Procedure

Early experience

1. Kittens kept in completely dark room for two weeks.

2. At two weeks old, the kittens were put in a cylinder (horizontal or vertical environment) for an average of five hours a day, otherwise they were kept in the dark room.

Exposure to normal environment

3. At five months the visual deprivation stopped.

4. For several hours each week the cats were taken to a small well-lit room with chairs and tables.

5. Cats were given artificial lenses so any visual difficulties were not due to astigmatism (causes blurred vision).

Testing

6. *Behavioural assessment* Cats' responses to new visual world observed over the following weeks.

7. *Neurophysiological assessment* At $7\frac{1}{2}$ months cats' eyes were shown lines of all possible orientations 'around the clock'. An electrode was inserted in each neuron to measure electrical firing of the neuron.

Results

Behavioural assessment

1. Some of the cats' reflexes were normal, e.g. eye pupils contracted normally in brighter light.

2. *Temporary deficit* Visual placing reflex (cats reach out with legs to nearby surface) not shown immediately after period of deprivation but recovered within 10 hours.

3. *Permanent deficit* Cats often reached out to touch something that was quite far away.

4. *Difference between 'horizontal' and 'vertical' cats* A long black rod held vertically and shaken was watched and played with by vertical cats but ignored by horizontal ones (and vice versa).

Neurophysiological assessment

5. In both cats, 75% of cells were binocular and responded as a normal animal would.

6. Responses to lines of certain orientations were completely abnormal, e.g. in horizontal cats visual cortex cells did not respond to lines within 20° of vertical orientation and only 12 of 52 neurons responded within 45° of the vertical orientation. This directional dependence (*anisotropy*) was significant at $p < 0.00001$.

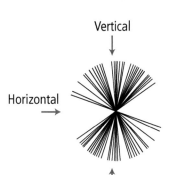

Recording of electrical firing from 52 neurons in the vertically-experienced cat, showing that only vertical neurons were responding.

Conclusions

Nature (the brain) is modified by nurture (experience of line orientation) so that the biological system fits the demands of the environment.

Unused parts of the innate nervous system adapt to match the actual visual input experienced.

Both demonstrate brain plasticity.

Links between the core study and the methodological issues

Research method and techniques

➕ Laboratory conditions mean extraneous variables can be controlled, e.g. kittens' first two weeks were in a completely dark room.

➖ The artificial environment itself may act as an extraneous variable. It might be that the distress caused by the experience affected the development of the kittens/cats. This means the effects of visual deprivation observed in this study may not generalise to everyday experiences.

Validity

➕ Validity is supported by studies with humans. For example, some children are born with squint eyesight (*strabismus*). If this is corrected with surgery before the age of four, children develop normal binocular vision but in older children the brain is permanently affected (Banks *et al.* 1975). This can be understood in terms of the cells in the visual cortex that change in response to early experience but which are no longer 'plastic' after a certain age.

Reliability

➖ There was no check on the reliability of the data – for example, it was not possible to see if another cat, reared with horizontal lines only, would respond in the same way to vertical lines.

➕ However, the fact that both cats responded in an almost identical way to the orientation of their rearing suggests consistency.

Sampling bias

➕ Cats are mammals and their visual systems are fairly similar to the human visual system, as shown in brain scans. This research could not be done with humans so it is necessary to use other animals in order to gain important insights about how the human visual system works.

Types of data

➕ Quantitative data, e.g. reaction of the neurons to the orientation of the lines, allowed comparisons between cats.

➕ Qualitative data, e.g. observations were made of the cats in a well-lit environment, such as tripping over table legs.

Ethical considerations

➕ Blakemore and Cooper suggest that the kittens were not unduly distressed. However, other research suggests that the kittens/cats might be affected by their visual and physical isolation.

➕ Costs versus benefits – the study provided important evidence about the nervous system response to deprivation and practical applications (see above).

➕ The three Rs offer a compromise: *replace* animal research with alternatives, *reduce* the number of animals, *refine* procedures to cause less suffering. Blakemore and Cooper did reduce and refine.

The kitten stood on a glass plate supported in the middle of the cylinder for five hours a day. The surface of the tube had black and white stripes (vertical or horizontal) of varying widths. The kitten wore a wide black collar to prevent it being able to see its own body.

Revision booster

Being able to link the core study theme (e.g. 'brain plasticity') to an aspect of the core study shows understanding. For example, Blakemore and Cooper showed how plasticity is linked to early visual experience as cats raised in the horizontal environment had visual cortex cells that did not respond to lines within 20° of vertical orientation.

Exam-style question examples

Component 2 Section A:

1. Outline **two** aims from Blakemore and Cooper's study. **[2]**

2. Identify the independent variable in Blakemore and Cooper's study. **[2]**

3. Outline the apparatus used by Blakemore and Cooper. **[2]**

4. Outline **two** results from Blakemore and Cooper's study. **[4]**

5. Describe a control used by Blakemore and Cooper. **[2]**

6. Give **one** limitation of the reliability of the data in Blakemore and Cooper's study. **[3]**

7. Give a strength of the research method used in the Blakemore and Cooper study. **[2]**

8. Describe **one** strength of the data used by Blakemore and Cooper. **[4]**

Biological core study 4 (contemporary)
Maguire *et al.* (2000) on *Taxi drivers*

Background

Hippocampus and spatial memory

There is one hippocampus in each hemisphere of the brain, located deep inside the temporal lobe.

Species that need spatial memory have larger hippocampi than species with less need for spatial memory.

Aims

To investigate:

- Whether the brain is capable of changing in response to environmental stimulation.
- The precise role of the hippocampus in humans.
- Structural changes in the human brain in response to behaviour requiring spatial memory.

Method

Design

Quasi-experiment, matched participants, repeated measures design.

IV: Whether a participant was a taxi driver or not.

DV: Volume of each hippocampus, measured in six areas: right and left hemisphere of the anterior, body and posterior hippocampi.

Sample

Experimental group: 16 right-handed taxi drivers (all men) who had passed 'The Knowledge'. Mean age 44 years (range 32–62 years), mean experience of taxi driving 14.3 years (range 1.5–42 years). Mean training time two years (range 10 months – 3.5 years). All had healthy medical, neurological and psychiatric profiles.

Matched control group: men who were not taxi drivers, matched to taxi drivers by health, mean age, age range, gender and handedness. Selected from a pool of 50 men whose records were held in a structural MRI scan database. Provided baseline data for the VBM. Only 16 used for pixel counting.

Materials/apparatus

MRI scanner used to measure the volumes in the hippocampus.

Procedure

Image analysis method 1: VBM

1. VBM = voxel-based morphometry. A 'voxel' is a three-dimensional pixel representing a single point on a graphic image.
2. VBM measured the volume of the hippocampus comparing it to the MRI scans of the 50 controls.
3. VBM identifies differences in density of brain grey matter.
4. VBM is an automatic procedure that uses Statistical Parametric Mapping.

Image analysis method 2: Pixel counting

5. MRI scans of the hippocampus were 'cut' into 26 slices (each 1.5 mm thick). Each slice produced a two-dimensional picture of the hippocampus.
6. Pictures were analysed by one person who counted the pixels in each slice.
7. Person counting was 'blind' to whether the participant was a taxi driver or non-taxi driver (control), and to VBM results.
8. Total hippocampal volume was measured.

Results

Results from VBM

1. Taxi drivers had significantly more grey matter in both left and right hippocampi (LH and RH) than controls.
2. This difference was only in the *posterior* portion of both LH and RH.
3. Controls had more grey matter in the *anterior* portion of both LH and RH.
4. No differences were observed elsewhere in the brain.

Results from pixel counting

5. Total hippocampal volumes and intercranial volume did not differ significantly between taxi drivers and controls.
6. LH and RH had greater volume in taxi drivers than controls but not a significant difference.
7. *Anterior* portion of both LH and RH had greater volume in controls than in taxi drivers.
8. *Posterior* portion of both LH and RH had greater volume in taxi drivers than controls.

Changes with navigational experience

9. There was a positive correlation between time spent taxi-driving and volume of the posterior RH. Negative correlation between time and volume of anterior RH and LH.

	LH (left hippocampus)	RH (right hippocampus)
Anterior	Control	Control
Body	No significant difference between groups	No significant difference between groups
Posterior	Taxi drivers	Taxi drivers

Table shows which areas of the hippocampi were larger for each group of participants.

Conclusions

Results support a relationship between hippocampus and navigational skills, suggesting that the brain changes in response to experience (plasticity).

The correlation with experience in taxi drivers confirms the role of nurture in development of a biological system.

Links between the core study and the methodological issues

Research method and techniques

✛ Quasi-experiments allow variables to be studied that could not be easily controlled, e.g. the long-term experience of using spatial memory. Taking advantage of taxi drivers' experience was a convenient way to assess the effect of spatial experience.

⊟ Quasi-experiments do not allow causal conclusions as participants are not randomly allocated to conditions. Other characteristics unique to taxi drivers may explain differences in hippocampal volume, e.g. taxi driving is a very social job, talking to people all day, and this may affect hippocampal development. This may have been partially overcome by matching participants.

Reliability

✛ Using MRI to measure brain volume is a standardised technique conducted in highly controlled conditions. This creates consistency, i.e. reliability and replicability.

⊟ However, only one person counted pixels, meaning results were not cross-checked.

Sampling bias

✛ Matching participants controlled for key variables that might explain differences between taxi drivers and non-taxi drivers (e.g. age and handedness).

⊟ The sample was made up of men only, women may respond differently.

⊟ Left-handed people may have been quite different as the right hemisphere may have greater spatial awareness.

Type of data

✛ Quantitative data, e.g. the density of the grey matter and the hippocampal volume.

⊟ Qualitative data could have been collected (but wasn't) by asking taxi drivers and controls to describe their experiences of using spatial memory.

Ethical considerations

✛ Participants gave consent for the MRI scan.

⊟ They may have found the experience more distressing than anticipated, e.g. a scanner is a very noisy environment.

Ethnocentrism

⊟ Only British participants were involved.

The experimental group consisted of people who lived in urban environments. People from rural settings may have developed different ways of using their spatial memory, e.g. they might not remember the relationships between names of roads and buildings but between things in the environment.

Revision booster

Showing the examiner you can apply your knowledge to the study is vital. For example, it is better to provide context from the core study such as 'the taxi drivers and non-taxi drivers were matched for age and handedness' rather than just 'participants were matched'.

Maguire et al. chose taxi drivers because their job requires spatial navigation around the streets of London. Taxi drivers use spatial navigation for different routes whereas bus drivers only follow the same route, thus using spatial navigation in a different way.

Exam-style question examples

Component 2 Section A:

1. Outline **two** aims from Maguire *et al.*'s study. [2]

2. Identify the independent variable in the Maguire *et al.* study. [2]

3. Identify the dependent variable in the Maguire *et al.* study. [2]

4. Outline the sample used by Maguire *et al.* [2]

5. Explain how participants were matched in the study by Maguire *et al.* [2]

6. Outline a strength of the way Maguire *et al.* reduced sampling bias in their study. [4]

7. Describe **one** weakness of the type of data collected by Maguire *et al.* [2]

8. Describe **one** way in which Maguire *et al.* ensured the reliability of their results. [3]

The individual differences area

The study of individual differences focuses on the way you are and the characteristics that make you stand out from the crowd.

Good answers always include the use of the specialist terms for the topic, e.g. personality, idiographic, quantifiable (measuring differences), uniqueness, characteristics.

Revision booster

Answers to questions about key concepts of an area should always include specialist terms and/or key concepts to improve your response. For example, a key concept of the individual differences area is the *differences* between people which means they are unique. This is an example of the *idiographic* approach.

Key concepts	**Eugenics** Aims to improve the quality of human beings through selective breeding. Galton (1884) collected data about people (e.g. visual acuity), and used this to estimate people's inherited intelligence.
	Differences and commonalities
	Differences – a focus on the uniqueness of people. This focus uses qualitative methods to build up a picture of subjective experiences. This is an idiographic approach, often used in case studies, e.g. Freud and Little Hans.
	Commonalities – a focus on characteristics people share. This is a nomothetic and quantitative approach, e.g. psychometric tests.
Everyday applications	**Treat psychological disorders** For example, Freud's research can be applied to psychoanalysis.
	Improve educational strategies For example, help autistic people understand others' emotions.
	Develop psychometric tests To assess the differences between people, e.g. different types of personality.
Similarities	The individual differences approach has developed psychometric measures that assess how we think, feel and behave. These measures are used in all areas of psychology (e.g. intelligence or personality tests).
Differences	The individual differences approach focuses on differences (e.g. intelligence) whereas other areas of psychology focus on the things people have in common (e.g. social behaviour).
Evaluation	➕ **Research on individual differences is useful** As our understanding of people with psychological disorders may provide insights into everyday experiences, e.g. Freud's case study of Little Hans's phobias can be related to everyday anxieties.
	➕ **Provides insights** Into what makes people different, e.g. Baron-Cohen *et al.* highlight autistic adults' lack of a Theory of Mind (ToM).
	➖ **Idiographic approach** This means that generalisations are not possible, e.g. Freud's unique insights on Little Hans cannot be presumed to be true for all people.
	➖ **Ethical issues** Related to informed consent, e.g. in Baron-Cohen *et al.*'s study on autism, participants may not have been fully able to give informed consent because their comprehension abilities were poor.

Links between the area and the perspectives/debates

The individual differences area is compared to the other four areas on page 97.

The perspectives and debates are explained on pages 90-94.

Behaviourist perspective In Freud's study, Little Hans's phobia could be explained through classical conditioning as horses become associated with fear.

Psychodynamic perspective Little Hans's phobia developed because of his unconscious thoughts and feelings that were repressed and became associated with horses, e.g. they reminded him of his father. Hancock *et al.* suggest psychopaths' use of language is not always under conscious control.

Nature/nurture Freud's study shows how a phobia develops through life experiences (nurture) yet the stages of development are biological (nature). Baron-Cohen *et al.* suggest that the basis of a theory of mind deficit might be genetic (nature).

Usefulness Research suggests ways psychological disorders might be treated, e.g. phobias treated using psychoanalysis, and social challenges associated with autism reduced through increased experience of reading other people's mental states.

Socially sensitive research There is the potential to have a negative impact on specific groups of people or society generally. Freud's study might influence the way parents interact with their children and Baron-Cohen *et al.*'s study could mean that employers avoid hiring autistic people because of their apparent deficit.

The debates on the left are examples of how you might link the area to the debates. All eight debates are explained on pages 91-94.

Extraverts tend to be happy, positive and sociable. They tend not to dwell on problems and, while they experience troubles like anyone else, extraverts don't let it affect them much.

Links between the area and the core studies

Core study 1
Freud on
Little Hans

The study illustrates the factors that make Little Hans both different and unique, e.g. his experience of phobia. It also tells us the similarities each of us have in the way that the Oedipus complex may be part of typical development.

Core study 2
Baron-Cohen *et al.* on
Autism

Mental health is one way in which people differ but the differences are not all-or-nothing. In the study by Baron-Cohen *et al.*, some people in the autistic group scored quite well on the Eyes Task. This shows a continuum in the ToM deficit.

Core study 3
Gould on a
Nation of morons

People are different in many ways, e.g. people differ in terms of their intelligence - their IQ score places them within the population range from low to high intelligence. Gould's review shows how Yerkes' tests divided recruits into one of several categories denoting intellectual ability.

Core study 4
Hancock *et al.* on
Psychopaths

Hancock *et al.*'s study on the testing of murderers highlighted differences between them by categorising them based on their scores on a psychometric test - they were either psychopaths or not.

Exam-style question examples

Component 2 Section A:

1. Outline how Baron-Cohen *et al.*'s study relates to the theme of understanding disorders. **[3]**

2. Explain how Freud's research links to the individual differences area. **[3]**

Component 2 Section B:

1. Outline **two** concepts of the individual differences area of psychology. **[4]**

2. Explain why the results of research into individual differences psychology may be socially sensitive. **[3]**

3. a) Outline **one** weakness of research into the individual differences area. **[3]**
   b) Outline **one** strength of research into the individual differences area. **[3]**

4. Outline **one** everyday application of research into the individual differences area. **[2]**

5. Describe how the individual differences area is useful. **[2]**

Individual differences core study 1 (classic)
Freud (1909) on *Little Hans*

Background

Freud's theories of personality and psychological disorder

Freud identified five stages of personality development. In each stage children must resolve specific conflicts to continue healthy psychological development.

The third stage is the phallic stage (age 3-6 years) where the conflict is about sexuality and identification. Boys experience the Oedipus complex (a desire for their mother, seeing their father as a rival). This is resolved (a) through ego defences such as repression, and (b) by identifying with their father. Ego defences protect ourselves (ego) from unpleasant feelings.

(Freud suggested girls go through a similar but less successful process.)

Aims

To use a case study to support Freud's ideas about:

- Child development and the Oedipus complex.
- The origins of psychological disorders such as phobias.
- The value of psychoanalysis (the 'talking cure') for treating psychological disorder.

Method

Design

Longitudinal case study.

Sample

One boy, 'Little Hans', from age three to five.

Hans and his family were selected because Hans's father was interested in Freud's work and wished to give Freud the opportunity to explore his theories about the origin of phobias and psychosexual development (an opportunity sample).

Research techniques

Data collected from conversations between father and son as recorded in writing by the father (i.e. self-report). The father also recorded the events in Hans's life.

Procedure

1. Data about Hans's life was written down by Hans's father and discussed with Freud.

2. Hans's father sent regular reports to Freud. The written record was similar to a diary, kept over a period of years.

3. The final account of this case consisted of data collected in the following ways:
   - Factual record (diary) of events in Hans's family life noted down by his father, e.g. birth of his sister. Some drawings were included.
   - Observations of Hans's behaviour made by his father, e.g. Hans touching his 'widdler' (penis).
   - Conversations between Hans and his father, recorded by Hans's father.
   - Analysis, by both Freud and Hans's father, of the events that unfolded and included their comments in the written account, e.g. Freud suggested that a horse represented Hans's father.

4. Once Hans was taken to meet Freud.

Results

Part I: Early life

1. Hans experienced the Oedipus complex.

2. Hans developed a fascination with his 'widdler' because he was in the phallic stage.

3. Hans feared castration because his mother said she would have his widdler chopped of.

Part II: Analysis

4. Ego defences: Hans's mother told him his penis would be cut off if he touched it, creating anxiety. This was expressed as a fear of horses that might bite if he touched them.

5. Hans's fear of horses: represented a subconscious fear of his father (the Oedipus complex → castration anxiety).

6. Hans's fear of carts: they represented pregnancy.

7. Hans's daydream about giraffes: evidence of his attraction to his mother.

Part III: Resolution

8. Hans's fantasy about the plumber and fantasy of being a father showed him now identifying with his father, having passed through the Oedipus complex.

Conclusions

The study supports Freud's ideas about the Oedipus complex. Hans repressed his desires for his mother and his jealousy towards his father.

The study shows how a psychological disorder (such as a phobia) can develop as a means of expressing repressed anxieties.

The study shows that the techniques of psychoanalysis can aid recovery.

Hans's dream about two giraffes was interpreted as the big giraffe being Hans's father or his penis, and the crumpled giraffe as his wife's genital organ.

Links between the core study and the methodological issues

Research method and techniques	⊕ Case studies focus on one individual so a lot of detailed information can be collected, e.g. about Hans's fears, dreams and fantasies.
	⊖ Data was entirely collected by Hans's father and interpreted by his father and by Freud, so the study lacked objectivity. Hans may have responded to his father's questions in the desired way because he wished to please his father and/or the questions were leading questions.
Validity	⊕ Freud argues that the anxieties that Hans experienced are relatively common in early childhood, so the study increases our understanding of typical development.
	⊖ However, Hans may not be representative of other children his age and so any generalisations about typical development should be made with caution.
	⊖ The use of leading questions and the lack of objectivity also reduce validity.
Sampling bias	⊕ The study of Hans, and his family, offered a unique opportunity to observe a child who had developed a phobia in the phallic stage of development, and collect a wealth of qualitative data about him.
	⊖ Hans may have been a nervous child so we cannot generalise the results from this study to other fears and phobias, e.g. a less anxious child may not have developed a sexual desire for his mother in the same circumstances. This is a different point from the one above about generalisation.
Type of data	⊕ Conversations and descriptions of events in Hans's life produced qualitative data, providing rich, in-depth insight into Hans's experiences, thoughts, feelings and phobias.
Ethical considerations	⊖ Hans's father provided informed consent, though the transcript represents an intrusion into the family's privacy. The intensive level of questions about why Hans felt as he did might have been quite stressful, causing psychological harm.
	⊖ Research into psychological disorders is socially sensitive as it suggests the reason people have phobias is because of repressed emotions from their childhood. Other simpler explanations are available, e.g. phobias are learned through an association between a neutral object (the horse) and something that provokes fear (being bitten).
Ethnocentrism	⊖ Freud explains the behaviour of middle-class, educated Europeans living in small family groups. Other people around the world have different experiences of family life, e.g. extended families. This means that the Oedipus complex may not apply to their experiences.
	Literacy may vary between cultures, which means that psychoanalysis (which requires developed verbal skills) may work less well.

Hans's fear of horses was related to the black around their mouths and the blinkers in front of their eyes, as they symbolised Hans's father's moustache and glasses.

Revision booster

Students sometimes find it difficult to summarise Hans's Oedipal complex. Here it is in three simple points:

- Attraction to his mother.
- Fear of his father.
- Identification with his father.

Exam-style question examples

Component 2 Section A:

1. Outline the aims of Freud's study. **[3]**

2. Describe the design in Freud's study. **[2]**

3. Explain why Freud used Hans and his family as an example of his theory. **[2]**

4. Outline the way in which data was collected in Freud's study. **[4]**

5. Describe **two** results from Freud's study. **[4]**

6. Explain why Freud's study can be considered to be low in validity. **[3]**

7. Explain **one** strength of collecting qualitative data in the study by Freud. **[2]**

8. Outline **two** ethical problems in the study by Freud. **[4]**

Individual differences core study 2 (contemporary)
Baron-Cohen *et al.* (1997) on *Autism*

*Autistic people are no longer divided into low- and high-functioning. Some autistic people have additional learning difficulties - those without such difficulties would previously have been described as 'high-functioning' or would have been diagnosed with Asperger syndrome. Now all people on the spectrum are either 'autistic' or 'autistic with learning difficulties'.

We have decided to both update and simplify the descriptions used in the original article for this core study:
- **AS** refers to autistic people who do not have additional learning difficulties and previously were called 'high-functioning' or were diagnosed with Asperger syndrome.
- **non-AS** refers to individuals without a diagnosis of autism.

Background

Theory of Mind (ToM)

The understanding that someone else has a separate mind to your own and therefore does not see or experience the world as you do.

Baron-Cohen *et al.* tested children's ToM using the Sally-Anne test, finding that autistic children did not have a ToM. Autism is a 'spectrum' condition, which means that autistic people share many characteristics (e.g. difficulties understanding other people) but experience these characteristics differently. People with Asperger syndrome are also on this spectrum.

Aims

To see if AS adults (with high-functioning autism or Asperger diagnosis*) have a ToM, using the Eyes Task (a more challenging test).

Method

Design and sample

Quasi-experiment, matched participants design (age and intelligence matched), and a snapshot study (one time frame).

Three groups each representing one level of the IV.

- IV 1: AS group. 'Average intelligence' (IQ > 85, mean 105.3), 13 men and 3 women.
- IV 2: non-AS group. Matched control, a random sample of 50 non-AS adults (25 men and 25 women), age matched with individuals in Group 1.
- IV 3: TS (Tourette syndrome), self-selected, mean IQ 103.5, age matched, 8 men and 2 women. (TS, like AS, is a developmental disorder linked to frontal lobe abnormalities but not linked to social deficits.)

DV: Scores on: Eyes Task, Strange Stories Task, Gender Recognition of Eyes, and Basic Emotion Recognition Task.

Materials/apparatus

Standardised magazine photographs - same size (15 × 10 cm), black and white, just showing the eye region of faces (men and women).

Procedure

Task A: Eyes Task

1. All participants were shown pictures of 25 pairs of eyes, each for three seconds.

2. Participants had to select between two mental state terms printed under each picture, e.g. attraction/repulsion, calm/anxious.

3. Participants were tested individually either in their own home, the researchers' clinic or a laboratory at Cambridge University.

Task B: Strange Stories Task

4. AS and TS participants (Groups 1 and 3) were tested on Happé's Strange Stories Task.

5. The AS and TS participants answered questions on what characters in the story were thinking and about physical events.

Task C: Gender Recognition of Eyes

6. AS participants had to identify the gender of the eyes.

Task D: Basic Emotion Recognition Task

7. AS participants had to identify basic emotions in whole faces.

8. The four tasks were presented in a random order.

Results

Task A: Eyes Task

1. The AS group did least well (mean score 16.3 out of 25).

2. Non-AS and TS groups did about the same (mean score 20.3 and 20.4 respectively).

3. The ranges of scores were similar.

4. There was a ceiling effect on this task.

5. Non-AS women performed significantly better than non-AS men on the Eyes Task (mean score 21.8 versus 18.8).

6. Non-AS men were significantly better than the AS men (mean score 18.8 versus 16.3).

Task B: Strange Stories Task

7. The AS group had more difficulty with this task than the TS group.

Tasks C and D: The control tasks

8. The AS group performed the same as the non-AS group on task C and task D.

Conclusions

AS adults may lack a Theory of Mind (ToM).

This is not due to a lack of intelligence, nor to frontal lobe damage.

The gender difference may be genetic or because girls are socialised differently from boys.

Task	Participants		
	AS	non-AS control	TS
A	×	×	×
B	×		×
C	×		
D	×		

This table will help clarify which tasks were completed by which participants.

Links between the core study and the methodological issues

Research method and techniques

⊕ Having control groups provided a baseline to judge the behaviour of the AS group, e.g. the TS group showed that, even with a neurological deficit, they could perform well on the Eyes Task.

⊕ The matched participants design means that one participant variable (age) was controlled.

⊖ The IV (AS, non-AS or TS) was not controlled meaning it may not be AS that causes a ToM deficit.

The research technique: The Eyes Task

⊕ The Eyes Task was given on paper, therefore there was no possible researcher bias in the way the questions were asked.

⊕ The bias due to differences between photographs was reduced as each photograph was identical except for the expression of the eyes.

⊖ The Eyes Task may not have been measuring what it claimed to measure (ToM in everyday life).

Reliability

⊕ Reliability is high as the Eyes Task was carried out the same way each time so the results could be interpreted in the same way each time.

Sampling bias

⊕ The sample was able to show that autistic adults (as well as children) have mind-reading deficits.

⊖ Group 1 had 13 men and 3 women, not matched for gender.

Types of data

⊕ Quantitative data, e.g. in the Eyes Task there was a numerical score.

⊕ Qualitative data, e.g. Happe's Strange Stories had questions about pictures such as, 'Why does Emma say this?'.

Ethical considerations

⊕ Participants were all adults and provided informed consent.

⊖ However, we might consider people who lack a ToM as vulnerable and unable to give truly informed consent.

⊖ Research into developmental disorders is socially sensitive because the discovery of a specific deficit in autistic people might lead to greater exclusion, e.g. jobs or education.

Ethnocentrism

⊖ The sample was British and also the symptoms of autism may be viewed more positively in some cultures if lack of social interaction is not seen as a problem to be solved.

Methodological issues are discussed in Chapter 1 and also on pages 95-96.

Revision booster

You should be able to explain how the individual differences area shows the uniqueness of people, e.g. AS adults may lack a Theory of Mind (ToM) as they scored lower on the Eyes Task than adults without a diagnosis. Such characteristics may have advantages.

The two terms for each photo consisted of one mental state term - the 'target', and its 'foil' - a term with the opposite meaning, e.g. 'friendly' and 'hostile'.

Exam-style question examples

Component 2 Section A:

1. From the study by Baron-Cohen *et al.*, outline what you understand by the term 'Theory of Mind'. **[2]**

2. Describe **one** of the sample groups used in the Baron-Cohen *et al.* study. **[2]**

3. Describe the Eyes Task used in the Baron-Cohen *et al.* study. **[4]**

4. Outline **two** results from the Baron-Cohen *et al.* study. **[4]**

5. Describe **two** conclusions from the Baron-Cohen *et al.* study. **[4]**

6. Outline **one** strength of using control groups in the Baron-Cohen *et al.* study. **[3]**

7. Explain why the Baron-Cohen *et al.* study can be considered to be reliable. **[3]**

8. Explain why the results of the Baron-Cohen *et al.* study might be considered to be ethnocentric. **[2]**

Individual differences core study 3 (classic)

Gould (1982) on a *Nation of morons**

> * The term 'moron' in the title has come to mean 'stupid' but originally was an IQ test classification for someone with a score of 51-70 (100 points is average).
>
> ** The term 'Negroes' was used in the original article but we have chosen to replace it with 'black Americans'.

Background

Early psychology

Before World War I, Yerkes sought to promote psychology as a science and thought the field of intelligence testing might show this. He created a set of intelligence tests and, using these, collected objective numerical data from large numbers of World War I Army recruits.

Aims

Gould's review aimed to show that Yerkes' intelligence tests were flawed and had far-reaching social consequences.

Method

Design

No design, an edited extract from Gould's book *The Mismeasure of Man*.

Sample

Opportunity sample of 1.75 million American Army recruits, all male, ethnically and culturally mixed, including white Americans, black Americans** and European immigrants.

Materials/apparatus

(1) Army Alpha test (written intelligence test for literate recruits), (2) Army Beta test (pictorial intelligence test for illiterate men and for men who failed the Alpha test), (3) Individual test (spoken for those who failed the Beta test).

Procedure

1. The Army tests were produced by Yerkes and other prominent psychologists.
2. Alpha and Beta tests each took less than an hour and were given to large groups.
3. The plan was to give certain tests to specific recruits:
   - Literate recruits would do the written test, the Alpha test.
   - Illiterate men and men who failed the Alpha test would do the Beta test.
   - Men who failed the Beta test would be recalled for an individual spoken test.
   - Army psychologists would then grade each man from A to E (with pluses and minuses) and offer suggestions for proper military placement.
4. The plan ran into difficulties:
   - There were too many illiterate recruits, so criteria for taking the Alpha test were lowered and criteria varied from camp to camp.
   - It was not possible to retest those men who failed the Alpha test, e.g. illiterate men who took the Alpha test.

Results

Systematic bias

1. Problems administering the tests led to a low mean score for illiterate immigrants and black Americans.
2. Boring confirmed this bias, e.g. the average 'mental age' [an outdated method of scoring IQ] for Alpha was 10.775 years, for Beta was 12.158.

The effect of the tests

3. Tests were used to screen 1.75 million recruits for officer training.
4. Tests established the first mass-produced intelligence tests.
5. Tests informed social policy, e.g. the American Immigration Restriction Act (1924).

Three key facts from the data

6. Average 'mental age' of white American Army recruits was equivalent to a 'moron'* (< 13 years of age).
7. Immigrants from southern and eastern Europe had lower scores than those from northern and western Europe (e.g. 'mental age'/IQ score for Russians was 11.34 and Italians was 11.01 years).
8. Black Americans had the lowest 'mental age' (10.41 years).

Problems

9. The positive correlation between average test scores and time in the US suggests that the tests assess familiarity with American ways, not innate intelligence.

Who has heard of Crisco?

Many of the items on the Army Alpha test were culturally specific.

Conclusions

Army tests were culturally biased because they required culturally-based knowledge and skills.

This explains the inferior score of black Americans and immigrants and not genetics.

The flawed data and conclusions had very serious and long-lasting negative consequences – both for intelligence testing and for immigration (e.g. strict quotas on people from south-eastern Europe).

Links between the core study and the methodological issues

Research method and techniques	⊕ Psychometric tests can be given to large numbers of people, allowing comparisons between different groups of people, e.g. intelligence of 1.75 million American Army recruits.
	⊖ Test results may be biased, favouring one cultural group (ethnocentric).
	⊖ Tests may lack construct validity because they do not measure what they aimed to measure, for example, intelligence.
Validity	⊖ The ethnocentric nature of the test items meant that construct validity was low as the Army IQ tests did not assess intelligence accurately (there was a bias towards culturally-based knowledge).
	⊖ The tests lacked face validity because many of the items did not assess intelligence.
	⊖ Validity of the hereditarian assumption that IQ/mental abilities are innate is low – it does not consider environmental influences on knowledge, e.g. more educated households.
Reliability	⊖ Test-retest reliability involves people taking the same test a second time to see if their scores are consistent. At one camp some men who took the Alpha were retested on the Beta version which was supposed to be equivalent. The result demonstrated extremely low reliability (86% got a higher grade on retesting).
Sampling bias	⊕ Very large sample (1.75 million American Army recruits) is representative of the target population of American men in the early 20th century.
	⊖ Many of the participants were illiterate and yet they were assessed using tests designed for literate people (they took the Alpha test).
Ethical considerations	⊖ Informed consent was an issue as the Army recruits did not give consent to the data being used in the way that it was.
	⊖ Using flawed data to inform social policy is problematic. Care should be taken when conducting socially sensitive research.
Ethnocentrism	⊖ Conclusions were drawn from the IQ data about black people and immigrants, based on the ethnocentric views of white American psychologists (the questions and methods of testing people were rooted in white, middle-class American experience).

Jews from south-eastern Europe trying to flee Europe before the Second World War were barred from entering America as a result of the 1924 Immigration Restriction Act. The consequence was that they died in concentration camps.

Revision booster

Try the revision technique of 'Just a minute'. It is based on the classic radio game. You can adapt it to any topic, e.g. talk for a minute on the Gould core study – no pauses, no hesitations, slips or repetitions. By self-explaining, you become more aware of your understanding – and any areas of confusion.

Exam-style question examples

Component 2 Section A:

1. Outline the sample used in Gould's study. [2]

2. Describe what you understand by the term 'Army Alpha test' from Gould's study. [2]

3. Explain **one** difficulty of Yerkes' plan to test US Army recruits, reported in the Gould study. [3]

4. Outline **two** key facts from Gould's results. [4]

5. Describe **two** conclusions from the Gould study. [2]

6. Outline **two** weaknesses of the tests used in the Gould study. [2]

7. Explain why Gould believed Yerkes' results can be considered ethnocentric. [3]

8. Explain **one** ethical issue from the Gould study. [3]

How psychology contributes to the success of the economy and society ...
This study is important in helping us appreciate the effect of prejudice and the importance of tolerance.

Individual differences core study 4 (contemporary)

Hancock *et al.* (2011) on *Psychopaths**

> * 'Psychopathy' is no longer a term used in the diagnosis of psychological disorder. It is now referred to as 'antisocial' or 'dissocial' personality disorder.
>
> As psychopathy was determined by the checklist used in the study, we have used the term 'psychopathy' and 'psychopath' in our descriptions.

Background

Language of psychopaths

Analysis of words reveals people's inner thoughts and psychological states, e.g. lying.

Psychopaths* are skilled at conversation but their language is less cohesive than non-psychopaths.

Aims

Text analysis of psychopaths describing their violent crimes, focusing on:

1. *An instrumental/predatory world view* – Psychopaths are more likely to be motivated by an external goal.

2. *Unique socioemotional needs* – Psychopaths show little need for others.

3. *Poverty of affect* – Psychopaths lack emotional intelligence.

Method

Design

Quasi-experiment, independent measures design.

IV: Psychopath or non-psychopath.

DV: Measures of language from text analysis.

Sample

Self-selected sample of 52 murderers in Canadian correctional facilities: 14 psychopaths and 38 non-psychopaths, all men.

Materials/apparatus

Assessment of psychopathy Psychopathy Checklist–Revised (PCL-R) measured affective/interpersonal traits (e.g. superficial charm) and impulsive/antisocial traits (e.g. criminal versatility).

A score of 25 or above indicated psychopathy.

Text analysis Wmatrix (types of words) and Dictionary of Affect in Language (DAL) (emotional content).

Procedure

1. Participants were told the purpose of the study was to assess the way that murderers recall the murder they committed.

2. Participants were tested for psychopathy (PCL-R).

3. Participants were asked to recall the murder they had committed.

4. Participants were interviewed by two senior psychology graduate students and one research assistant.

5. Step-Wise semi-structured interviews began with participants recalling their offence in as much detail as possible.

6. Interviews lasted for 25 minutes, were audiotaped, and put into written form.

7. Using Wmatrix, text was classified into:
   - Parts of speech, e.g. nouns, verbs.
   - Semantic categories, e.g. 'money'.
   - Major discourse fields, e.g. social actions.

8. Text analysed using the DAL (Dictionary of Affect in Language).

Results

Number of words

1. No significant difference in the number of words used to describe the murder by the psychopaths and non-psychopaths (average 2,201 and 2,554 respectively).

Instrumental language analysis

2. Psychopaths produced more subordinating conjunctions, e.g. 'because'.

Hierarchy of needs analysis

3. Psychopaths used twice as many of Maslow's 'basic needs' words, e.g. food.

4. Non-psychopaths used significantly more words related to 'higher' social needs, e.g. family.

Emotional expression in language

5. Psychopaths used more past tense verbs and fewer present tense verbs, e.g. 'stabbed' and not 'stab'.

6. Psychopaths used more concrete nouns and more articles, e.g. 'the'.

7. No difference in emotional language (DAL scores).

Disfluency

8. Psychopaths' language was less fluent (e.g. more 'ums').

Conclusions

Significant differences exist in the language used by psychopaths and non-psychopaths.

This is predicted from their behaviour, e.g. a lack of emotion.

Data supports the notion that psychopaths operate in a primitive but rational manner.

Psychopaths typically show an incapacity for love and a lack of empathy.

Links between the core study and the methodological issues

Research method and techniques

✛ Using semi-structured interviews allowed the participants to determine what they wished to include and meant that the psychopaths had more leeway to reveal their unconscious thoughts and feelings.

✛ Semi-structured interviews also let the interviewer ask some questions or give prompts to include more detail so there was in-depth description recorded for analysis.

⊟ Some participants may have forgotten specific details of their crime and recalled more if given specific questions.

⊟ The interview only concerned one event – the murder. The differences between psychopaths and non-psychopaths might have been different when recalling a less emotional event.

Validity

✛ High internal validity as researchers were testing the language of psychopaths.

⊟ Low in external validity as it is difficult to generalise to other populations, e.g. women, other cultures, non-murderers.

Sampling bias

✛ It was easy to collect a large sample of psychopaths because 15-25% of the prison population are likely to be psychopaths compared to 1% in the general population.

⊟ Psychopathic murderers may have a different personality profile from psychopaths who do not commit murders, e.g. they are more violent.

⊟ The behaviours exhibited by the psychopaths who volunteered were perhaps not typical of psychopathic murderers, e.g. they were much prouder of their murder than those who did not volunteer.

Types of data

✛ Quantitative data - the rich data from the transcripts was reduced to categories of speech, e.g. disfluencies such as 'um' to count occurrences.

✛ Qualitative data - audiotaped transcripts of what the participants said. This provided a rich record of participants' thoughts, feelings and attitudes. In total over 100,000 words were collected.

Ethical considerations

⊟ Participants were told the purpose of the study, but not the full purpose of the study (no fully informed consent).

⊟ Social sensitivity is an issue due to potential negative consequences for psychopaths, e.g. results might be used to identify psychopathic tendencies of prisoners.

Ethnocentrism

✛ All prisoners were Canadian so are representative of one, typically individualist culture.

⊟ It is possible that psychopathic behaviour does not manifest itself in the same way in other cultures, e.g. psychopaths in collectivist cultures such as China might show more concern for others and have a greater sense of conscience.

Even if you don't speak fluently, and you 'umm' and 'ahh' a lot, that doesn't mean you are lying or have a lack of emotion intelligence.

Revision booster

Students sometimes forget the Step-Wise Interview involves three steps:
- Free recall.
- Follow-up questions that are open-ended and not leading.
- Specific questions to clarify information.

Exam-style question examples

Component 2 Section A:

1. Describe the aims of the Hancock *et al.* study [2]

2. Outline the independent variable in the Hancock *et al.* study. [2]

3. Describe the sample in the Hancock *et al.* study. [2]

4. Describe how Hancock *et al.* assessed psychopathy. [3]

5. Explain how the data was analysed in the Hancock *et al.* study. [3]

6. Outline **two** strengths of the type of data collected by Hancock *et al.* [4]

7. Outline **one** weakness of the sample used by Hancock *et al.* in their study. [3]

8. In what way might the Hancock *et al.* study lack validity? [3]

The exam questions above are just representative examples. Read the guidance for Component 2 exam questions on page 7.

Perspectives

Good answers always include the use of the specialist terms for the topic, e.g. tabula rasa (blank slate), operant and classical conditioning, positive and negative reinforcement, stimulus-response.

Skinner trained pigeons during World War II to peck landmarks on a screen so that a missile could be directed to its target. However, the plan never got off the ground.

Some useful specialist terms for the psychodynamic perspective are: idiographic, unconscious, subconscious, defence mechanisms, psychosexual stages.

Exam-style question examples

Component 2 Section B, for each perspective:

1. Outline **one** concept of the perspective. **[2]**

2. Describe **one** application of the perspective. **[2]**

3. Explain how the perspective relates to **one** core study. **[3]**

4. Describe **one** similarity **and one** difference between one perspective and any other perspective/area. **[3]**

5. Outline **one** weakness **and one** strength for the perspective. **[3 + 3]**

Behaviourist perspective

Key concepts	**Classical conditioning** (Pavlov) Dogs associate sound of bell with arrival of food, then salivated at bell only.
	Operant conditioning (Skinner, Bandura) Reinforcement, punishment, vicarious reinforcement.
Application	**Therapy** Systematic desensitisation uses classical conditioning to overcome phobia (associate fear with relaxation).
Links to core studies	**Bandura** *et al.* Aggressive behaviour is learned by observing role models.
	Chaney *et al.* Positive reinforcement increased adherence through the Funhaler.
Similarities and differences	Similar to the cognitive area (excludes emotional influences).
	Differs from the individual differences area (focuses on experimentation and direct observation).
Evaluation	✚ **Scientific** For example, Bandura *et al.* controlled variables to show that aggressive models increase aggression.
	▬ **Reductionist** Complex behaviours are represented as stimulus-response, e.g. Funhaler creates pleasure.

Psychodynamic perspective

Key concepts	**The unconscious mind** Contains unresolved conflicts that we access through dreams (fulfilment of wishes).
	Importance of early childhood experiences Adult disturbances have roots in early experiences.
Application	**Therapy** (psychoanalysis, dream analysis) Unresolved conflicts in the unconscious cause psychological disorders.
Links to core studies	**Freud** Explains little Hans's phobias through his unconscious mind and the events of his childhood.
	Hancock *et al.* Discuss ego development and suggest that language is likely to be beyond conscious control.
Similarities and differences	Similar to the individual differences area (case studies).
	Differs from all areas (more an ideology than a science).
Evaluation	✚ **Interactionist** The approach combines nature and nurture, e.g. Little Hans's innate urges + life experiences.
	▬ **Determinist** People are controlled by their unconscious, e.g. Little Hans's unconscious motivations.

Component 2 Psychological themes through core studies

Chapter 7 Perspectives, debates and methodological issues

Nature/nurture

Key concepts	**Nature** Characteristics determined by genes that may be present at birth or appear later as you mature. **Nurture** Behaviour learned through experience and interactions with the environment.
Application	**Eugenics** Aims to improve the quality of humans through selective breeding. But selective breeding only improves quality if the behaviour (e.g. IQ) is inherited.
Links to core studies	**Bandura** *et al.* Are children born to be aggressive (nature) or do they learn it (nurture)? **Milgram** Considered why people obey authority and speculated that we have a genetic tendency to be obedient (nature).
Similarities and differences	Nature and nurture are both similar to determinism (genetic and environmental influences can control our behaviour and there is very little we can do about it). Nurture is similar to (and nature is different from) situational explanations (both explain environmental influences).
Evaluation	➕ **Interactionist** Makes us consider what makes each of us unique – a mix of our genetic make-up and life experiences. ➖ **Reductionist** The debate suggests the answer is either nature or nurture when it is always a combination of both.

Free will/determinism

Key concepts	**Determinism** Every event, including human cognition, is directly caused by chains of prior events. **Free will** The idea that we are able to make choices about our behaviour.
Application	**Brain scanning** Might be used to identify people for certain jobs or identify criminality (Raine *et al.*).
Links to core studies	**Milgram** Participants' obedience was determined by the situation rather than their spontaneous choice. **Bandura** *et al.* Children's aggressiveness was determined by the behaviour of the adult model.
Similarities and differences	Free will differs from nature and nurture (genes/environment don't determine behaviour because we can make choices). Determinism is similar to reductionism (behaviour is largely controlled by single, simplified factors, e.g. genetics).
Evaluation	➕ **Scientific** Emphasis on cause and effect, which is useful as it allows us to predict behaviour. ➖ **Reductionist** Suggests that our choices are limited by e.g. biology (i.e. they are determined), thus discouraging people from exercising their free will.

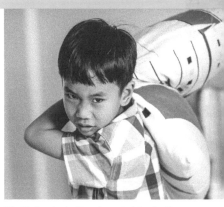

The Bobo study (Bandura et al.) asks the question about whether children are born to be aggressive or whether they learn it.

Revision booster

In reality, debates are more of a continuum but it is easier, when answering exam questions, to polarise them.

Exam-style question examples

Component 2 Section B:

1. Describe what you understand by the term 'nurture'. **[2]**

2. Describe **one** application of the nature/nurture debate. **[3]**

3. Describe how Bandura *et al.*'s study relates to the nature/nurture argument. **[3]**

4. Outline how the nature/nurture debate is similar to determinism. **[2]**

5. Outline **one** strength of the nature/nurture argument. **[3]**

6. Describe what you understand by the term 'free will'. **[2]**

7. Outline **one** reason why conducting determinist research is useful. **[3]**

8. Explain how Milgram's study relates to determinism. **[2]**

9. Describe how free will is different from the nature/nurture debate. **[2]**

10. Outline **one** weakness of the free will/determinism debate. **[3]**

Debates (continued)

Revision booster

Students often only view reductionist arguments as being negative and therefore miss out on the chance to counterargue that simplifying complex arguments can be beneficial.

People who plead not guilty by reason of insanity (NGRI) argue their crime was determined by inherited tendencies. This supports individual, reductionist and nature arguments.

Exam-style question examples

Component 2 Section B:

1. What do you understand by the term 'holism'? [2]

2. Outline **one** reason why conducting reductionist research is useful. [3]

3. Describe how Baron-Cohen *et al.*'s study relates to reductionism. [3]

4. Explain how reductionism differs from the situational explanation of behaviour. [2]

5. Outline **one** weakness of the holism argument. [3]

6. Describe what you understand by the term 'individual factors'. [2]

7. Outline **one** application of the situational explanation. [2]

8. Explain how Sperry's study links to an individual explanation. [3]

9. Outline how individual explanations are similar to nature explanations. [2]

10. Outline **one** strength of the reductionist argument. [3]

Reductionism/holism

Key concepts	**Reductionism** Complex explanations can be reduced to the sum of more fundamental things.
	Holism Living matter is made up of unified wholes that are greater than the simple sum of their parts.
Application	**Medical models** Help reduce complex psychological disorders to simple chemical changes in the brain leading to psychological disorders (e.g. depression).
Links to core studies	**Casey** *et al.* Explained delay of gratification in terms of brain structures (e.g. frontal lobe).
	Baron-Cohen *et al.* Reduced explanations of autism spectrum disorder to a lack of Theory of Mind.
Similarities and differences	Reductionism is similar to determinism (reduce behaviour to chemical changes which control our behaviour).
	Reductionism differs from situational explanations (where a more holistic approach is needed because behaviour is harder to quantify).
Evaluation	⊕ **Scientific** Breaking complex systems down to lower-level units may enhance understanding.
	⊖ **Oversimplification** May fail to represent the true complexity of behaviour, e.g. emotions.

Individual/situational explanations

Key concepts	**Individual factors** Enduring aspects of an individual - their disposition or personality.
	Situational factors Anything in the environment, including other people.
Application	**IQ tests** Need to consider people's upbringing (situation) as this may determine how well they can answer the questions.
Links to core studies	**Bandura** *et al.* Aggressive behaviour is due to situational events in the environment.
	Sperry The split-brain participants' behaviour was due to an individual influence (severed corpus callosum).
Similarities and differences	Individual factors are often similar to nature explanations (behaviour explained by biology).
	Situational factors are similar to nurture (our social and physical environment).
Evaluation	⊕ **Adaptability** Being able to respond to situations makes humans adaptable.
	⊖ **Unresolvable** Both individual and situational factors contribute to development, so the debate can't be resolved.

Usefulness of psychological research

Key concepts	**Moral dimension** Who is the research useful for?
	Practical dimension What are the benefits?
	Knowledge dimension What new insights?
Application	**Therapy** For example, psychoanalysis or cognitive behaviour therapy.
Links to core studies	**Loftus and Palmer** The research informs court decisions and improves our understanding of eyewitness testimony.
	Chaney *et al.* Useful in providing a Funhaler device to improve adherence to medication in children.
Similarities and differences	Similar to behaviourism (train people with rewards and punishments to behave in such a way to be well and be happy).
	Similar to ethics (researchers balance usefulness against costs, e.g. psychological harm to participants).
Evaluation	➕ **Focuses attention** Rather than thinking too much about technical issues (e.g. sample sizes), we can focus on more important questions (e.g. is research useful?).
	➖ **Research doesn't have to be useful** We should do research just for the sake of it because it may turn out to be useful in the future.

Ethical considerations

Key concepts	**Morals** The rules of right and wrong to guide our behaviour based on socially agreed principles.
	Ethics A moral framework that is applied to a narrow group of people, e.g. psychologists.
Application	**Research** Psychologists should follow the BPS ethical guidelines and try to ensure their results are used to help people rather than to harm them.
Links to core studies	**Milgram** Participants experienced a stressful situation that stayed with some of them for the rest of their lives.
	Bocchiaro *et al.* Took great care to design an ethical study, considering the moral choices of the participants.
Similarities and differences	Similar to usefulness (the decision to promote human welfare is an ethical one).
	Differs from determinism (assumption that rewards/punishments can determine behaviour is unethical).
Evaluation	➕ **Responsibility** Makes psychologists take personal responsibility for their work and treat participants with respect.
	➖ **Narrow** Tends to be about a limited set of issues, ignoring the broader context of how research is used.

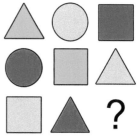

choose answer

An item from an intelligence test – quantifying and measuring human qualities (e.g. intelligence) is done using psychometric tests. Such tests are useful in education, health and business.

Revision booster

The British Psychological Society's (BPS) code of ethics and conduct provides four ethical principles for carrying out research in psychology; respect, competence, responsibility and integrity.

Exam-style question examples

Component 2 Section B:

1. Outline what you understand by the term 'usefulness of psychological research'. **[2]**

2. Describe how psychological research can be useful. **[2]**

3. Explain how the study by Loftus and Palmer is useful. **[2]**

4. Explain how the usefulness of psychological research is similar to behaviourism. **[2]**

5. Describe **one** strength of the usefulness of psychological research. **[3]**

6. Outline what you understand by the term 'ethics'. **[2]**

7. Outline **one** application of ethical research. **[2]**

8. Describe the ethical considerations of Milgram's study. **[2]**

9. Describe how ethical considerations are different from determinism. **[2]**

10. Describe **one** weakness of the debate about ethical considerations. **[3]**

Debates (continued)

Fortune-telling is not a science - it is a pseudoscience because its claims cannot be disproved (see falsification on page 38).

The topic of psychology as a science is also covered in Chapter 1 on Research methods.

Exam-style question examples

Component 2 Section B:

1. Outline what you understand by the term 'social sensitivity'. [2]

2. Describe **one** application of conducting socially sensitive research. [2]

3. Explain how Loftus and Palmer's study links to conducting socially sensitive research. [3]

4. Explain how conducting socially sensitive research is similar to ethical considerations. [2]

5. Outline **one** strength of conducting socially sensitive research. [3]

6. Describe what you understand by the term 'science'. [2]

7. Outline **one** reason why conducting scientific research is useful. [3]

8. Describe how Bandura *et al.*'s study is scientific. [3]

9. Outline how psychology as a science is similar to determinism. [2]

10. Outline **one** strength of viewing psychology as a science. [3]

Conducting socially sensitive research

Key concept	**Socially sensitive research** Considers the extent to which studies can have a negative impact on specific groups of people or society generally.
Application	**False memory** Research helps clarify the claims surrounding recovered memories of childhood abuse.
Links to core studies	**Milgram** Investigated why people are capable of acts of gross inhumanity.
	Loftus and Palmer Has a social impact with regard to unreliability of memory and eyewitness testimony.
Similarities and differences	Similar to ethical considerations (both about making moral decisions).
	Differs from usefulness (some useful research may lack social sensitivity if it has negative effects on people).
Evaluation	⊕ **Broader approach** Aims to explore areas that are generally not spoken about, e.g. men have a tendency to ignore health problems.
	⊖ **Ethical issues** May distress the participants and/or the target social group for no measurable benefit.

Psychology as a science

Key concept	Science values systematic observation, identification, description and empirical investigation. This contrasts with approaches that value subjective experience.
Application	**Predicting future behaviour** Through the use of objective, verifiable methods that build up coherent theories.
Links to core studies	**Bandura** *et al.* Demonstrated a causal relationship between observation and aggression using the experimental method.
	Freud Did not provide testable hypotheses and so his theory cannot be refuted (lacks falsifiability).
Similarities and differences	Similar to determinism (science aims to discover how behaviour is determined by identified causes).
	Differs from the psychodynamic perspective (cannot be falsified).
Evaluation	⊕ **Useful** Allows us to develop a body of knowledge that can be tested and developed.
	⊖ **Reductionist** Science reduces behaviour to a small set of variables which may not represent complex interactions.

Ethnocentrism

Key concept	**Ethnocentrism** Using our own cultural (ethnic) groups' beliefs, attitudes and behaviour to judge others.
Application	**Interpreting psychological research** Consider the potential ethnic biases of researchers.
Links to core studies	**Gould** Ethnocentric bias in intelligence tests and the misapplication of the findings to immigration laws.
	Sperry A US/European focus on split-brain reductionism rather than considering the whole brain.
Similarities and differences	Similar to socially sensitive research and psychology as a science (concerned with ensuring research is unbiased).
	Differs from cross-cultural psychology (where the viewpoint of many cultures is considered).
Ethnocentrism in psychological research	Spotting ethnocentric bias in psychological research is best done by considering how the results would be different if the study was carried out with different groups.

Validity

Key concepts	**Validity** Authenticity of results, representing something 'real'.
	Internal validity Whether a researcher is testing what they intended to test.
	External validity Whether the results of a study can be generalised beyond the original research setting to other settings (**ecological**) or to other people (**population**).
Application	**Self-report** Closed and leading questions may reduce validity, as can social desirability bias.
	Observations Limited behavioural categories may mean that some events are missed, reducing validity.
	Experiments Extraneous variables mean that changes in a dependent variable may not be due to the independent variable.
Links to core studies	**Loftus and Palmer** Watching film clips of a car accident lacks the emotion of a real accident (low ecological validity).
	Bocchiaro *et al.* Participants didn't know researchers were noting their ethical behaviour (high ecological validity).
Similarities and differences	Similar to ethnocentrism (research that only represents some people and not all people is low in external validity).
	Differs from reliability (validity is about the accuracy of a measure whereas reliability concerns its consistency).
Validity in psychological research	When replications confirm original results, they show external (ecological) validity because the same results are produced in different settings, i.e. are generalisable.

Field experiments may increase external validity (participants' behaviour is more natural if they are not aware of being studied). But internal validity may be lower because variables are not so easy to control.

Other types of validity:

Face validity = whether a test appears (at face value) to measure what it claims to.

Construct validity = the degree to which a test measures what it claims to be measuring.

Exam-style question examples

Component 2 Section B:

1. Outline what you understand by the term 'ethnocentrism'. **[2]**

2. Explain the usefulness of understanding ethnocentrism. **[2]**

3. Explain how Gould's study links to ethnocentrism. **[2]**

4. Explain how ethnocentrism is similar to conducting socially sensitive research. **[2]**

5. Explain ethnocentrism in psychological research. **[2]**

6. Describe what you understand by the term 'internal validity'. **[2]**

7. Describe **one** application of validity in psychological research. **[2]**

8. Explain how Bocchiaro *et al.*'s study relates to validity. **[2]**

9. Outline how validity is different from reliability. **[2]**

10. Explain validity in psychological research. **[2]**

Tyres are reliable. They have been made using a standardised procedure, so they are consistent in their appearance.

Revision booster

You can often make connections between methodological issues. For example, sampling bias is related to validity because it reduces the ability to generalise results to the target population (low population validity).

Validity (previous page), reliability and sampling bias are topics covered in Component 1.

Exam-style question examples

Component 2 Section B:

1. Outline what you understand by the term 'reliability'. [2]

2. Describe **one** application of reliability in psychological research. [2]

3. Outline how Bandura *et al.*'s study is reliable. [2]

4. Explain how validity is similar to reliability. [2]

5. Describe reliability in psychological research. [2]

6. Describe what you understand by the term 'sampling bias'. [2]

7. Outline **one** application of sampling bias in psychological research. [2]

8. Explain how Grant *et al.*'s study relates to sampling bias. [2]

9. Describe how ethnocentrism is similar to sampling bias. [2]

10. Describe sampling bias in psychological research. [2]

Reliability

Key concepts	**Reliability** Measure of consistency. **Internal reliability** Consistency of items within a set of scores or questions on a questionnaire. **External reliability** Consistency of results when a measure is used on subsequent occasions.
Application	**Good science** Depends on replication to demonstrate the validity of any results – if we repeat a study and find the same results this suggests the results must be 'real' (valid) rather than just a fluke.
Links to core studies	**Bandura** *et al.* The dependent variable (aggressiveness) was measured by making observations of the children playing. A second observer checked the observations for half of the participants and inter-rater reliability was reported as high. **Baron-Cohen** *et al.* The Eyes Task (a questionnaire) assessed ability to understand the emotion shown. All items on the test must be assessing the same thing for high internal reliability.
Similarities and differences	Reliability is similar to validity (if reliability is low this then threatens the validity of the measure). Reliability differs from validity (reliability is about the *consistency* of a measure, whereas validity is about *authenticity* – are we measuring what we meant to measure?).
Reliability in psychological research	Repeating a standardised procedure with each participant is necessary in order to make comparisons between participants.

Sampling bias

Key concept	**Sampling bias** This is a systematic error where the sample does not accurately represent the population of interest.
Application	**Getting a good sample** Requires balancing costs against using the most representative sampling methods.
Links to core studies	**Milgram** The sample consisted of American men only. **Grant** *et al.* The sample were men and women but all Americans.
Similarities and differences	Similar to ethnocentrism (both are biases related to the group of people studied). Differs from ethnocentrism (ethnocentrism is about being prejudiced which may lead to a sampling bias).
Sampling bias in psychological research	The best psychologists can do is remove as much bias as possible and try to ensure that some groups of people are neither over- nor under-represented in psychological research.

For further information consult the OCR Guides:

- *Relating core studies to psychological areas and perspectives*
- *Debates (Teacher Guide)*

Sampling bias	Reliability	Validity	Ethnocentrism	Psychology as a science	Conducting socially sensitive research	Ethical considerations	Usefulness of research	Individual/situational explanations	Reductionism/holism	Free will/determinism	Nature/nurture	Psychodynamic perspective	Behaviourist perspective	Core study	AREAS →
×	×	×	×	×		×	×	×		×	×	×	×	Milgram	SOCIAL
×	×	×		×		×	×	×		×				Bocchiaro et al.	SOCIAL
×	×	×	×	×		×	×	×		×	×			Piliavin et al.	SOCIAL
×	×	×	×	×		×	×	×		×	×			Levine et al.	SOCIAL
×	×	×		×	×	×	×	×				×	×	Loftus and Palmer	COGNITIVE
×	×	×		×		×	×	×						Grant et al.	COGNITIVE
×	×	×	×	×		×	×			×	×	×		Moray	COGNITIVE
×	×	×	×	×		×	×			×	×	×		Simons and Chabris	COGNITIVE
×	×	×		×		×	×	×		×	×	×	×	Bandura et al.	DEVELOPMENTAL
×	×	×		×		×	×	×		×	×		×	Chaney et al.	DEVELOPMENTAL
×	×	×	×	×	×	×	×	×		×	×			Kohlberg	DEVELOPMENTAL
×	×	×	×	×	×	×	×	×		×	×		×	Lee et al.	DEVELOPMENTAL
×	×	×		×		×	×	×	×	×	×			Sperry	BIOLOGICAL
×	×	×		×		×	×	×	×	×	×	×	×	Casey et al.	BIOLOGICAL
×	×	×		×		×	×		×		×			Blakemore and Cooper	BIOLOGICAL
×	×	×		×		×	×		×		×			Maguire et al.	BIOLOGICAL
×	×	×	×	×	×	×	×	×		×	×	×	×	Freud	INDIVIDUAL DIFFERENCES
×	×	×		×	×	×	×	×	×		×			Baron-Cohen et al.	INDIVIDUAL DIFFERENCES
×	×	×	×	×	×	×	×				×			Gould	INDIVIDUAL DIFFERENCES
×	×	×	×	×	×	×	×			×	×	×	×	Hancock et al.	INDIVIDUAL DIFFERENCES

How to use this grid

Exam questions often ask you to make comparisons between areas, perspectives, debates and methodological issues in psychology.

You should always provide examples from core studies to support your answer and you can use this grid to identify which core studies might be appropriate.

You may think others would work too.

Each area is discussed at the beginning of the relevant chapter, e.g. the social area is discussed on pages 40-41.

Use this grid to put yourself in pole position for the exams.

Revision booster

The rule of two!

In any comparison question, you must always explain the similarity/difference, and then support this using relevant evidence from *two* appropriate core studies.

Background
Historical views of mental illness

The terms 'mental illness' and 'abnormality' are used in the specification (and therefore in exam questions). However, since attitudes about psychological disorder as an 'illness' or 'abnormality' have changed, we have used terms such as 'disorders' or 'differences' in our descriptions.

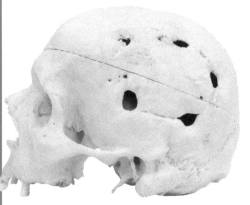

Trephining (also called trepanning) was used to deal with 'strange' or 'abnormal' behaviour in prehistoric times. It involved holes being drilled into the skull using sharp stones to release the demons that were causing the 'madness'.

Anti-psychiatry

In the 1960s a number of people started to speak out against the medical model of 'mental illness' and the associated biological treatments. Psychiatrists are medically-trained doctors who specialise in psychiatry – so 'anti-psychiatry' means 'against the medical model'.

This shift away from the medical model explains why we prefer to use the phrase 'psychological disorder' instead of 'mental illness'.

Exam-style question examples

Component 3 Section A questions are different from the rest of Component 3 Section B questions - there are a series of questions rather than one question split into related parts. In Section A the questions range from 2 to 10 marks. Questions on background (this spread) are usually short (between 2 and 4 marks).

1. Outline **one** historical view of mental illness. [2]

2. Explain why there are differing views of mental illness. [3]

3. Outline **one** difference between two historical views of mental illness. [4]

Historical views of mental illness

Whether any behaviour is classed as 'mental illness' (psychological disorder) depends on many factors, e.g. culture, context and historical time period. Each historical view offers its own *aetiology* (explanation) of psychological disorder and each of these views leads to its own treatments.

Prehistory **Supernatural explanation**	**Aetiology** 'Strange' or 'abnormal' behaviour was attributed to witchcraft, religion and demonic possession. People also believed that psychological disorders were a punishment for wrongdoing. **Treatments** Saying prayers and immersing the individual in holy water are examples of the treatments. Exorcisms were also used to rid the individual of their demonic possession, e.g. trephining (see left).
Greek culture **Humoral theory**	**Aetiology** Hippocrates said that four bodily humours (fluids) were each related to a different personality dimension. (1) Black bile → introversion, (2) yellow bile → impulsiveness, (3) blood → being courageous, (4) phlegm → being calm. Psychological disorders were due to an imbalance/excess of one of the four humours, e.g. excess yellow bile leads to mania. **Treatments** To redress the balance between the four bodily humours, clinicians would 'purge' the person, by using laxatives or, in extreme cases, bloodletting (*phlebotomy*). Leeches were used to drain blood. Symptoms were also treated with changes to lifestyle, e.g. diet and exercise.
Psychogenic approach	**Aetiology** In the late 19th century, disturbed behaviour was attributed to psychological factors, e.g. Freud introduced the idea of unconscious influences on behaviour. **Treatments** Freudian psychoanalysis used free association to gain an insight into past experiences and the unconscious mind. Freud also used dream analysis. Psychoanalysis led to many types of talking therapy, e.g. cognitive behaviour therapy.
Somatogenic approach	**Aetiology** This approach focuses on biological dysfunction, e.g. something different about a person's brain structure, neurotransmitters and genes. This is associated with the medical model. **Treatments** Drugs (*psychopharmacology*) are the dominant treatment, based on the assumption that psychological disorders are largely caused by dysfunctional neurotransmitters. There is also electroconvulsive therapy (ECT) and psychosurgery (e.g. lobotomy).

Defining abnormality

Statistical infrequency	**Explaining the concept** Behaviours that occur infrequently are classed as 'abnormal'.
	Thinking about the concept Some statistically *infrequent* behaviours are actually desirable, e.g. very low scores on a depression scale are unusual and indicate no depression. But some statistically *frequent* behaviours are undesirable, e.g. many people experience some characteristics of depression.
Deviation from social norms	**Explaining the concept** Anyone who behaves differently, or 'deviates', from socially created norms is classed as 'abnormal'.
	Thinking about the concept This definition distinguishes between desirable and undesirable behaviour, e.g. a low depression score is not 'abnormal' as society agrees it is not a negative attribute (i.e. it is desirable).
Failure to function adequately	**Explaining the concept** 'Abnormality' is judged in terms of not being able to cope with everyday living, e.g. not managing to go to work or not managing to eat regularly.
	Thinking about the concept This definition recognises the subjective experience of a person with a psychological disorder and is relatively easy to judge objectively because clinicians can list clearly identifiable behaviours, e.g. person has a regular job, person can dress themselves.
Deviation from ideal mental health	**Explaining the concept** Jahoda (1958) listed characteristics of mental health: good self-attitudes (high self-esteem), personal growth and self-actualisation, integration (e.g. coping with stress), autonomy (independence), accurate perception of reality, mastery of the environment (can function at work). Absence of any one of these criteria shows 'abnormality'.
	Thinking about the concept These criteria are ideal and most of us do not fulfil all of them all the time – so most of us are 'abnormal' (i.e. not psychologically healthy). The criteria are also difficult to measure and are highly culture-bound.

Categorising mental disorders

The *International Classification of Diseases* (ICD-10) and *Diagnostic and Statistical Manual of Mental Disorders* (DSM-5) are systems that give clinicians a means to communicate about their clients, provide a diagnosis and begin treatment for it.

ICD-10	Produced by the World Health Organisation and used in the UK and internationally. ICD codes mental and behavioural disorders (F00–F99), e.g. F30–39: Mood (affective) disorders, such as bipolar disorder, and F20–29: Schizophrenia, schizotypal and delusional disorders.
DSM-5	DSM-5 is used in the USA and lists around 300 disorders divided into three sections, e.g. Section II includes 20 categories of disorders, such as depressive disorders.

DSM-5 describes internet gaming disorder as causing deception of family, withdrawal symptoms (e.g. anxiety when not playing) and risks to relationships and education/occupation.

Revision booster

You don't need to know lots of the disorders that appear in ICD-10 and DSM-5 but you do need to be able to describe briefly how disorders are categorised. For example, ICD-10 has a code and description for each disorder (see bottom left).

ICD-11 replaced ICD-10 in January 2022. The principles of both versions are the same. For consistency with our Student book, we have continued with ICD-10.

Exam-style question examples

Component 3 Section A:

1. Outline **one** definition of abnormality. [2]

2. Compare definitions of abnormality. [4]

3. Describe **one** way of categorising mental disorders. [3]

Key research

Rosenhan (1973) on *Being sane in insane places*

* 'Insane' is the term used in this article and refers to a person with a psychological disorder.

** 'Sane' is also a term used in this article and refers to a person without a psychological disorder.

Background

Rosenhan observed that the prosecution and defence in murder trials each called their own psychiatrists who often disagreed on the defendant's sanity. This led Rosenhan to wonder whether there is any way to reliably identify who is 'insane'*.

Aims

Study 1: To see if 'sane'** people presenting with a disorder would be diagnosed as 'insane' by staff at psychiatric hospitals.

Study 2: To see if psychiatrists and other mental health workers would be undercautious rather than overcautious because they had been told about the mistaken diagnosis in study 1.

Mini-experiment: To see if staff behaved differently towards patients compared with a non-patient who was asking similar questions.

Method

Design

Study 1: Participant observation.

Study 2: Questionnaire.

Mini-experiment: Self-report.

Sample

Study 1: Patients and staff at 12 American psychiatric hospitals. Eight 'pseudo-patients'.

Study 2: Staff in one psychiatric hospital.

Mini-experiment: Staff and pseudo-patients from four of the hospitals, plus a confederate.

Procedure

Study 1

1. Pseudo-patients made an appointment at the hospital admissions office.

2. They complained about hearing voices that sounded like they were saying 'empty', 'hollow' and 'thud'.

3. Once admitted to the psychiatric ward, pseudo-patients exhibited no more symptoms and behaved as they usually would.

4. Pseudo-patients had to display exemplary behaviour to be released, e.g. obeying instructions.

5. Pseudo-patients recorded their observations in a notebook.

Study 2

1. Hospital staff were told pseudo-patients would be admitted in the next three months. None were actually presented.

2. Hospital staff were asked to rate patients on a 10-point scale (1 = high confidence that the patient was a pseudo-patient).

Mini-experiment

1. Pseudo-patient asked hospital staff a question: *Excuse me, Mr/Mrs/Dr X, could you tell me when I will be presented at the staff meeting?*

2. A confederate asked staff members on a university campus a similar question ending: *Do you know where … is?*

Results

Study 1

1. All but one pseudo-patient were diagnosed with schizophrenia (and later discharged with 'schizophrenia in remission').

2. Pseudo-patients were in hospital for 7–52 days (mean 19).

3. No pseudo-patient was suspected by the hospital staff.

4. 35 of 118 patients were suspicious about the pseudo-patients saying, e.g., 'You're not crazy'.

5. 'Normal' behaviours were interpreted as symptoms of their disorder, e.g. queueing early for lunch was seen as pathological behaviour.

6. Depersonalisation and powerlessness: Patients lacked privacy, e.g. toilets with no doors.

Study 2

Number judged to be pseudo-patients after three months:

1. 41/193 patients identified by at least one staff member.

2. 23/193 patients identified by one psychiatrist.

3. 19/193 patients identified by one psychiatrist and one other staff member.

Mini-experiment

1. 4% of the pseudo-patients received an answer from a psychiatrist (185 attempts).

2. All 14 requests at the university were responded to.

Conclusions

Diagnosis is not valid as psychiatrists failed to distinguish the 'sane' from the 'insane'.

All except one pseudo-patient was diagnosed with the same disorder (schizophrenia), suggesting diagnosis is reliable.

Rosenhan noted the 'stickiness of psychiatric labels' – once a person was labelled 'insane', all behaviours were interpreted according to this label.

How the key research explains ... categorising mental health	This study indicates that there is a lack of validity in categorising and diagnosing psychological disorder.
	Pseudo-patients were categorised as having a psychological disorder simply by telling staff they had symptoms. This labelling led to pseudo-patients' usual behaviour being interpreted according to the context (situation) and so it lacked validity.
	The study supports the anti-psychiatry movement in that it criticises the idea that psychological illnesses can be diagnosed in the same way that physical illnesses can.

Rosenhan's study broke many ethical guidelines but it was important as a warning of the lack of validity in categorising and diagnosing psychological disorder.

Links between the topic and the methodological issues

Validity	✚ Rosenhan used real hospitals, with real staff and patients who were unaware of the study, so behaviours were representative and had high external validity.
	✚ The mini-experiments were conducted using standardised procedures, creating high internal validity.
Reliability	✚ Observations were consistent with each other, with all pseudo-patients reporting similar experiences.
	⚊ There was no direct comparison of observations between the pseudo-patients in different hospitals, which questions inter-observer reliability.
Sampling bias	✚ Rosenhan tried to ensure the study was generalisable by using a variety of hospitals across America.
	⚊ The hospitals were only in America, whereas other countries have different systems for psychiatric diagnosis and hospitalisation.
Ethnocentrism	⚊ Classification systems (e.g. DSM) are based on social norms in individualist cultures and related to white middle-class people. Yet the same criteria are applied to people from different subcultures, which is ethnocentric.

Links between the topic and the debates

Individual/ situational explanations	Rosenhan's study supports the individual view of psychological disorder as some pseudo-patients took longer to be released from hospital than others, e.g. 7-52 days.
	The study also supports a situational explanation in the labelling and interpretation of psychological disorder.
Ethical considerations	Psychiatrists were deceived - they were told the pseudo-patients were hearing voices and that they were real patients.
	None of the medical staff were able to provide informed consent nor did they have the right to withdraw from the study.
Conducting socially sensitive research	Many nurses complained that Rosenhan's study made their profession look bad but overall the benefit to society has been enormous. The study raised awareness of the flaws in psychiatric diagnosis and subsequent treatment. As a consequence, diagnostic systems became more stringent.

Revision booster

Students often get confused over how Rosenhan's study shows problems with the reliability of diagnosis.

The first study illustrated a failure to detect 'sanity', and the secondary study demonstrated a failure to detect 'insanity'. Overall this shows a lack of consistency (reliability) in how psychological disorder was diagnosed.

Exam-style question examples

Component 3 Section A:

1. Outline **one** way in which the psychiatric hospitals in Rosenhan's study failed to diagnose the pseudo-patients as sane. **[2]**

2. Explain how Rosenhan's research highlights the 'stickiness of labels' in relation to mental health. **[3]**

3. Discuss the extent to which Rosenhan's findings can be seen to be reliable. **[5]**

4. Discuss ethical considerations in relation to Rosenhan's study on being sane in insane places. **[5]**

How psychology contributes to the success of the economy and society ...
Understanding how to reliably diagnose psychological disorders is fundamental to a safe and caring society.

Application

Characteristics of three different types of disorder

The OCR specification uses the term 'characteristics' instead of 'symptoms' - they basically refer to the same thing but 'symptoms' suggests a medical/physical explanation. We have used 'symptoms' where it seems more appropriate.

Major depression

It is called 'major depression' (or major depressive disorder) to distinguish it from 'depression' which is a symptom of many other psychological disorders. It is estimated that around one in five people are likely to experience major depression in their lifetime. It occurs more in young people (20-30 years) than older people. Almost twice as many women are diagnosed with major depression than men, and it is found in all cultures throughout the world.

The high incidence of schizophrenia in cities may be due to people moving there for treatment rather than urban environments being a high-risk factor for schizophrenia.

On this spread we are looking at the application of Topic 1 (The historical context of mental health). The specification states that this application involves knowing the characteristics of an affective disorder, a psychotic disorder and an anxiety disorder.

We have selected major depression as an example of an affective disorder, schizophrenia for psychotic disorder and specific phobias for anxiety disorder. However, you can choose other examples, e.g. OCD for anxiety disorder.

Mental health disorders

Disorders are grouped into broad categories, e.g. affective, psychotic and anxiety disorders.

Each disorder has a set of key characteristics which can be used for diagnosis. The characteristics are listed in a manual, e.g. ICD or DSM (see page 99).

Disorder 1

Affective disorders

Affective disorders (e.g. major depression) are referred to as 'mood disorders' as they have a significant effect on an individual's emotional state.

ICD-10 characteristics of major depression

- Mild: Two key characteristics (see below) plus at least two 'other' characteristics.
- Moderate: Four or more characteristics in total.
- Severe: Seven or more characteristics in total.

Characteristics should be present all or most of the time, and should persist for longer than two weeks.

Key characteristics

1. Low mood, e.g. feels sad, empty, hopeless.
2. Loss of interest and pleasure, e.g. in almost all activities.
3. Reduced energy levels, e.g. lethargy.

Other characteristics

4. Sleep pattern changes, e.g. reduced sleep (insomnia) or premature waking.
5. Appetite, e.g. increase or decrease, weight change.
6. Self-confidence and self-esteem reduced.
7-10. Including: reduced concentration, feelings of guilt, thoughts of self-harm/suicide.

Topic 1

Chapter 1 Issues in mental health

Component 3 Applied psychology

| Disorder 2
Psychotic disorders | A person with psychosis has lost touch with reality. They may experience unusual perceptions and thinking. |

The most well-known psychotic disorder is schizophrenia. It tends to develop in early adulthood and rates of diagnosis are higher in cities than the countryside and for working-class rather than middle-class people.

ICD-10 characteristics of schizophrenia ICD-10 recognises a range of subtypes of schizophrenia. Paranoid schizophrenia is characterised by powerful delusions and hallucinations but relatively few other characteristics. Hebephrenic schizophrenia involves primarily negative characteristics.

For a diagnosis of schizophrenia at least one clear positive or negative symptom (two or more if less clear) should be present for one month:

Positive symptoms Behaviours are exaggerated or 'added' to 'normal' behaviour, e.g.

1. Hallucinations - unusual sensory experiences, e.g. hearing voices or seeing something that is not there.

2. Delusions - irrational beliefs, e.g. thinking you are someone famous (delusions of grandeur) or believing you are being persecuted.

Negative symptoms The person lacks usual behaviours, e.g.

3. Avolition - reduced motivation to carry out a range of activities.

4. Alogia (speech poverty) - reduced amount and quality of speech.

Cognitive deficits The person's mental processes are affected, e.g.

5. Disorganised thought or speech - e.g. jumping between thoughts due to 'loose associations' between concepts or words.

6. Thought insertion - believing your thoughts are being placed there by someone else.

| Disorder 3
Anxiety disorders | Anxiety disorders (e.g. phobias) are characterised by feelings of anxiety and fear, often about things that will happen in the future. In addition to psychological characteristics, anxiety disorders often create biological reactions, e.g. increased heart rate. |

Specific phobias A strong, persistent and irrational fear of a specific stimulus (object, situation or activity), e.g. acrophobia (fear of heights). The fear is out of proportion to the risk that the stimulus presents. People take extreme measures to avoid contact with the phobic stimulus. The behaviour is considered a *clinical* phobia when it interferes with everyday life.

ICD-10 characteristics of specific phobias

1. Marked fear or avoidance of a specific stimulus.

2. Characteristics of anxiety caused by the feared stimulus, at least two present, e.g. trembling, sweating.

3. Significant emotional distress due to avoidance of feared stimulus or due to the anxiety characteristics, and a recognition that this distress is excessive or unreasonable. Characteristics are restricted to the feared stimulus.

Revision booster

In exam questions such as questions 1 and 2 below, don't simply list the characteristics of a disorder. You must remember to describe and apply them to the context of the scenario.

Phobias are the most common type of anxiety disorder, and the most common phobia is arachnophobia (fear of spiders). This is a picture of a spider monkey - we don't want to scare anyone.

Exam-style question examples

Component 3 Section A:

1. Sarah is a clinical psychologist who has recently diagnosed a client with a psychotic disorder.

   How might Sarah describe the characteristics of a psychotic disorder to her client? **[5]**

2. Pete and Louise have noticed a change in their son's behaviour and refer him to a doctor who diagnosed him with an affective disorder.

   How might the doctor outline to Pete and Louise the characteristics of an affective disorder? **[5]**

3. Compare the characteristics of a psychotic disorder with the characteristics of an anxiety disorder. **[6]**

See exam guidance on Component 3 Section A questions on page 8.

Background
Medical model explanations of mental illness

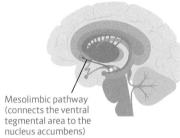

Mesolimbic pathway (connects the ventral tegmental area to the nucleus accumbens)

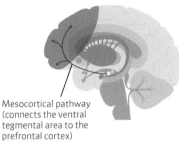

Mesocortical pathway (connects the ventral tegmental area to the prefrontal cortex)

Two neural pathways associated with schizophrenia.

Concordance rate

This is a measure of similarity (usually expressed as a percentage) between two individuals or sets of individuals on a given trait.

A twin study is a quasi-experiment in which concordance rates for identical (monozygotic, MZ) and non-identical (dizygotic, DZ) twins are compared.

The biochemical explanation of mental illness

The physical causes of 'mental illness' (psychological disorder) may be due to atypical biochemistry, genes or brain structure.

Affective disorder e.g. major depression	**Monoamine hypothesis** Low levels of monoamines: • **Serotonin** Regulates monoamine neurotransmitters, deficiencies are related to low mood and erratic thinking. • **Noradrenaline** Regulates heart rate and alertness, deficiencies lead to lack of energy. • **Dopamine** Regulates motivation, deficiencies are related to lack of interest in pleasure and reward.
Psychotic disorder e.g. schizophrenia	**Dopamine hypothesis** Unusually high level of dopamine (DA) in the brain is a cause of schizophrenia. **Revised dopamine hypothesis** Excessive amount of dopamine receptors (especially *D2* subtype), leading to excess dopamine in brain pathways. **Positive symptoms** Linked to high DA activity in the mesolimbic pathway (responsible for motivation and emotion). **Negative symptoms** Linked to erratic DA function in the mesocortical pathway (responsible for self-regulation).
Anxiety disorder e.g. specific phobias	**Gamma-aminobutyric acid** (GABA) Responsible for counterbalancing the excitatory action of the neurotransmitter glutamate. Decreased levels of GABA means that neuronal firing in glutamate pathways is higher, leading to feelings of anxiety.

The genetic explanation of mental illness

The genes we inherit from our parents determine many aspects of our behaviour and personality. Similarity is measured in terms of the correlation or concordance rates between any two individuals. This is done using family, twin, adoption and gene association studies.

Affective disorder e.g. bipolar disorder	**Family study** Gottesman *et al.* (next spread) used a family study to show the increased risk of a child with one parent with bipolar disorder being diagnosed with the same disorder (4.4%), compared with a 0.63% risk of diagnosis for the general population.
Psychotic disorder e.g. schizophrenia	**Twin studies** Glatt (2008) found that the concordance rate for schizophrenia in MZ twins is about 50% (range of 46–53%). In other words, if one MZ twin develops schizophrenia, the other has about a 50% chance of developing it. Concordance rate in DZ twins is about 15%. The greater concordance for MZs implies a substantial genetic component to schizophrenia.
Anxiety disorder e.g. specific phobias	**Twin studies** The results are inconsistent. Kendler *et al.* (1992) found concordance rates for animal-type specific phobias (anxiety disorder) were 25.9% for MZ twins and 11% for DZs, implying genetic causation. However, they found no significant differences in concordance rates for blood-injection-injury or situation-specific phobias.

The brain abnormality explanation of mental illness

There are differences in the brain of someone with a psychological disorder compared to the brain of the same person before they developed their disorder, and also compared to the brain of a neurotypical person.

Affective disorder e.g. major depression	**Limbic system** Differences in the amount of grey matter and the levels of activity in the limbic system are linked to major depression.

- **Amygdala** Regulates emotions, and is disrupted in people with major depression, e.g. increases in activity have been found when depressed people are presented with negative stimuli such as a sad face.
- **Hippocampus** Significantly smaller in people with major depression and the more severe the depression, the more severe the loss of grey matter in the hippocampus. This may explain why people with major depression process emotionally-charged memories in dysfunctional ways.

Psychotic disorder e.g. schizophrenia

Enlarged ventricles People with schizophrenia (psychotic disorder) have enlarged ventricles (spaces) in their brain. These spaces hold cerebrospinal fluid which provides nutrients to the brain and protects the brain from damage.

Reduced grey matter The enlarged ventricles lead to a reduction in the total amount of grey matter in the brain, particularly in these areas:

- **Temporal lobes** (verbal and acoustic memory) Loss of grey matter in these lobes may explain auditory hallucinations.
- **Frontal lobes** (planning and coordination) Loss in these lobes may explain incoherent speech and perceptual disturbances such as delusions.
- **Thalamus** (integrating sensory and motor information) Loss in this area may lead to auditory and verbal hallucinations.

Smaller brain size People with schizophrenia have a reduced overall brain size, with less grey matter in total compared with neurotypical brains. The longer that people have had schizophrenia, the less grey matter there is in their brain.

Anxiety disorder e.g. specific phobias

Prefrontal cortex (contains emotional centres) If the prefrontal cortex is not functioning effectively it fails to suppress the fearful urges from the amygdala.

Amygdala (detects and responds to threats) People with anxiety disorders (e.g. phobias) have a smaller amygdala, which is associated with the inability to control behavioural and biological responses to fearful objects or situations.

Hippocampus (involved in memory, e.g. learning associations - classical conditioning) Reduced hippocampal functioning may mean that a person only recalls the link between a stimulus and a previous fearful experience, rather than neutral or positive feelings.

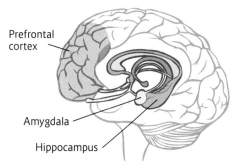

Prefrontal cortex
Amygdala
Hippocampus

The limbic system (amygdala and hippocampus) plays an important role in emotion. Disruption in this system is related to major depression and phobias.

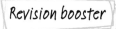

Revision booster

Good answers always include the use of the specialist terms for the topic, e.g. monoamine, serotonin, amygdala, ventricles.

Exam questions will always refer to an affective or psychotic or anxiety disorder but you then use the specific examples (e.g. major depression, schizophrenia, specific phobias).

Exam-style question examples

Component 3 Section A:

1. Outline a biochemical explanation for **one** specific affective disorder. **[3]**

2. Explain a brain abnormality explanation for **one** specific affective disorder. **[5]**

3. Explain a biochemical explanation for **one** specific anxiety disorder. **[5]**

4. Outline a genetic explanation for **one** specific anxiety disorder. **[3]**

5. Describe a brain abnormality explanation for **one** specific psychotic disorder. **[3]**

6. Outline a genetic explanation for **one** specific psychotic disorder. **[4]**

7. Compare the brain abnormality explanation of **one** specific disorder with any **one** other explanation. **[6]**

How psychology contributes to the success of the economy and society ... Understanding the causes of psychological disorder should help us reduce their incidence, making our society healthier.

Key research

Gottesman *et al.* (2010) on *Genetic explanations*

Background

Past research has shown that, when one parent has a psychological disorder, the risk of their child having a psychological disorder increases. However, only small samples have been used in research, lacking generalisability.

Aims

- To use a large sample to investigate the likelihood of offspring being diagnosed with schizophrenia, bipolar disorder or another disorder if one or both of their parents had been diagnosed with one of these psychological disorders.
- Specifically, to see if some of the same genes underlie more than one disorder and whether a 'double dose' of these genes from both parents would increase the risk.

Method

Design
Secondary data from a database.

Sample
2,685,301 Danish children aged 10 and over, plus their parents (total 3,391,018). Names obtained from the Danish Civil Registration System of children born between 1968 and 1997 and data from the Danish Psychiatric Central Register (650,000 people).

There were four main groups of participants: (1) couples who were both on the psychiatric register (279 couples and their 416 children), (2) couples where one partner was on the register (20,001 couples and their 37,030 children), (3) neither parent had any psychological disorder = 'cleaned' population, (4) people with no data on a diagnosis = 'uncleaned'.

Procedure

1. Using the Civil Registration the researchers were able to identify the parents of each child.

2. Each child and parent was checked to see if they were on the Psychiatric Register.

3. The specific diagnosis was identified.

4. Data on each offspring was linked with their parents' psychiatric history so that the likelihood of a diagnosis of psychological disorder could be calculated.

Results

Incidence of developing schizophrenia by age 52

1. If both parents had a schizophrenia diagnosis, the incidence of a schizophrenia diagnosis in offspring was 27.3% (and 67.5% for any diagnosis).

2. If one parent had a schizophrenia diagnosis and the other parent had no diagnosis, the incidence of a schizophrenia diagnosis in offspring was 7%.

3. If one parent had a schizophrenia diagnosis and the other had a bipolar diagnosis the incidence of a schizophrenia diagnosis in offspring was 15.6%.

4. The incidence of a schizophrenia diagnosis was 0.86% if neither parent had been admitted (compared with 1.12% in the general population).

Incidence of developing bipolar disorder by age 52

5. If both parents had a bipolar diagnosis the incidence of a bipolar diagnosis in offspring was 24.95% (and 44.2% for any diagnosis).

6. If one parent had a bipolar diagnosis and the other parent had no diagnosis, the incidence of a bipolar diagnosis in offspring was 4.4%.

Age of onset and development

7. There is a variable age of onset.

8. After age 45 there were only a few new diagnoses of schizophrenia but there were still new diagnoses of bipolar disorder.

The results of this study may be useful for genetic counsellors to help people make decisions in relation to having children.

Conclusions

If both parents have a serious psychological disorder, this significantly increases the risk of their child developing not just that particular psychological disorder, but other psychological disorders.

Having one parent with a psychological disorder increases risk compared with the general population but having two parents with a psychological disorder creates an even greater risk (Gottesman called this 'a super-high-risk sample').

This research provides support for the genetic explanation of psychological disorders because it demonstrates the increased chance of developing a serious psychological disorder if direct relatives have that or another serious psychological disorder.

How the key research explains ... the medical model	Gottesman *et al.*'s study supports the medical model because it is a biological explanation of psychological disorder (genetics).
	For example, they found an increased risk of children being diagnosed with schizophrenia if one or both parents had been diagnosed with schizophrenia.
	The research also demonstrates that there is an increased risk of developing a psychological disorder if parents have any psychological disorder, suggesting that the same genes may underlie a number of psychological disorders.

Links between the topic and the methodological issues

Validity	⊕ The diagnosis of the psychological disorders in Gottesman *et al.*'s research was based on the ICD classification system, deemed to be valid.
	⊖ Some diagnoses in the study may not have been valid in the first place because the characteristics of schizophrenia and bipolar disorder have some overlap.
Reliability	⊖ Research related to the medical model (e.g. studying brain abnormality) often uses MRI scans, but the reliability of MRI scans as a brain imaging technique is variable. Therefore, such research should be treated with caution.
Sampling bias	⊕ Gottesman *et al.*'s sample was very large so the conclusions can be generalised to the target population of Danish citizens.
	⊖ Gottesman *et al.* only included people with hospital admissions for schizophrenia and bipolar disorder, excluding those with less severe characteristics. Therefore, the conclusions may only apply to severe cases.
Ethnocentrism	⊖ Gottesman *et al.*'s results provide an individualist explanation of psychological disorder whereas other cultures may focus on social, cultural and spiritual factors as primary causes of psychological disorders.

Links between the topic and the debates

Nature/nurture	The genetic explanation of psychological disorder predominantly supports the nature side of the debate. It suggests that we are born with certain characteristics which underlie psychological disorder.
	Brain abnormality and biochemical explanations support nurture as they take into account the role of events that occur after birth, e.g. brain damage (as the result of an accident) or use of drugs (such as cannabis).
Free will/ determinism	The medical model is largely determinist as disorders are explained by neurotransmitters, genes and brain structure that are factors beyond personal control.
Reductionism/ holism	All three of the explanations within the medical model are reductionist. They each break down a complex behaviour into the simplest form, whether that is at the level of biochemistry, genes or brain structures.

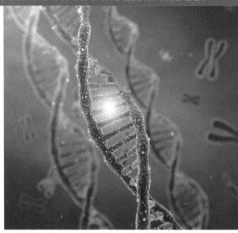

Knowledge of genetic risk factors could lead to eugenic beliefs - that reproduction should be prevented in certain groups of people, such as those with serious psychological disorders, because of the 'damage' to the human gene pool. This makes this research socially sensitive (one of the debates you could link to this topic).

The links on the left are explained on page 115.

Revision booster

Make sure you relate Gottesman's key research to the medical model. For example, show how the results highlight the role of genes in psychological disorder.

Exam-style question examples

Component 3 Section A:

1. Outline how the key research by Gottesman *et al.* (2010) explains the medical model of mental illness. **[5]**

2. Discuss sampling bias in relation to the key research by Gottesman *et al.* (2010). **[6]**

3. Discuss research into explanations of mental illness in relation to the nature/nurture argument. **[10]**

The debates on the left are examples of how you might link the topic to the debates. You need to prepare responses for all of the debates - or be ready to think on your feet in the exam.

All the debates are explained on pages 91-94.

Application

Biological treatment of one specific disorder

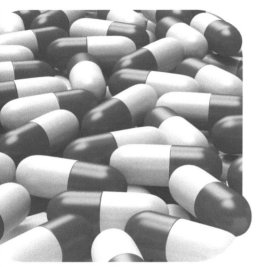

Finding the most effective drug treatment is important because it allows people with psychological disorders to have better health prospects and to be able to better function within society, for example being able to find employment and keep a job.

Before the 1950s, schizophrenia was treated with psychosurgery or electroconvulsive therapy (ECT). Since the 1950s, drug treatments have been developed and become the preferred method, allowing a person with a psychological disorder to lead a relatively regular life.

Revision booster

We have provided two biological (medical model) application strategies on this spread. This gives you a choice of which treatment you want to use when answering an exam question.

If the question says 'a', which is how it is presented in the exam (and in our question examples on the facing page), then you must only use one application.

Where these questions ask for 'one specific disorder', make sure you actually *name* the specific disorder in your answer.

Questions will not ask for two applications or two specific disorders – though you could always use this knowledge as part of your evaluation in a discuss question.

Biological application 1

Treatment for schizophrenia

Antipsychotic medication

If neurotransmitter irregularities cause schizophrenia, then drug treatments that modify those neurotransmitters should alleviate the symptoms of schizophrenia.

How antipsychotics work The drug blocks dopamine by occupying postsynaptic receptor sites, particularly D2 receptors. This reduces activity in postsynaptic neurons resulting in less activity in the mesolimbic pathway (see page 104) and a decrease in positive symptoms of schizophrenia.

Types of antipsychotics There are two types of antipsychotics used in the UK:

- *Typical* ('first generation') antipsychotics (e.g. chlorpromazine and haloperidol) were introduced in the 1950s as tranquilisers used to calm people with schizophrenia. Typical antipsychotics are effective at reducing the positive symptoms of schizophrenia but they do not reduce the negative symptoms.
- *Atypical* ('second generation') antipsychotics (e.g. clozapine and risperidone) are newer and are more widely used. They still work by blocking dopamine receptors, but in a more gradual way. They tend to also reduce the negative symptoms.

How antipsychotics are taken The drugs are given in tablet form, or sometimes by injection which requires a less frequent dose. The drugs change the levels of dopamine available in the brain, therefore it is important that the person takes the medication regularly to stabilise their dopamine levels. If they stop taking the medication it is likely they will relapse quite quickly. The effects of the medication build up slowly in the brain so the person will need to take the medication over several weeks before symptoms show any real signs of reducing.

Do antipsychotics work for schizophrenia?

Usefulness A strength of antipsychotic medications is that they have benefits in reducing symptoms. Leucht *et al.* (2012) found that antipsychotic medication reduces both the relapse rate of schizophrenia and hospital readmissions. It creates a better quality of life for people with schizophrenia and reduces aggressive acts.

Effectiveness Clozapine is the most effective antipsychotic in terms of reducing hospital admissions and reducing the use of other medications (Stroup *et al.* 2015). It has also been found to be effective for those people for whom other antipsychotic medications have not been effective.

Practicalities Side effects are a weakness of typical antipsychotics, particularly when a person experiences tremors, spasms, jerky movements, slow movements or restlessness. In many cases the severity of the side effects can lead to reduced adherence to the medication, which of course makes the medication become less effective and may raise ethical concerns in relation to protection from harm.

Biological
application 2

**Treatment for
major depression**

**Electroconvulsive
therapy (ECT)**

ECT is a controversial therapy, today mainly used only for severe depression.

How ECT is administered

- The person is usually in hospital due to the severity of their depression. A full medical examination is carried out including heart monitoring, blood tests and X-rays.
- They are given a general anaesthetic and muscle relaxant to prevent physical injury, as well as oxygen to prevent brain damage.
- Once the person is unconscious, electrodes are placed on their head and a small amount of electric current (approximately 0.6 amps) is passed through their brain for about half a second. The current causes a convulsion (seizure) that can last 20–50 seconds.
- Usually six to eight treatments are given over a three- to four-week period (two per week).

How ECT works Doctors are not sure exactly how ECT works. It may be that the electric current changes the activity of the neurotransmitters implicated in depression (e.g. serotonin). Other explanations suggest blood flow in areas of the brain (e.g. the limbic system) is stimulated. ECT may even stimulate the growth of new cells and new pathways in the brain.

Types of ECT There are two types of ECT used in the UK:

- *Unilateral ECT* where electrodes are attached to only one temple.
- *Bilateral ECT* where electrodes are attached to both temples. Bilateral ECT is the preferred method because it works more quickly and effectively but it is reported that it may cause more side effects.

Does ECT work for major depression?

Usefulness ECT is more likely to be used for people whose depression is so severe that they cannot wait several weeks for drug treatment to take effect, and also for people who are at serious risk of suicide or for when drug treatment has not succeeded in reducing the depression. However, there are questions in relation to whether severely depressed people can give informed consent for ECT.

Effectiveness The UK ECT Review Group (2013) found that ECT is significantly more effective at reducing the symptoms of major depression than either drugs or simulated ECT (no electrical current used). The Review Group also found that bilateral ECT is slightly more effective than unilateral, and that high doses are more effective than low doses.

Practicalities Side effects include headaches, aching muscles, feeling dizzy and being distressed. Most people who have had ECT also report temporary memory loss. The Review Group found more memory loss with bilateral ECT.

As with any treatment involving general anaesthetic, there are risks of death or serious injury. This means there are ethical concerns regarding ECT in relation to protection from harm.

Although ECT may be initially effective for people with major depression, there is a relatively high relapse rate and many people develop further depressive symptoms.

It is important to note that, unlike most medications for physical disorders, medications for psychological disorders do not 'cure' the disorder – they merely alleviate the symptoms.

Exam-style question examples

Component 3 Section A:

1. Outline a biological treatment of **one** specific disorder. **[5]**

2. Discuss **one** strength and **one** weakness of the biological treatment referred to in your answer to question 1. **[6]**

3. Discuss ethical considerations concerning the biological treatment of **one** specific disorder. **[8]**

4. Discuss the usefulness of a biological treatment of **one** specific disorder. **[5]**

Background
Alternative explanations of mental illness

You are required to study the medical model as an explanation of psychological disorder (mental illness). This is covered in Topic 2 (pages 104-109).

Five alternative explanations of psychological disorder are also identified in the specification. You are required to know the behaviourist and cognitive explanations (this spread) plus one other (humanistic, psychodynamic or cognitive neuroscience - see next spread).

There is more information on the behaviourist perspective on page 90.

Revision booster

Exam questions like the ones on the facing page may ask you to discuss explanations of psychological disorder (mental illness) using the debates, so you should prepare for this.

More information on debates can be found on pages 91–94.

If you observe someone who stays calm when facing a snake, social learning theory suggests you will learn and then imitate this calm behaviour when in the presence of snakes, instead of learning and then imitating a fear response.

The behaviourist explanation of mental illness

The behaviourist approach suggests that 'mental illness' (psychological disorder) is learned as a consequence of external events.

Affective disorder e.g. major depression	**Classical conditioning** Early experiences of lack of control mean that, later in life, when faced with similar situations, people may respond with passivity, inaction and depression. This is called *learned helplessness*. **Operant conditioning** Depression can occur when positive reinforcers from the environment are removed, e.g. interactions with colleagues (a positive reinforcer) may cease if a person loses their job. This can lead to avoidance where people no longer seek out other social situations. Other people may unconsciously encourage depressive behaviour by giving attention to the depressed individual.
Anxiety disorder e.g. specific phobias	**Classical conditioning (initiation)** Watson and Rayner (1920) conditioned 11-month-old Albert to develop a fear of white furry objects through association with a loud noise:

- Neutral stimulus (NS) = white rat. Albert initially showed no fear of a white rat.
- Unconditioned stimulus (UCS) = banging a steel bar to make a loud noise.
- Unconditioned response (UCR) = crying and falling forward.
- NS paired with UCS = Albert reached out to touch the white rat (NS) and the experimenters banged the bar near Albert (UCS).
- Several pairings of the white rat (NS) and loud noise (UCS) meant that just seeing the rat alone, even without the steel bar being struck, caused Albert to cry. In this way, the white rat became the conditioned stimulus (CS) producing a conditioned response (CR) of crying.
- Albert had been conditioned to fear the rat, creating a phobia.

Operant conditioning (maintenance)

- **Positive reinforcement** People who produce an emotional reaction to an object often receive attention. This extra attention acts as a reinforcer of the phobic reactions.
- **Negative reinforcement** Avoiding the phobic object reduces fear and reinforces the continued avoidance of the object because it reduces the unpleasant feeling.

Social learning theory Phobias are acquired by observing and then imitating the behaviour of others - especially if the person is someone you identify with.

Research Askew and Field (2007) showed that children acquired phobias when images of unfamiliar animals were paired with a scared (rather than happy) adult face.

The cognitive explanation of mental illness

The cognitive approach to 'mental illness' (psychological disorder) focuses on faulty (maladaptive) thinking.

Affective disorder e.g. major depression	**Beck's cognitive triad** (Beck 1967):

- **The self** The person believes that they are worthless, e.g. feels unattractive or not likeable.
- **The future** The person thinks the future is going be negative, e.g. they will never find a job.
- **The world** The person thinks that everyone around them, and every situation, is negative, e.g. the world is a cold, hard place with no hope.

These beliefs form negative cognitive *schemas* - the person expects situations to be negative and therefore interprets them in this way (*systematic negative cognitive bias*).

The negative schemas stem from criticism and rejection early in life from parents/teachers, and may also come from over-expectations in childhood.

Research A meta-analysis of over 300 studies found improvement in depressive characteristics through the use of cognitive therapies, which suggests that faulty cognitions may be related to depression (Butler *et al.* 2006).

Psychotic disorder
e.g. schizophrenia

Deficits in schizophrenia Many symptoms are cognitive, e.g. speech poverty, disorganised speech and thought insertion. So, it makes sense to have a cognitive explanation. The main assumption is that the characteristics of schizophrenia are caused by disordered thinking.

Attention deficit theory Frith (1979) suggests that people with schizophrenia are more consciously aware of the many cognitive processes that usually take place out of awareness. Clinically healthy people are unaware of these processes (and therefore can deal better with the cognitive tasks they have to process).

The result, for people with schizophrenia, is that too much information is being processed, leading to sensory overload.

Anxiety disorder
e.g. specific phobias

Beck *et al.* (2005) suggested that fear responses are caused by a person's *interpretation* of the situation/object rather than the situation/object itself.

Cognitive biases:

- **Attentional bias** People who develop specific phobias pay extreme attention to situations and objects that produce fear and anxiety.
- **Negative appraisal bias** People who develop specific phobias interpret harmless situations and objects as dangerous.
- **Systematic attentional bias** Pflugshaupt *et al.* (2005) found that people with a spider phobia detected spiders more quickly in photographs than controls without a phobia.

If the cognitive deficits of schizophrenia can be explained, then the disorder we know as schizophrenia no longer needs to be explained. It can be understood just in terms of the individual deficits.

Exam-style question examples

Component 3 Section A:

1. Outline the behaviourist explanation of mental illness. **[5]**

2. Describe how a cognitive psychologist would explain mental illness. **[5]**

3. Compare the behaviourist explanation of mental illness with the cognitive explanation of mental illness. **[8]**

4. To what extent do alternatives to the medical model of explaining mental illness support psychology as a science? **[10]**

5. Discuss alternative explanations of mental illness in relation to the individual/situational explanations debate. **[10]**

6. Compare the medical model explanation of mental illness with either the behaviourist **or** cognitive explanation of mental illness. **[8]**

Study the examples above carefully - there are lots of different ways you may be assessed on this topic. For example, some exam questions may ask you to use explanations from both the medical model and alternatives to the medical model.

Background
Alternative explanations of mental illness

Topic 3

Chapter 1 Issues in mental health

Component 3 Applied psychology

Rogers proposed that, in order to be able to accept yourself, you need unconditional positive regard from others (e.g. love, respect, being valued) without giving anything in return. Only then can you reach your potential.

Remember you are required to know the behaviourist and cognitive explanations (previous spread) plus one other explanation from this spread (humanistic, psychodynamic or cognitive neuroscience).

Rogers and Maslow were two of the key figures in early humanistic psychology.

Maslow suggested that our behaviour is motivated by the desire to satisfy basic needs (e.g. food, safety) and, if these are satisfied, we move higher up the hierarchy of needs (e.g. need for love and self-esteem). The ultimate need is to seek self-actualisation (SA) - being the best person we can be. This is an important characteristic of mental health.

Pyramid of needs

Maslow's hierarchy was mentioned in Hancock's study of psychopaths (see page 88) - psychopaths used twice as many 'basic needs' words compared to non-psychopaths.

The humanistic explanation of mental illness

Humanistic psychologists (such as Rogers and Maslow) suggest that *self-actualisation* is one of the key characteristics of mental health — the ability to realise potential, to accept ourselves, develop relationships with others and to find a meaning to life.

Affective disorder e.g. major depression	**Taking personal responsibility** Major depression occurs because external factors (over which people have no control), inhibit the growth of an individual.
	Reduced self-esteem An individual's failure to live up to their ideal self creates a threat which reduces their self-esteem. People use defence mechanisms (e.g. *distortion*) to reduce the perceived threat but this does not lower the threat itself and this diminishes a person's contact with reality.
	Downward spiral Threats to the self increase and it becomes harder to defend against such 'threats'. The person is trapped in a depressive downward spiral because they need to use more and more defence mechanisms with less and less effect.
Psychotic disorder e.g. schizophrenia	**Active and holistic** People with schizophrenia are not passive carriers of symptoms. The humanistic approach does not focus on a narrow aspect of psychological functioning but instead considers the whole person.
	Striving for meaning and growth Schizophrenia is an interruption of the usual developmental process towards emotional maturity. The humanistic approach believes that a person with schizophrenia does not have an 'illness' but is experiencing a form of immaturity - their development into a healthy and fulfilled person has been affected by circumstances (e.g. stress).
	Self-esteem and parenting According to the humanistic approach, harsh, neglectful parenting can drastically lower a child's self-esteem, causing greater vulnerability to schizophrenia in adulthood.

The psychodynamic explanation of mental illness

Psychodynamic explanations of 'mental illness' (psychological disorder) focus on unconscious forces, conflicts and motivations. These stem from childhood experiences, e.g. of loss and failed attachments.

Affective disorder e.g. major depression	**Loss and depression** Depression develops when an adult experiences a loss (real or symbolic) and they re-experience repressed unconscious feelings of self-directed anger and loss from childhood.
	Attachment theory A child who 'loses' their mother figure (e.g. through death or divorce) cannot fully understand the experience of loss at such a young age. This means they grow up with unresolved mourning which could be triggered by later adult experiences of loss, resulting in depression (Bowlby 1980).

The psychodynamic explanation of mental illness (continued)

Psychotic disorder
e.g. schizophrenia

Regression to primary narcissism Freud suggested that adults with schizophrenia had coped with a harsh childhood (e.g. cold, rejecting parenting) by regressing to an earlier state of development called *primary narcissism*. The child can no longer distinguish between fantasy and reality and their only concern is to meet their own needs. Freud believed this infantile state could be detected in the symptoms of schizophrenia (e.g. delusions of grandeur), triggered by extreme stress.

Re-establishing ego control The adult's regression to primary narcissism triggers an attempt by the ego to re-establish control by regaining contact with reality. However, this only results in other symptoms of schizophrenia emerging (e.g. auditory hallucinations - an internal substitute for external reality).

Anxiety disorder
e.g. specific phobias

Ego defence mechanisms Anxiety acts as a threat to a person's ego. This is resolved by displacing the anxiety on to a neutral object that represents the real feared object (e.g. on to a spider).

In the Freud core study (page 82), Hans displaced his real fears of castration onto a fear of horses because the horses' black harnesses represented his father's moustache.

The cognitive neuroscience explanation of mental illness

Cognitive neuroscience considers how biological factors (e.g. the limbic system in the brain) have an impact on cognitive processes (e.g. perception).

Affective disorder
e.g. major depression

Role of the corticolimbic circuit An impairment of this mood-regulating circuit means connections between the prefrontal cortex and the limbic system are disrupted and depression is one possible consequence of this dysregulation.

Psychotic disorder
e.g. schizophrenia

Hallucinations A faulty neural circuit linking the prefrontal cortex with the septo-hippocampal system may cause the delusions associated with schizophrenia (Frith 2005). The result is a positive symptom, e.g. people hear voices.

Language Difficulties (e.g. poverty of speech) stem from an atypical temporal-prefrontal neural circuit linking the primary auditory cortex to areas in the prefrontal cortex, both of which are central to processing the meaning of language.

Anxiety disorder
e.g. specific phobias

Dual brain circuits The fear response is controlled:

- Circuit 1: Thalamus to the amygdala, an 'early warning system' that is fast but inaccurate.
- Circuit 2: Thalamus to the prefrontal cortex and then to the amygdala. This allows us to perceive more accurately what is causing the fear response.

Both of these dual brain circuits are probably impaired in people with specific phobias. This means they have greater amygdala activity than people without a phobia, and so have a stronger fear response.

Revision booster

Students often mix up cognitive neuroscience explanations with medical model explanations (both include biochemical and brain abnormalities).

Make sure you clearly show how cognitive neuroscience is different from the medical model by highlighting the *impact* the biology has on cognitive processes.

Exam-style question examples

Component 3 Section A:

1. Outline **either** the humanistic **or** the psychodynamic **or** the cognitive neuroscience explanation of mental illness. **[5]**

2. Compare the cognitive explanation of mental illness with **either** the humanistic **or** the psychodynamic **or** the cognitive neuroscience explanation of mental illness. **[10]**

3. Compare the behaviourist explanation of mental illness with **either** the humanistic **or** the psychodynamic **or** the cognitive neuroscience explanation of mental illness. **[10]**

4. To what extent are explanations of mental illness determinist? **[10]**

Chapter 3.1 Topic 3: Alternatives to the medical model

Key research

Szasz (2011) on *The myth of mental illness* *

*We have retained the term 'mental illness' on this spread as the concept of 'illness' is integral to Szasz's article.

Background

Szasz wrote a book in 1961, *The myth of mental illness*. The 2011 article was a review of his ideas and of the situation 50 years later.

Note: This essay is not a study. It is a commentary on Szasz's beliefs about mental illness.

Aims

Szasz's aims in the 1961 book and 2011 article were to:

- Challenge the medical concept of 'mental illness'.
- Reject psychiatric treatments based on the medical model.
- Encourage people to avoid labels (e.g. 'psychoses', 'neuroses', 'mental illness') and instead think of individual behaviours that disturb or disorient others or the self.
- Reject the image of people with mental illness as the helpless victims of pathobiological events.
- Stop coercive psychiatric practices which are incompatible with free societies.

1. Fifty years of change

In the 1950s in the USA no one thought that the government should provide health care. People with mental illness were seen as incurable and locked away.

Fifty years later, government has taken on a legal responsibility for mental health care to prevent people being a danger to themselves or others.

2. Mental illness - a medical or legal concept?

In the 21st century, mental illnesses are defined by political and economic criteria. Many 'disorders' (e.g. homosexuality) are no longer considered disorders. If mental illness was a real phenomenon it could not change so readily.

The politicalisation of mental illness means that those in power have determined that mental illness is like any other physical illness. This argument is not based on scientific research but shows that mental illness is a metaphor - a phrase used to represent something that is a real physical change.

Psychiatric hospitals are like prisons - people labelled with mental illness are treated like prisoners rather than receiving treatment for their illness. Psychiatrists act as judges rather than healers. Traditional psychiatric viewpoints should be discarded, and replaced with morals and laws.

3. 'Mental illness' is a metaphor

A person diagnosed with a mental illness may later be found to have a physical illness. This shows they were misdiagnosed - they didn't have a 'mental illness', they had an undiagnosed bodily illness.

If all mental illnesses were found to be brain diseases, then the term 'mental illness' would become devoid of meaning.

'As quiet as a mouse' is a metaphor - it describes something in a way that isn't literally true.

4. Changing perspectives

Medicalisation of the soul began in the late 16th century, e.g. Shakespeare's Lady Macbeth reported internal experiences (hallucinations). Her husband sent for a doctor who prescribed religion (internal self-conversation) rather than medicine. By the end of the 19th century, the physician took on the task of curing the soul.

5. In the eye of the beholder

Diseases of the body have causes (e.g. infection) which can be cured. Mental illnesses must be understood, they cannot be cured. Feelings don't matter in physical illnesses.

There is the ethical principle of 'do no harm' - people with physical diseases have a choice which is not given to people diagnosed with a mental illness.

6. Revisiting *The myth of mental illness*

Critics continue to see *The myth of mental illness* as a radical effort to recast mental illness from a medical problem into a linguistic problem (i.e. the way mental states are described).

However, some non-psychiatrists believe that psychiatry, without reference to the medical model, is a method of social control which violates freedom and autonomy.

7. Having an illness doesn't make a person a patient

One of the worst assumptions of psychiatry is that if someone is labelled as 'mentally ill', then they require some form of treatment, whether they choose the treatment or not.

This leads to two different ways of treating people:

- Curing or healing by using conversation, e.g. talking therapy.
- Controlling or coercing patients forcefully, which has been authorised by the state.

How the key research explains ... the alternatives to the medical model	**Explaining psychological disorder** Szasz claims that if a disorder has a physical basis then it should be diagnosed as a physical illness rather than a 'mental' illness. Alternatively, behaviours that are disturbed/disturbing should be explained psychologically because these are psychological symptoms.
	Treating psychological disorder Szasz identified two types of treatment: (1) talking therapy that the person consents to, or (2) controlling people against their will, involving medication.

Links between the topic and the methodological issues

Validity	⊖ Szasz's essay is based on his own views and not on empirical research. This reduces validity as the arguments are not based on objectively gathered data.
Reliability	⊖ fMRI scans can be used to study brain function (e.g. in schizophrenia). The reliability of such scans can be variable, e.g. depends on tasks being undertaken (Bennett and Miller 2010).
Sampling bias	⊖ Case studies are used (e.g. Little Albert and Little Hans - each from culturally distinct backgrounds). It may be wrong to assume that we can generalise from such restricted and unique samples.
Ethnocentrism	⊕ The medical model assumes the universality of psychological disorders, due to its biological roots.
	⊖ Szasz talks about the politicalisation of mental illness in the USA, suggesting that the assumptions of the dominant political groups affect the cultural view of psychological disorders.

Links between the topic and the debates

Nature/nurture	Cognitive neuroscience explanations support nature. Genes may underlie the faulty neural circuits related to psychological disorders.
	Behaviourist explanations of psychological disorders support the nurture side of the debate as they explain how psychological disorders are learned through experiences, e.g. conditioning.
Free will/ determinism	The humanistic explanation supports free will as it explains how our choices reduce the gap between the real and ideal self.
	The behaviourist explanation suggests psychological disorders are due to conditioning experiences, showing environmental determinism.
Reductionism/ holism	Cognitive neuroscience reduces psychological disorder to aspects of neuronal activity in the brain.
	Humanistic explanations are more holistic as the individual as a whole is taken into account - the 'self' is a psychological entity.

- In the Component 2 exam (covered in Chapters 2.2-2.6) you are required to link the *core study* to the methodological issues.
- In the Component 3 exam (covered in Chapters 3.1-3.5) you are required to link the *topic* to the methodological issues.
- In the Component 2 exam you are required to link the *area* with the debates *and perspectives*.
- In the Component 3 exam you are required to link the *topic* with the debates.

Revision booster

Szasz's article can be difficult to understand. Use the subheadings from the article to guide you. Also learn a few key terms (e.g. metaphor, medicalisation, politicalisation).

Methodological issues are explained on pages 95-96 and the debates are explained on pages 91-94.

Exam-style question examples

Component 3 Section A:

1. How does Szasz (2011) defend his claim that 'there is no such thing as mental illness'? **[3]**

2. Evaluate the usefulness of the key research by Szasz (2011). **[6]**

3. Assess methodological issues in research into alternative explanations of mental illness. **[10]**

4. Discuss nature/nurture in relation to alternative explanations of mental illness. **[10]**

Application
Non-biological treatment of one specific disorder

Phobias can be learned via classical conditioning - this is explained on page 110, with the case of Little Albert.

If phobias can be learned then they can be unlearned through classical conditioning - this time a new association is formed between the now conditioned stimulus (phobic object) and a new response (relaxation).

This is called 'counterconditioning' - a new response 'counters' the original conditioning.

The end result is that the person is desensitised because they cannot feel anxious and relaxed at the same time (reciprocal inhibition).

Non-biological application 1
Treatment for phobias
Systematic desensitisation

Systematic desensitisation (SD) is based on the principle of classical conditioning, so it is a behaviourist therapy. It is often used to help overcome phobias and other anxiety disorders.

There are four main stages of SD:

1. **Functional analysis** The therapist and client discuss reasons for the phobia, how the client responds to the phobic stimulus and feared scenarios.

2. **Construction of an anxiety hierarchy** The therapist and client develop a hierarchy of phobic situations, from the least to the most fearful.

3. **Relaxation training** The client is taught relaxation techniques, e.g. breathing exercises.

4. **Gradual exposure** Starting with the least phobic situation, the client experiences the fear response and practises relaxation in the presence of the phobic stimulus. When the client is coping and reports no anxiety, they move up the anxiety hierarchy to a slightly more anxiety-provoking phobic situation.

Treatment usually takes place over a number of sessions, depending on the severity of the phobia and the client's ability to relax.

Revision booster

The systematic desensitisation application strategy described on this page has a staged structure. You can use the structure of such a strategy to help organise your answer to exam questions, such as question 1 on the facing page.

Plutophobia is a phobia of money or wealth.

Does SD work for phobias?

Usefulness It is not necessarily the actual treatment itself that is useful for reducing the phobia - the symptomatic benefits may come from learning useful processes that can be applied in new situations (e.g. learning how to relax and focus on emotions).

Effectiveness Lang and Lazovik (1963) found that people with snake phobias who had undergone SD displayed less avoidance of snakes when presented with them and reported fewer self-reported phobic behaviours, even up to six months later.

Practicalities Cost and ease of use are practical issues. SD is significantly cheaper and quicker than treatments such as psychoanalysis, which can go on for years.

However, although a client may appear to have reduced symptoms of the phobia, such treatments may not address the root cause of the phobia and therefore the phobia may reappear in a different form. Other types of therapy, such as psychoanalysis (on the facing page), focus on the underlying causes.

Another practical issue is that some phobic objects are too dangerous or impractical to have in a therapy room, such as wild animals or flying in an aeroplane.

The solution is to practise SD in a controlled environment where the phobic object may be represented in photographs and/or imagined rather than being physically present.

Psychoanalysis is based on the idea that individuals are unaware of the many unconscious factors that cause their depression. For example, unconscious repressed memories of loss and anger in childhood may resurface when triggered by adult experiences of loss.

During psychoanalysis, the therapist (*psychoanalyst*) attempts to trace unconscious memories to childhood events, such as the real or symbolic loss of a parent or having parents who were cold and rejecting. The psychoanalyst then helps the client (*analysand*) to deal with these newly recalled repressed memories. The psychoanalyst uses special techniques to uncover the repressed material and help the depressed analysand deal with it.

Two important techniques are:

1. **Free association** The depressed analysand is encouraged to express their thoughts exactly as they occur.

   Freud believed that the value of free association lies in the fact that the analysand is making associations that are determined by the unconscious factors that the analysis is aiming to uncover.

   The psychoanalyst listens carefully as their analysand talks, looking for clues and drawing tentative conclusions about the possible cause(s) of the depression.

2. **Dream analysis** The real meaning of a dream (*latent content*) is transformed into the content you actually experience (*manifest content*).

   Dream analysis consists of reversing the processes that created the manifest content. Free association can uncover latent content through discussion of each dream element.

   The psychoanalyst then selects the interpretation that makes most sense based on the free associations and life experiences of the analysand.

Free association and dream analysis can involve painful discussions and interpretations that an analysand may resist. The analysand transfers their current feelings about past conflicts onto the therapist.

Non-biological treatments are based on the assumption that disorders are caused by psychological rather than biological factors.

Does psychoanalysis work for major depression?

Usefulness Schofield (1964) argued that psychoanalysis is only useful for 'youthful, attractive, verbal, intelligent and successful' people ('YAVIS'). This means that psychoanalysis could be less useful for people with major depression who do not fit into these categories.

Effectiveness Fonagy (2015) investigated people who experienced CBT plus medication or psychoanalysis. Those clients who received psychoanalysis showed a significant decrease in symptoms of major depression after two years, in comparison with the CBT plus medication group. This suggests that psychoanalysis can be an effective long-term treatment for depression.

Practicalities Psychoanalysis is not a brief form of therapy. Together, psychoanalyst and analysand examine the same issues over and over again, sometimes for years, in an attempt to gain greater clarity concerning the causes of the major depression. Therefore, psychoanalysis is not a quick fix and is quite expensive.

Exam-style question examples

Component 3 Section A:

1. Outline a non-biological treatment of **one** specific disorder. [5]

2. Discuss **one** strength and **one** weakness of the non-biological treatment referred to in your answer to question 1. [6]

3. Explain how a non-biological treatment can contribute to the success of the economy and society. [4]

4. Discuss ethical considerations concerning the non-biological treatment of **one** specific disorder. [8]

How psychology contributes to the success of the economy and society ... Finding successful ways to alleviate the distress experienced by people with psychological disorders is a key feature of any successful society.

Background

What psychologists mean by intelligence and what biological factors could affect intelligenc

Is intelligence more than simply academic ability?

A twin study is a quasi-experiment comparing concordance rates for identical (monozygotic, MZ) and non-identical (dizygotic, DZ) twins.

MZ twins are 100% identical genetically because they develop from one fertilised egg (zygote).

DZ twins share, on average, 50% of their genes (the same as any pair of siblings). MZ and DZ twins are assumed to share the same environment with their co-twin, therefore environment is not an extraneous variable when comparing MZ and DZ twins.

Using the background research

Consider how you could use the background research to support answers to the following questions. See exam guidance on Component 3 Section B questions on page 8.

(a) Outline the key research by Van Leeuwen *et al.* (2008) and explain how intelligence is affected by biological factors. **[10]**

(b) Assess the validity of research into intelligence. **[15]**

(c) Lara is an organisational psychologist advising companies on how to use intelligence testing for job interviews.

Outline the advice Lara might give to a computer software company looking to appoint new job applicants. **[10]**

Defining intelligence

Psychologists suggest that intelligence involves at least three abilities:

- Understanding complex ideas.
- Adapting effectively to the environment.
- Learning from experience.

Different kinds of intelligence

General (*g*) and specific (*s*) intelligences

Spearman (1904) believed our ability to behave intelligently on a cognitive task depends upon a combination of both:

- *g* (intelligence that applies in all tasks).
- *s* (intelligence required in a particular task e.g. maths, but not necessarily in others).

Fluid and crystallised intelligences

Horn and Cattell (1966) suggested that *g* has two main aspects:

- **Fluid intelligence** The ability to reason in abstract ways and solve problems logically without experience. This declines with age.
- **Crystallised intelligence** The ability to acquire knowledge through learning and experience. This increases with age.

Multiple intelligences: Gardner's theory

Gardner (1983) argued that we all have eight independent intelligences but each of us blends them differently, e.g. a person may have moderate logical-mathematical intelligence, but little musical intelligence.

Biological factors in intelligence

Genes

Twin studies About 50% of the variation in IQ scores between MZ and DZ twins is due to genetic inheritance (Plomin and Spinath 2004).

Adoption studies MZ twins who are brought up in different families have more similar IQs than the IQs of DZ twins brought up together, supporting the role of genes in intelligence (McGue *et al.* 1993).

Brain structure

Brain size There is a moderate link between brain size and intelligence (Rushton and Ankney 2007).

Areas of the brain Jung and Haier (2007) suggest intelligence may be correlated with the volumes of the prefrontal cortex, Broca's area and Wernicke's area.

Grey matter Luders *et al.* (2009) showed that higher IQ scores are correlated with higher amounts of both grey and white matter.

Nutrition

The consistent 'generational gain' in IQ (*Flynn Effect*) is due to improved diet. Our brains benefit from key micronutrients (e.g. neurons become more efficient), so people are performing better on IQ tests now than they did 50 years ago (e.g. Qian *et al.* 2005).

Application 1

Wechsler intelligence scale for children (WISC)

WISC is the most widely used intelligence test in the USA (and other countries) for children aged six to 16. It has been revised five times since first being introduced in 1950.

What the test measures WISC measures five main forms of intellectual functioning (the primary indexes, assessed by two subtests, so ten tests in total). There are five ancillary indexes. The test can also give complementary index scores which can be useful in diagnosing learning-related difficulties.

Administering the test Trained testers administer the test face-to-face with individual children in a session lasting between 15 minutes and three hours.

Does WISC-V work?

Usefulness The WISC is not considered a very culturally-fair test because of its dependence on language skills. It may underestimate the intelligence of people from cultures that value nonverbal skills over verbal ones.

Effectiveness It has been found to have an internal reliability of +.96 (Canivez and Watkins 2016), which is exceptional. The WISC, with its many subscales measuring specific intellectual abilities, fits well with Gardner's multiple intelligences, and so has a high degree of construct validity.

Practicalities The WISC can be administered and scored online. It provides lots of scores from many subtests, which can be used in different ways depending on purpose. However, this also means the test can be difficult to interpret.

Application 2

Raven's progressive matrices

Raven's test assesses fluid intelligence. It is a nonverbal test (no language involved) and therefore considered to be 'culture-fair'.

Description of the test The standard progressive matrices (SPM), which is used for children, has 60 tasks arranged into five sets (A to E) each with 12 tasks which are progressively more difficult. Each item has a matrix of six or nine items (see illustration at top right). One item is missing and the testee has to select the appropriate one from a set of six (sometimes eight) alternatives.

Administering the test The SPM takes between 15 and 45 minutes. The test produces a standard IQ score to be used in comparison with the wider population.

Do Raven's progressive matrices work?

Usefulness The SPM is a reasonably culture-fair test, which means it is ideal for comparing cultures in cross-cultural research.

Effectiveness The split-half reliability of the SPM is around +.90, and test-retest reliability is above +.80 (Domino and Domino 2006). Split-half reliability of the advanced progressive matrices (APM) test is +.85 (Raven and Court 1998). However, the construct validity of the SPM has been questioned because the test is based on the idea of a single *g* factor, which is not universally accepted.

Practicalities The SPM test is flexible to administer and simple to interpret. However, the fact that only a single score is produced means the various subscales produced by the WISC are better for diagnosing specific difficulties.

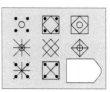

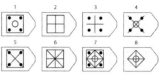

A task from the Raven's SPM test. The correct answer is number 2. The study by Leeuwen et al. (next page) used both the SPM and also the adult version, the APM.

Revision booster

In application questions such as those below, students often solely focus on outlining the strategy. Remember to also write about the benefits of the strategy to the person in the scenario.

Exam-style question examples

Component 3 Section B part (c):

(c) Pooja is an eight-year-old girl who has been referred to an educational psychologist by her teachers who are worried about her level of intelligence because she is performing very poorly at school.

Outline **one** strategy the educational psychologist could use to test Pooja's level of intelligence. **[10]**

(c) Celine is a clinician who uses intelligence tests in the diagnosis of neurological and psychiatric disorders as a component of a comprehensive assessment procedure for her clients.

Outline **one** strategy Celine might use to help assess the cognitive strengths and weaknesses of her clients. **[10]**

The exam questions above are just representative examples. Read the guidance for Component 3 exam questions on page 8.

Key research

Van Leeuwen *et al.* (2008) on a *Twin-family study*

Background

Assumption 1: Parents' phenotypes are not correlated Phenotype = a person's actual behaviour which results from an interaction between genes and environment. Some people have suggested that parental phenotypes are not correlated - but research evidence suggests this view is wrong, i.e. parental phenotypes are correlated, because of either:

- Phenotypic assortment - people mate with partners of similar intelligence.
- Social homogamy - people mate with partners from similar environments.

Assumption 2: Genotype and environment are not correlated This is not true because parents provide children with environments that match the parents' genes (= their genotype), called *cultural transmission*.

Aims

- To carry out an extended twin study to consider the two assumptions:
    1. Is phenotypic assortment or social homogamy the better explanation of variation in IQ score?
    2. Do biological factors (genotype) or environmental factors (phenotype) affect intelligence more?
- To calculate an unbiased heritability estimate for IQ.

Method

Design
Correlation of the IQs of twins, their siblings and parents.

Sample
112 families from Netherlands Twin Registry. 48 MZ twins (identical) and 64 DZ twins (non-identical). Twins' age ranged from 8.9 to 9.5 years, additional siblings' age ranged from 9.9 to 14.9 years.

Materials/apparatus
Raven's SPM (children) and Raven's APM (parents).

Procedure

1. Children and their parents visited the Free University of Amsterdam, and were tested in separate rooms.

2. Children's intelligence was assessed using Raven's SPM and their parents' was assessed using Raven's APM.

3. The lowest and highest test scores in the groups (Min and Max), and the mean and standard deviation of each group's test scores were calculated.

4. Procedure took five hours.

5. Twin status was established by parents taking cheek swabs from themselves and their children.

6. University's medical centre used a standardised genetic testing technique to determine whether each twin pair was MZ or DZ (MZ twins are monozygotic = come from one egg/zygote).

7. A questionnaire determined zygosity for two of the twin pairs.

Results

Descriptive and inferential statistics

1. There were no significant differences in IQ scores between men/boys and women/girls, nor for adults and children.

2. Correlations between pairs of IQ scores were higher for MZ twins than those between twin and parent or twin and other siblings.

Heritability of IQ

3. If we assume that phenotypic assortment is true, then:
    - Genetic variation contributes 58% to the variation in intelligence in children as well as parents.
    - The remaining 42% is explained by environmental variation - but it is 'unshared' environment (i.e. environment that the parents and children do not share).

4. If we assume that social homogamy is true, then:
    - 15% is explained by genetic variation.
    - 19% is explained by one dominant gene (dominance variation).
    - 27% is explained by environmental variation - where the environment was shared between parents and child (shared environment).
    - 39% is explained by environmental variation - where the environment was not shared between parents and child (unshared environment).

5. The heritability estimate for IQ (effect of genes) was 67%, with 33% due to random environmental effects.

6. The interaction between genes and environment was higher for people with low IQ than people with high IQ.

DZ twins.

Conclusions

There is no evidence for cultural transmission, that intelligent parents (phenotypic assortment) create more stimulating environments for their children. However, children with high IQ will seek out stimulating environments more than children with low IQ.

Individual differences in intelligence are largely accounted for by biological factors, i.e. genetic differences.

Environmental factors are more important in children with a genetic predisposition for low IQ than in children with a genetic predisposition for high IQ.

| How the key research explains ... intelligence | **Genes cause intelligence (IQ)** Results show intelligence is mostly, but not entirely, genetically transmitted. Genes are how parents influence their children's IQs, rather than influence through cultural transmission, e.g. education. |
| | **Higher estimate for genetic influence** Van Leeuwen *et al.* suggest a greater role for genes in intelligence than was previously given by, for example, Plomin and Spinath (2004) who reported 50% genetic influence. Earlier studies may have underestimated the role of genes, especially in childhood. |

Jeans can also be inherited from your parents.

Links between the topic and the methodological issues

Validity	⊖ The validity of Raven's SPM (used in Van Leeuwen *et al.*'s study) is limited as it depends on the validity of Spearman's *g* as an explanation of intelligence, which is increasingly rejected in favour of a multidimensional theory, e.g. Gardner's.
Reliability	⊕ Reliability in Van Leeuwen *et al.*'s study is high as they used standardised protocols to measure zygosity.
	⊕ Van Leeuwen *et al.* used reliable tests to measure IQ, e.g. the Raven SPM and APM tests that have good internal and external reliability (see previous spread, under 'Effectiveness').
Sampling bias	⊖ Participants were selected from the Netherlands Twin Register. The sampling method was unknown but may have been biased.
	⊖ Families of children with a significant medical history, psychiatric problems, special educational needs or physical disabilities were excluded from participation.
Ethnocentrism	⊕ Van Leeuwen *et al.* used a culture-fair intelligence test (SPM/APM) as it provides a measure of intelligence that is independent of language and education.
	⊖ The notion of 'intelligence' is based on an assumption that logical and rational thinking is superior - other cultures may view intelligence quite differently, e.g. common sense.

Links between the topic and the debates

Nature/nurture	Van Leeuwen *et al.* showed the heritability of IQ to be 67%, appearing to support nature. However, Van Leeuwen *et al.* do not account for how genes and environment interact. For example, parents' reactions to a child's play behaviour are environmental influences on the development of intelligence.
Free will/ determinism	Van Leeuwen *et al.* support biological determinism - children's IQ is determined by genes inherited from their parents.
	However, phenotypic assortment suggests some free will because we choose our partner, and generally we choose someone similar in intelligence to ourselves.
Reductionism/ holism	Research into biological factors (e.g. genes) in intelligence is often considered reductionist.
	But psychologists also appreciate that genotype and environment interact providing a more holistic approach to understanding intelligence.

Revision booster

Students often get confused by the terms phenotypic assortment and social homogamy. Make sure you know the difference.

Phenotypic assortment refers to people mating with partners who are similar in intelligence to themselves.

Social homogamy refers to people tending to form relationships with partners who share similar environments to themselves.

Don't forget that you need to be ready for questions on all eight debates.

Exam-style question examples

Component 3 Section B part (a):

(a) Use the key research by Van Leeuwen *et al.* (2008) to explain intelligence. **[10]**

Component 3 Section B part (b):

(b) Evaluate the reliability of research into intelligence. **[15]**

(b) Discuss nature/nurture in relation to research into intelligence. **[15]**

How psychology contributes to the success of the economy and society ... Understanding the factors that determine intelligence may help improve children's intellectual abilities.

Background
Brain development and the impact of this on risk-taking behaviour

Don't worry, in time synaptic pruning will fine-tune his brain for eating.

Effects of early stress

There is evidence that early stressful experiences can predispose individuals to later risk-taking behaviour by affecting brain development.

For example, prolonged physical abuse (an uncontrollable and chronic stressor) has been associated with negative outcomes in adolescence, including addiction and suicide (Romer 2010).

Using the background research

Consider how you could use the background research to support answers to the following questions. See exam guidance on Component 3 Section B questions on page 8.

(a) Outline the research by Barkley-Levenson and Galván (2014) and use it to explain risk-taking behaviour. **[10]**

(b) Assess the validity of research into pre-adult brain development. **[15]**

(c) Julia drives dangerously and often overtakes on bends.

Outline a strategy a psychologist may suggest to reduce Julia's risk-taking behaviour. **[10]**

Brain development and structures

The focus of this page is on the development of the human brain in terms of the structures and developmental processes that are related to risk-taking behaviour.

We are born with all our brain structures present. The primitive structures essential for survival develop in the first few months of life. The more advanced areas (towards the front of the brain) are present at birth but continue to develop into adolescence.

Limbic system	This system includes the amygdala, which is connected to the ventral striatum and the nucleus accumbens. The limbic system helps to process emotional experiences and regulate emotions, e.g. controlling impulsive behaviour.
Cerebral cortex	A very thin covering of most of the brain. It is where thinking takes place. It includes the frontal cortex which controls higher cognitive functions, e.g. abstract thinking.
	There is extensive development during childhood and adolescence of the limbic system and the cortex.

Developmental processes

Synaptogenesis	The process by which new synapses are formed between neurons. This takes place before birth and continues postnatally. Synaptogenesis contributes to greater complexity in the brain and cognitive processes, e.g. thinking.
Myelination	Much of early brain growth is due to myelination. Myelin is the fatty substance that insulates many neurons. It allows neurons to conduct electrical impulses more efficiently in the nervous system.
Synaptic pruning	After the age of three, inactive synapses die off – they are 'pruned' out when not used. Synaptic pruning creates organisation in the brain, so areas become specialised for certain functions, e.g. auditory.

Risk-taking and the brain

Dual systems theory	Steinberg (2008) suggested that risk-taking in adolescence (e.g. drug-taking) is directed by the interaction of two brain systems that mature at different times.
	Ventral striatum (VS) An emotion-regulating system matures in response to changes in the VS due to increased dopamine activity in early adolescence. The VS is involved in sensation-seeking behaviour and addiction, and has greater sensitivity in adolescence to rewards than at any other age.
	Prefrontal cortex (PFC) This is a cognitive control system. It matures later than the emotion-regulating system and cannot exert control over risk-taking behaviours. This imbalance during adolescence results in more impulsive behaviour than in childhood or adulthood.

Strategies to reduce risk-taking behaviours using knowledge of brain development

Application 1

Nurse visitation programmes (NVP)

Early stressful experiences can damage the prefrontal cortex, limiting its influence on the ventral striatum (VS) later in life. This can lead to more impulsive behaviour and greater risk-taking.

Reducing stress The principle behind the NVP intervention is to reduce stress in parents. A nurse visits the parent(s)-to-be at home before childbirth and for some time afterwards. The programme trains parents to cope with stressors that could provoke mistreatment and they are put in touch with health services and social support, e.g. friends. Such stress reduction will have a long-term effect on reducing risk-taking later in life.

Do nurse visitation programmes work?

Usefulness Preventing child mistreatment avoids the risk of damaging brain structures and processes at a sensitive period in development. The intervention stimulates brain development by encouraging parents to provide better nurturing care for their child.

Effectiveness Izzo *et al.* (2005) conducted structured interviews with mothers 15 years after they were part of the NVP. They were able to cope better with uncontrollable life stressors than mothers who were not part of the programme.

Practicalities NVP intervention is better (i.e. outcomes for adolescents were more positive) if mothers were visited before *and* after the birth rather than only before the birth.

Application 2

Graduated driver programmes

An obvious form of intervention is to target risk-taking behaviours directly.

Driving and the pre-adult brain Adolescents are frequently involved in driving accidents possibly due to the delay in the maturation of the cognitive control system relative to the emotion regulation system (which matures earlier). This imbalance leads to underdevelopment of cognitive skills crucial to driving, e.g. distance judgement.

Reducing the impact of arousal Two high arousal situations for adolescents are driving and being with friends. So interventions must aim to reduce the impact of such toxic combinations.

Stages of the GDP This programme is available for inexperienced drivers. In the 'learner' stage, the driver is always supervised. In the second 'intermediate' stage the adolescent can drive unsupervised but only during daylight. They can only reach stage 3 ('full privileges') after passing stage 2 and reaching the age of 18.

Do graduate driver programmes work?

Usefulness One of the most useful restrictions in GDPs is that friends are only allowed in stage 2 and only with an adult present.

Effectiveness Research (e.g. Dee *et al.* 2005) shows that GDP participation reduces driving fatalities. The more restrictive the programme the greater the effectiveness.

Practicalities The most effective component of GDPs in reducing accidents is the first extended period of supervision. The longer it takes for adolescents to drive unsupervised, the less risky their driving behaviour.

Risk-taking behaviours amongst adolescents are most likely when the prefrontal cortex cannot exert control over the ventral striatum.

Revision booster

Do not forget to use psychological research to support the strategies you suggest. For example, one strategy to reduce risk-taking behaviour is nurse visitation programmes (e.g. the Nurse-Family Partnership).

Exam-style question examples

Component 3 Section B part (c):

(c) Nadine is a mother-to-be who is considered at high risk of mistreating her baby.

Outline **one** strategy a psychologist might suggest to reduce any stress the baby may experience.   **[10]**

(c) Despite attending school lectures on driving safety, Devon and his friends enjoy driving quickly around the roads surrounding their school during lunchtimes.

Outline the advice a psychologist might give to Devon to reduce his risk-taking behaviour.   **[10]**

How psychology contributes to the success of the economy and society ... Understanding brain development may help improve our children's future.

Key research

Barkley-Levenson and Galván (2014) on the *Adolescent brain*

Background

In past research adolescents have shown heightened sensitivity to rewards and an associated increase of activity in the ventral striatum (VS). This observation may only apply when money is a reward.

Aims and hypotheses

To investigate whether adolescents value money more than adults.

Hypotheses:

H1 Adolescents would be more sensitive than adults to increased expected value (EV = the sum of all of the possible outcomes of a choice multiplied by their probabilities).

H2 Adolescents would show greater VS activation as EV increased, compared to adults.

H3 Adolescents would show a heightened VS response even after matching with adults on the number of gambles accepted.

Method

Design

Laboratory-based quasi-experiment, independent measures.

IV: Adolescent or adult.

DV: Number of gambles in a 'spinner' game and activity in the VS.

Sample

Self-selected sample of 19 adults aged 25 to 30 years (8 men, 11 women) and 22 adolescents aged 13 to 17 (11 boys, 11 girls). All right-handed.

Materials/apparatus

fMRI scans

Procedure

Intake session

1. Informed consent was given by adults and by parents (or legal guardians) for adolescents.

2. Participants detailed their monthly spending money and where it came from.

3. Mean figure for adults = $467.11, for adolescents = $52.50.

4. Participants were each given $20 to be used as 'playing money' in the next session.

fMRI session

5. Each participant did a gambling task while being scanned.

6. On-screen spinner showed potential gains (on one side) and losses (on the other side).

7. Trials - there were 192 gambles (trials) per participant:
   - 24 × fixed loss, EVs ranged from -$6 to -$19.
   - 24 × fixed gain, EVs ranged from +$6 to +$19.
   - 144 × 50:50, EVs ranged from -$7.50 to +$7.50.

8. Participants had to decide on each trial whether or not they would accept the gamble for real money.

Results

H1

1. Increasing the EV made acceptance of a gamble significantly more likely for adolescents.

2. Amount of disposable income had no effect on the link between EV and gamble acceptance.

3. Gamble acceptance did not change for either adolescents or adults in no-risk (gain- or loss-only) trials.

H2

4. As the EV increased, activation in the superior medial prefrontal cortex (PFC) increased.

5. An increased EV was linked to decreased activation in other brain areas, e.g. amygdala and hippocampus.

6. Adolescents showed greater activation to an increased EV in the left VS than did adults but not right VS or medial PFC.

H3

7. A comparison was made between adolescents and adults who had a high rate of gambling acceptance (over 80%), using matched participants. The difference in VS activation in adolescents and adults remained.

Conclusions

The adolescent brain has a uniquely heightened sensitivity to rewards.

The brain's 'valuation system' is confirmed to be located in the medial PFC.

The VS is important in representing valuation in adolescents which is not true in adults.

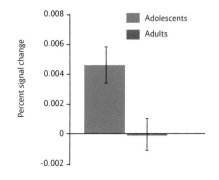

Graph showing the difference in average activation in the left VS between adolescents and adults.

The difference in activation in the left VS between adults and adolescents has been used to explain the difference in their risk-taking behaviours.

How the key research explains ... pre-adult brain development	**Neural sensitivity to rewards** Adolescent risk-taking is underpinned by biological processes that occur in a specific part of the brain.
	Role of ventral striatum There is hyperactivation of the VS (specifically the left VS) in adolescents in response to a reward. The same response does not occur in adults.
	Dual-systems theory Results confirm that the relatively early-maturing VS plays a dominant role in adolescent risk-taking behaviour. The study offers only partial support for the dual-systems theory as it did not investigate the role of the PFC.

Learning how to make sensation-seeking fun can still give your left VS the rewards it wants and help the PFC develop the control it needs.

Links between the topic and the methodological issues

Validity	✛ Internal validity is high as extraneous variables were controlled, e.g. all participants believed they earned $20 during the intake session, controlling the 'house money effect' (people gambling recklessly if money is not theirs).
	▭ The study lacks ecological validity because the gambling decision task bears little resemblance to the kinds of risks adolescents and adults take in real life.
Reliability	✛ High reliability because the researchers used standardised procedures, e.g. gambling task was the same for everyone.
	✛ fMRI scanning followed an established protocol so it was conducted and analysed consistently.
Sampling bias	▭ Defining adolescence as no older than 17 years was arbitrary and may have created a biased sample.
	▭ Self-selected samples may result in volunteers who are very outgoing and more impulsive than non-volunteers, a trait thought to be central to risk-taking.
Ethnocentrism	▭ Individualist cultures value independence which may stem from risk-taking. This view is not necessarily shared in other cultures where individual needs are secondary.

Links between the topic and the debates

Nature/nurture	The process of synaptic pruning is innate (nature), based on a genetically-determined blueprint.
	However, synapses that are underused are removed, showing environmental stimulation.
Reductionism/ holism	Risk-taking is portrayed solely in terms of adolescent brain structure, so this is a reductionist account.
	However, variations in environmental experiences create subtle differences in brain development which is an interactionist view that is more holistic.
Individual/ situational explanations	Risk-taking in terms of brain structure and function is an individual-level explanation.
	Situational influences, e.g. peer and friend relationships, can promote or limit risk-taking behaviours.

Revision booster

Remember to use and explain specific terminology from the key research. This shows the examiner you understand the main psychological concepts of the topic, e.g. 'expected value' (or 'EV', but only use initials after you have used the full term).

Exam-style question examples

Component 3 Section B part (a):

(a) Outline how the research by Barkley-Levenson and Galván (2014) explains risk-taking in adolescents. [10]

Component 3 Section B part (b):

(b) Discuss research into pre-adult brain development in relation to nature/nurture. [15]

(b) Evaluate the reliability of research into pre-adult brain development. [15]

The text on the left provides examples of how you might link the topic to the debates. You need to prepare responses for all of the debates - we haven't got room to cover all of them here.

Background

Perceptual development in children and how this can be studied in babies and animals

Fantz (1966) showed babies the two images above. Babies younger than three months showed no preference but after three months they preferred the image on the left.

How babies perceive faces

At one month, babies look at the 'edges' or contours of faces but at two or three months babies look at the centre of the face and start to perceive the human face as a 'whole' rather than as a collection of parts.

Using the background research

Consider how you could use the background research to support answers to the following questions. See exam guidance on Component 3 Section B questions on page 8.

(a) Outline how the research by Gibson and Walk (1960) explains perceptual development in children. **[10]**

(b) Assess the validity of research into perceptual development in children. **[15]**

(c) Jean is a psychologist and is running a course for kindergarten teachers who want to encourage children's perceptual development.

Outline **one** play strategy Jean might give to the kindergarten teachers to help develop perception in young children. **[10]**

Perceptual development

Perception is the organisation and interpretation of sensory information.

Nature Humans (and other animals) are born with some genetically-determined perceptual abilities.

Nurture Perceptual abilities develop through learning and experience.

Interactionist We are born with predispositions to develop perceptual abilities important for survival (e.g. depth perception), but these develop through experience (e.g. cues to depth such as shadows).

Development of depth perception

Perceiving three dimensions	Promotes survival, e.g. not falling off a cliff. Our brain interprets depth cues - features of the environment that provide information about how far away objects are and where they are in relation to each other.
Research into the role of nature	Bower *et al.* (1971) tested depth perception in 8- to 17-day old babies. Babies raised their arms defensively when shown a smaller object 8 cm away heading towards them, but not a larger object 20 cm away heading towards them (both had same retinal size). This suggests the babies had some depth perception only days after birth.
Research into the role of nurture	Hudson (1960) showed two-dimensional drawings to South African children and adults who were schooled (had formal primary education) or unschooled) The unschooled participants could not correctly interpret the depth cues in the image in the way the schooled participants could. This implies that depth perception is (at least partly) learned through experience of drawings that represent three dimensions.

How perceptual development is studied in babies and animals

Preferential looking	If babies spend longer looking at one stimulus than another stimulus (i.e. they show a preference), this indicates they can distinguish between the two. Researchers can film the baby's eye movements to get a reasonably objective and accurate measure of what the baby can do.
Habituation-dishabituation	Once a stimulus no longer interests babies they look elsewhere (*habituation*). If a baby looks at a new stimulus for a longer time, they are *dishabituated*, i.e. they recognise a difference between the two stimuli.
Electro-encephalogram (EEG)	Babies' EEG activity can be related to what they are viewing, e.g. viewing faces. Babies' EEGs are similar to those of adults, confirming other evidence (e.g. Fantz).
Dark-rearing	Dark-reared animals are deprived of perceptual stimulation. If they are capable of the same perceptual feats as light-reared animals, then this suggests the ability is innate.

Application 1

Sensory integration therapy (SIT)

SIT can be used to aid all children, but specifically those who have difficulties processing sensory information. Some children are hyposensitive to sensory stimuli (e.g. they don't feel pain) whereas others are hypersensitive (e.g. overwhelmed by sounds).

Assessment The child is observed by an occupational therapist who uses checklists to diagnose sensory problems.

The sensory diet A structured programme of sensory experiences, tailored to the individual child (the sensory diet) is devised including play activities (e.g. messy play). Activities become more challenging over time. The programme involves accommodations (adjustments in the child's environment). For example, schools provide sensory-friendly classrooms with reduced lighting and glare, and offer special training for teachers.

Does sensory integration therapy work?

Usefulness The sensory diet can become a daily home routine, and one that fits into the child's and family's schedule. SIT is flexible and realistic about what parents can achieve.

Effectiveness There are serious doubts over the effectiveness of SIT, e.g. Case-Smith *et al.* (2015) found little evidence for SIT's effectiveness after reviewing 19 studies of the therapy.

Practicalities SIT usually requires an occupational therapist specially trained in the diagnosis and treatment of sensory processing disorder. However, the therapy is planned and provided in close consultation with parents and teachers due to the consequences for home and school, e.g. accommodations.

Application 2

Developing form constancy

Form constancy refers to how our perceptual system 'knows' the properties of an object, e.g. shape does not change even when viewed from a different angle. The aim of the application is to develop those constancies that are essential for functioning in everyday life (e.g. through play).

Activities to develop shape constancy Activities can use household objects or toys. For example, the child is asked to identify all the rectangular shapes in a room. Then he or she stands in a different place and repeats the activity.

Activities to develop auditory perceptual constancy Games involve saying the same words but in high and low pitches. This helps the child understand that speech sounds are the same no matter who says them. Listening to music is beneficial for understanding that sounds remain constant under changing conditions, because an instrument (e.g. a guitar) remains that instrument even if its tone or pitch changes.

Does developing form constancy work?

Usefulness Form constancy is fundamental to reading, writing and speech. For example, in whatever way the letter 'L' is represented, it is still the letter 'L' even though the projection of it on our retinas varies.

Effectiveness Newman *et al.* (2016) showed it took just five play sessions of 30 minutes for children to improve their ability to mentally rotate an object.

Practicalities Many activities can be carried out with no specialised equipment (i.e. toys) but toys easily capture a child's enthusiasm and direct their motivation.

Cooking is the sort of activity that could well be part of the sensory diet but it does require a lot of 'accommodation' from parents.

Revision booster

Don't forget to read our exam advice on pages 4–15. Pay particular attention to the advice on how to improve application skills (AO2) on page 10.

Exam-style question examples

Component 3 Section B part (c):

(c) Esther is concerned that her daughter's 'temper-tantrums' are due to overstimulation from her school environment.

Outline advice a psychologist might give to Esther to improve her daughter's difficulties with processing sensory information. **[10]**

(c) Malcolm is a nursery teacher working with children who find it difficult to distinguish between similar sounds in speech (for example 's' and 'f').

Outline the advice a psychologist might give to Malcolm to improve the speech of the children in his nursery. **[10]**

Always look for opportunities to discuss how psychology contributes to the success of the economy and society.

Key research
Gibson and Walk (1960) on the *Visual cliff*

Background

Previous research on early depth perception used animals (e.g. rats, in Lashley and Russell 1934). This research had low validity due to extraneous variables.

Aims

To investigate:

- Whether the ability to perceive and avoid a drop is learned through experience or is part of the child's 'original endowment' (i.e. innate).
- If babies can perceive depth before, after or at the same time as they develop the ability to move around independently.
- Which is more important in depth perception: the density of pattern in the environment (texture) or motion parallax.

Method

Design

Laboratory experiment, repeated measures.

IV: Mothers encouraged their babies either across the shallow or the deep side.

DV: Baby's or young animal's behaviour.

Sample

36 human babies aged six to 14 months, all could crawl. Animal species: chicks, lambs, kids (baby goats), kittens, rats, pigs, dogs and aquatic turtles.

Materials/apparatus

Visual cliff apparatus (see below).

Procedure

1. Participants tested individually. Baby placed on centreboard. Their mother stood to right or left of the shallow or deep side.

2. Mother encouraged baby to crawl towards her across the glass surface.

3. Researchers observed if the baby complied or refused.

4. When young animals were tested, the centreboard was raised so they either descended onto one side or the other.

Controls

5. The chequered sheets were lit from below so there were no reflections.

6. Control experiments with a patternless grey sheet and the chequered sheet was directly against the underside of glass.

7. Controlling for texture density - on some trials, the size of squares on the deep side was increased to appear the same size as squares on the shallow side.

8. Controlling motion parallax - on some trials, the chequered material was attached directly to the glass on both sides. The squares in the pattern were made larger on the shallow side (so they appeared closer).

Results

Human babies

1. Nine refused to move from centreboard.

2. 27 crawled onto shallow side at least once.

3. Three crawled onto the deep side.

4. When mothers called from the deep side, some babies crawled in the opposite direction.

5. Some babies cried with frustration because they did not want to cross the deep side.

Young animals

6. Chicks, kids and lambs never stepped onto the deep side.

7. Hooded rats showed no preference for deep or shallow side.

8. Kittens at four weeks old always chose the shallow side.

9. 76% of the aquatic turtles preferred the shallow side.

Conclusions

Depth perception for young animals is innate.

Human depth perception appears to develop before controlled movement.

Motion parallax is probably an innate cue for depth perception, whereas perception of pattern texture density is learned.

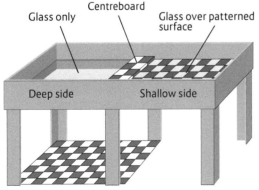

The visual cliff apparatus. Will a baby move across what appears to be a visual cliff? What would a kitten or lamb do?

Glass only • Centreboard • Glass over patterned surface

Deep side • Shallow side

Pattern seen through glass

How the key research explains ... perceptual development	**Development of depth perception in children** Cliff avoidance in humans appears to develop by six months. In that time babies have had opportunities to acquire depth perception through experience, suggesting that depth perception is not innate in humans.
	Contribution of animal research Gibson and Walk's results from animals show that depth perception can be innate, e.g. lambs and kids showed cliff avoidance from birth. However, this cannot be generalised to humans.
	Evolutionary value In order to survive, animals develop depth perception by the time they can move independently. In humans this seems to be an innate predisposition to learn at a certain time rather than an innate ability.

When an observer is moving, things nearby appear to move faster than things relatively further away. This is motion parallax.

Links between the topic and the methodological issues

Validity	✚ Gibson and Walk controlled many potentially extraneous variables enhancing internal validity, e.g. the two sides of the visual cliff were identical in every way except the appearance of depth (the IV).
	▭ Gibson and Walk used their non-human animal results to show that depth perception is innate. But this involves an extrapolation from animals to humans which may not be justified (low external validity).
Reliability	✚ Gibson and Walk's methodology is reliable as they used standardised procedures, e.g. the starting position for each baby or young animal. It also meant that the procedure was easily replicated.
Sampling bias	▭ Animal observations involved species where independent movement is possible from birth. This tells us little about how and when it develops in humans that do not move for some time after birth. This makes it difficult to make valid comparisons of perceptual development.
Ethnocentrism	▭ As people from different cultures have different experiences of the environment, it is possible that depth perception does not develop in every culture as it did in the babies tested by Gibson and Walk.

Links between the topic and the debates

Nature/nurture	Human babies in Gibson and Walk's study were old enough that environmental influences on depth perception cannot be ruled out (nurture).
	However, results from, for example, chicks support the influence of nature as they avoided the deep side essentially from birth.
Reductionism/ holism	Gibson and Walk's research is reductionist as it attributes perceptual development to innate genetic factors.
	A more holistic approach accounts for wider influences on perceptual development, e.g. mother's facial expressions.
Usefulness of research	This research highlights the importance of correcting certain perceptual disorders (e.g. *amblyopia* - 'lazy eye') which might prevent the development of depth perception if they are not treated early on.

Revision booster

Gibson and Walk's control of variables (e.g. controlling for texture density) meant they could more easily infer cause and effect between the IV (shallow or deep) and the DV (cliff avoidance). It is a good example of psychology as a science.

Exam-style question examples

Component 3 Section B part (a):

(a) Using the research by Gibson and Walk (1960), explain perceptual development. **[10]**

Component 3 Section B part (b):

(b) Discuss nature/nurture in relation to research into perceptual development. **[15]**

(b) Discuss methodological issues of research into the development of perception. **[15]**

The debates on the left are examples of how you might link the topic to the debates (you can read about the debates on pages 91-94). In the exam be prepared to think on your feet.

Background

Cognitive development in children and the impact of this on education

Piaget claimed that knowledge was actively constructed by the child with some guidance from the teacher. In contrast, Vygotsky described the process as a collaboration between child and teacher.

The term more knowledgeable other (MKO) *refers to someone who has a better understanding of a task or concept than the learner. This may be a teacher but could be classmate.*

Using the background research

Consider how you could use the background research to support answers to the following questions. See exam guidance on Component 3 Section B questions on page 8.

(a) Using the research by Wood *et al*. (1976), explain how teachers can help children's learning. **[10]**

(b) Discuss the usefulness of research into cognitive development. **[15]**

(c) Anna is a psychologist who has been asked to provide training for primary school teachers.

Outline the advice Anna might give to improve pupils' learning. **[10]**

Cognitive development

Cognitive development refers to the way that people become more skilful learners and thinkers as they get older. There are two contrasting theories.

Theory 1: Piaget's theory of cognitive development

Schemas, disequilibrium and equilibration	Schemas are organised mental structures containing knowledge of some aspect of the world. They develop through two main processes: • **Assimilation** We add new experiences to existing schemas. • **Accommodation** New experiences may mean that existing schemas need to change or a new schema must be created. **Disequilibrium** Children are motivated to learn when new experiences mean they feel 'out of balance' with the world. *Equilibration* is the cycle of assimilation and accommodation that helps restore that balance.
Stages of cognitive development	**Sensorimotor stage** (approximately 0 to 2 years) This includes *object permanence* - a child realises that objects continue to exist even when they cannot be seen. **Pre-operational stage** (approximately 2 to 7 years) Children lack consistent logic and make reasoning errors. **Concrete operational stage** (approximately 7 to 11 years) Logical reasoning is used with physical objects only. A child is capable of *conservation* - understanding that quantity stays constant even if its appearance changes. **Formal operational stage** (approximately 11 years+) Children can now apply logical reasoning to abstract ideas.

Theory 2: Vygotsky's theory of cognitive development

Sociocultural context	Experts (adults or peers) pass on knowledge, skills and cultural values. Language is crucial in learning.
Zone of proximal development (ZPD)	Cognitive development occurs in the gap (ZPD) between what a child understands on their own, and what they could understand in collaboration with an expert.

The impact of cognitive development on education

Piaget: Readiness and discovery learning	A child must have reached the appropriate stage of development in order to be 'ready'. Teachers plan goal-directed discovery learning activities in a variety of contexts to create disequilibrium in the child, motivating them to learn in order to restore equilibrium.
Vygotsky: Scaffolding and collaborative learning	'Scaffolding' a task enables a child to climb to a higher level. Once a task is mastered, scaffolding is removed. Collaborative learning (e.g. peer tutoring) involves a few students at different performance levels working together to achieve a common goal.

Application 1

Context-dependent memory

Cues (or 'triggers') can be powerful aids that help when trying to recall information, especially for students in exams.

Importance of context A cue can help us remember something if the cue is present at encoding (when we learn material) and at retrieval (when we recall the material).

The memory palace Select somewhere that is really familiar, e.g. inside a building (hence 'palace') or a street you often walk down. Form mental images of everything you want to remember and 'place' them in various locations in your 'palace'. To recall the items, take a mental walk through the 'palace'. Each location acts as a cue to trigger your memory of the item placed at the location.

Does context-dependent memory work?

Usefulness Context cues are less useful when answering multiple-choice questions because such questions test recognition not recall. In any case, items in a multiple-choice question act as cues.

Effectiveness The core study by Grant *et al.* (1998) found that students performed better on a test when the context of recall matched the context of learning (i.e. silence in both cases), demonstrating the importance of context.

Practicalities Most exams are taken in large halls that are unfamiliar, so students do not encode material in the place they will have to recall it (so no contextual cues). However, using a mental technique (e.g. memory palace) is a possible use of context because all you need is your imagination.

Application 2

Mind-mapping

Basic mind map elements A mind map has a central element (the main concept) and several lines branching out from it to sub-elements (aspects of the main concept, strictly one per branch). There could be further lines (twigs) leading to lesser elements.

Further elements A complex mind map could include other lines connecting related concepts, using different colours and images.

Psychological basis of mind maps Mind maps help structure knowledge in a meaningful way, and creating mind maps forces a learner to process material meaningfully (semantically). This means information is easier to recall, so *producing* a mind map (process) may be more beneficial than *having* it (outcome).

Does mind-mapping work?

Usefulness Mind maps are helpful because visual representations allow an almost instant appreciation of an area of knowledge (e.g. how concepts relate to each other).

Effectiveness Farrand *et al.* (2002) found that students using mind maps maintained a small but significant increase in recall of material one week later compared with a group not using mind maps.

Practicalities Mind-mapping can be 'learned' reasonably well without help, from materials available online. But to develop it as a useful skill, some training is helpful.

You don't have to live in a palace to use the memory palace technique. Just choose a place you know really well so that you can later 'walk' round it easily.

Revision booster

Choose one of the cognitive strategies outlined on this page to improve your own learning. Use it to create a revision aid for a piece of research of your choice. You can of course apply this to any of the studies/information you need to learn for the exams.

Exam-style question examples

Component 3 Section B part (c):

(c) Martin is an educational consultant who has been asked to provide advice to year 11 pupils about the best way to prepare for their GCSE exams.

Outline **one** strategy Martin might recommend to the pupils to improve their exam revision. **[10]**

(c) Jhumpa has just made her revision timetable and now needs to decide how to revise for her psychology exam.

Outline the advice you might give to Jhumpa to help her prepare effectively for her psychology exam. **[10]**

Key research

Wood *et al.* (1976) on the *Role of tutoring*

Background and aims

Bruner (1973) suggested that children are natural problem-solvers. However, with the intervention of a more skilled tutor who provides scaffolding, children can achieve a goal beyond their present capabilities.

Aims

To investigate a 'natural' tutorial session to gain knowledge about how children respond to different types of help.

Method

Design

Controlled observation in a laboratory environment.

Sample

30 children aged 3-, 4-, or 5-years-old (YO), five boys and five girls in each age group, mainly middle- or lower-middle-class families living within a five-mile radius of Cambridge, Massachusetts, USA. The children's parents responded to ads asking for volunteers (self-selected sample).

The task

To construct a pyramid from a set of jumbled blocks.

Procedure

Tutoring procedure

1. Each child was tutored individually and sat at a small table with the 21 blocks spread out on it.

2. Children had five minutes of free play, then the tutor took two blocks and demonstrated how to join them (each block had a peg and a hole so they fitted together).

3. The tutor gave three possible responses:
   - If the child ignored the tutor and continued to play → tutor repeated how to join two blocks together.
   - If the child selected blocks and assembled them like the tutor but missed out parts → tutor said the construction was incomplete, and suggested that the child compares it with the tutor's and tries to make it similar.
   - If the child used the blocks presented by the tutor → tutor corrected any mistake the child made.

4. The tutor would only intervene if the child stopped building or got into difficulty.

Scoring system

5. Each act of construction was classified as either assisted or unassisted.

6. Tutor interventions were classified into:
   - Direct assistance, e.g. tutor indicated blocks to use.
   - Verbal error prompt, e.g. *Does this look like this?*
   - Verbal attempt to get the child to make more constructions, e.g. *Can you make any more like this?*

The pyramid task had to be fun, interesting, easy enough to be within each child's capabilities, but complex enough to extend each child.

Results

Observations on tutorials

1. Median number of construction 'acts' (e.g. putting blocks together): 3YOs = 39, 4YOs = 41, 5 YOs = 32 (no significant differences between groups).

2. Proportion of 'pairing acts' to complete the pyramid (out of 15): 3YOs = 10%, 4YOs = 50%, 5 YOs = 75%.

3. Reconstructions: 3YOs = 13, 4YOs = 4, 5 YOs = 4.

4. There were no significant differences in overall total number of construction acts between age groups.

Tutorial relationship

5. *Tutorial help* Younger children needed more tutorial help: 3YOs = 64.5% constructions unassisted, 4YOs = 79.3%, 5YOs = 87.5%.

6. *Help from tutor* Median number of assisted constructions: 3YOs = 9, 4YOs = 6.5, 5YOs = 3.

7. *Verbal assistance* 4YOs and 5YOs received a significantly greater proportion of verbal assistance than 3YOs.

8. *Tutor's type of interaction* The number of direct interventions by the tutor dropped by half from 3YOs to 4YOs, and dropped by half again from 4YOs to 5YOs.

Conclusions

Six steps occur during the process of scaffolding (1 = recruitment, 2 = reduction in degrees of freedom, 3 = direction maintenance, 4 = marking critical features, 5 = frustration control, 6 = demonstration).

Comprehension precedes production, e.g. 3YOs were able to recognise a correct solution before they could provide it.

The tutor plays different roles related to age of the child.

How the key research explains ... cognitive development and education	**Implications for children's cognitive development** Tasks which 'push' a child's understanding slightly beyond their current capabilities can advance their thinking abilities. But this only happens if they can recognise what counts as a solution to the problem.

Impact on education A more knowledgeable other (MKO) can assist a child's cognitive development by:

- Providing appropriately demanding tasks.
- Helping a child to recognise possible solutions, e.g. through demonstrations.
- Organising tasks so they are achievable.
- Gradually withdrawing help as the child's thinking develops.

One of the important elements of scaffolding is when the tutor simplifies the task to reduce the number of 'acts' needed by the learner to complete it successfully (reduction in degrees of freedom).

Links between the topic and the methodological issues

Validity	⊕ The task of constructing a pyramid had high validity as it was appealing and similar to the kind of activity children would engage with.
	⊖ Low validity as Wood *et al.*'s study was a controlled observation in a laboratory setting so children may not have behaved naturally.
Reliability	⊕ Wood *et al.* standardised the tutoring procedure, e.g. five minutes' free play for all children. Therefore, there was good reliability.
Sampling bias	⊖ Wood *et al.*'s sample of children was limited because it was drawn from a very narrow geographical area and socioeconomic grouping (middle class).
Ethnocentrism	⊖ Vygotsky valued collaborative activity (a collectivist view) but saw the end goal as individual independent activity (an individualist perspective). Ultimately collaboration was a means to independent behaviour – an ethnocentric perspective.

Links between the topic and the debates

Nature/nurture	Piaget believed the stages of cognitive development progressed in the same biological sequence for every child, supporting the nature argument.
	Vygotsky highlighted the role of experts in the child's cognitive development, which supports nurture.
Free will/ determinism	Children learn best when they are active but they have to choose to be active learners (i.e. exercise their free will).
	Scaffolding of a task is the responsibility of the tutor – a form of environmental determinism.
Usefulness of research	Wood *et al.* demonstrate that scaffolding is a useful way of guiding the teaching/tutorial process. Scaffolding encourages the teacher to be responsive which is useful in promoting cognitive development.

Revision booster

Remember there are 5 marks for AO1 (description) for Component 3 Section B part (a) questions like the one below. So, practise writing a detailed summary of the key research by Wood *et al.*

The other 5 marks are for AO2 (application), explaining what Wood *et al.* tells us about problem-solving in children.

You have about 15 minutes to write such an answer (see advice on page 8 and timings on page 9).

Exam-style question examples

Component 3 Section B part (a):

(a) Outline the research by Wood *et al.* (1976) and explain what it tells us about problem-solving in children. **[10]**

Component 3 Section B part (b):

(b) Discuss methodological issues in relation to research into cognitive development and education. **[15]**

(b) Discuss research into cognitive development and education in relation to determinism. **[15]**

How psychology contributes to the success of the economy and society ... The research on this spread can be used to improve quality of education.

Background

The development of attachment in babies and the impact of failure to develop attachment

The behaviourist explanation for attachment is sometimes called a 'cupboard love' theory because it focuses on food.

Bowlby first proposed the maternal deprivation hypothesis and later proposed a broader theory of attachment.

Using the background research

Consider how you could use the background research to support answers to the following questions. See exam guidance on Component 3 Section B questions on page 8.

(a) Using the research by Ainsworth and Bell (1970), explain the development of attachment. **[10]**

(b) Discuss research into the development of attachment in relation to nature/nurture. **[15]**

(c) Maureen advises day nurseries on how to improve their provision for children.

Outline the advice Maureen might give to a day nursery on high-quality care for young children. **[10]**

The development of attachment

Attachment is a close two-way emotional bond between two individuals, e.g. babies and caregivers. Emotional attachment is indicated by:

- **Proximity-seeking** Staying physically close to an attachment figure.
- **Separation distress** Being upset when an attachment figure leaves.
- **Secure-base behaviour** Being content to leave an attachment figure but touching base when anxious.

Learning theory of attachment

Classical conditioning	Food is an unconditioned stimulus (UCS) → pleasure in the baby. Pleasure is an unconditioned response (UCR).
	Baby associates caregiver (neutral stimulus, NS) with food. Caregiver is now a conditioned stimulus (CS).
	Caregiver (CS) then produces sense of pleasure → conditioned response (CR).
Operant conditioning	**Positive reinforcement** Baby cries and is then comforted. The crying is reinforced and therefore will be repeated.
	Negative reinforcement Caregiver experiences relief when crying stops and therefore repeats the comforting.
Drive reduction	**Primary drives** (e.g. hunger, thirst) These are satisfied by primary reinforcers (e.g. food, water).
	Secondary reinforcers When a caregiver provides food, a baby associates the caregiver with a reduction of primary drives.

Bowlby's (1969) theory of attachment

Monotropy	A baby's attachment is to one (mono) caregiver.
Social releasers and the critical period	Social releasers (e.g. smiling) trigger an innate disposition in caregivers to respond by giving, for example, affection. The first six months is a critical period for attachment.
Internal working model	The caregiver creates a template (working model) of what a relationship is like. This is 'transmitted' between generations.

The impact of failure to develop attachments

Privation and deprivation	**Privation** Baby forms no bond with a caregiver at all.
	Deprivation Bond formed but broken through separation.
Maternal deprivation hypothesis	Bowlby (1944) proposed that deprivation of a maternal bond in the first 30 months leads to emotional maladjustment, e.g. affectionless psychopathy.
Effects of privation	Extreme privation can have permanent effects but may be reversed if sensitive care is given later in childhood (Rutter 1981). Therefore, the first six months may be more of a 'sensitive period' rather than critical.

Application 1

High-quality day nurseries

Features of high-quality day care

- The lower the number of children per caregiver the better.
- Staff should be well-qualified, experienced and knowledgeable about child development.
- Staff turnover should be as low as possible.
- Staff should be responsive and sensitive to children's emotional needs.

Central importance of consistency Consistency of care is a feature of high-quality day nurseries that can contribute to an attachment-friendly environment.

Do high-quality day nurseries work?

Usefulness Consistency of care and affection can provide an attachment that is not identical to the bond between baby and main caregiver (e.g. mother), but is good enough to be beneficial.

Effectiveness High-quality care features caregiver sensitivity. Howes *et al.* (1998) gave 20 hours of sensitivity training to day nursery staff. Staff whose sensitivity improved were more likely to have a secure attachment with the children they were caring for.

Practicalities The 'key person approach' assigns each child (and family) a specific member of staff who cultivates an attachment bond with the child by being approachable, warm, sensitive and responsive.

Application 2

Improving the experience of hospitalisation

Maximise family contact Parents and children can stay with each other on hospital wards. Charities have extended this by building houses or rooms near children's hospitals. With this 'rooming-in', families can stay in close proximity and the bond between primary caregiver and child is maintained.

Provide suitable substitute emotional care Substitute carers in hospital should be sensitive and responsive to a child's emotional needs. They should maintain a child's normal routines as much as possible. Other caregivers in the child's life (e.g. grandparents) should visit regularly to maintain an emotional connection to the family.

Does improving the experience of hospitalisation work?

Usefulness It reduces the stress families come under during hospitalisation, which could otherwise create even more disruption to attachment bonds during separation.

Effectiveness Robertson and Robertson (1971) provided substitute emotional care for children briefly separated from their hospitalised mothers. The care was sensitive and responsive to the children and ensured plenty of contact with their families, including their mothers. The children adjusted well and were happy on reunion with their parents.

Practicalities Hospital staff, working together in teams, place caregiver-child attachment at the forefront of their plans, policies and ward arrangements, e.g. mothers are encouraged to breastfeed to strengthen attachment. All staff are trained to provide emotional support.

The 'key person approach' - high quality day care involves assigning each child in day care to one carer who develops an attachment bond with the children in his/her care.

Revision booster

For section B part (c) questions like those below, make sure you describe how to carry out a strategy that will develop an attachment-friendly environment. Don't simply name it.

Exam-style question examples

Component 3 Section B part (c):

(c) Mercedes has a six-month-old baby and knows she wants to return to her job in six months' time, so has started thinking about childcare arrangements.

Outline the advice a psychologist might give to Mercedes so she can provide substitute emotional care for her baby. **[10]**

(c) Florence is two years old and has to go into hospital for three weeks for treatment. Her mother is concerned about the effects of their separation.

Outline **one** strategy you would recommend to the hospital to help improve Florence's experience of hospitalisation. **[10]**

How psychology contributes to the success of the economy and society ... Understanding the healthy development of babies may help improve their physical and mental futures.

Key research

Ainsworth and Bell (1970) on the *Strange Situation*

Background and aims

Hamburg (1968) believed exploratory behaviour is evolutionarily important. Babies are genetically predisposed to be interested in new features of their environment, leading them to explore and learn.

Aims

To investigate the evolutionary concept of attachment by observing:

- How much one-year-old babies use their mother as a secure base for exploration.
- The extent to which attachment behaviour overcomes exploratory behaviour when alarm is caused by a stranger.
- The baby's behaviour during separation and reunion with their mother.

Method

Design
Controlled observation.

Sample
56 babies (B) and their mothers (M) from white, middle-class families, recruited via paediatricians. 33 babies were 49 weeks old, 23 were 51 weeks.

A confederate acted as the stranger (S) and two observers (O) recorded babies' behaviour.

The Strange Situation
Eight episodes (E) in standard order: (E1) M+B+O, (E2) M+B, (E3) S+M+B, (E4) S+B, (E5) M+B, (E6) B alone, (E7) S+B, (E8) M+B.

No Es were more disturbing than babies' everyday life situations.

Procedure

1. Observation through a one-way observation window.
2. Two Os dictated running commentaries into a tape recorder with a timer clicking every 15 seconds.
3. Commentaries were transcribed and coded.
4. Os recorded the frequency of crying and exploratory behaviour (locomotor, manipulatory and visual).
5. In each 15-second interval a score of 1 was given for each behaviour (maximum of 12 per three-minute episode).

Classifying behaviour

6. E2, E3, E5, E8 were scored for interaction with mother.
7. E3, E4, E7 were scored for interaction with stranger.
8. Behaviour categories rated on seven-point scales:
   - Proximity- and contact-seeking behaviours, e.g. approaching, reaching.
   - Contact-maintaining behaviours, e.g. clinging, embracing, resisting release.
   - Proximity- and interaction-avoiding behaviours, e.g. ignoring adult, moving away.
   - Contact- and interaction-resisting behaviours, e.g. pushing away, angry screaming.
   - Search behaviour scored in separation episodes E4, E6, E7, e.g. following mother to the door.

Results

Exploratory behaviour

1. E2 to E3: Significant reduction in exploration.
2. E5 and E6: Visual and manipulatory exploration increased in E5, declined in E6.
3. E7: Exploration at lowest.
4. E2: Baby looked mostly at toys and the room and only glanced occasionally at mother.
5. E3: Baby looked more at stranger.

Crying

6. Minimal crying in E2 which did not increase significantly in E3.
7. Crying increased in E4 and reduced in E5. It increased significantly in E6 and did not decrease significantly in E7.

Search behaviour during separation

8. Mean search behaviour was moderate (3.0) in E4. It was significantly stronger (4.6) in E6 and moderate (2.5) in E7.
9. E6: 37% of babies cried minimally but searched strongly, 20% cried a lot but searched weakly, 32% cried and searched.

This key research involved mothers – but a considerable number of babies are more strongly attached to their fathers than their mothers.

Conclusions

Attachment and attachment behaviours are not identical – the predisposition to seek proximity is the attachment. Attachment *behaviour* increases in threatening situations of danger or separation.

Strong attachment behaviour (seeking proximity) cannot co-exist with exploratory behaviour, but mother (safe base) overcomes this.

Attachment behaviours are often stronger after separation.

There are individual differences in the quality of attachments.

| How the key research explains ... the development of attachment | **Bowlby's evolutionary theory** The Strange Situation supports Bowlby's view that infant–mother attachment is 'adaptive' (promotes survival), e.g. the presence of the mother encouraged exploratory behaviour and her absence discouraged it. Absence also increased attachment behaviours (e.g. crying and searching) which are related to protection from threat. |
| | **Failure to develop attachments** Romanian adoptees (Kumsta *et al.* 2015) failed to form attachments because of a lack of early emotional care (privation). These adoptees were clingy and proximity-seeking, behaviours that matched the way some babies reacted to separation in the Strange Situation. This suggests that lack of attachment may underlie clingy behaviour in both the short- and long-term. |

One-way observation window

The Strange Situation puts a baby in a strange environment and observes their responses to a stranger and also to being left alone.

Links between the topic and the methodological issues

Validity	✛ High internal validity because controlled laboratory conditions allowed comparisons of exploration and attachment behaviours.
	⊂ The Strange Situation was artificial. A mother might behave differently towards her child than she would at home, so low in external validity.
Reliability	✛ Observations were standardised using five behavioural categories. Inter-rater reliability of four babies in the Strange Situation was very high (e.g. +.99 for exploration).
	⊂ Some mothers diverged from the Strange Situation 'script' so Strange Situation experiences may not have been consistent from one infant–mother pair to the next.
Sampling bias	⊂ Babies were all from white, middle-class families, a restricted sample. This means that generalisations about attachment and exploration are questionable.
Ethnocentrism	⊂ The Strange Situation is an ethnocentric measure of attachment, based on the values of one culture (USA). It means that infant–mother behaviour from other cultural groups may appear 'abnormal'.

Revision booster

Students often forget that social sensitivity is an ethical consideration – see below left.

Links between the topic and the debates

Nature/nurture	Attachment behaviours are the result of nature, e.g. safe base behaviour is important for safety and survival.
	Attachment behaviours are also influenced by nurture because they are situationally determined, e.g. the quality of the relationship with the mother.
Usefulness of research	Attachment theory and research have been influential in changing attitudes towards parenting of young babies, e.g. by showing that distressed babies can be comforted without learning to be over-dependent.
Ethical considerations	It seems ethically questionable to design the Strange Situation to cause distress.
	The research is socially sensitive because it has important implications for parents who work away from the home.

Exam-style question examples

Component 3 Section B part (a):

(a) Outline the research by Ainsworth and Bell (1970) and use it to explain the development of attachment. **[10]**

Component 3 Section B part (b):

(b) Discuss methodological issues in relation to research into the development of attachment. **[15]**

(b) Discuss ethical considerations in relation to research into the development of attachment. **[15]**

How psychology contributes to the success of the economy and society ... Mothers and fathers make important contributions to the economy, so research on the best forms of care for babies is important.

Background

The influence of television advertising on children and the stereotyping in such advertising

Children's toys (e.g. Ken and Barbie above) often communicate stereotypes about how men and women should act, dress, think and talk.

Food advertising and childhood obesity

Research shows that obesity in children is due partly to their susceptibility to food-related cues which trigger eating.

Using the background research

Consider how you could use the background research to support answers to the following questions. See exam guidance on Component 3 Section B questions on page 8.

(a) Using the research by Johnson and Young (2002), explain the impact of advertising on children **[10]**

(b) Discuss the reliability of research into the impact of advertising on children. **[15]**

(c) Karel is a marketing psychologist who advises advertising media companies.

Outline the advice Karel might give an advertising executive to reduce the impact of advertising on children. **[10]**

Effects of TV advertising on children

The effects depend on the age of the child and features of the ad. Ads have intentional and unintentional effects (the latter are almost always negative).

Intentional effects

Greater brand awareness	**Recognition** There is a positive correlation between the amount of television children watch and the number of brand logos they recognise from a collection shown to them.
	Recall Younger children find it more difficult to recall brands than older children (15–18 years). This is because they: • Are not able to tell the difference between ads and, for example, TV programmes. • Cannot understand that an ad has persuasive intent, e.g. it is trying to sell them something.

Unintentional effects

Parent-child conflict	Parent-child conflict arises out of child 'pester power', with the many requests for a preferred advertised brand refused by parents. The conflict begins early, e.g. two years old.
Dissatisfaction and unhappiness	**Social comparison theory** Children view ads and compare themselves with people who are happy because of the products they buy. The children then experience dissatisfaction because of the contrast between what they expect and what they get. The more ads they watch, the greater the dissatisfaction.

Stereotyping in children's TV advertising

Gender stereotyping	**Active and passive** Boys and girls are equally likely to appear in ads, but boys tend to be portrayed as active and aggressive whereas girls tend to be portrayed as passive.
	Types of toys Linked to traditional gender-role stereotypes, e.g. ads for boys' toys feature activity, competition, battle and destruction, ads for girls' toys emphasise the importance of an attractive physical appearance.
	Language used Narratives in ads aimed at girls include words related to appearance, e.g. 'sparkly'. Boys' ads include more aggressive and power-related language as well as more references to science (Owen and Padron 2015).
Effects of gender stereotyping	**Social learning theory** (e.g. Bandura 1986) Suggests that gender-stereotyped roles can be learned from media models through imitation, identification and vicarious reinforcement. For example, girls who watch ads where girl or women characters are rewarded (e.g. for passivity) are more likely to imitate this.
Ethnic stereotyping	Historically, African-American characters were almost absent from children's TV ads (or indeed any ads). Frequency of portrayal has increased, but African-American characters are still often presented in stereotyped roles, e.g. an athlete rather than a scientist.

Application 1

Limiting television advertising

Total ban Norway has a total ban. The US *Campaign for a Commercial-Free Childhood* (CCFC, now called *Fairplay*) has proposed a total ban on advertising to children under 12 years.

Partial ban The *UK Code of Broadcast Advertising* bans ads that appeal to children shown during children's programmes.

Self-regulation Encourage companies to sign up voluntarily, e.g. Mars pledged not to advertise during children's programmes.

Does limiting television advertising work?

Usefulness Interventions to restrict advertising have been closely linked to preventing and reducing childhood obesity, with economic and health benefits to individual children and their families.

Effectiveness Research has shown that, if all TV advertising of unhealthy foods was banned in the US, somewhere between one in seven and one in three American children would not be obese (Veerman *et al.* 2009).

Practicalities The Obesity Health Alliance (2016) proposals:

- Ban all ads promoting unhealthy foods and drinks before 9 pm.
- Limit the use of advertising techniques that appeal to children.
- Stricter definition of the foods that cannot be advertised.

Application 2

Media literacy interventions

Cognitive defence An appropriate strategy involves teaching children directly about the purposes of ads and ways of thinking critically about advertising, marketing and consumer culture.

Affective defence *Affective* refers to 'emotion-based'. Children should be encouraged to develop critical attitudes towards ads, especially those that appeal to the emotions. The more cynical children's attitudes are towards TV in general, the less vulnerable they are to the persuasive intent of ads.

A complete intervention should aim to strengthen both cognitive and affective defences.

Do media literacy interventions work?

Usefulness Interventions that avoid the negative consequences of advertising are useful because they reduce parent-child conflict over buying advertised products. They also decrease the dissatisfaction and unhappiness that children experience due to failure to fulfil their high expectations.

Effectiveness Increasing children's knowledge of persuasive intent (cognitive defence) increases their scepticism of ads, encouraging more negative attitudes towards the messages in ads. Children will then have less of a preference for specific advertised brands and are less likely to ask for them.

Practicalities Provide children with the knowledge to understand advertising critically. Give them practice in retrieving and using it to process an ad while they watch it. Develop in children a disbelieving attitude towards all they watch on TV.

Limiting junk food ads during children's programmes may not reduce the impact of advertising because a lot of children watch other programmes and these aren't covered by the UK Code of Broadcast Advertising.

Revision booster

It pays to take breaks during revision. Why not relax and watch some TV? And you can kill two birds with one stone – relax and watch children's TV, and think about what you have learned about the impact of advertising!

Exam-style question examples

Component 3 Section B part (c):

(c) Shirley is an influential child psychologist who is concerned about the impact of TV advertisements on children under 12 years old.

Outline **one** strategy Shirley might recommend to the government to reduce the impact of TV advertisements on children. **[10]**

(c) Ramone works with primary school children to increase their awareness of the impact of TV advertising.

Outline the advice you would give to Ramone to increase the children's awareness of the effects of advertising. **[10]**

Key research

Johnson and Young (2002) on *Gendered voices*

Background

Ads and TV programmes are a cultural resource for children – they provide information and role models about how to act as consumers and in terms of gender roles (e.g. Kline 1993).

Aims

To investigate:

- Whether the language of ads aimed at preschool/early elementary school children is scripted differently for boys and girls.
- How gender is used as a discourse code to link products to gender roles.

Method

Design

Discourse analysis, content analysis.

Sample of commercials

Children's TV cartoons from American commercial networks, independent stations in New England and the TV channel *Nickelodeon* during the autumn of 1996, 1997 and 1999.

The 1996 and 1997 samples were 15 half-hour programmes. The 1999 sample was 24 half-hour programmes. The total number of commercials was 478 (149 from 1996, 133 from 1997, 196 from 1999). There were between 8.2 and 8.9 commercials per programme.

Procedure

Gendered voice

1. Analysis of discourse was used to categorise the gender of any speaker.
2. Gender was assessed in: (i) voice-overs, (ii) verb elements, (iii) speaking lines given to boys and girls, (iv) use of the word 'power' in ads aimed at boys.

Targeting

3. Ads were categorised into: food, toys, educational/public service messages, recreational facilities and video/film promotions.
4. 188 toy commercials were used, 147 of them different.
5. Ads were classified in terms of target audience: (i) target audience boys, boys only portrayed, (ii) target audience girls, girls only portrayed, (iii) both boys and girls.

Voice-overs

6. Voice-overs were considered to be gendered in terms of two aspects: (i) the gender of the voice-over, (ii) whether the voice-over was gender-exaggerated.

Verbs

7. Ads were classified into verbs that were related to: action (e.g. fly), competition/destruction (e.g. crush), agency/control (e.g. rule), limited activity (e.g. look), feeling and nurturing (e.g. cuddle).

Results

Gendered voice

1. 55% of the girl-oriented and 53% of the boy/girl-oriented ads included a verbal utterance.
2. 21% of the ads aimed at boys contained the words 'power' or 'powerful'.

Targeting

3. More ads were targeted at boys than at girls.
4. 37% of toy ads for boys were action figures.
5. 44% of toy ads for girls were 'posable figures' (e.g. Barbie dolls).

Voice-overs

6. 100% of ads featuring boys had masculine voices.
7. 89% of girl-oriented ads had feminine voices but also some masculine voices.
8. 80% of voices in boy-oriented ads were gender-exaggerated, and same in 87% of girl-oriented ads.

Verbs

9. There were significantly more feeling/nurturing verb elements in girl-oriented ads.
10. Boy-oriented ads had over 12 times more competition/destruction verb elements than girl-oriented ads.

Conclusions

Language that polarises gender continues to be presented in consumer culture for children to model.

Children accept exaggerated gender in voice-overs.

Ads present children with stereotypical language which communicates that boys prefer action and girls like to talk.

Names for boys' toys (e.g. 'Big Time Action Hero') reflect a gender polarisation in how toys are advertised to children.

How the key research explains ... the impact of advertising on children	**Children's play is gender-based** Children tend to play in different ways that match their gender, e.g. boys are active and powerful, and girls are quiet and generally passive.
	Boys and girls communicate differently Ads use gendered rather than neutral language, and exaggerate the gender features of voices. Voice-overs indicate that boys and girls have different, traditionally-defined roles.
	Social learning and modelling The gendered language of ads provides models for children, essentially telling them how it is appropriate for boys and girls to speak, behave and buy.

Children may be presented with quite different gender representations in ads aimed at adults or a family audience. This runs counter to the messages of gender equality that children often receive from their parents and teachers.

Links between the topic and the methodological issues

Validity	✚ Johnson and Young's categories for 'gendered voice' (e.g. use of the word 'power') were relevant to gender stereotyping in children's advertising, so had high internal validity.
	▭ The research was correlational (e.g. obesity and exposure to food ads with lack of exercise), so lacks internal validity due to uncontrolled extraneous variables.

Reliability	✚ The key research used standardised procedures to analyse the ads, e.g. the content analysis categories were clear and did not overlap.
	▭ Some measures were not objective as they were hard to operationalise, e.g. the degree of gender exaggeration.

Sampling bias	▭ The sample of ads may not be representative of all advertising aimed at children because the ads were all from children's cartoon programmes, which is not the only type of programmes that children watch.

Ethnocentrism	✚ Johnson and Young focused on one culture (the USA) to understand the meanings of ads. They did not assume that their conclusions applied to any other culture.

Methodological issues are discussed in Chapter 1 and also on pages 95-96.

Revision booster

We need to appreciate this topic is socially sensitive. It concerns gender differences and whether they should be encouraged or downplayed in children. At the same time, we need to consider the tension between the rights of advertisers to sell their products as they wish and their wider social responsibilities.

Links between the topic and the debates

Nature/nurture	Children learn gender roles from the language and behaviour presented in ads, supporting nurture.
	If children are born predisposed to behaving in gender-stereotyped ways (e.g. aggression due to male hormones), it would be as a result of nature.

Usefulness of research	Research could be used to make parents and advertisers more aware of the extent of gender stereotyping in children's ads, especially in terms of language.

Individual/ situational explanations	Children model their behaviour on environmental experiences, e.g. TV ads (situational).
	But children's internal cognitive processes (e.g. expectations) determine how they respond to TV ads (an individual explanation).

Exam-style question examples

Component 3 Section B part (a):

(a) Outline the research by Johnson and Young (2002) and use it to explain the impact of advertising on children. **[10]**

Component 3 Section B part (b):

(b) Discuss the validity of research into the impact of advertising on children. **[15]**

(b) Discuss nature/nurture in relation to research into the impact of advertising on children. **[15]**

Background

Physiological and non-physiological explanations of criminal behaviour

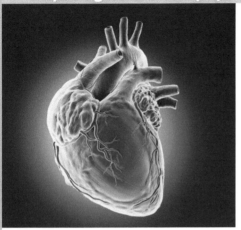

Criminal behaviour can be understood in terms of biology (physiology). Biological markers (such as heart rate) are characteristics that can be objectively measured. They may be used in research to demonstrate that criminal behaviour may have a biological (physiological) basis. But don't forget there are also non-biological explanations, such as learning the behaviour from people around you.

What's the difference between 'physiological' and 'biological'? See page 70 for an explanation.

Revision booster

It is important to know some background research as it allows you to show top level AO3 evaluation skills by making comparisons and contrasts with key research.

Using the background research

Consider how you could use the background research to support answers to the following questions. See exam guidance on Component 3 Section B questions on page 8.

(a) Use the key research by Raine *et al.* (1997) to explain criminal behaviour. **[10]**

(b) Discuss nature/nurture in relation to research into what makes a criminal. **[15]**

(c) Renee is a criminal psychologist who works with prisoners to help reduce recidivism.

Suggest **one** biological strategy Renee might teach the prisoners she works with to prevent them from reoffending. **[10]**

What makes a criminal?

Advances in neuroscience have meant that new evidence has been produced for the role of biology (physiology) in criminal behaviour.

However, other psychologists look at non-physiological factors that may explain why people commit crime, such as their upbringing or cognitive factors.

Physiological explanations of criminal behaviour

Hormones (Glenn and Raine 2014) Low levels of cortisol and increased testosterone in childhood predict later aggressiveness.

Low resting heart rate (Choy *et al.* 2017) Resting heart rate is an early biological marker for a gender gap in later criminal behaviour (e.g. violence and drug-related crime).

Genes (Brunner *et al.* 1993) Case study of a violent Dutch family identified a mutation in the MAOA gene ('warrior gene').

Brain dysfunction (Raine *et al.* 1997) Possible links between brain dysfunction and violence, e.g. people with exaggerated amygdala reactivity show impulsive aggression whereas people who are aggressive but more cold and calculating have reduced amygdala volume and functioning (Glenn and Raine 2014).

Non-physiological explanations of criminal behaviour

Social explanation: Families Farrington *et al.* (2006) conducted longitudinal research, interviewing 411 boys/men periodically from the age of 8 up to 48 years of age. Criminal records and data from teachers about aggressive behaviour was collected. Results suggested that criminal behaviour is influenced by risk factors.

Social explanation: Norms Sutherland's (1947) differential association theory proposed that criminal behaviour is learned through the frequency and intensity of interactions primarily with family members, close friends or groups (e.g. gangs in the community). Through this interaction, people acquire the norms and values of the criminal group in preference to the norms and values of non-criminal groups.

Cognitive explanations Kohlberg's (1984) theory of moral development was based on levels of moral reasoning. Additionally, Palmer and Hollin (1998) found clear differences in moral reasoning between delinquents and non-delinquents, with young men showing the least mature reasoning (pre-conventional morality).

Application 1

Drug treatments

Psychopharmacology Looks at the effects drugs have, e.g. effects on treating psychological disorders. They can help prevent associated criminal behaviour.

Antipsychotic drugs These work by altering the effect of chemicals in the brain, e.g. blocking dopamine receptor sites, particularly D2 receptors. Reduced dopamine activity means a decrease in the positive symptoms of schizophrenia.

An example of an antipsychotic drug - Clozapine Used to treat severe schizophrenia. The drug should be kept in its blister pack until taken. The initial dose is usually 12.5 mg, taken once or twice a day.

Do drug treatments work?

Usefulness Drug treatments can address criminal and violent behaviour across a range of mental health issues and are prescribed to both juveniles and adults.

Effectiveness Antipsychotic drugs effectively reduce violent crime amongst prison populations particularly amongst those with a psychological disorder.

Practicalities Psychopharmacologists build a therapeutic alliance with the offender. Side effects and non-adherence to medication are also issues that need to be addressed.

Application 2

Nutritional supplements

Omega-3 Deficiencies may result in limited regulation of the limbic system, leading to self-control problems and aggressive behaviour. Antisocial behaviour in prisons, including violence, is reduced by supplementing young offenders' diets with vitamins, minerals and essential fatty acids, e.g. omega-3 found in salmon.

Example of a nutritional supplement regime for prisoners (Gesch *et al.* 2002) Nutritional supplements are packed into blister packs labelled with the prisoner's name, cell and prison number. An omega-3 capsule is taken four times per day and a vitamin/mineral capsule at lunchtime. The omega-3 and vitamin/mineral supplement dosages should equal the recommended daily intake and be taken every day for a month. Supplements are consumed under the watch of prison guards to ensure compliance.

Do nutritional supplements work?

Usefulness Supplements are useful to HM Prison Service as a strategy to reduce disruption in prisons or to prevent recidivism if combined with a nutrition education programme that prisoners follow after their release.

Effectiveness Gesch *et al.* reported a 26% improvement in the disciplinary record of young offenders (men) who took supplements though effectiveness may depend on the concentration of omega-3 given to offenders.

Practicalities Nutritional supplements may be relatively easy to enforce in prison as there is a network of support to ensure the prisoner continues to take the supplements. However, this may not be the case once an offender is released.

Fish oil (often found in vitamin supplements) is associated with decreased aggression in the general population as well as in violent individuals.

Revision booster

We have provided a choice of two application strategies. Knowing both of them can be useful as it gives you more to write when answering an exam question – however, if the question says 'one' (as in the first question below) then you must only use one application. Questions never ask for two applications so you can always just focus on one (but it may enhance your mark if you cover two).

Exam-style question examples

Component 3 Section B part (c):

(c) Andrew is a prison governor. He wants to apply biological interventions while offenders are in his prison, with the aim of preventing any criminal behaviour once they leave prison.

Outline **one** biological strategy a criminal psychologist may recommend to Andrew that could be used to prevent offenders from committing crime in the future. **[10]**

(c) Seemab works with families of criminals as part of the Troubled Families Programme. Her job is to prevent them from engaging in future criminal behaviour.

What advice might a psychologist give to Seemab about biological strategies to prevent criminal behaviour in the families she works with? **[10]**

Key research
Raine *et al.* (1997) on *Murderers*

Background

Previous research
This has shown that violent offenders have poorer brain functioning than non-offenders (Raine 1993).

Brain scanning techniques (e.g. Positron Emission Tomography, PET) allow researchers to localise brain areas that may be dysfunctional in violent offenders.

Hypotheses
H1 Seriously violent individuals have localised brain dysfunction in the prefrontal cortex, angular gyrus, amygdala, hippocampus, thalamus and the corpus callosum.

H2 There is no dysfunction in other brain areas, e.g. caudate, putamen, globus pallidus, midbrain and cerebellum.

Method

Design
Quasi-experiment, matched participants design.

IV: NGRI (see below) murderer or not murderer.

DV: Activity in specified brain regions assessed by PET scans.

Sample
41 murderers, 39 men and 2 women, with a mean age of 34.3 years. They had all been charged with murder or manslaughter and had pleaded not guilty by reason of insanity (NGRI).

Psychological disorders: schizophrenia (6), history of head injury (23), history of psychoactive drug abuse (3), affective disorder (2), epilepsy (2), history of hyperactivity and learning disability (3) and personality disorder (2). A control group of people with no history of psychological disorders was matched to the murderers by age and sex.

Materials/apparatus
PET scanner, continuous performance task (CPT) thermoplastic head holder, glucose tracer (flurodeoxyglucose or FDG).

Procedure

1. Participants took part under protocols, e.g. consent forms approved by the university.
2. Participants worked for 32 minutes on the CPT (target recognition).
3. CPT designed to test target areas of the brain.
4. Participants practised the CPT for 10 minutes before the FDG injection.
5. Participants started the CPT 30 seconds before the FDG.
6. 32 minutes after the FDG a PET scan was carried out on each participant.
7. Ten slices (pictures) at 10 mm intervals were taken of the cortical and subcortical regions.

Results

Brain differences

1. Murderers had reduced activity in the prefrontal cortex, left angular gyrus and corpus callosum (areas linked to violent behaviour).
2. Murderers also had reduced activity in the amygdala, thalamus and hippocampus in the left hemisphere.
3. Murderers showed higher activity in the cerebellum and amygdala, thalamus and hippocampus in the right hemisphere.
4. No differences between the NGRIs and the control group in the caudate, putamen, globus pallidus and midbrain.

Behavioural performance on the CPT

5. Groups didn't differ on any aspect of the CPT.

Other characteristics (not used when matching participants)

6. Handedness: Left-handed murderers (6) had less amygdala symmetry and higher medial prefrontal activity than right-handed.
7. Ethnicity: Comparison between 14 murderers of different ethnicities and white murderers showed no difference in metabolic activity in the brain.
8. Head injury: No difference in brain activity between murderers with a history of head injury and murderers without a history of head injury.

Reduced activity in the prefrontal cortex may explain why violent criminals experience loss of self-control.

Conclusions

There is preliminary evidence that NGRI murderers have different brain functioning from non-murderers.

But Raine *et al.* warn that results do not show that violent behaviour is determined solely by biology, nor that murderers pleading NGRI are not responsible for their actions.

The results do not show that brain dysfunction causes violence - the results relate only to criminal behaviour.

Evaluation of research on what makes a criminal

How the key research explains ... what makes a criminal	Murderers have reduced activity in the prefrontal cortex and the left hippocampus. This may explain their loss of self-control and increased aggression.
	Damage to the amygdala could mean murderers are less likely to perceive threatening situations as dangerous, supporting the 'fearlessness theory' of violence.

Links between the topic and the methodological issues

Validity	▭ Quasi-experiments may be affected by extraneous variables and so brain areas per se may not cause murderous behaviour but other factors are responsible, e.g. early experience. This lowers validity.
	▭ Self-reports used by Farrington *et al.* (see page 142) may have low validity if the boys lied about their level of offending.
Reliability	⇧ The PET scans of the NGRIs and the control group have high external reliability as there is a standardised procedure.
	▭ Farrington *et al.*'s results may also be seen as having low reliability as data about parents' attitudes to discipline and separation from their sons was conducted by different social workers.
Sampling bias	▭ Murderers who pleaded not guilty by reason of insanity (NGRI) are not representative of all violent murderers or all examples of aggressive behaviour.
Ethnocentrism	▭ Farrington *et al.*'s understanding of family relationships is from an individualist perspective. Therefore, the way in which the families approached disruption may be different from collectivist cultures where the family unit may have strategies to maintain cohesion.

A 'broken mind' is often related to violent behaviour. However, brain dysfunction alone does not determine aggression, though clearly it is a contributory factor.

Links between the topic and the debates

Nature/nurture	The nature argument suggests that innate characteristics of murderers (e.g. reduced activity in the prefrontal cortex) explain their violent crime.
	However, NGRI murderers could have been born with their brain dysfunction (nature) or it could have been a result of their life experiences (nurture).
Free will/ determinism	Brain dysfunction alone does not determine violent behaviour, e.g. low amygdala activity in the left hemisphere is related to violence but does not cause it.
	People can exert free will, e.g. people who grow up in a criminal family do not always become criminals.
Reductionism/ holism	Physiological explanations reduce causes of violent crimes to structures, e.g. the 'warrior gene' MAOA.
	Raine *et al.* (1997) believe violent behaviour is explained by the disrupted interaction of brain networks and is therefore a holistic perspective.

Revision booster

On Paper 3, part (a) 10-mark questions ask you to use the key research to explain the topic area. For example, in the first question below you would need to include good knowledge and understanding of the Raine *et al.* study and, importantly, you would need to show how the results and conclusions explain criminal behaviour.

Exam-style question examples

Component 3 Section B part (a):

(a) Use the key research by Raine *et al.* (1997) to explain criminal behaviour. **[10]**

Component 3 Section B part (b):

(b) Evaluate the validity of research into what makes a criminal. **[15]**

(b) Discuss the extent to which research into criminal behaviour can be considered determinist. **[15]**

How psychology contributes to the success of the economy and society ...
Understanding physiological and non-physiological explanations of criminal behaviour may lead to ways to deal with criminal behaviour.

Background
Motivating factors and bias in the collection and processing of forensic evidence

Fingerprints are unique patterns, made by raised ridges and recessed furrows on fingers and thumbs. They are used successfully as a means of identification because of their uniqueness.

Types of forensic evidence

Forensic evidence takes the form of solid evidence, e.g. firearms, fired bullets, drugs and paraphernalia or computers.

Forensic evidence may also include fragile evidence, e.g. hairs, DNA, body fluids or unsolved (latent) fingerprints from a crime scene.

Using the background research

Consider how you could use the background research to support answers to the following questions. See exam guidance on Component 3 Section B questions on page 8.

(a) Using the key research by Hall and Player (2008), explain how bias can be reduced in the collection and processing of forensic evidence. **[10]**

(b) Discuss methodological issues in relation to the collection and processing of forensic evidence. **[15]**

(c) Imran's work with the Metropolitan Police Fingerprint Bureau has led him to work on many crimes that have a highly emotional context, such as murder investigations.

Outline **one** strategy Imran may have been given in his training with the Metropolitan Police that may help him to reduce any bias when making fingerprint identifications. **[10]**

Collection and processing of forensic evidence

Forensic experts should guard against factors that lead to predictable errors in making judgements when collecting forensic evidence.

- 'Motivating factors' may be an issue because experts are under pressure to solve a case.
- Cognitive biases may be an issue, e.g. the effects existing beliefs have on the way a situation is perceived.

Motivating factors and forensic evidence

Emotional motivation in fingerprint analysis Charlton *et al.* (2010) used semi-structured interviews with 13 experienced fingerprint experts. They concluded that experts are influenced by psychological factors, e.g. job satisfaction and emotional rewards associated with catching criminals.

Influence of crime type on emotions Dror *et al.* (2005) used low- and high-emotional contexts from a violent or non-violent crime scene. Twenty-seven student participants had to match unambiguous or ambiguous fingerprints. When a match between fingerprints was ambiguous, participants were influenced by contextual information.

Need for cognitive closure Kruglanski *et al.* (2006) found that, when the need to conclude a decision-making process is high, quicker and more confident judgements are made. Better decision-making occurs when the need for cognitive closure is low.

Biases and forensic evidence

People make information processing errors known as *cognitive biases*. These may lead to errors in judgement:

Contextual bias Irrelevant contextual information of a crime (e.g. details of the suspect or the way information is presented) influences reasoning.

Confirmation bias Experts may look only for confirming evidence for pre-existing beliefs rather than potentially conflicting evidence, especially when under pressure to solve a case.

Role effects Experts identify either with the prosecution or defence teams. This may introduce a subconscious bias that can influence decisions.

Integrated automated fingerprint identification system (IAFIS) Examiners may favour identifications at the top of the search list, creating a cognitive bias (Dror 2013).

Application 1

Analysis, comparison, evaluation and verification (ACE-V)

ACE-V minimises the effects of bias in fingerprint identification.

1. Analysis phase Latent (unsolved) prints are taken from a crime scene and examined to determine the overall pattern of the ridges, including magnified analysis. Causes of distortion of the print are assessed.

2. Comparison phase Fingerprints are taken from the suspect and inked. The inked prints are examined to find an image that is consistent with the level of detail found in the latent print.

3. Evaluation phase Inked and latent prints are examined side by side and corresponding features are evaluated to see if they are similar in terms of clarity.

4. Verification phase Positive identifications are verified by a second expert who repeats the process without knowing there is a positive identification, i.e. 'blind.'

Does ACE-V work?
Usefulness ACE-V provides a structured approach that allows experts to conduct an initial identification that is cross-checked to determine the accuracy of the identification.

Effectiveness ACE-V is a scientific process that compares features in the inked and latent print. The 'blind' verification process reduces the errors due to bias.

Practicalities Each phase requires caution, time and effort but this is justified given the importance of reducing cognitive bias.

Application 2

Linear sequential unmasking (LSU)

LSU is a technique that adopts a linear line of reasoning where the expert first examines the evidence from a crime scene before seeing known reference material, e.g. a case report.

The process of LSU An initial analysis of the evidence is only followed by other case information when necessary. Information is gradually unmasked in sequence of importance, e.g. details of whether a crime involved violence.

An example of LSU Dror *et al.* (2015) suggest that examiners should be permitted to revisit and alter their initial analysis of trace evidence but should not be allowed to remove any evidence. Examiners can also express their confidence about fingerprint identifications.

Does LSU work?
Usefulness It means evidence is interpreted consistently and offers restrictions that reduce bias while providing examiners with flexibility in their work.

Effectiveness The decision to provide case information to the examiner is based on weighing up the relative contribution made to the examiner's work against the potential bias - a cost-benefit analysis.

Practicalities Consider which and how many pieces of additional evidence should be given to the examiner.

Revision booster

Students often forget to use the context of an exam scenario when describing application strategies. Always mention details from the scenario so you can show how you are applying the strategy.

Forensic experts are motivated to find the offender by collecting evidence from the crime scene as quickly as possible (cognitive closure).

Exam-style question examples
Component 3 Section B part (c):

(c) Michelle has just qualified as a forensic expert and has been asked to process fingerprints from a door handle on a house that has been used in a drug-related crime. She has been given the crime scene report from the police.

   Outline the advice a criminal psychologist might give to Michelle to reduce the potential for bias in her identification of the fingerprints. **[10]**

(c) Celine is a fingerprint expert with Greater Manchester Police and is concerned that her fingerprint identifications are influenced by the case reports she is given.

   Suggest **one** strategy a criminal psychologist could suggest to Celine which would help reduce the influence of the case reports. **[10]**

How psychology contributes to the success of the economy and society ... Careful collection and processing of forensic evidence ensures that criminals are caught.

Key research
Hall and Player (2008) on *Fingerprint analysis*

Background

Previous research

Fingerprint experts use their ability to analyse and compare fingerprints from a crime scene with those from a suspect.

However, experts are capable of making mistakes due to emotional bias.

Aims

To test the effect of context on fingerprint identification by fingerprint experts:

- Does the written report of a crime, as routinely supplied with the fingerprint evidence, affect a fingerprint expert's interpretation of a poor-quality mark?
- Are the fingerprint experts emotionally affected by the circumstances of the case?

Method

Design

Field experiment, independent measures design.

IV: Low-emotional context or high-emotional context.

Participants were asked to consider the following:

DV 1: Whether the print was a match, not a match, not enough detail to make a comparison or insufficient detail for identification.

DV 2: Whether experts referred to the crime scene examination report prior to their assessment of the prints.

DV 3: Whether information contained in examination reports affected experts' analysis and confidence to present it in court.

Sample

Self-selected sample of 70 fingerprint experts working for the Metropolitan Police Fingerprint Bureau.

Materials/apparatus

Post-experiment questionnaire, right forefinger impression scanned onto a £50 note, Canon laser 1000 printer, crime scene examination report, 10-print fingerprint form.

Procedure

1. Participants tested during work time and in a typical fingerprint examination room at the New Scotland Yard Fingerprint Bureau.
2. Participants given no time limit and told to consider the material as an ordinary case.

Tasks

3. Participants assigned to low- or high-emotional context.
4. Low-emotional context (LEC) = allegation of forgery.
5. High-emotional context (HEC) = allegation of murder.
6. Participants given printed fingerprint and asked if it matched the suspect's fingerprints.

Post-experiment questionnaire

7. Demographic information, e.g. where they worked, number of years' experience.
8. Feedback sheet, e.g. whether they read the crime scene examination report before assessing the marks and if this affected them.

Results

Effect of written report

1. 57 of the 70 participants read the crime scene examination report prior to examining the prints.
2. 30 of this 57 were in the HEC group.
3. 52% of the HEC group were affected by the information in the examination report.
4. This is significantly more than in the LEC group ($p < 0.0001$).

Emotional context

5. No significant difference between final decisions regardless of emotional context ($p < 0.05$).
6. Some experts in the HEC group thought they were affected by the examination report, but this did not affect their final fingerprint identification.

Conclusions

Even if experts think that a serious crime-type has influenced their analysis, the final outcome is not affected.

Experienced fingerprint experts are less affected by cognitive bias than the non-experts.

Fingerprint examiners may regard details of an individual crime that are provided with the fingerprints as surplus to requirements.

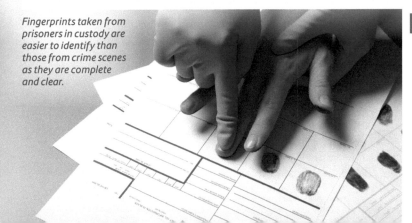

Fingerprints taken from prisoners in custody are easier to identify than those from crime scenes as they are complete and clear.

Evaluation of research on the collection and processing of forensic evidence

How the key research explains ... the collection and processing of forensic evidence	**Can experts be influenced?** Even experienced fingerprint experts are open to the effects of cognitive bias, as shown by the results of *perceived* influence on the two conditions ($p < .0001$). They could be emotionally motivated to make identifications based on the contextual information.
	Are they actually influenced? There was no significant difference in the final identifications between the high- and low-emotional contexts ($p < 0.05$). This means that experts appear to be able to minimise the risk of misidentification due to the high level of training they are given.

Links between the topic and the methodological issues

Validity	✛ Techniques to control variables increased the internal validity of the study, e.g. experts were given the same right forefinger fingerprint.
	▭ The research design means internal validity can be questioned, e.g. fingerprint experts knew they were not dealing with a 'live' mark which could potentially create demand characteristics.
Reliability	✛ Each copy of the right forefinger fingerprint would be consistent as it was standardised using a Canon laser printer. This would increase the reliability of the method.
	✛ Information gathered from the experts was consistent, e.g. they were all given a feedback sheet asking whether they had referred to the crime scene examination report.
Sampling bias	✛ Participants were experienced Metropolitan Police Fingerprint experts, a representative sample of fingerprint experts.
	▭ As the experts came from a trained fingerprint bureau in London, the effects of motivating factors and cognitive bias might not apply to less well-trained fingerprint experts.
Ethnocentrism	▭ Hall and Player's results might be ethnocentric because the lack of cognitive bias observed was in people from an individualist culture. Experts from other cultures might be more prone to be affected by culturally-related cognitive biases.

Links between the topic and the debates

Free will/ determinism	Contexts provided for fingerprint experts (e.g. examination reports in highly emotional contexts) may determine their final decisions, a form of environmental determinism.
	However, there was no difference in the final decisions, suggesting cognitive bias does exist but experts exert free will in deciding whether there is a fingerprint match.
Usefulness of research	Research is useful as training programmes can be developed to reduce the possible effects of cognitive bias in fingerprint identification.
Conducting socially sensitive research	Public money should be spent on training fingerprint experts so that their analysis is sufficiently reliable in courts of law leading to fewer miscarriages of justice.

Your fingerprints hold the key to lots of valuable information - don't leave home without them!

Revision booster

Create a continuum to show the extent to which research evidence is explained by debates, e.g. how far fingerprint experts' decisions are determined by emotional contexts.

Exam-style question examples

Component 3 Section B part (a):

(a) Use the key research by Hall and Player (2008) to explain how bias can be reduced in the collection and processing of forensic evidence. **[10]**

Component 3 Section B part (b):

(b) Evaluate the validity of research into the collection and processing of forensic evidence. **[15]**

(b) Assess the social sensitivity of research into the collection and processing of forensic evidence. **[15]**

Remember to be ready for questions on all eight debates (you can read a summary of them on pages 91-94).

Background
Collection and use of evidence from witnesses and suspects

Building a rapport with distressed witnesses helps them recall information from the crime.

The ECI

1. Establish rapport.
2. Help communication so witnesses can report everything.
3. Free reporting and context reinstatement.
4. Use open-ended questions.
5. Use questions to gather new information.
6. Leave the witness in a positive frame of mind.
7. Evaluate the interview recording.

Using the background research

Consider how you could use the background research to support answers to the following questions. See exam guidance on Component 3 Section B questions on page 8.

(a) Use the key research by Memon and Higham (1999) to explain the collection of evidence. **[10]**

(b) Discuss the usefulness of research into the collection of evidence. **[15]**

(c) John is a police Chief Inspector and wants to improve the validity of evidence from police interviews.

Outline advice a psychologist might suggest to John to improve police interviews. **[10]**

Collecting evidence from witnesses and suspects	Questioning a person regarding their involvement or suspected involvement in criminal offence(s) is regulated by the 1984 Police and Criminal Evidence Act (PACE). All interviews must be carried out under caution.
Evidence from witnesses – The cognitive interview (CI)	**The CI protocol** (Fisher and Geiselman 1992) Consists of four components to maximise information retrieval and communication from witnesses: context reinstatement, report everything, recall from a changed perspective and recall using a changed order. **A toolbox** The CI should be used as a toolbox of skills and adapted to the situation as required. **Original development** The CI is based on research on context-dependent and eyewitness memory. **Research evidence** Fisher *et al.* (1989) used interviews with real witnesses conducted by 16 police detectives from the robbery division of Dade County, Florida. Analysis was by a team blind to the conditions. They found 63% more information was obtained by the detectives trained in CI than those who were untrained. **The enhanced cognitive interview** (ECI) Fisher and Gieselman (1992) improved the CI, introducing seven structured phases (see left).
Evidence from suspects	**A suspect's rights when being questioned** People suspected of having committed a crime are questioned by police under caution ('You do not have to say anything. But it may harm your defence…'). **Interviews and interrogations** Interview techniques aim to psychologically manipulate suspects into confessions and are non-accusatory. In contrast *interrogation* of suspects aims to be accusatory, coercive and discourages talking unless it is to confess, e.g. Reid technique (suspect is isolated and confronted with a strong assertion of guilt, the interrogator interrupts all denial efforts and must keep the suspect's attention, e.g. by showing sympathy). **False confessions** Suspects sometimes confess to crimes they did not commit. Interrogators should always re-evaluate their evidence but there are factors that mitigate against this: • Confirmation bias – interrogators seek to confirm existing beliefs. • Willingness of people to comply – some suspects are vulnerable because they are eager to please (Gudjonsson 2010). • Psychological disorders – offenders with such disorders have a higher false confession rate (Redlich 2007). • Youth – adolescents are more compliant and suggestible than adults and immature in their judgements (Kassin *et al.* 2010).

Application 1

PEACE framework

The PEACE Model was developed to reduce false confessions.

Planning and preparation Create and record a written interview plan, including characteristics of the interviewee and practical arrangements for the interview.

Engage and explain Interviewers establish a rapport with witnesses to encourage conversation.

Account, clarification and challenge Use of open-ended prompts initiate a witness's account of the crime (e.g. 'Tell me what happened'). Permitting the witness to pause and reflect is important. The interviewer also clarifies and expands on the witness's account to ensure everything is covered.

Closure This should be planned and the interviewer should announce the date and time before turning the recording equipment off.

Evaluation The interviewer needs to assess how the witness's account fits in with the rest of the investigation.

Does PEACE work?

Usefulness It is best practice for interviewing people ethically and is suitable for any type of interviewee: victim/survivor, witness or suspect.

Effectiveness It assumes that suspects or witnesses who lie will build up a series of false explanations that will eventually lead to their story breaking down due to inconsistencies.

Practicalities Special training is necessary for the PEACE framework to be effective, especially for the planning and preparation phase.

Application 2

Audio recording interviews

Making the recording The interviewer should load a clearly unused tape into the recorder and:

- Explain that the interview is being audibly recorded.
- Give their name and rank.
- Ask the suspect and any other party present (e.g. a solicitor) to identify themselves.
- State the date, time and place of the interview.
- State that the suspect will be told what will happen to the recording.

Ending the interview The interviewer cautions the suspect and reminds them of their entitlement to free legal advice. The time is recorded and the recording stopped.

Does audio recording interviews work?

Usefulness They are useful as a safeguard both for the police and for the suspect to prevent the police fabricating confessions or suspects retracting admissions.

Effectiveness They provide accurate records of complex interviews which avoids unnecessary disputes or trials.

Practicalities If recording equipment fails it can be replaced. But interview transcriptions of witnesses' statements is time-consuming and expensive, and is a drain on police resources.

Audio recordings are effective in providing consistency between what was said in an interview and the statement that has to be signed by a witness or criminal.

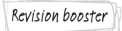

Revision booster

Students often focus only on the original cognitive interview and forget to mention the enhanced cognitive interview – you only need to mention a few of the extra phases.

Exam-style question examples

Component 3 Section B part (c):

(c) Bernice is accused of a number of cybercrimes across Europe. She is interviewed in relation to these crimes and the police want to ensure they collect all relevant evidence in their interview.

Suggest **one** strategy the police could use in their interview to improve the collection of evidence from Bernice. **[10]**

(c) Mirka is a psychologist who advises the police on interview strategies with witnesses and suspects.

Outline the advice Mirka may give to police officers to help them collect evidence from witnesses and suspects. **[10]**

The exam questions above are just representative examples. Read the guidance for Component 3 exam questions on page 8.

Key research
Memon and Higham (1999) on the *Cognitive interview*

Background

This article reviews the cognitive interview (CI) around four themes:

- The effectiveness of various components of the CI.
- The relationship between the CI and other interviewing methods.
- Different measures of memory performance.
- The effect of training quality on interviewer performance.

Aims

To make comments on the:

- Theoretical and methodological issues to be considered in CI research.
- Practical considerations relating to the use of the CI in the field.

Results 1: Effectiveness of the CI

Four components

Memon and Higham reviewed the four components of the CI:

1. *Context reinstatement (CR)* Interviewers help witnesses recreate the context of the crime scene, creating images of the original scene, e.g. location of objects in a room.

2. *Report everything (RE)* Witnesses are encouraged to report any detail that they can remember regardless of how trivial. It is valuable to combine details from different witnesses to the same crime.

3. *Change perspective (CP)* Witnesses are encouraged to view the scene as others may have seen it, e.g. the victim (though this may confuse witnesses).

4. *Change order (CO)* Recall events in different orders, e.g. starting halfway through a sequence of events and then working backwards.

Isolating the effective components of the CI

There is no single component of the CI that is more effective than another when using children as participants (Memon and Stevenage 1996).

However, research using adults indicates that CR provides the most recalled information and is the single most effective component of the CI (Milne 1997). The effectiveness of the ECI is due to improved communication and retrieval of information.

Results 2: Comparing the CI with other interviews

Standard interview

This is the technique typically used by the police but is far from standardised and has undesirable characteristics, e.g. frequent interruptions.

Memon and Higham recommend against using the standard interview as a comparison group to evaluate the efficacy of the CI because it is so different from the CI.

Guided memory interview (GMI)

The GMI is a reasonable comparison group for determining whether CI effects are due to context reinstatement alone or a combination of cognitive techniques.

Structured interview (SI)

Many of the positive aspects of the SI are also present in the enhanced CI, e.g. rapport with witnesses, a non-interruptive approach and the use of open questioning. However, context reinstatement is only used with the CI, so more information is received from witnesses using CI.

Results 3: Measures of memory

Performance is usually measured using the percentage of correct interview statements, but this ignores the amount and nature of *unreported* information.

The more information that is reported by witnesses, the less accurate it becomes.

The CI does improve retrieval of correct details and monitoring relative to the SI (Memon and Stevenage 1996).

Results 4: Suggestions for training quality

1. A two-day training programme is best.

2. The quality of training is governed by available resources.

3. Interviewers w potential should be guided toward the role of investigative detective.

Conclusions

Research into the effectiveness of the CI remains inconclusive.

Further research is needed on how the various elements of the CI work.

Interviewers differ in their ability and motivation to conduct a good interview.

The trick in relation to this study is to focus on learning the four components of the cognitive interview. Also recognise that cognitive reinstatement (CR) is most effective in helping recall of information by witnesses.

Evaluation of research on collection of evidence

How the key research explains ... collection and use of evidence	**Using the cognitive interview (CI)** Memon and Higham explain how context reinstatement is the single most effective component of the CI at collecting more evidence from witnesses. But it is not as effective as the use of the whole CI protocol to collect evidence.
	Enhanced cognitive interview (ECI) The effectiveness of the ECI in collecting evidence is due to improved communication between interviewer and witness and this leads to increased retrieval of information.

Links between the topic and the methodological issues

Validity	✛ Fisher *et al.* (1989) developed the cognitive interview and tested it with real witnesses. Their study is high in validity because they used a blind procedure, e.g. witness interviews were analysed by a team who didn't know if the interview was by a trained CI detective or not, eliminating bias in judgements.
	⊖ Testing the CI in the field reduced control of extraneous variables, limiting the validity of the research.
Reliability	✛ The standardised approach of the CI means that the witness testimonies collected by Fisher *et al.* (1989) are reliable, e.g. police detectives all used the CI protocol.
	⊖ The standard interview used by the police adopts a less standardised approach to interviewing, e.g. many interruptions means testimonies are likely to be inconsistent.
Sampling bias	✛ Samples in the research critiqued by Memon and Higham have been partially replicated using adults, with similar results to those in child studies. This confirms that the full CI is more effective than each of its components.
	⊖ These samples often used children of primary school age who find it difficult to use the cognitive techniques. This means the results may lack generalisability.
Ethnocentrism	⊖ The CI stems from an individualist perspective of police interviewing, e.g. a presumption that the police, witnesses and suspects should tell the truth in all situations. Such 'truth telling' may not be universal.

Links between the topic and the debates

Free will/ determinism	Information recalled by a witness is determined by the CI, e.g. Fisher *et al.* (1989) found trained detectives obtained 63% more information than those who were untrained.
	The opportunity to report everything means witnesses have free will to report as much information as they wish.
Usefulness of research	Memon and Higham's research increases our understanding of how police interviewers collect evidence from witnesses. The research also suggests that police interviewers should be given adequate training in CI techniques to be effective.
Ethical considerations	Gudjonsson (2010) suggests that ethical interview procedures should be non-coercive and the witness or suspect should not be put in stressful conditions when providing evidence.

Interviewers can use cues from the crime scene to help witnesses recall information during the interview.

Revision booster

In Section B part (a) questions, students make the mistake of simply regurgitating the details of the key research. Obviously it is important to include such details but it is equally important to show how the key research explains the topic in question.

Exam-style question examples

Component 3 Section B part (a):

(a) Explain the collection of evidence from witnesses using the key research by Memon and Higham (1999). **[10]**

Component 3 Section B part (b):

(b) Discuss the usefulness of research into collecting evidence from witnesses and suspects. **[15]**

(b) Discuss the extent to which research into collecting evidence from witnesses and suspects is determinist. **[15]**

Background
How juries can be persuaded by the characteristics of witnesses and defendants

The Halo effect

This is a cognitive bias where an observer's overall impression of a person influences their perception of that person's character.

For example, attractive people are more likely to be viewed as having socially desirable personalities and are less likely to be convicted of a crime.

Using the background research

Consider how you could use the background research to support answers to the following questions. See exam guidance on Component 3 Section B questions on page 8.

(a) Explain how the key research by Dixon *et al.* (2002) could be used to show how the characteristics of a defendant can affect whether they are found guilty. **[10]**

(b) Discuss the usefulness of research into psychology and the courtroom. **[15]**

(c) Kris, a defendant, believes the jury in his trial may be exposed to biased information that may affect their verdict.

Suggest **one** strategy a psychologist might suggest to improve the jury's decision-making in Kris's trial. **[10]**

The jury system

The function of a jury is to evaluate trial evidence in order to reach an unbiased verdict.

The UK and US use an adversarial system where defendants are represented by lawyers who argue against prosecution lawyers who represent the Crown or State. A judge gives direction to the jury about matters of law. The defendant is considered innocent until proven guilty.

Characteristics of the witness

Participant factors can affect the decision of a jury, e.g. confidence and age:

Witness confidence Penrod and Cutler (1995) found that the more confident a witness is in providing their evidence to a jury, the more likely the jury is to return a guilty verdict. For example, if a witness in a videotaped trial was 100% confident that she had correctly identified a robber, 67% of the 'jury' voted that the robber was guilty compared to 60% when the witness was 80% confident.

Children as witnesses Rozell (1985) reported that children are good observers who provide reliable identifications of perpetrators but they have difficulty in translating their observations into verbal accounts of events. Children's recollection of events can be distorted by leading questions.

Characteristics of the defendant

Characteristics of a defendant may increase or decrease the likelihood of a jury finding the accused guilty:

Attractiveness of the defendant and of the survivor Castellow *et al.* (1990) investigated the *halo effect* (see top left). When a defendant in a mock trial was rated attractive, guilty verdicts were passed 56% of the time compared to 76% for an unattractive defendant. When a survivor was attractive, the guilty verdict followed 77% of the time with 55% for an unattractive survivor.

The attractiveness of the defendant and the type of crime Sigall and Ostrove (1975) found that good-looking people are more likely to get away with crime or receive reduced sentences. However, if a jury thinks a defendant used their looks to get away with crime, then attractiveness leads to longer sentences.

The ethnicity of the defendant Maeder *et al.* (2015) studied sexual assault trials and found that when the defendant was white, attractive survivors were rated as more responsible for the assault than when the survivor was unattractive - but this effect was reversed for black defendants and nonexistent for aboriginal Canadian defendants.

The effect of accent on juries Seggie (1983) found that more guilt was attributed to a person with an RP (Received Pronunciation) accent when the crime was theft and more guilt was attributed to a person with an Australian accent when it was a violent crime.

Application 1

Present evidence in story order

Pennington and Hastie (1992) proposed both prosecution and defence lawyers should present their evidence in chronological order to help juries in decision-making.

Lawyers create a timeline Evidence is organised and presented into a 'story order'.

Jurors develop a coherent story Jurors make sense of the trial information by making their own story based on their knowledge of the events given to them at the trial.

Judge gives direction The judge sums up the evidence at the end of the trial and advises the jury on how to come to a verdict.

Juror matches story to possible verdicts Possible verdict decisions are presented by the judge, and jurors try to match their story to one of these possible verdict decisions. It is thought that those lawyers who create clear timelines are more likely to be believed.

Does story order work?

Usefulness It provides lawyers with a strategy to influence the decision-making of jurors to the benefit of their client. It also helps jurors to understand information at the trial.

Effectiveness Pennington and Hastie (1992) showed that story order is more effective as a persuasive strategy than witness order (where lawyers present witnesses in the order they feel would be most persuasive).

Practicalities Counsel need to make sure they categorise all evidence before the trial so it can be put in the order that will best influence the jury's decision-making.

Application 2

Using expert witnesses

What is expert testimony? Expert witnesses provide independent, impartial and unbiased evidence to assist a court in reaching its decision where a specialised area needs explaining.

Qualities required of an expert witness Expert witnesses have detailed knowledge of their subject and the ability to communicate opinions clearly.

Evidence for using expert psychological witnesses Cutler *et al.* (1989) found expert psychological testimony improved juror sensitivity to eyewitness evidence, meaning jurors had improved knowledge of factors influencing memory.

Does using expert witnesses work?

Usefulness The usefulness of expert evidence depends on a high level of detail and clear explanations.

Effectiveness Expert witnesses provide an effective safeguard against jurors' over-reliance on witness confidence when assessing the evidence.

Practicalities Courts usually allow more than one expert if evidence is required in more than one area of expertise, but the cost should be proportionate to the value of the case.

Mock jury trials (e.g. using videotapes) are much shorter than real trials and lack the realism of a real trial. However, it would be unethical to use a real trial for research purposes.

Revision booster

Do not forget to use psychological research or knowledge to support the strategies you suggest. For example, one strategy that is used to influence jury decision-making is the presentation of evidence in story order. This is based on the research by Pennington and Hastie (1992).

Exam-style question examples

Component 3 Section B part (c):

(c) The new Government Justice Secretary is concerned that too many verdicts in jury trials are later overturned. She asks a psychologist to suggest ways to improve jury decision-making.

What advice might a psychologist suggest to the Justice Secretary to improve jury decision-making? **[10]**

(c) Nigel is a lawyer who often represents high-profile defendants accused of criminal behaviour.

Suggest **one** strategy Nigel could use to influence the jury to help his clients. **[10]**

Don't forget to read all the exam advice on pages 4-15.

Key research
Dixon et al. (2002) on Accents and guilt

Background

Received Pronunciation (RP) is the English accent not associated with any region. It is rated more positively than non-standard accents, e.g. a Brummie (Birmingham) accent.

Attributions of guilt may be affected by a suspect's use of non-standard English, their ethnicity and the type of crime committed.

Aims

To investigate whether:

- A suspect with a 'Brummie' accent would receive a higher rating of guilt than a suspect with a standard accent.
- Ethnicity or type of crime would have an effect on how the suspect using either a Brummie or standard accent was judged.

Method

Design

Laboratory experiment, a 2 × 2 × 2 factorial (independent measures) design.

IVs: Accent type (Brummie or standard), ethnicity of suspect (black or white), crime type: armed robbery (a blue-collar crime) or cheque fraud (a white-collar crime).

DV: Participants' attribution of guilt, 1 = innocent and 7 = guilty.

Sample

119 white psychology undergraduates, 24 men and 95 women from University College Worcester, mean age of 25.2 years.

Materials/apparatus

Speech evaluation instrument (SEI), tape recording of a mock interview.

Procedure

Tape recording of suspect

1. Participants listened to a two-minute tape recording of a mock interview.
2. Students played the roles of police inspector and suspect.
3. The police inspector and suspect spoke RP.
4. The role of suspect was played by a 'code-switcher' (able to switch between a Brummie and standard accent). The same person made both tapes.
5. The suspect description was altered to either black or white.

Rating the dependent variables

6. After listening to one version of the tape-recorded exchange, participants completed two sets of rating scales.
7. Suspect's guilt was rated on a 7-point scale ranging from innocent to guilty.
8. Suspect's language attitudes were rated on superiority, attractiveness and dynamism using the SEI.

Results

Independent variables (IVs)

1. **Accent type** There was a significant effect of the suspect's accent on the attribution of guilt.
2. The suspect with the Brummie accent was rated higher on guilt than the suspect with standard English (4.27 compared to 3.65, $p < 0.05$).
3. **Ethnicity of suspect** Black participants were not rated significantly more guilty than white participants.
4. **Crime type** Blue-collar participants were not rated significantly more guilty than white-collar participants.
5. **Interaction between the IVs** The participant in the black, Brummie-accented, blue-collar crime condition received the highest guilt rating.

Speech evaluation instrument (SEI)

6. The Brummie suspect was rated lower in superiority than the standard accent suspect.
7. Superiority and Attractiveness predicted guilt but Dynamism did not.
8. Superiority and Attractiveness factors accounted for 13% of the variance in respondents' guilt ratings ($p < 0.002$).

Conclusions

Non-standard English speakers tend to be perceived as more guilty than standard speakers.

Non-standard speakers tend to be perceived as less competent than standard speakers.

Perception of a suspect's language superiority and attractiveness may predict their guilt.

It is not just speaking with a British accent that is important, it is also which regional accent you have!

Evaluation of research on psychology and the courtroom

How the key research explains ... psychology and the courtroom	**Effect of accent on perceived guilt** A person with a Brummie accent is more likely to be found guilty than a person with an RP accent as it suggests the speaker is working class and, together with their poor language competence, arouses a criminal stereotype. **Other factors** Crime type and skin colour also affect jurors' attributions of guilt, so an awareness of these factors is important in order for the suspect to receive a fair trial in court.

A 'blue-collar' worker. Remember it is the interaction of having a Brummie accent + black ethnicity + committing a blue-collar crime (armed robbery) that leads to increased attribution of guilt – rather than any one variable alone.

Links between the topic and the methodological issues

Validity	⊕ Mock interviews enhance internal validity because a high level of control is possible, as evidenced by the fact that more than 95% of people were able to identify the region of the Brummie accent in Dixon *et al.*'s research. ⊖ The ecological validity of mock interviews may be low, e.g. playing a tape recording of a police interview does not represent what would happen in a real courtroom.
Reliability	⊕ The internal reliability of the SEI is high, e.g. +.95 for Superiority using the split-half method. ⊕ Dixon *et al.* used a standardised procedure (e.g. the exchange between police officer and suspect), and Penrod and Cutler (1995) used the same videotaped trial of a robbery, increasing the reliability of their results.
Sampling bias	⊖ The psychology undergraduates used by Dixon *et al.* may not be a representative sample, e.g. juries are not solely made up of students. Therefore, it may be difficult to make generalisations of how guilt is judged based on this sample.
Ethnocentrism	⊖ Dixon *et al.* chose a Brummie accent because it signalled stereotypes associated with a working-class culture. In some cultures accents may simply be viewed as regional variations and not linked to any social stereotypes.

Links between the topic and the debates

Free will/ determinism	This study suggests that jurors' decisions are determined by social factors, e.g. a suspect's accent may generate social stereotypes. However, jurors may exercise their free will if they base their verdict solely on the evidence rather than the defendant's accent or their attractiveness.
Individual/ situational explanations	Individual explanations propose that some witnesses or suspects have more confident personalities than others, e.g. Penrod and Cutler (1995) showed that participants who were more confident (100% versus 80%) when giving evidence had a greater effect on the jury members. Situational explanations suggest that the courtroom, how evidence is presented by lawyers and the characteristics of witnesses and defendants all influence the decision of jury members.
Usefulness of research	Judges and juries need be aware that physical attraction, accent, ethnicity and type of crime affect jurors' perception of guilt.

Revision booster

You should use research to support your evaluation but do not include lots of description about the procedure. Instead, analyse the research to find the specific evidence to support your argument.

Exam-style question examples

Component 3 Section B part (a):

(a) Explain how the key research by Dixon *et al.* (2002) could be used to show how the characteristics of a defendant can affect whether they are found guilty. **[10]**

Component 3 Section B part (b):

(b) Discuss the validity of research into psychology and the courtroom. **[15]**

(b) Discuss the usefulness of research into psychology and the courtroom. **[15]**

How psychology contributes to the success of the economy and society ...
The conduct of court cases is important for a successful society.

Chapter 3 Criminal psychology   Topic 5

Component 3 Applied psychology

If your car is in poor condition, don't leave it in a run-down area as it may be even further damaged when you return!

Defensible space

This term refers to residents adopting a protective attitude towards the shared area outside their property and leads to the upkeep of the area and reduced crime (Newman 1973).

Using the background research

Consider how you could use the background research to support answers to the following questions. See exam guidance on Component 3 Section B questions on page 8.

(a) Explain how the research by Wilson and Kelling (1982) could be used to reduce crime. **[10]**

(b) Discuss ethnocentrism in relation to research into crime prevention. **[15]**

(c) Sarah has noticed an increase in vandalism in the areas surrounding her block of flats and she is keen to address this problem.

What crime prevention strategy might a psychologist suggest to help Sarah address this problem of vandalism? **[10]**

What is crime prevention?	Governments attempt to reduce and deter crime in society. The UK Government's (2016) *Modern crime prevention strategy* targets: **Opportunity** Remove opportunities for criminals to offend. **Character** Interventions with those at high risk of committing crime. **Effective Criminal Justice System** Should act as a deterrent to would-be offenders. **Profit** Should be reduced for benefits of crime. **Drugs** Develop strategies to restrict the drugs trade. **Alcohol** Consumption should be made safer, reducing fear of alcohol-related crime.
Features of a neighbourhood **Newman's theory**	Newman argued that a lack of *defensible space* (see left) led to reduced satisfaction with one's neighbourhood. Defensible space can be created by changing: • **Territoriality** Create zones by providing boundary markers (e.g. fences) where residents have ownership and privacy. • **Natural surveillance** Provide unobstructed views of communal areas with improved lighting. • **Image** Maintain and improve appearance of buildings to increase pride. • **Milieu** (surroundings) Make entryways more visible from the road to enhance surveillance. Newman compared Van Dyke and Brownsville housing projects and showed how physical design was related to differences in crime and graffiti.
Broken windows theory	Zimbardo (1969) abandoned two cars – one in the Bronx (poor area, stripped in three days) and one in Palo Alto (affluent area, left untouched for a week until Zimbardo vandalised it, quickly copied by others). **Developing an explanation** If broken windows remain unrepaired, vandals will soon break a building's remaining windows. The broken windows are a metaphor for ways that behavioural norms break down in a community (Wilson and Kelling 1982).
Zero tolerance policy and crime	Zero tolerance policing strategy involves relentless order maintenance and aggressive law enforcement. **Research evidence for zero tolerance** Zero tolerance policies reduced violent crimes by 5% from 1989-1998 in New York City (Kelling and Sousa 2001). **Challenges to zero tolerance** Harcourt and Ludwig (2006) attributed the crime reduction to falling crack cocaine use in 1990s with accompanying large declines in violent crime.

Application 1

Neighbourhood watch schemes

Neighbourhood watch (NHW) schemes Aim to reduce crime by directly involving the community in activities that promote safety or assist with the detection of crime.

Setting up a neighbourhood watch scheme Neighbours need to form a group and register with the Neighbourhood and Home Watch Network and local police authority. The group should decide how NHW can help to make the community more secure. A group coordinator ensures a smooth flow of information between the police and scheme members who receive regular alerts from their local policing team.

Do neighbourhood watch schemes work?

Usefulness NHW is useful as residents can keep an eye open for suspicious activity and is especially useful for the elderly or those who live alone. It helps in preventing burglaries and antisocial behaviour and other forms of crime, e.g. fraud.

Effectiveness NHW acts as a deterrent to offenders by increasing their awareness that local residents will be looking for and reporting suspicious activity. NHW also reduces the perceived opportunity for crime by increasing signs of occupancy in vacant homes, e.g. moving bins.

Practicalities Setting up a NHW scheme is free except for associated costs, e.g. time and running costs for setting up meetings and producing newsletters.

Application 2

'Pulling levers' policing

The pulling levers deterrence framework involves:

- **Selecting a particular crime problem** For example, targeting street drug dealing and pulling together a law enforcement group to deal with it.

- **Key offenders are identified** Law enforcement operation is directed at offenders by using any and all legal 'levers' to sanction those who commit serious crime.

- **Police communicate directly with offenders** Police let the offenders know they are under scrutiny and how they can avoid enforcement action.

Therefore, criminals are deterred from committing future crime as they become aware that the costs outweigh the benefits.

Does 'pulling levers' policing work?

Usefulness It increases the benefits of not being involved in crime and acts as a driver for crime prevention by reducing the opportunities for crime.

Effectiveness Police departments can engage in a variety of partnerships and tailor an array of tactics to address criminal activity.

Practicalities The pulling levers deterrence framework is expensive, e.g. creating job training opportunities for gang members and providing drug abuse treatments for offenders. Therefore, the effectiveness of the deterrents is dependent on the funding from central government.

Neighbourhood watch schemes are designed to catch cat burglars.

Revision booster

For section B part (c) questions, make sure you describe how to carry out a crime prevention strategy not simply name it.

Exam-style question examples

Component 3 Section B part (c):

(c) Simon manages a sport retail store and believes people are stealing trainers from it. He wants to tackle this problem.

Suggest advice a psychologist might give Simon to help address the problem of trainers being stolen from his sport retail store. **[10]**

(c) Elizabeth works with a law enforcement agency that works to deter drug crime.

Outline **one** crime prevention strategy that Elizabeth may suggest to police to deter criminals from becoming involved in drug crime. **[10]**

Key research
Wilson and Kelling (1982) on *Broken windows*

Background

The 1970s 'Safe and Clean Neighborhoods Program' in New Jersey involved officers walking beats rather than driving in patrol cars. It did not reduce crime rates but residents felt more secure, officers had greater job satisfaction, and citizens and officers had more favourable opinions of each other.

Aims

To outline:

- How features of neighbourhoods can influence crime rates.
- The changing role of the police in the US.
- Strategies for maintaining order.

Safe neighbourhoods

Foot-patrol officers

1. Foot-patrol officers improved the level of public order in Newark, so the fear of being bothered by disorderly people (e.g. drunks) was reduced.

2. Officers enforced the law and protected the neighbourhood rules for public order.

3. Officers kept an eye on strangers.

4. Officers knew the neighbourhood 'regulars' and the regulars knew them.

5. Officers ensured disreputable regulars observed informal rules, e.g. drunks could sit but not lie down on the stoops (building steps).

Broken windows

6. Neglected property (e.g. with broken windows) shows a breakdown in community controls. Then many residents wish to move and these areas are vulnerable to crime and disorderliness.

Community controls

7. One broken window becomes many, acting as a metaphor for the disorderliness that weakens the interaction between people and community controls.

The changing role of the police

New developments in policing

1. The role of the police changed from maintaining order to one of detecting and apprehending criminals.

2. Society had to decide what constitutes an undesirable person and what behaviours should be criminalised.

Ensuring police treat people fairly

3. Consider selection, training and supervision of police.

4. Three solutions: Newark 'Safe and Clean Neighborhoods Program', informal social control (e.g. community rules) and citizen patrols (e.g. Guardian Angels).

Maintaining order

1. Police are key to maintaining order but substantial cuts in officers.

2. Some neighbourhoods are so crime-ridden that foot patrols are useless, whereas some are so stable that foot patrols are unnecessary.

3. The key objective is to identify neighbourhoods at a tipping point – public order is deteriorating but not unreclaimable.

4. However, few police departments systematically identify areas that need officers. They need to decide where officers will make the greatest difference.

Suggestions

5. Private security guards can be employed to help communities maintain order, or tenant organisations can hire off-duty police officers to patrol area.

6. Patrol officers should be encouraged to use public transport and enforce rules on drinking and disorderly conduct.

7. Police should protect communities as well as individuals, and ought to recognise the importance of maintaining communities without broken windows.

Conclusions

Policing focuses on high-crime areas because police mistakenly think they are judged on ability to fight crime.

Police ought to protect communities as well as individuals.

Police should focus on the value of maintaining intact communities that don't have broken windows.

Newark programme: Moving officers from patrol cars to walking the beat did not reduce the amount of crime but people felt safer.

How the key research explains ... crime prevention	**Safe neighbourhoods** Using a zero tolerance policy and creating foot-patrol officers reduced people's fear of being bothered by disorderly people (e.g. drunks), and the level of public order was elevated.
	The changing role of the police and maintaining order Police are the key to order maintenance and central to crime prevention. Their strategies seek to maintain order by reinforcing the community controls in neighbourhoods.

Links between the topic and the methodological issues

Validity	⊕ Zimbardo's (1969) field experiment demonstrates high ecological validity as residents of the Bronx and Palo Alto behaved naturally towards the abandoned cars in a real-world situation. Kelling's observations of foot-patrol officers in run-down areas would also suggest high ecological validity.
	⊖ Kelling's observations were subjective with no other corroboration. This questions their validity.
Reliability	⊖ Broken windows theory is based only on Kelling's observations of foot-patrol officers in Newark. The reliability of this data is difficult to assess as it is from one source only. We have no measure of inter-observer reliability.
Sampling bias	⊖ Zimbardo's research was in cities where there was already breakdown in community controls. The findings may not generalise to all cities, especially less affluent ones where breakdown hasn't started.
Ethnocentrism	⊖ Research into broken windows takes place in America where zero tolerance policing exists to deal with the types of crime experienced in individualist cultures. Collectivist cultures may deal with crime through family and community support and would not need relentless order maintenance and aggressive law enforcement.

Links between the topic and the debates

Reductionism/ holism	Research often tends to oversimplify the number of factors at work in reduction of crime figures, e.g. Kelling and Sousa's (2001) use of broken windows policing ignores a number of other key explanations, such as the economy and drug use.
Individual/ situational explanations	Research supports the situational explanation, e.g. Wilson and Kelling's observations showed that features of neighbourhoods (run-down areas with broken windows) influence crime rates.
	Individual explanations can be seen in the way residents of Newark demonstrated self-restraint in terms of reduced crime and this was a factor in the increased feeling of security in the neighbourhood.
Usefulness of research	Newman's (1973) research can be regarded as useful because of the social benefits it brings to neighbourhoods, e.g. architectural design reduces crime.
	Similarly, the article by Wilson and Kelling is useful because it highlights the important role the police have in crime reduction.

Disorderly people create fear of crime. It is the role of the police to keep community controls so that public order is maintained.

Background
Punishment and reform as responses to criminal behaviour

Prison education can open up opportunities and build offenders' self-confidence. It can increase their awareness of options, giving them a real choice of a life away from crime.

Revision booster

Don't forget to focus on both the positive and negative effects that prison has on offenders (e.g. rehabilitation and poor mental health), and not simply discuss how prison acts as a punishment.

Using the background research

Consider how you could use the background research to support answers to the following questions. See exam guidance on Component 3 Section B questions on page 8.

(a) Using the key research by Haney *et al.* (1973), explain the effects of imprisonment. **[10]**

(b) Discuss ethnocentrism in relation to research into the effects of imprisonment. **[15]**

(c) Velma is a psychologist who works in the Prison Service to prevent prisoner reoffending.

What advice might Velma give to inmates about how to reduce reoffending after they are released from prison? **[10]**

Punishment and reform	Her Majesty's Prison & Probation Service is responsible for running prison and probation services. They also provide rehabilitation services to stop people reoffending.
Punishment as a response to criminal behaviour	**Types of punishment** • **Non-custodial punishments** Usually involve a fine, community sentence or probation. • **Custodial sentences** Involve the offender being put in a prison or secure hospital for the term of their sentence. **Prison as a form of punishment** • A prison sentence is designed to punish offenders and to protect the public. • Prison is also a form of retribution where a victim feels that justice has been served. • Prison also aims to act as a deterrent or has a reforming effect so offenders do not commit more crimes in the future. **Effects of imprisonment** Overcrowding, fear of violence from other prisoners, lack of freedom and boredom can lead to mental health issues. Dooley (1990) attributed suicides and unnatural deaths in prison to overcrowding and prisoners' stress. This suggests that prison may make matters worse for offenders rather than better.
Reform as a response to criminal behaviour	**Are prisons effective?** Extremely violent offenders need to be locked up to protect the public. However, imprisonment does not work well as a deterrent - 25% of prisoners reoffend. On the other hand, prisons do provide offenders with opportunities to learn new skills or change their behaviour. **Why reform is necessary** Prison as a deterrent does not work for everyone and offenders find it very difficult not to reoffend due to poor job prospects. **The role of prisons in offender rehabilitation** Development of working prisons means inmates get the chance to work during their sentence to improve their opportunities on release. Prisons also offer therapeutic programmes (e.g. anger management therapy) to encourage rehabilitation. **Research supporting reform** Gillis and Nafekh (2005) found that offenders who are employed while on conditional release (parole), are less likely to return to prison during that time. This shows that planned employment at the time of release from prison is important for offenders' reintegration into society.

Application 1
Restorative justice (RJ)

Six principles of restorative justice (RJ)

Restoration The harm that has been caused is repaired.

Voluntarism Participants take part of their own free will.

Neutrality Practitioner neutrality ensures no one feels disadvantaged or discriminated against during RJ process.

Safety Risk assessments are carried out and practitioners should be appropriately trained.

Accessibility RJ is available to anyone who has experienced harm or conflict.

Respect Practitioners need to manage the highly emotional process.

Does restorative justice work?

Usefulness RJ helps provide closure for both the victim/survivor and the offender after the crime. Offenders who are part of RJ programmes are significantly less likely to reoffend.

Effectiveness RJ programmes are flexible so they can be adapted and tailored to the needs of the individual situation. The success of the RJ programme may depend upon the extent to which the offender feels remorse for their actions.

Practicalities The meeting between offender and victim is likely to be an emotional event and trained, skilled practitioners are required to act as mediators. There are high dropout rates.

Application 2
Cognitive behaviour therapy (CBT)

CBT programmes such as JETS (Juvenile Estate Thinking Skills) are a powerful means of changing behaviour patterns.

What is the psychology behind JETS? JETS is based on Ellis's (1957) ABC model of irrational beliefs where *A* is the activating event (e.g. situations that led to the crime), *B* is the negative beliefs attached to the crime, *C* is the negative consequences that happen as a result of negative beliefs.

What does a JETS programme involve? 25 sessions of two-and-a-half hours with young offenders firstly completing exercises in a workbook, followed by a group session that focuses on support in the community.

Engagement in JETS programmes JETS focuses on the offenders' family and the Young Offending Team that attempts to reduce youth recidivism.

Does JETS work?

Usefulness JETS reduces reoffending in both the short and long term for 14- to 17-year-old offenders. It can be tailored to the specific needs of each offender.

Effectiveness Research using JETS shows positive results in terms of recidivism after 12 months - only 54% of offenders on a JETS programme had been reconvicted compared to 74% of a control group.

Practicalities Young people in custody struggle to maintain motivation for interventions and JETS requires trained facilitators.

The process of RJ

Practitioners of RJ invite victim and offender to an introductory meeting. The offender usually talks about the crime, why they have agreed to RJ and often apologises for their actions. Victims explain the impact of the crime on them. Finally, a contract may be signed, detailing actions agreed by the offender to ensure the crime does not happen again.

CBT challenges and changes faulty thinking, improves emotional regulation, and develops coping strategies to target problem behaviours such as crime.

Exam-style question examples

Component 3 Section B part (c):

(c) Sara is a criminal psychologist who spends part of her time working with young offender institutions to find out what can be done to reduce rates of recidivism.

Suggest **one** strategy Sara might investigate to reduce reoffending. **[10]**

(c) Ellie has been in and out of prison for a range of different crimes. She is determined not to return and is working with her probation officer, Aleema, to find a strategy to prevent her reoffending.

What advice could Aleema give to Ellie to prevent her from returning to prison? **[10]**

Key research
Haney *et al.* (1973) on *a Simulated prison*

Background

In the 1970s, American prisons were failing and recidivism rates were high. A situational rather than dispositional explanation might account for this (i.e. bad conditions not bad people).

Aims and hypothesis

To create a 'mock' prison, a functional representation of a real prison.

The general hypothesis was assigning a person to the role of 'guard' or 'prisoner' would result in significantly different reactions in terms of behaviour, emotion and attitudes toward self.

Method

Design

Laboratory experiment, independent measures design.

IV: Role of prisoner or guard, allocated randomly.

DV: Behaviour of the prisoners and guards.

Sample

21 men, all college students, largely middle-class and strangers to each other.

Materials/apparatus

Audio and video recordings of prisoners and guards, personality tests, interviews and guard reports. Outfits (see 'Uniforms' below).

Procedure

Physical aspects of the prison

1. There were three small cells for the prisoners, a bedroom for the 'superintendent' (Zimbardo) and 'warden', an interviewing room, and a 'yard' with an observation screen for video recording equipment and space for observers.

Operational details

2. Prisoners remained in prison and guards worked three-man eight-hour shifts, leading normal lives at other times.

3. Participants were all guaranteed adequate diet, clothing, housing, medical care in return for playing their role for duration of the study (up to two weeks).

4. Prisoners had little privacy and no civil rights, with the exception of no physical abuse.

5. Guards should 'maintain a reasonable degree of order within the prison necessary for its effective functioning'.

6. Uniforms - guards wore khaki shirts and trousers and sunglasses. Prisoners wore a loose-fitting muslin smock.

7. 'Prisoners' were arrested by police, taken to the 'prison', stripped, deloused and made to stand naked in the yard.

8. Guards referred to the prisoners by number. Prisoners lined up three times a day to be counted.

Results

Behaviour of prisoners and guards

1. Guards and prisoners showed progressively more negative feelings towards each other and themselves.

2. Prisoners expressed more intentions to harm others.

3. Guards were prevented from using physical abuse but often expressed aggression using verbal affronts.

4. Guards were distressed at prisoner suffering.

5. Guards turned up for work on time and some did extra hours without pay.

Reactions of prisoners

6. Five prisoners were released early due to extreme emotional depression, crying, rage and acute anxiety.

Individual differences

7. Some guards were fair and passive, others went beyond the rules to engage in creative cruelty and harassment.

End of experiment

8. The experiment was terminated early (after six days) because of the effect on both prisoners and guards.

Conclusions

Prison environments have negative effects on the feelings of both guards and prisoners.

Prison guards may develop a pathology of power.

Prisoners may develop a pathological prisoner syndrome.

Prisoners expressed initial disbelief, followed by rebellion and flattened emotions, becoming passive and ill (the pathological prisoner syndrome).

How the key research explains ... the effect of imprisonment	**Punishment** The study shows that prisoners and guards in prisons adopt the social role they believe is expected of them, e.g. the guards' role is to confine prisoners, thereby restricting their freedom. The study also demonstrates that prison is a stressful place, e.g. prisoners showed symptoms of extreme emotional depression.
	Reform Haney *et al.* suggest their research provides a model for better guard training and operation of penal institutions.

Offenders are often more worried about the freedom that release brings rather than being worried about being imprisoned (where they have a sense of security).

Links between the topic and the methodological issues

Validity	⊕ Haney *et al.*'s participants reacted to the situation as though it was real, e.g. 90% of prisoners' conversations were about prison conditions.
	⊝ The study could be seen as low in ecological validity as the simulated prison was not completely realistic, e.g. there were no threats to life.
Reliability	⊕ The official statistics that measured employment status and community outcomes come from the Correctional Service of Canada's automated database and are considered reliable.
	⊝ The reliability of Haney *et al.*'s data is difficult to assess as the observations were only made by the researchers, so we have no evidence of inter-observer reliability.
Sampling bias	⊕ Gillis and Nafekh's (2005) data is reasonably representative (23,525 offenders from Canadian prisons, both men and women).
	⊝ Haney *et al.*'s sample is unrepresentative as it only involved college students, all of whom were men. Female prison guards may not act so aggressively.
Ethnocentrism	⊝ Using prison as an effective punishment can be viewed as a response to criminal behaviour more typical of individualist countries. Some cultures focus on programmes aimed at reforming offender behaviour rather than punishing it.

Links between the topic and the debates

Free will/ determinism	The poor guard behaviour in Haney *et al.*'s study was due to the power they were given over the prisoners and their deindividuation. They no longer felt responsible for their behaviour due to lack of personal agency.
	However, the 'good' guards showed free will and were less willing to abuse their power.
Individual/ situational explanations	Haney *et al.* suggest social roles (situational) caused the guards' behaviour as participants were randomly allocated to the role of prisoner or guard.
	However, some of the guards were far more aggressive than others, an individual dispositional factor.
Ethical considerations	Haney *et al.*'s study is unethical due to a lack of fully informed consent. Also, prisoners were not protected from psychological harm, e.g. humiliation arising from being stripped naked.

Revision booster

Remember that recidivism refers to criminal acts that result in rearrest, reconviction or return to prison following the prisoner's release with or without a new sentence.

Read the guidance for Component 3 exam questions on page 8.

Exam-style question examples

Component 3 Section B part (a):

(a) Use the key research by Haney *et al.* (1973) to explain the effects of imprisonment. **[10]**

Component 3 Section B part (b):

(b) Evaluate the validity of research into the effects of imprisonment. **[15]**

(b) Discuss whether research into the effects of imprisonment is ethnocentric. **[15]**

How psychology contributes to the success of the economy and society ... Imprisonment and reform are important for maintaining a safe society.

Background

Environmental stressors and their impact on our biological responses

Your heart starts pounding when you are scared due to adrenaline produced by the sympathetic nervous system.

Using the background research

Consider how you could use the background research to support answers to the following questions. See exam guidance on Component 3 Section B questions on page 8.

(a) Using the key research by Black *et al.* (2007), explain the impact of stressors in the environment. **[10]**

(b) Discuss determinism in relation to research into the impact of environmental stressors. **[15]**

(c) Ajaz lives next door to a family with children learning to play brass musical instruments.

Outline **one** strategy Ajaz could use to cope with the stress he feels when the children practise their brass instruments. **[10]**

Stress and stressors	Stress arises when individuals perceive they cannot adequately cope with the demands made on them (Lazarus 1966).
	Two elements of stress (1) the stressor, which causes (2) a stress reaction (i.e. a biological response).
	Internal stressors Include anxiety and pressure that we put on ourselves.
	External stressors Include things in the environment, e.g. noise and temperature.
Stress caused by noise	Noise is a loud or disturbing sound. It can be unpleasant depending on its pitch, duration, predictability, whether it is continuous or intermittent, and to what extent we can control it.
	Stansfeld *et al.* (2000) found that environmental noise is associated with increased anxiety in adults.
	Lundberg and Frankenhaeuser (1978) revealed increased levels of stress in participants who were not in control of noise played during a mental arithmetic task.
Stress caused by temperature	Increases in temperature can lead to an increase in negative emotional reactions, e.g. stress.
	Peng *et al.* (2017) found significantly more psychiatric hospital admissions occurred within 24 hours of a very hot day, compared to a cold day.
The impact of stressors on our biological responses	**Short-term stress**
	Cannon (1932) suggested a fight or flight model for short-term stressful situations.
	This short-term response is controlled by the SAM system (**S**ympathetic — **A**drenaline — **M**edulla).
	Stressor perceived → Sympathetic nervous system aroused → Adrenaline released from adrenal medulla → Causes increased heart rate and blood pressure → Instantaneous response.
	The impact of short-term stress Creates cardiovascular problems because sympathetic arousal leads to high blood pressure.
	Long-term stress
	The hypothalamic-pituitary adrenal system (HPA) activates the body's response to long-term (chronic) stress.
	Stressor perceived → Hypothalamus aroused, producing corticotropin releasing factor (CRF) → Pituitary gland releases adrenocorticotropic hormone (ACTH) into the bloodstream→ Adrenal cortex releases cortisol → Increases glucose metabolism to power the stress response → Takes at least 20 minutes to produce cortisol after a stressor is first perceived
	The impact of long-term stress Immunosuppressive effects, making us more susceptible to illness, e.g. colds.

Application 1

 Stress inoculation therapy (SIT)

SIT is a form of cognitive behaviour therapy (CBT).

Conceptualisation phase The aim is for the client to understand that stressors (e.g. aircraft noise) are challenges that can be overcome.

Skills acquisition and rehearsal phase The client learns skills needed to cope with stress (e.g. relaxation), tailored to their specific needs.

Real-life application and follow-through phase Therapists create opportunities for the client to try out their skills in a safe environment (e.g. role play) with gradual transfer to everyday life through homework tasks.

Does SIT work?

Usefulness Coping with environmental stressors (e.g. noise) reduces long-term illnesses. Consequently, people take fewer sick days from work, leading to higher productivity.

Effectiveness Sultan *et al.* (2016) found significant positive differences pre- and post-SIT, e.g. assessing emotional state and severity of symptoms of coronary heart disease.

Practicalities SIT is flexible and tailored to suit the requirements of a client, e.g. group sessions, varying duration of sessions. However, SIT requires commitment from the client to complete the homework tasks.

Application 2

Mindfulness

Mindfulness focuses a client on the present situation rather than thinking of the past, future or other people.

What mindfulness involves The client concentrates on their own breathing and feelings at a particular moment and does not let external distractions interfere.

Undertaking mindfulness It is usually taught in an eight-week programme with group sessions of two to three hours a week. Clients are encouraged to practise meditation and awareness techniques between these sessions, so they can then easily use their breathing and relaxation techniques when real stressors (e.g. traffic noise) occur.

Does mindfulness work?

Usefulness Mindfulness has the potential to reduce stress levels and improve the long-term health of many people. However, people who have mental health issues may have their troubles amplified by undertaking mindfulness.

Effectiveness Mindfulness-based interventions have been found to have long-term positive effects on the psychological well-being of the parents of children with autism spectrum disorder (Cachia *et al.* 2016).

Practicalities The focus and skills needed in mindfulness can take a long time to acquire, and the therapy can therefore be quite expensive overall. Once the skills are mastered, individuals can use the technique without an instructor and use it wherever they are.

Mindfulness is not the same as mindlessness.

Revision booster

Don't forget that you should be able to discuss how any topic contributes to the success of the economy and society. On some spreads (see bottom of this column) we have given you some ideas about how to do this. But be ready to think on your feet.

Exam-style question examples

Component 3 Section B part (c):

(c) Mirka has moved to a new house close to a main road. She didn't realise how much the noise would be a problem and has started feeling stressed living there.

Outline **one** strategy a psychologist might give to Mirka to reduce her stress levels. **[10]**

(c) An airline has started flying to a small regional airport and the noise increase has had an impact on the number of local residents experiencing stress-related illness.

Outline the advice a psychologist might give to the local residents to cope with the increase in aircraft noise. **[10]**

How psychology contributes to the success of the economy and society ... Knowledge about the effects of environmental stressors is important for health.

Key research
Black *et al.* (2007) on *Aircraft noise*

Background

One important environmental stressor is noise, a major issue for people living near an airport.

Aims

To answer two questions:

- Is health-related quality of life worse in a community chronically exposed to aircraft noise than in a community not exposed?
- Is long-term aircraft noise exposure associated with hypertension in adults, with noise stress as a mediating factor?

Method

Design

Quasi-experiment, independent measures, matched control group.

IV: Living near airport (noise exposure group) or further away.

DV: Scores on health measurement questionnaire.

Settings

Highly exposed, noise-affected area near Sydney Airport experiencing more than 50 aircraft per day over 70 decibels (dB).

The control area, South Penrith, is an area about 55 km from Sydney Airport, not exposed to aircraft noise.

Sample

1500 participants aged 15–87 years, 704 responded to the questionnaire.

Materials/apparatus

Health measurement questionnaire.

Procedure

Pilot study

1. Questionnaire given to 100 residents of a suburb south of Sydney Airport to check the reliability of the measurement scales.

Health measurement

2. Questionnaire measured seven participant characteristics:
   - Health-related quality of life (HRQoL).
   - Noise stress.
   - Noise annoyance.
   - Confounding factors.
   - Hypertension condition.
   - Noise sensitivity.
   - Demographic characteristics.
3. Questionnaire out of 100, higher scores meaning a more positive health status.

Noise measurement

4. Noise gap index (NGI) - difference between background noise and aircraft noise - taken at 26 stations around Sydney Airport.
5. Also measured at three stations in the control area.

Results

Health measurement

1. Most of the health scores of the noise exposure group were lower than the control group, including the mental health score, general health and vitality.
2. The noise exposure group had lower physical functioning, general health, vitality and mental health than the control group.

Chronic aircraft noise, stress and hypertension

3. Participants chronically exposed to high aircraft noise levels were 2.61 times more likely to report chronic noise stress.
4. Chronic noise stress participants were 2.74 times more likely to report hypertension compared to those without chronic noise stress.

Conclusions

People who have long-term aircraft noise exposure are likely to:

- Develop symptoms of chronic noise stress.
- Show symptoms of hypertension.

Lower physical functioning, general health, vitality and mental health in the noise group suggests that noise exposure reduces health-related quality of life.

Airports can reduce the impact of noise on residents by developing more runways or flight paths. Sound insulation in houses can also be improved.

How the key research explains ... stressors in the environment	**Effect of noise on physical health** Hypertension was significantly more prevalent in the noise-affected group than the control group, demonstrating the physical effects of stress.
	Effect of noise on psychological health Aircraft noise led to chronic stress, feelings of annoyance and reduced mental health in the noise-affected group but not the control group. This suggests that problems were caused primarily by noise stress, not other demographic variables.

Links between the topic and the methodological issues

Validity	⊖ Black *et al.*'s use of self-reports may be problematic as self-reports are subject to truth distortions (social desirability bias), which could reduce the validity of the responses about environmental stressors.
Reliability	✚ Black *et al.* checked the health questionnaires for reliability during the pilot study. They used a comparison analysis known as *Cronbach's Alpha*. This found that the self-reported measures of noise were highly consistent with each other.
Sampling bias	✚ Black *et al.*'s sample was very large (704 respondents), providing a varied set of data.
	⊖ However, this data set may be biased as only around 50% responded out of the original 1500 participants contacted, and these people may have been disproportionately bothered by aircraft noise. Therefore, the data may not represent what everyone feels and may exaggerate the unpleasant effects of noise.
Ethnocentrism	✚ Negative consequences of transport noise exist in many other cultures, e.g. Japan and many European countries (Clark and Stansfeld 2007). This suggests results apply to many other cultures and thus are not ethnocentrically biased.

Links between the topic and the debates

Free will/ determinism	The biological account of our response to stressors is determinist, e.g. the SAM system is seen as an inevitable reaction to a short-term stressor, and the HPA inevitably starts after a period of time.
	In terms of free will, it is unlikely that people would *choose* to experience stress or related ill-health.
Reductionism/ holism	Biological explanations are reductionist as they focus only on the biological causes of stress, e.g. hormones.
	A more holistic explanation of stress considers how biological, social and psychological explanations of stress interact, e.g. physiological arousal is moderated by social support (Ogden 2004).
Individual/ situational explanations	Stress is seen as situational rather than individual, e.g. living close to an airport (and its noise) triggers the biological stress response rather than something individual, e.g. personality.

Persistent and regular noise can be considered to be unlawful if it has a bad effect on you or your enjoyment of your home.

Revision booster

When evaluating the key research, you should consider that environmental stressors other than aircraft noise may have impacted the participants' physical and mental health, e.g. traffic congestion around an airport.

Exam-style question examples

Component 3 Section B part (a):

(a) Outline the research by Black *et al.* (2007), and use it to explain the impact of environmental stressors. **[10]**

Component 3 Section B part (b):

(b) Assess the extent to which research into stressors in the environment is determinist. **[15]**

(b) Discuss the validity of research into stressors in the environment. **[15]**

The debates on the left are examples of how you might link the topic to the debates. You need to prepare responses for the other five debates – we haven't got room to cover all of them here.

Background
Biological rhythms and the impact of their disruption on our behaviour

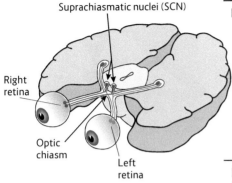

Suprachiasmatic nuclei (SCN)

Right retina

Optic chiasm

Left retina

The SCN receives information about light levels from both eyes, lying at the point where the optic nerves cross over (optic chiasm).

Revision booster

Students often make the mistake of not recognising that endogenous pacemakers and exogenous zeitgebers interact with one another. Do consider these concepts together.

Using the background research

Consider how you could use the background research to support answers to the following questions. See exam guidance on Component 3 Section B questions on page 8.

(a) Outline the key research by Czeisler *et al.* (1982) and use it to explain the impact of disrupting biological rhythms. **[10]**

(b) Discuss the nature/nurture debate in relation to research into biological rhythms. **[15]**

(c) Joe lives in the US and has an important business meeting in Glasgow. He is worried about the effects of jet lag after the long flight.

Outline **one** strategy a psychologist could recommend to Joe to help him reduce the effects of jet lag. **[10]**

Biological rhythms	Biological rhythms are governed by the body's internal biological 'clocks':
	Endogenous pacemaker The suprachiasmatic nucleus (SCN) is the main body clock. At low light levels the SCN triggers the pineal gland to release melatonin, inducing sleep. The pineal gland is inhibited by light.
	Exogenous zeitgebers These are external cues that 'fine tune' the SCN and other body clocks, e.g. daylight which signals waking up time.
Different types of biological rhythms	**Ultradian rhythms** Occur many times during the day, e.g. sleep cycles.
	Circadian rhythms Last for around 24 hours, e.g. the sleep–wake cycle.
	Infradian rhythms Take longer than a day to complete, e.g menstruation cycles.
	Circannual rhythms These happen on an annual basis, e.g. seasonal affective disorder.
A circadian rhythm: The sleep-wake cycle	**The sleep-wake cycle** Regulated by exogenous zeitgebers (e.g. darkness) or endogenous pacemakers (e.g. the SCN causing fluctuations in melatonin).
	A 'free-running' biological rhythm occurs if the biological clock is 'left to its own devices'.
	Siffre's (1975) cave study Siffre's 'free-running' biological rhythm more or less remained the same when he lived in a cave for two months, suggesting that circadian rhythms must be biological. Internal cues must have governed his biological rhythms as there were no exogenous zeitgebers (e.g. light).
The impact of disruption of biological rhythms on our behaviour	**Jet travel** Jet lag occurs when exogenous zeitgebers do not match our endogenous pacemakers.
	Travelling east to west is easier because we can stay up later (phase delay) but getting up earlier (phase advance) is harder to do.
	Effects of jet travel Jet lag can lead to negative cognitive and physiological effects, e.g. loss of concentration or increased anxiety (Green 2011).
	Shift work This is necessary in many jobs but requires people to work against their natural circadian rhythms. A circadian trough occurs between midnight (when cortisol levels are lowest) and 4 am (when core body temperature is at its lowest). The consequence is that we experience decreased alertness (Boivin *et al.* 1996).
	Effects of shift work Shift lag creates impairments in reaction times and decision-making abilities of shift workers, deteriorating as the number of night shifts increases (Tilley *et al.* 1982).

Application 1

Reducing the effects of jet lag

Melatonin supplements Used in phase advance travel (travelling east) because we are not ready for sleep. Taking melatonin supplements can help to induce sleep.

Melatonin supplements taken orally after dark on the day someone arrives at their destination may help them sleep and settle into the new time zone more quickly.

Do strategies to reduce the effects of jet lag work?

Usefulness There are few side effects from melatonin supplements if they are taken around normal bedtime and taken according to administration guidelines. However, if taken earlier in the day the supplements may actually have detrimental effects on a person's adjustment to jet lag.

Effectiveness Herxheimer and Petrie (2002) found melatonin was effective at reducing the effects of jet lag when taken between 10 pm and midnight. Supplements significantly reduced the effects of jet lag when crossing five or more time zones, particularly travelling west to east.

Practicalities Melatonin should not be taken with other medications (e.g. sedatives) or whilst pregnant or breastfeeding (WebMD.com 2016). A doctor should be consulted before a person takes melatonin supplements.

Application 2

Reducing the effects of shift work

Changing schedules Businesses could adjust shift patterns to reduce the negative effects, e.g. changing shifts by phase delay rather than phase advance, or making changes to shift patterns less frequently.

Businesses could also attempt to use continuous shifts, where employees complete the same shift permanently rather than rotating between shift patterns.

Light box treatment Employees on shift work can use phototherapy. This involves sitting near a 'light box' that emits artificial bright light. This bright light reduces melatonin levels, tricking the body into thinking that it is daytime. This can reduce drowsiness, for example, during a night shift.

Do strategies to reduce shift work effects work?

Usefulness Evidence has shown that changing shift patterns to match circadian rhythms (Czeisler *et al.*) and using light therapy (Costa *et al.* 1993) can have positive effects on shift workers.

Effectiveness Czeisler *et al.* found that a change in shift patterns that closely matched circadian rhythms was beneficial to both employees and their employers. However, Czeisler *et al.* only studied a very specific job and so positive effects may not be equally strong in other types of employment.

Practicalities Not all companies have the flexibility to adjust shift patterns in line with research evidence on circadian rhythms. Educating employers about circadian rhythms might have beneficial effects on workers if changing shift patterns is not possible, e.g. using light box treatments to change biological rhythms.

Using a sleep mask (properly) can help night shift workers adjust to sleeping during the daytime as it tricks the SCN into thinking it is dark, producing more melatonin.

Revision booster

If a Component 3 Section B part (c) question simply asks for 'advice' (as in the first question below), you can take either a 'depth' or 'breadth' approach. Your advice may centre on one suggestion (depth) or more than one suggestion (breadth).

Exam-style question examples

Component 3 Section B part (c):

(c) Elaine wants to visit her sister in Perth, Australia (travelling west to east). A direct flight takes 17 hours and she wants to minimise the effects of jet lag after the long flight.

Outline the advice you would give to Elaine to help reduce the effects of jet lag after such a long flight. **[10]**

(c) Lenka is the CEO of a chemical company that is introducing night shifts to increase production but she wants to maintain worker job satisfaction.

Outline **one** strategy a psychologist could suggest to Lenka about how to best increase production and also to make sure changes in shifts do not reduce workers' job satisfaction. **[10]**

How psychology contributes to the success of the economy and society ...
Improving performance for shift workers can increase productivity and decrease accidents at work.

Key research

Czeisler *et al.* (1982) on *Shift work*

Background

Recruiting workers for fixed night shifts is difficult because shift work disrupts circadian rhythms. However, it is the most practical way of ensuring 24-hour productivity. Rotating shifts is a reasonable compromise in some industries.

Aims

- To investigate levels of job satisfaction, personnel turnover, health and productivity in shift workers.
- To implement a new schedule for shift work based on knowledge of circadian rhythms.
- To test the impact of the new shift schedule on satisfaction, health and productivity. (The new schedule had less frequent shift rotation and rotation according to phase delay rather than phase advance.)

Method

Design

Quasi-experiment, independent groups.

IV: Shift pattern of the workers, phase delay (two groups) or phase advance.

DV: Sleep attitudes, sleep behaviours and job satisfaction.

Sample

Experimental group: 85 men, 19-68 years (mean age 31.4 years), worked on rotating shifts at the Great Salt Lake Minerals and Chemicals Corporation in Ogden, Utah (USA).

Control group: 68 men working on non-rotating shifts at the same plant, aged 19-56 years (mean age 27.3 years).

Materials/apparatus

Questionnaire which included: sleep-wake preference questionnaire, schedule preference questionnaire (shift rotation), job descriptive index, health index.

Procedure

Prior to the study

1. Workers were on a phase advance programme.
2. Three, eight-hour shifts per day - midnight to 8 am, 8 am to 4 pm, 4 pm to midnight.
3. Shift workers 'rotated' to the preceding eight-hour shift after one week - 'anticlockwise rotation' (phase advance).

Stage 1 of the study

4. Participants completed the questionnaire.

Stage 2 of the study

5. Workers and managers attended a presentation on the sleep-wake cycle and were given an information booklet on circadian rhythms.
6. Experimental group had their rotating shifts changed to phase delay:
   - 33 participants, shift pattern changed every week.
   - 52 participants, shift pattern changed every three weeks (21-day phase delay).
7. Workers completed questionnaires after three months.
8. Turnover and productivity was reviewed after nine months.

Results

Stage 1 of the study

1. Participants on rotating shifts (phase advance) reported significantly more problems with insomnia than the control group.
2. 29% of the 'rotators' reported falling asleep at work at least once in three months.
3. 81% of the rotators reported that it took 2-4 days to adjust to sleep pattern changes.
4. 26% reported that they never adjusted before the shift pattern changed again.
5. 90% felt that the shifts changed too frequently.

Stage 2 of the study

6. Complaints about frequent shift changes dropped from 90% to 20% of workers on the 21-day phase delay schedule.
7. There was a significant increase in satisfaction at work and an improvement in health measures for the 21-day schedule.
8. There was a reduction in staff turnover (same level as control group) and a significant increase in productivity.

People prefer longer (three-week) shift rotations to get used to the pattern of work compared to a short rotation (weekly). They also prefer this to fixed night shifts.

Conclusions

Phase advance schedules create a permanent state of desynchronisation between exogenous zeitgebers and endogenous pacemakers.

Phase delay shift work is more compatible with the circadian rhythm than phase advance rotations.

Shift patterns should be designed using knowledge of circadian rhythms to minimise disruption to health.

How the key research explains ... biological rhythms	Czeisler *et al.*'s study supports the negative impact that shift work has on performance, e.g. many people on rotating shift patterns had fallen asleep at work and struggled to adjust to the regular changes.
	When shift patterns changed less frequently, staff reported more satisfaction and showed more productivity and lower staff turnover. This shows that having time to adjust can help in coping with disruption to circadian rhythms and sleep patterns.

Links between the topic and the methodological issues

Validity	⇨ Czeisler *et al.*'s quasi-experiment meant they could not randomly allocate participants to conditions. Therefore, participant variables may have affected the results, reducing validity.
	⇨ Using questionnaires means participants may have exaggerated their negative feelings towards shift patterns, potentially reducing the validity of their responses.
Reliability	⇧ Czeisler *et al.*'s different measures of satisfaction all demonstrated a similar pattern, suggesting high internal reliability.
Sampling bias	⇨ Participants in Czeisler *et al.*'s study were all from one chemical plant in America, and had been on the same shift pattern for ten years. This is not highly representative of people working shift patterns.
	⇨ The sample consisted of men only, all of whom worked in a factory, which is not true of all shift workers.
Ethnocentrism	⇨ Czeisler *et al.*'s study is ethnocentric as it solely looked at the mismatch between endogenous pacemakers and exogenous zeitgebers in an individualist culture (the US).

It is more difficult to wake up earlier than you want (phase advance) than going to bed later than usual (phase delay).

Methodological issues are discussed in Chapter 1 and also on pages 95–96.

Links between the topic and the debates

Nature/nurture	Endogenous pacemakers show the influence of nature because they are determined by our biological systems.
	Circadian rhythms (endogenous pacemakers) are also influenced by external factors in our environment (exogenous zeitgebers), supporting the nurture argument.
Free will/ determinism	Biological rhythms (e.g. circadian rhythms) are an example of biological determinism because they are governed by biological activity (e.g. brain activity and hormone levels).
	We can exercise free will through changing shift patterns to work with our biological rhythms, creating conditions that cause minimum disruption.
Reductionism/ holism	Endogenous pacemakers setting circadian rhythms is a reductionist explanation because it is attributing a complex behaviour solely to a biological clock.
	Exogenous zeitgebers (e.g. mealtimes and how busy the environment is) also influence our daily rhythms, representing a more holistic approach.

Revision booster

Set yourself achievable 'bite-size' targets for your revision, e.g. learn the different types of biological rhythms and test yourself before moving on to the impact of disruption on biological rhythms.

Exam-style question examples

Component 3 Section B part (a):

(a) Use the research by Czeisler *et al.* (1982) to explain how disruption to biological rhythms impacts behaviour. **[10]**

Component 3 Section B part (b):

(b) Discuss the validity of research into the impact of disruption to biological rhythms. **[15]**

(b) Evaluate the reliability of research into the impact of disruption to biological rhythms. **[15]**

How psychology contributes to the success of the economy and society ... Research on factors that reduce productivity and individual health is important to the economy.

Background

Conservation behaviours and the factors which influence the tendency to conserve or recycle

Recycling has many benefits for the environment, e.g. less air pollution, less waste going to landfill and fewer greenhouse gases.

Revision booster

Remember to use both background research (e.g. TPB) and the key research (e.g. Lord) to explain behaviours (e.g. conservation and recycling).

Using the background research

Consider how you could use the background research to support answers to the following questions. See exam guidance on Component 3 Section B questions on page 8.

(a) Use the research by Lord (1994) to explain factors that influence recycling behaviour. **[10]**

(b) Discuss the validity of research into recycling and conservation behaviour. **[15]**

(c) Jamie works ten minutes' walk from home but he drives his car to work each day. His wife, Michelle, thinks that he should walk to work and help the environment.

Outline the advice you would give to Michelle to help persuade Jamie to walk to work rather than use his car. **[10]**

Conservation behaviours	Conservation behaviours are anything that individuals, organisations and governments do that is environmentally friendly, e.g. recycling household waste. There are physical factors that influence the tendency to conserve or recycle (e.g. being able to take out recycling to bins) and situational factors (e.g. the frequency of collections).
Recycling	Recycling is the process of converting waste materials into reusable objects. Recycling is commonly available for materials such as glass, paper, cardboard, plastics and aluminum. Some parts of Britain also recycle nappies, textiles and food. Household recycling can be done either by kerbside collections of recyclable waste, or by taking recycling to a collection centre.
Theory of planned behaviour (TPB) (Ajzen 1985)	The TPB is a cognitive model used to explain why people behave as they do. Intentions to conserve (and subsequent behaviour) are a consequence of: • **Personal attitudes towards conservation** Based on whether a person sees the outcomes of conservation as positive or negative. • **Subjective norms** Based on what other people, especially significant people (e.g. friends or family), think about conservation. • **Perceived behavioural control** This increases if people believe they have the ability to do it (i.e. to conserve). This may be influenced by external factors, e.g. frequency of recycling. **Outcome** Personal attitudes + subjective norms + perceived behavioural control form the likelihood of having intentions to perform conservation behaviours. If the three factors are high, then an individual is more likely to have the intention to conserve and then more likely to behave in this way.
Cognitive dissonance theory (Festinger 1957)	If a person has two cognitions (attitudes) about something that conflict, this creates tension (*dissonance*) due to cognitive inconsistency. **Changing cognitions** People are motivated to change negative states of inconsistency. Therefore, they change their cognitions to become consistent with other cognitions or consistent with their behaviour. This change is achieved by finding out new information, or minimising the perceived importance of the cognitions. **Changing behaviours** People may also change behaviours to match cognitions. For example, Lord (1994) found that people were more likely to change their behaviour if they were told the negative consequences of their behaviour rather than being given messages about the benefits of recycling.

Application 1

Antecedent techniques

Antecedent techniques encourage conservation or recycling *before* a person is faced with the decision to conserve or not.

Examples of antecedent techniques Two examples are providing more recycling bins and offering more frequent collections. Recycling can also be increased by clarifying for residents what can and can't be recycled in their area.

Changing perceptions This works by increasing the public's perception of the benefits of recycling and reducing their perception of the drawbacks of recycling or other conservation behaviours.

Framing the advice Focus on the financial benefits and the positive feeling people get from recycling.

Do antecedent techniques work?

Usefulness Uzzell (2014) suggests if a whole community undertakes recycling behaviours, it encourages others and recycling becomes the 'subjective norm', increasing the amount of recycling.

Effectiveness Promotional messages given to residents improve recycling behaviour (Lord 1994). However, messages phrased negatively are most likely to have a positive behavioural impact.

Practicalities Advertising on a mass scale is very expensive and some people may not be physically able to move recycling bins, e.g. elderly people.

Application 2

Consequent techniques

Consequent techniques are those that occur during or after conservation behaviour.

Rewards For example, raffle tickets can be given with a prize for each box of recycling that is left out. This uses operant conditioning because people anticipate a reward for conservation behaviour.

Punishments People who do not conserve may be punished by systems such as 'pay as you throw'. This is a system used in over 4000 communities in the US whereby households pay per bag of rubbish that isn't for recycling.

Do consequent techniques work?

Usefulness Incentives may not always be the most effective way to encourage conservation behaviours. However, they are likely to be more effective than creating regulations in the form of laws.

Effectiveness Incentives (e.g. raffle tickets) can be effective at encouraging recycling (Couch *et al.* 1978). However, as soon as the incentive stops, the conservation behaviour may stop too.

Practicalities One problem with trying to change people's behaviour is that a lot of recycling is habit bound rather than being a thoughtful process of weighing up the pros and cons of recycling.

Choosing an electric car can help with conservation because such cars reduce carbon footprints by emitting fewer greenhouse gases and air pollutants than petrol or diesel cars.

Revision booster

The Wrap Recycling Action Program message 'Most people recycle me' is used to nudge people into recycling more. You could use this type of strategy as a useful example when answering the part (c) questions below.

Exam-style question examples

Component 3 Section B part (c):

(c) Kaoru is the school liaison officer for a water company and has been asked to give a presentation on water conservation to a year 10 group.

Outline the advice Kaoru could include in her water conservation presentation to the school pupils. **[10]**

(c) Joel is a primary school teacher who wants to increase the amount of plastic his pupils recycle.

Outline **one** strategy a psychologist would recommend to Joel to help his pupils recycle more. **[10]**

Key research

Lord (1994) on *Recycling behaviour*

Background

Previous research has looked at the effectiveness of a variety of methods to encourage recycling, e.g. financial incentives or making a public commitment.

Aims and hypotheses

To investigate whether more personally-directed messages might encourage recycling, based on eight hypotheses:

Advocacy messages ...

- H1 ... positively affect attitudes.
- H2 ... lead to an increase in observed recycling behaviour.

Positive framing of messages ...

- H3 ... leads to more positive beliefs about the benefits of recycling.
- H4 ... leads to more favourable attitudes.

When there is an interaction between framing and source of message ...

... Negative framing affects ...

- H5 ... *beliefs* about recycling most if the advocacy message comes from a news story and least from an advertising appeal.
- H6 ... *attitudes* towards recycling most coming from a news story.

... Personal appeals have more effect on ...

- H7 ... *attitudes* towards recycling when framed positively than when phrased negatively.
- H8 ... recycling *behaviour* than the other sources, particularly when negatively framed.

Method

Design

Field experiment, independent groups.

IV: 3 × 2 design - three sources of information (news, advertising, personal letter) framed either positively or negatively (six experimental groups).

DV: recycling behaviour observed, attitudes/beliefs assessed on questionnaire.

A control group received no message about recycling.

Sample

140 households from Buffalo, USA, respondents aged 19-65 years (mean 34.9 years). 57% of respondents were women.

Materials/apparatus

News, advertising or personal letter.

Questionnaire assessing beliefs and attitudes.

Procedure

1. Recorded number of items each household recycled.
2. Recorded how many different categories the items belonged to, e.g. glass, paper.
3. The next day participants were given one advocacy message, either positively or negatively framed.
4. Assessing behavioural impact of advocacy message - recycling observed on the following week's kerbside collection.
5. Assessing impact of message on attitudes and beliefs:
   - Day after collection the person responsible for recycling in the household completed the questionnaire.
   - Beliefs: 7-point rating scale (from 1 for definitely false to 7 for definitely true).
   - Attitudes: semantic differential rating scale (e.g. good-bad, wise-foolish).

Results

1. H1: Any message encouraged a significantly more positive attitude to recycling than no message.
2. H2: Advocacy message showed significantly more recycling behaviour than no message.
3. H3: Participants with positively-framed message believed advocacy messages significantly more than those with negative messages or no message.
4. H4: Positively-framed messages led to significantly more positive attitudes and beliefs to recycling than negatively-framed messages.
5. H5: Message source made little difference to credibility of the source.
6. H6: Negatively-framed messages affected attitudes most when presented as part of a news story.
7. H7: A positively-phrased personal appeal created significantly more positive attitudes towards recycling than when phrased negatively.
8. H8: Households with a negatively-framed personal letter recycled significantly more than other groups.

Conclusions

Negatively-framed messages in a personal letter or from advertising are effective methods to increase recycling.

Positive messages lead to attitudinal changes.

The most effective way to encourage recycling is to use more than one technique at the same time.

How the key research explains ... recycling and other conservation behaviours	Lord found that, although positively-framed messages improved attitudes towards recycling, they did not necessarily lead to behaviour change. Instead, he found that negatively-framed messages led to more behaviour change.
	Lord also found that subjective norms influence recycling, as the personal letter written by an acquaintance of the participant had the biggest impact on recycling behaviour, but this was only for negatively-framed messages. People whose opinions are important to us influence our recycling behaviours.

Links between the topic and the methodological issues

Validity	⊕ Lord's study was high in validity as typical recycling routines were monitored and participants were unaware they were monitored, so recycling behaviour was natural.
	⊖ Lord could not be sure if the respondent of the questionnaire was involved in recycling or had seen the information. This questions the validity of the responses to the questionnaires.
Reliability	⊕ Lord controlled variables by using standardised observation categories and a fixed questionnaire, enhancing reliability.
	⊕ The semantic differential rating scales used in the self-report were tested and found to be reliable (+.88 for attitudes).
Sampling bias	⊕ Lord used quota sampling to get a representative sample, making results about recycling more generalisable.
	⊖ Data came solely from people in Buffalo with a high socio-economic status and perhaps a more positive attitude towards recycling than other subgroups in society.
Ethnocentrism	⊖ Collectivist cultures who value the group over the individual may be more influenced by subjective norms than individualist cultures, so may recycle more items. Therefore, this research may underestimate the effect of personally-directed messages on behaviour.

Links between the topic and the debates

Reductionism/ holism	The theory of planned behaviour is a holistic model as it combines cognitive factors (attitudes towards conservation), social factors (e.g. what other people think) and also practical elements (e.g. whether people can actually do that conservation behaviour).
	Lord concluded that recycling behaviour is complex, thus recognising that a reductionist approach is unlikely to work.
Individual/ situational explanations	Situational factors (e.g. frequency of kerbside collections) can influence an individual's tendency to conserve or recycle.
	People's perception of what other people think of their recycling behaviour is an individual explanation of conservation.
Usefulness of research	If society understands why people don't conserve, then governments can implement strategies to encourage it, thereby reducing the pollution caused by waste.

There is no single effective way of promoting recycling but the biggest behaviour change came from a negatively-framed personal letter.

Revision booster

Students often forget to highlight that, although changing attitudes to recycling is good, it is changing recycling behaviours that is most important.

Exam-style question examples

Component 3 Section B part (a):

(a) Use the research by Lord (1994) to explain how to increase people's tendency to conserve or recycle. [10]

Component 3 Section B part (b):

(b) Discuss the validity of research into recycling and conservation behaviour. [15]

(b) Discuss the usefulness of research into recycling and conservation behaviour. [15]

The exam questions above are just representative examples. Read the guidance for Component 3 exam questions on page 8.

Background
Cognitive overload and the impact of observation in the workplace environment

Novice readers have to sound out unknown words which increases the information that has to be held in working memory. This increases the cognitive load of the reader.

If workstations are not appropriate for a user, this can lead to poor mental health, lower productivity, higher staff turnover and lower job satisfaction.

Using the background research

Consider how you could use the background research to support answers to the following questions. See exam guidance on Component 3 Section B questions on page 8.

(a) Outline the research by Drews and Doig (2014) and explain what it tells us about ergonomics in the workplace. **[10]**

(b) Discuss the extent to which research into ergonomics in the workplace is scientific. **[15]**

(c) Mike manages an NHS call centre dealing with out-patient appointments. He wants to improve the office layout so his staff can better focus on the out-patients' calls.

Outline **one** strategy a psychologist could teach Mike about how to apply ergonomic research to improve the call centre design. **[10]**

Ergonomics – human factors	*Ergonomics* is the process of developing products, systems or workplaces so that they fit the people who use them. Ergonomics can refer to: **Physiological suitability** For example, arranging a workspace to reduce back pain. **Cognitive suitability** For example, designing a flexible workspace to allow users to be more productive, as in the case of hot-desking.
Cognitive overload	*Cognitive load* (Sweller 1988) refers to the amount of information working memory can hold at one time. *Working memory* refers to the information stored in short-term memory and used whilst working on a task. Some of this information may be passed to the long-term, permanent memory store. Too many demands on our cognitive load lead to cognitive *over*load, leading to stress, anxiety, poor decision-making and reduced performance at work.
Working memory model (WMM)	Baddeley and Hitch (1974) proposed that working memory consists of several stores: **Phonological loop** Deals with sound information. **Visuo-spatial sketchpad** Deals with visual information. **Central executive** Controls and coordinates the operation of the two subsystems above.
Social facilitation	Social facilitation is when our performance on a task is improved, just because other people are present. **Zajonc's explanation** Arousal increases due to the presence of an audience. This increase means we are more likely to respond with our dominant response (i.e. how we would most naturally act). When performing a simple task in front of an audience (e.g. adding digits), we would do it well. But when performing a complex task in front of an audience (e.g. reading a difficult passage out loud), even the most effortless, 'dominant response' is likely to be poorly performed.
Audience effects	Audience effects in the workplace can lead to both positive and negative changes in behaviour. **Positive effects** Dashiell (1930) showed that students completed a higher number of multiplication problems in a set time with an audience. **Negative effects** Dashiell also found that participants made more mistakes in the multiplication tasks they were undertaking. This suggests that having an audience reduces the accuracy of the task being performed. **Other factors** The impact of being observed by others (audience effects) in a workplace environment largely depends on the performer (employee), task (complex or simple, familiar or new) and audience (manager, stranger or friend).

Application 1

Adjusting the lighting in the workplace

It is easier to change the environment in which someone works rather than trying to change their cognitive abilities and performance.

For example, the lighting can be changed from fluorescent to LED lights. Lighting is necessary for practical purposes at work but it can also have a profound impact on productivity and well-being. 'Cooler' LED light has positive effects on worker alertness, fatigue and productivity.

Does adjusting the lighting in the workplace work?

Usefulness Hawes *et al.* (2012) observed US Army members performing both cognitive and visual tasks. There was no increase in task accuracy in the different lighting conditions. This may mean that change in lighting is less useful in jobs where accuracy is more important than speed of completion.

Effectiveness On the positive side, Hawes *et al.* found that 'cooler' lighting conditions were associated with positive effects on the speed of work and depression scores of participants than in the 'warmer' lighting conditions.

Practicalities Adjusting any fixtures and fittings can cost a lot of money for a company, so it may not always be financially viable to change the lighting. Changing the lighting also may not be appropriate in all workplaces, e.g. operating theatres.

Application 2

Closed office spaces

Workplaces can introduce closed offices rather than using an open-plan set-up or hot-desking.

What is a closed office? This is where employees are sectioned off in individual rooms or cubicles.

Reduced cognitive load Fewer people in closed offices means reduced noise levels and stimulation from talking, technology and movement. This means the worker is less likely to experience cognitive overload.

Other advantages There is more privacy because fewer people can see the employee's work and behaviour. Closed offices also allow for more perceived control because people do not have to agree on elements that need adjustment, e.g. temperature. Also a closed office allows for greater personalisation, benefitting mental health.

Do closed offices work?

Usefulness Positive effects from closed offices could lead to lower staff absences and higher productivity, as well as higher job satisfaction. However, many people do not work in offices, e.g. workers in hospitals and on building sites.

Effectiveness Lusk *et al.* (2002) showed that reduced noise at work is associated with lower levels of stress (both self-reported stress levels and physiological measurements). This suggests that working in a quieter office benefits an individual's well-being.

Practicalities Changing working environments is expensive or may not be well received. If open-plan offices are needed, the negative effects can be mitigated by creating higher boundaries between desks, and introducing policies to reduce extra noise, e.g. using headsets when on the phone.

Not all offices are improved by making them 'closed'. Often open-plan offices allow enhanced communication between employees, which for some businesses will speed up and improve service.

Revision booster

In application questions such as those below, students are often solely focused on outlining the strategy. Remember to also write about the strategy benefits to the person in the scenario.

Exam-style question examples

Component 3 Section B part (c):

(c) Penny is head of sales at a boutique selling handbags. She finds that she feels very tired working under bright, fluorescent lights.

Outline the advice a psychologist may give the manager about the boutique's lighting so that Penny feels more alert at work. **[10]**

(c) Ji-hyun is an architect who is designing a new office space for a large Korean bank.

Outline the advice a psychologist may give to Ji-hyun about how best to apply ergonomic research to the design of the new office space. **[10]**

Don't forget to read our exam advice on pages 4–15.

Key research
Drews and Doig (2014) on *Visual displays*

Background and aims

In an intensive care unit (ICU), a patient's vital signs are constantly displayed on a monitor. Traditionally this has only featured the current status of vital signs. Drews and Doig wanted to develop a display that showed both recent and current data about a patient's vital signs graphically. This would enable changes in status to be identified quickly and easily, reducing cognitive demands on ICU nurses.

Aims

- To develop a configural vital signs (CVS) display.
- To evaluate this CVS display in terms of its ability to reduce cognitive demand on ICU nurses.

Method

Design

Field experiment, independent measures design.

IV: CVS display or a traditional display (a control group).

DV1: Nurse response time.

DV2: Accuracy of the interpretation of the clinical data.

Sample

42 registered ICU nurses with critical care training and at least one year of experience. Mean age of the nurses was 44.59 years. 69% of the nurses were women. Their experience in ICU ranged from two to 30 years, with a mean of 8.48 years' ICU experience.

Materials

Four different scenarios to test the displays: early sepsis, septic shock, pulmonary embolus, stable patient.

Assessment of workload questionnaire.

Procedure

1. Participants received 20 minutes' training on using the displays.

2. Participants given patient case information.

3. Participants given patient vital signs information (CVS or traditional display).

4. Participants asked to verbally evaluate patients' physiological status.

5. Participants had to recommend appropriate interventions as quickly and accurately as possible.

6. Participants given five minutes to complete each of the four scenarios.

7. Participants completed the Assessment of workload questionnaire.

8. Participants answered questions on the clinical desirability of the CVS display and the realism of the study scenarios.

Results

Dependent variable 1: Nurse response time

1. In all four scenarios, participants in the CVS condition identified the patients' state on average 30% faster than those in the traditional display condition.

2. Improvement varied between the different scenarios, e.g. septic shock response was 48% quicker for CVS than traditional display.

Dependent variable 2: Accuracy of the interpretation of the clinical data

3. Overall, nurses using the CVS display correctly identified the patients' condition more frequently than nurses in the control group.

4. Only the septic shock and pulmonary embolus scenarios showed a significant difference between the two groups.

Responses regarding cognitive demand

5. Nurses reported less cognitive demand using the CVS screens (mean = 3.95 out of 7) compared to the traditional display (mean = 4.71).

6. Nurses rated the scenarios as realistic (a median rating of 6 out of 7), and they rated the CVS display as desirable (also a median rating of 6 out of 7).

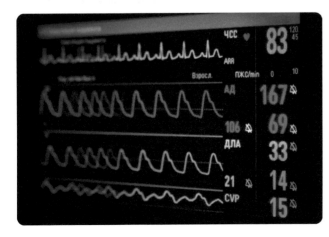

Ergonomics is all about designing equipment so that it is easy for people to use. Drews and Doig's CVS display was designed so it suited the needs of the hospital nurses.

Conclusions

CVS displays improve the speed and accuracy of interpretation of data by ICU nurses.

CVS displays put all the data in one place, using colours and geometric shapes to make the data more accessible. This reduces nurses' workload.

CVS displays improve patient safety.

How the key research explains ... ergonomics	ICU nurses deal with many complex tasks, often several of them simultaneously, and this could lead to reduced performance. The CVS display was designed to reduce the nurses' cognitive demand by simplifying their task, thereby increasing the speed and accuracy of their response to patients.
	Nurses using the CVS system were also likely to find it less stressful than using traditional ICU displays.

Links between the topic and the methodological issues

Validity	⊕ The simulated scenarios in Drews and Doig's study allowed for tight control of variables and for all patient data in each scenario to be standardised. This increases validity of the study.
	⊖ The study lacked ecological validity as there were no real consequences to the diagnoses for patients. Therefore, the participants may not have treated the task in the same way they would in everyday work.
Reliability	⊕ The questionnaire Drews and Doig gave to the ICU nurses to assess subjective workload is called the NASA-TLX, which has a high split-half reliability of +.80.
Sampling bias	⊖ The findings for ICU nurses may not apply to other users of CVS displays in hospitals as they are used differently and for different purposes by different groups of medical staff.
	⊖ Students are used to performing cognitive tasks for an assessing audience and so Dashiell's (1930) results may not be applicable to other target populations.
Ethnocentrism	⊖ American culture is monochronic (people prefer to finish one task at a time), which would suggest that cognitive overload may occur more easily than in, for example, Asian countries that are polychronic (prefer to undertake several tasks at once).

Links between the topic and the debates

Individual/ situational explanations	The change in the environment with the CVS display for Drews and Doig's nurses supports a situational explanation for improved speed and accuracy of responses.
	Zajonc's (1965) research shows that individual factors (e.g. perceived complexity and familiarity of the task) influence whether the presence of others affects behaviour.
Usefulness of research	If CVS displays can increase the speed and accuracy of nurses' responses in ICU, this could have profound effects on the lives of the ICU patients, as well as benefits for the well-being of the nurses.
	However, it is not clear how much of an improvement the CVS display would have for other areas of nursing.
Ethical considerations	Drews and Doig used simulations rather than real ICU patients. Therefore, there was no risk of physical harm and nurses did not face any real-life consequences to their actions.

People often work in the same space and need to collaborate with each other. Therefore, social factors are important (in addition to environmental factors) in determining an individual's work-related performance.

Revision booster

Dual-coding refers to using both words and visuals (i.e. coding information in two different ways). It is a way of improving your memory, e.g. you could draw and label a storyboard of Drews and Doig's study to aid your revision.

Exam-style question examples

Component 3 Section B part (a):

(a) Use the key research by Drews and Doig (2014) to explain the benefits of ergonomics to nurses in hospitals. **[10]**

Component 3 Section B part (b):

(b) Evaluate methodological issues in research on ergonomics. **[15]**

(b) Discuss the problems that arise when conducting research into ergonomics. **[15]**

The debates on the left are examples of how you might link the topic to the debates (you can read a summary of the debates on pages 91–94). In the exam be prepared to think on your feet.

Background
The impact of the built environment and urban renewal on our well-being

Ulrich's study may be considered socially sensitive because it has the potential to affect the specific groups of people in the research (i.e. hospital patients) – though the effect is likely to be positive.

Impact of the built environment	The *built environment* refers to aspects of our surroundings that are human made, e.g. buildings and roads. Such urban areas often have high noise and population density. People living in urban areas are less psychologically healthy than those in rural areas (Alcock *et al.* 2014).
Effect of noise on well-being	Noise might come from, for example, transport, industry and increased amounts of people. Cities and other built-up environments are often noisier than rural areas. This noise can have a negative impact on well-being.
	Ng (2000) found that the students living closest to high levels of noise from a construction site found it more difficult to study and relax than students living further away from the construction noise.
Effect of overcrowding on well-being	In the built environment, *overcrowding* can refer to a high number of residences in an area or to a high number of people within a limited space.
	Overcrowding can have detrimental effects on physical and mental health, performance on tasks and social behaviours.
	Fleming *et al.* (1987) found that overcrowded environments increase stress levels and have a negative impact on our well-being.
Impact of urban renewal	*Urban renewal* (also called 'urban regeneration') is the process of redeveloping urban (city) areas by demolishing and rebuilding structures, adjusting the layout of an area or developing green areas within the city.
	This is done in an attempt to improve the economic status of the area and to increase the satisfaction and health of residents.
Effect of green spaces on well-being	Successful green spaces are enclosed yet accessible and include parks, play areas, farms, forests, sports fields and allotments. Developing green spaces in urban areas is important due to their benefits on physical and mental health.
	Effects on mental health White *et al.* (2013) found that people living near green spaces experienced lower psychological distress and improved well-being than those living further away. The availability of green spaces had more impact on psychological health than local crime rate. Green spaces should be freely available to all members of society, regardless of income, culture or age.
	Effects on physical health Haluza *et al.* (2014) found that contact with outdoor, natural environments was associated with improved health, a stronger immune system, better cardiovascular health and a healthier endocrine system (hormones).

Using the background research

Consider how you could use the background research to support answers to the following questions. See exam guidance on Component 3 Section B questions on page 8.

(a) Using the research by Ulrich (1984), explain psychological effects of the built environment. **[10]**

(b) Discuss methodological issues relating to psychological effects of the built environment. **[15]**

(c) Residents of a housing estate have complained to their local council that many of them are experiencing stress from long-term roadworks at a nearby junction.

Outline the advice a psychologist might give to the council in order to avoid such roadworks having a negative effect on the well-being of the estate's residents. **[10]**

Application 1

Defensible space

Defensible space refers to an area of physical space that can be perceived as clearly belonging to someone, e.g. the garden in front of a house. In multiple-occupancy homes (e.g. a block of flats), residents often lack the feeling of defensible space in areas such as corridors and hallways. This can be improved by providing shared ownership of gardens which can lead to greater feelings of well-being.

Creating defensible space New estates could have fewer people or families sharing any public area (e.g. fewer people sharing a corridor), enabling them to have a greater sense of ownership. Defensible space can also be achieved by having clear boundary markers for gardens. Windows that overlook communal areas in blocks of flats further give the sense of defensible space.

Does defensible space work?

Usefulness Brown and Altman (1983) found that houses that had not been burgled had territorial markers that indicated privacy. Burgled houses tended to have cues of being unoccupied.

Effectiveness Moore (1975) found that military wives living in houses felt happier and healthier than wives living in flats. They also felt less isolated and lonely despite having the same number of friends as the women in flats.

Practicalities There are costs of creating defensible space and there may be restrictions imposed by the council or landlords. It is easiest to create defensible space when building new neighbourhoods.

Application 2

'Walkability'

Walking is the most common form of exercise in adults and *walkability* (Villanueva *et al.* 2013) is the number of attributes in the neighbourhood that make the area pedestrian-friendly, e.g. street lighting.

Factors that encourage walking Saelens *et al.* (2003) found that roads that were laid out in straight-line grids plus improved footpaths, encouraged short-distance walking.

Town planning Traditional town planning that uses 'high land use mix' areas (residential and commercial properties mixed in together) encourages walking.

Changing attitudes Education should be provided to change people's attitudes so they are more likely to use walking as a mode of transport or as exercise (Saelens *et al.* 2003).

Does 'walkability' work?

Usefulness Increased physical activity is also closely linked with longer life expectancy, less illness and better mental health. This means that encouraging walking, through environmental design, could be useful for health and well-being.

Effectiveness Frank *et al.* (2006) found that people living in neighbourhoods with high walkability were 32% more active and had a reduced body mass index.

Practicalities Creating 'walkable' environments is difficult in neighbourhoods that already exist but for new developments, town planners could take these ideas about walkability into account.

Developing boundary markers such as fences can be the responsibility of the homeowner or of the town planners when creating new housing.

Revision booster

Remember to use and explain specific terminology from the key research. This shows the examiner you understand the main psychological concepts of the topic, e.g. use the term 'defensible space'.

Exam-style question examples

Component 3 Section B part (c):

(c) Emily has been asked to design a new housing estate on the outskirts of a town.

Outline **one** strategy a psychologist might suggest to Emily so that she can ensure the health and well-being of the new residents. **[10]**

(c) Erik has noticed an increase in vandalism in the areas surrounding his house and wants it to stop.

Outline the advice a psychologist might suggest to Erik to address this problem of vandalism. **[10]**

Key research

Ulrich (1984) on *Recovery from surgery*

Background

Ulrich proposed that pictures of rural views may have a positive impact on hospital patients' anxiety and stress, and therefore on their recovery.

Aim

To investigate whether having a view of a natural scene from a hospital window would have positive effects on the recovery of patients.

Method

Design

Matched participants design (matched on gender, age [within a range of five years], smoking status, weight bracket, year of surgery, floor level and general nature of previous hospitalisation), repeated measures design.

IV: Window view of a wall or window view of a tree.

DV: Patients' hospital records.

Sample

46 patients (30 women and 16 men) who had gall bladder surgery, given a room on the second or third floor of a three-storey wing of a suburban hospital in Pennsylvania between 1972 and 1981 in the months of May to October.

Materials/apparatus

Rooms on the ward had two beds and were all of similar dimensions, layouts and had a similar-sized window. The window was large and at a height that meant patients could get a clear view out of it from their bed.

Procedure

1. Data was gathered at the time of the hospital stay as part of the hospital records, this is therefore secondary data.

2. The data was analysed by an experienced nurse who was blind to the experimental conditions.

Information for each patient

3. Days of hospitalisation - Number of days.

4. Analgesics - Number and strength, each day.

5. Anti-anxiety drugs - Number and strength of doses, each day.

6. Minor post-operative complications - For example, persistent headache or nausea requiring medication.

7. Nurses' notes - Relating to a patient's condition or course of recovery, classed as positive (e.g. 'in good spirits') or negative (e.g. 'upset and crying'). This was the only qualitative data used.

Results

1. **Days of hospitalisation** The tree-view patients spent significantly less time in hospital after their operation.

2. **Analgesics**
   - No difference was found between the two experimental groups (wall versus tree view) on the initial day after the surgery.
   - Days 2-5 after the operation: The tree-view patients took significantly fewer moderate and strong analgesics than the wall-view patients.
   - Day 6 onwards: There was no difference between the two groups in the number and type of analgesics taken.

3. **Anti-anxiety drugs** There was no difference in the amount of drugs given between the experimental groups.

4. **Minor post-operative complications** Tree-view patients had fewer minor complications.

5. **Nurses' notes** Significantly more negative notes were made about those patients with the wall view than tree view.

Conclusions

Rural landscapes have a positive physical and psychological effect on patient recovery.

Hospital design should consider the views from patients' beds as a means of aiding recovery.

Urban views that are more stimulating than a featureless wall (e.g. a lively city street) might be more interesting and have a more therapeutic benefit than the wall.

Not a very nice view from your window and, as it turns out, not good for your psychological health.

Evaluation of research on psychological effects of built environment

| How the key research explains ... the psychological effects of built environment | Ulrich's study found that patients with a tree view recovered more quickly from surgery compared with patients with a wall view. This shows the potential negative impact of the built environment on physical well-being.

Patients with a wall view also reported significantly more negative emotions during their stay than patients with a tree view. This shows how the built environment can have a negative impact on psychological well-being. |

Doesn't matter which way you look at a tree, it is still good for you.

Links between the topic and the methodological issues

Validity	➕ Ulrich's data was collected from hospital records by a nurse who did not know whether a patient had a wall or tree view, meaning the nurse's judgements were unbiased. ➕ Ulrich controlled many variables, e.g. matching patients to eliminate participant variables. This increased internal validity.
Reliability	➕ Ulrich used standardised procedures to control variables, e.g. the rooms, windows and beds were of similar dimensions and layouts. This made the results highly reliable.
Sampling bias	➖ Ulrich's study involved patients in one specific ward of one hospital, all having had the same operation. Their reactions to the view from the window may be different from those of other patients who have different levels of discomfort and mobility, and those staying in hospital for a longer duration.
Ethnocentrism	➖ Collectivist cultures may not experience the same psychological impact of the built environment. For example, Evans *et al.* (2000) found Americans (individualist) experienced greater psychological distress from high density housing than Vietnamese-Americans (more collectivist).

Links between the topic and the debates

Free will/ determinism	Environmental determinism is when our surroundings cause our behaviour, attitudes or beliefs, e.g. military wives living in houses felt happier and healthier than wives living in flats (Moore 1975). However, Ng (2000) found that people sometimes deal with construction noise by shutting windows or leaving the room, demonstrating an element of free will.
Individual/ situational explanations	Ulrich found views from the hospital room affected patients' well-being and recovery rates. This is a situational explanation, based on the built environment. The negative impact of environmental stressors (e.g. overcrowding) is only felt if the individual perceives it to be stressful, supporting an individual explanation.
Ethical considerations	Ulrich's patients did not give informed consent as they were unaware their data was being used for research purposes. However, Ulrich did not have access to patient names so confidentiality was protected.

Revision booster

To help understand the demands of Section B part (b) questions, underline the command word (e.g. 'discuss'), and then put a ring around the content words (e.g. 'psychological effects'), and finally put a box around the issue or debate (e.g. 'determinism').

Perspectives, debates and methodological issues are explained on pages 90–96.

Exam-style question examples

Component 3 Section B part (a):

(a) Outline the research by Ulrich (1984) and use it to explain the psychological effects of the built environment. **[10]**

Component 3 Section B part (b):

(b) Assess the psychological effects of the built environment in relation to situational explanations. **[15]**

(b) Discuss the extent to which research into the psychological effects of the built environment can be considered determinist. **[15]**

How psychology contributes to the success of the economy and society ...
Understanding the effects of our environment creates a healthier society.

Background
Territory and personal space in the workplace

Invasion of personal space can lead to cognitive overload and reduced job satisfaction.

Intimate space refers to cuddling. Personal space is for friends. Social space is for people we do not know personally but meet regularly. Public space is for people we don't know.

Using the background research

Consider how you could use the background research to support answers to the following questions. See exam guidance on Component 3 Section B questions on page 8.

(a) Using the research by Wells (2000), explain territory and personal space in the workplace. **[10]**

(b) Discuss the validity of research into territory and personal space in the workplace. **[15]**

(c) Roseanne is the CEO of a large IT company which is moving into new office space. She is meeting consultants regarding the proposed layout of the new offices.

Outline **one** strategy based on research into territory or personal space that the consultants could recommend to Roseanne to help her new office design. **[10]**

Territory and personal space	*Territory* is a fixed area owned by someone, usually with visual boundaries or perimeters that are marked out. *Personal space* is an area surrounding someone which has invisible boundaries. Personal space is portable and changes size depending on the situation and who is there.
Territory (Altman 1975)	**Primary territory** Permanent, clearly belongs to someone and tends to be highly personalised. **Secondary territory** Slightly more temporary than primary territory and it may have several users, e.g. your seat in a classroom. **Public territory** Temporary and may have a large number of possible users. It is not personalised, except during use, e.g. a bus seat. Edney (1974) suggests that territory provides three elements that are necessary for well-being – security, social stimulation from others and a sense of identity.
Territory in the workplace	**Territorial markers** Often created by office workers by personalising their workspace, e.g. family photos. **Open-plan offices** Many desks in one large room. This may involve hot-desking, where employees find an empty desk at which to work when they arrive, saving office space when a number of employees work from home. Brown and Zhu (2016) found participants who feel they have territorial ownership over an area have positive feelings towards it. However, too much territorial behaviour lowers a person's perceived status as judged by colleagues.
Explaining personal space	The level of personal space with which we feel comfortable depends on: • Situational factors such as social context, e.g. in a nightclub. • Dispositional factors that affect our personal space boundaries, e.g. age, culture and gender. Middlemist et al. (1976) studied men in a men's lavatory and found that invasion of personal space caused physiological arousal and discomfort. Negative effects of invasion of personal space can also be found in the workplace.
Personal space in the workplace	Personal space is often invaded in the workplace as open-plan offices have no, or few, physical boundaries between workspaces. Sinha and Sinha (1991) found that performance on a complex cognitive task was diminished when students were in a crowded room and their personal space was invaded. No such effect was found for a simple cognitive task.

Application 1

Activity-based working

Removing the opportunity for territoriality at work may improve relationships, comfort levels and productivity at work. Turning office space into public territory can be achieved through hot-desking, but activity-based working takes this a step further.

How activity-based working can be achieved The office is set up with various different areas, e.g. meeting spaces and team desks designed to serve different functions rather than people having their own desk.

These areas support the current activities of the employees to enable greater efficiency and effectiveness.

Does activity-based working work?

Usefulness Appel-Meulenbroek *et al.* (2011) reported that if not used properly, activity-based working can lead to illness, dissatisfaction and loss in productivity.

Effectiveness In activity-based working environments, employees are satisfied with certain aspects, e.g. seclusion rooms. However, people in traditional work environments have higher levels of satisfaction with other aspects of their workplace, e.g. their privacy.

Practicalities Specially-designed areas is a potentially expensive way of redesigning an office space and may not be feasible for all types of work.

Application 2

Changing perceptions of open-plan offices

Personalisation Workers should be encouraged to design the space in which they work. Personalisation gives people a sense of territory and personal space.

Furniture arrangement Fisher and Byrne (1975) found women felt more stressed when their personal space was invaded from the side, whilst for the men invasion of personal space from the front was more uncomfortable. This suggests that the gender of the employee must be taken into consideration when planning furniture arrangement to increase personal space in offices.

Increased natural light Offices that have more natural light and more windows tend to have employees who are more satisfied at work, have better well-being and have lower intention to leave the job (Leather *et al.* 1998).

Does changing perceptions of open-plan offices work?

Usefulness If workers are happy, they are likely to be more productive, which in turn would boost profits and is therefore worth the investment from the company.

Effectiveness Invasions of personal space can be detrimental to performance and physiological well-being, so maintenance of personal space protects us from these negative effects.

Practicalities Different people have different personal space preferences (e.g. gender differences), so a technique that works for one person may not work for others. One way to resolve this is to give each individual as much control over their own areas as possible.

Women will sit closer to people than men will, demonstrating gender differences in personal space boundaries.

Revision booster

Use retrieval practice when revising. This involves pulling information 'out' from your mind rather than the simpler revision methods of repeating what you have memorised or rereading notes. Retrieval dramatically improves recall. Tests and quizzes are good methods to promote retrieval, e.g. be able to recall two ways to change perceptions of open-plan offices.

Exam-style question examples

Component 3 Section B part (c):

(c) Eta wants to redesign and make the school staffroom open plan.

Outline the advice a psychologist might give to Eta to redesign the school staffroom, based on psychological knowledge of territory and personal space. **[10]**

(c) Insiya is the manager at an IT company who wants to design special workspace areas to improve the efficiency of her team.

Outline **one** strategy Insiya might use to create an effective team environment in her office. **[10]**

Key research
Wells (2000) on *Office personalisation*

Background

Previous research has tested gender differences in personalisation, but not whether personalisation of a workspace can enhance well-being.

Aims and hypotheses

H1 – Women personalise their offices more than men do, with different items and for different purposes.

H2 – Personalisation is positively associated with satisfaction with the physical work environment, which is positively associated with job satisfaction, which is positively associated with employee well-being.

H3 – Workspace personalisation is more integral to the well-being of women than of men.

H4 – Companies with more lenient personalisation policies report higher levels of organisational well-being than companies with stricter personalisation policies.

Method

Design

Self-report, case studies with structured interviews, observation.

Sample of companies

20 companies in Orange County, California with at least 30 employees, 15 working in offices.

Sample of employees

338 employees, 55% of respondents were men, 41% were women, 4% did not report their gender. Most were aged 25-44, a mixture of ethnicities and marital statuses.

23 employees (8 men, 15 women) from five of the 20 companies were involved in a more in-depth case study.

Procedure

Surveys

1. Details about personalisation at work, e.g. number of items and type of items.

2. Measures of satisfaction with work environment, using nine 5-point scales.

3. Measures of job satisfaction, on five 5-point scales.

4. Well-being measures (global, physical and mental).

5. Employee perception of organisational well-being, e.g. morale, productivity.

6. Personality traits linked with personalisation, e.g. need for affiliation.

7. Demographic information, e.g. type and quality of workspace.

Case studies

8. Structured interviews (10-15 minutes) with open questions about personalisation, conducted at the employee's desk.

9. Observations included a checklist of behavioural categories listing different personalisation items.

Results

H1

1. Women personalised workspace more compared with men.

2. Women personalised to express their identity, emotions and improve the feel of the workspace.

3. Men were more likely to personalise to show company status than women, and had more sport paraphernalia.

H2

4. Personalisation is positively associated with satisfaction with the physical work environment. This was positively associated with job satisfaction, which was positively associated with employee well-being.

H3

5. Survey data showed personalisation was no more important for women than men.

6. Case study data found women valued personalisation more than men.

H4

7. Companies that allow more personalisation have a more positive organisational climate.

Secondary analyses

8. Employees' workspace personalisation positively correlated with the amount of personalisation allowed by the company.

One way to personalise the office.

Conclusions

Personalisation of workspaces keeps a workforce satisfied, productive and healthy.

Allowing personalisation can help employers retain employees long term.

Other variables may confound the results, so causality cannot be claimed between personalisation, gender and well-being.

| How the key research explains ... territory and personal space | Wells' study showed how employees personalise their primary territory at work with territorial markers such as photos (for women) and sporting memorabilia (for men). |
| | Wells found that when employees were able to personalise, they had more job satisfaction, indirectly leading to better mental health. Additionally, Wells' interviews showed if employees were no longer allowed to personalise, they would express dissatisfaction with their employment. |

Links between the topic and the methodological issues

Validity	✚ Wells used a combination of questionnaires, interviews and objective data from photographs. The use of different methods permits triangulation between research methods.
	⬌ Participants may have felt this was an opportunity to complain about their workplace, so what they said may not be fully representative of their real feelings.
Reliability	✚ Wells' use of structured case study interviews had high reliability because there was consistency in the questions.
	⬌ Survey data showed personalisation was no more important for women than men but case study data found women did value personalisation more than men, indicating a lack of consistency in responses.
Sampling bias	⬌ In Wells' study only 20 companies out of 2000 possible companies responded to the request. This very low response rate suggests the sample may have consisted of a certain type of company and was not representative.
Ethnocentrism	⬌ Negative reactions to personal space invasion or to being unable to personalise a workspace may not necessarily be found in 'contact' cultures (e.g. Italy and Spain), where people are comfortable with a smaller personal space.

Links between the topic and the debates

Nature/nurture	Territoriality is adaptive and due to nature, e.g. marking territory is an inherited behaviour to reduce fighting between animals (especially males).
	Wells found that personalisation is more important for women than for men, suggesting that socialisation (nurture) may have an effect.
Individual/ situational explanations	Wells found employees are affected by external factors in the environment at work, e.g. employers allowing workers to personalise workspaces. Therefore, it is a situational concept.
	However, men and women use territorial markers in different ways and display different types of personalisation, which is an individual factor.
Ethical considerations	Wells' self-selecting participants all consented to be involved. Questionnaires were anonymous, so confidentiality was protected. There was no deception and there were no distressing questions.

Managers, those on higher salaries, older employees, those who are married and people who are more creative tend to personalise the most.

Revision booster

You should monitor what you are writing in an exam answer (called 'metacognition'). You can do this by asking yourself questions as you write, e.g. 'Have I included both knowledge and understanding?', 'Have I included specific examples?'.

Exam-style question examples

Component 3 Section B part (a):

(a) Explain what the key research by Wells (2000) tells us about territory and personal space in the workplace. **[10]**

Component 3 Section B part (b):

(b) Assess methodological issues that arise in research into territory and personal space in the workplace. **[15]**

(b) Discuss the nature/nurture debate in relation to research into territory and personal space in the workplace. **[15]**

Background

Optimising arousal, controlling anxiety and measuring anxiety in sport

Penalty shootouts are often seen as a lottery, but they are about being able to perform a skill under pressure and this requires control of arousal and anxiety, even for elite footballers.

Revision booster

It is worth remembering that, as optimal levels of arousal can vary between sports, coaches need to personalise their players' preparations for performance in order to optimise arousal.

Using the background research

Consider how you could use the background research to support answers to the following questions. See exam guidance on Component 3 Section B questions on page 8.

(a) Using the key research by Fazey and Hardy (1988), explain arousal and anxiety in sport. **[10]**

(b) Discuss the validity of research into arousal and anxiety in sport. **[15]**

(c) Frank is a trainer at a boxing club and is concerned that some of his fighters are not performing at their best because they are worried about their opponent.

Suggest **one** strategy you could give to Frank to help him optimise the performance of his boxers. **[10]**

Arousal	In a sporting context, *arousal* is a physiological state of both alertness (e.g. increased heart rate) and anticipation (e.g. increased attention), both of which prepare the body for action.
Optimising arousal	**Drive theory** As arousal increases so will performance. However, experts are more able to be skilful when arousal is high compared to beginners. Elite-level expert performers also make mistakes under pressure, suggesting that arousal only benefits sport performance up to a certain point, after which performance decreases. **The inverted-U hypothesis** A gradual increase in arousal levels leads to a gradual increase in performance up to an optimal point. If arousal is too high or too low, there will be a detrimental effect on performance. Athletes aim for optimal (moderate) levels of arousal for best performance. **Criticisms** The inverted-U hypothesis fails to explain differences in optimal arousal for simple or complex tasks (e.g. running versus golf putting). Also, the hypothesis does not quantify high or low arousal (Oxendine 1976). **Individual zones of optimal functioning (IZOF)** These are low, moderate, or high - there isn't one optimal level. This zone depends on the individual, and is not dependent on complexity or type of activity.
Controlling anxiety in sport	**Trait-state anxiety** (Spielberger 1966) • State anxiety (A-state) is an emotional state of apprehension and tension. • Trait anxiety (A-trait) is a predisposition to perceive certain situations as threatening and to respond with varying levels of state anxiety. **Cognitive and somatic anxiety** A-state is multidimensional. • Cognitive anxiety (cog A-state) is the negative expectations of success and self-evaluation. • Somatic anxiety (som A-state) is the physiological response from arousal, e.g. sweaty palms. Cog and som A-state can have detrimental effects on performance.
Measuring anxiety in sport	**Sport competition anxiety test (SCAT)** Assesses situations performers find threatening in sport by measuring competitive A-trait. SCAT involves respondents selecting whether each of 15 items 'rarely', 'sometimes' or 'often' reflect their behaviour. **Competitive state anxiety inventory (CSAI-2)** Coaches need to understand how anxiety mediates performance - one performer may respond to a sport situation with mainly cog A-state and another performer with som A-state. CSAI-2 measures the separate constructs of cognitive anxiety, somatic anxiety and self-confidence.

Application 1

Principles of biofeedback Individuals learn to exert voluntary control over involuntary (autonomic) behaviours.

The Wingate five-step approach (W5SA) (Blumenstein and Orbach 2014)

- **Step 1 Introduction** Learning self-regulation strategies, e.g. imagery and biofeedback.
- **Step 2 Identification** The most effective type of biofeedback for the performer and their sport is selected.
- **Step 3 Simulation** Biofeedback training coupled with simulated competitive stress, e.g. using videos of an athlete's performance.
- **Step 4 Transformation** Transferring mental preparations to the field setting, e.g. before and after warm-up.
- **Step 5 Realisation** Athletes applying self-regulation skills in precompetitive activities and routines.

Biofeedback is based on the principles of operant conditioning because any control over behaviour that an athlete can exert is rewarding which reinforces the behaviour.

Does biofeedback training work?

Usefulness W5SA is a flexible strategy to help control and optimise arousal and anxiety in a wide range of sporting situations and different populations, e.g. children and elite performers (Blumenstein and Bar-Eli 2005).

Effectiveness It provides the athlete with objective feedback of their physical and mental control, e.g. display showing heart rate (Blumenstein and Bar-Eli 2005).

Practicalities Using remote communication of data limits the use of biofeedback training in the field. Sport psychologists require specialist preparation to deliver biofeedback training.

Revision booster

In application questions such as those below, students often solely focus on outlining the strategy. Remember to also write about the benefits of the strategy to the person in the scenario.

Application 2

Lidor and Mayan (2005) proposed three phases in a pre-performance routine:

Phase 1 Readying (mechanical, mental and emotional) Athlete attempts to generate positive thoughts and emotions about performance expectations.

Phase 2 Focusing attention Athlete focuses their attention on one aspect of performance or thought to block out internal distractions, e.g. symptoms of physiological arousal such as raised heart rate.

Phase 3 Evaluating Performers judge the outcome of their previous performance and assess the strategies that produced the movement to make future improvements in performance.

Do pre-performance routines work?

Usefulness Develops attentional focus, reducing distractions and triggering well-learned movement patterns, reducing cognitive anxiety and increasing self-confidence.

Effectiveness Most effectively used with closed skills such as a golf shot or long jump as such skills allow time for systematic routines to be followed (Cotterill *et al.* 2010).

Practicalities Coaches need to consider how to measure the impact of a pre-performance routine and consider at what stage of learning pre-performance routines should be taught to athletes.

Exam-style question examples

Component 3 Section B part (c):

(c) Freddy is an Olympic swimmer who often worries about his performance before finals compared to qualifying rounds.

Outline advice a sport psychologist could give to Freddy to reduce his anxiety before finals. **[10]**

(c) Gary is a sport psychologist who has been employed by a golf club to improve the performance of their top players.

Outline **one** strategy Gary could suggest to the golfers to manage their arousal and anxiety. **[10]**

Do read our exam advice on pages 4–15.

Key research

Fazey and Hardy (1988) on the *Inverted-U hypothesis*

Background

Fazey and Hardy (1988) identified three issues with the predictive validity of the inverted-U hypothesis in practice:

1. There is no sound experimental evidence for the detailed predictions of the inverted-U hypothesis.

2. The inverted-U hypothesis does not account for differences in athletes' performance when exposed to the same stressor.

3. The inverted-U hypothesis does not consider how different situations affect stress responses.

Aim

To develop a new catastrophe model based on these criticisms.

Method

Design

A monograph was produced (a detailed article on a specialised subject).

Fazey and Hardy identified difficulties with the basic constructs, corroborative evidence and application of the inverted-U hypothesis.

Results: The catastrophe model

1. Performance increases as arousal increases until a critical point is reached where it suddenly falls to a very low level.

2. A multidimensional model, with two components:
   - Cognitive, e.g. negative expectation about performance.
   - Physiological arousal, e.g. increased heart rate.

3. There are four relationships between cognitive anxiety, physiological arousal and performance:
   - Low cognitive anxiety - Performers with low cognitive anxiety, physiological arousal and performance show an inverted-U relationship where increases in arousal have corresponding increases and then decreases in performance.
   - Low physiological arousal - When physiological arousal is low then, as cognitive anxiety increases, so will performance.
   - High physiological arousal - When physiological arousal is high then, as cognitive anxiety increases, performance will decrease.
   - High cognitive anxiety - When cognitive anxiety is high any increases in physiological arousal leads to a catastrophic drop in performance.

Predictions of the model

4. Prediction 1 - When a performer's cognitive anxiety is high, *hysteresis* occurs (when arousal is increasing, performance will increase and when arousal is decreasing, performance will decrease).

5. Prediction 2 - Physiological arousal is not always harmful to performance when there is high cognitive anxiety.

6. Prediction 3 - When physiological arousal and cognitive anxiety are both high, performance will be either catastrophic or excellent.

7. Butterfly catastrophe model:
   - Task difficulty - as the cognitive demand of the task increases, the arousal level reduces at which point catastrophes occur.
   - Self-confidence - when self-confidence is very high or anxiety very low, the performer can regain stable performance.

Tennis players such as Dominika Cibulková (left) need to ensure that their cognitive anxiety is controlled if they are to maximise their performance.

Conclusions

The interaction of cognitive anxiety, physiological arousal and performance explains the anxiety-performance relationship in sport.

The catastrophe model is a more credible explanation of the anxiety-performance relationship than the inverted-U hypothesis.

Difficult tasks with a high processing load mean hysteresis will occur at lower levels of arousal.

Intermediate levels of performance are possible only for confident performers or at relatively low levels of cognitive anxiety.

How the key research explains ... arousal and anxiety	**Arousal** The catastrophe model predicts that when:
	• Physiological arousal is low then any increases in a performer's cognitive anxiety will lead to increases in performance.
	• Physiological arousal level is high, their performance will decrease in line with any increase in their cognitive anxiety.
	Anxiety (the splitting factor) Cognitive anxiety determines whether or not the effect of arousal is smooth and small or whether the effect is large and catastrophic.
	Therefore, performers and coaches must optimise arousal levels and control cognitive anxiety to maximise performance.

It is hard to imagine that crown green bowlers' physiological arousal levels can get high!

Links between the topic and the methodological issues

Validity	⊝ Fazey and Hardy question the validity of the inverted-U hypothesis as gradual declines in performance are unlikely in practical situations.
	⊝ It is also difficult to make valid measures of arousal and anxiety during performance.
Reliability	⊕ SCAT has been tested on children. The mean test-retest reliability score was +.77, indicating acceptable levels of reliability (Martens *et al.* 1990).
	⊕ SCAT uses standardised scoring procedures so data can be compared from one trial to another, aiding consistency.
Sampling bias	⊝ Samples used to test the catastrophe model are small (e.g. eight crown green bowlers), so unrepresentative of all sport performers. It is therefore difficult to generalise the catastrophe model and to assume that hysteresis occurs.
Ethnocentrism	⊝ Hysteresis may be more typical of highly competitive sports in individualist cultures, but may not occur in non-individualist cultures and also in activities where players' attitudes focus towards the team.

Links between the topic and the debates

Reductionism/ holism	The catastrophe model is reductionist as it reduces performance to numerical values, e.g. arousal and cognitive anxiety measures to predict performance.
	However, the catastrophe model also looks at the interaction of arousal and cognitive anxiety, an example of a holistic approach.
Individual/ situational explanations	Individual levels of arousal and anxiety can affect performance. For example, a gymnast's optimal arousal range may be low, moderate or high, depending on the individual and not the complexity or type of activity.
Usefulness of research	Predictions of the catastrophe model are useful for coaches and performers because knowing when and how arousal and cognitive anxiety can affect performance means they can develop interventions to minimise the effects of arousal and anxiety.

Revision booster

Simplify the catastrophe model by explaining the four relationships between cognitive anxiety, physiological arousal and performance as outlined on the facing page.

Exam-style question examples

Component 3 Section B part (a):

(a) Use the key research by Fazey and Hardy (1988) to explain the relationship between arousal and anxiety in sport. **[10]**

Component 3 Section B part (b):

(b) To what extent does research into arousal and anxiety in sport support the individual explanation? **[15]**

(b) Discuss the usefulness of research into arousal and anxiety in sport. **[15]**

The debates on the left are examples of how you might link the topic to the debates. You need to prepare responses for the other five debates - we haven't got room to cover all of them here.

Background
Benefits of exercise to mental health

Go dancing before your exams – it will make you feel better!

Benefits of exercise

Aerobic and resistance exercise programmes significantly reduce symptoms of depression.

Exercise has been found to be as effective as psychotherapy as a treatment for anxiety. The more people exercise, the lower their anxiety levels.

Mood states in high intensity aerobic dance classes are enhanced in comparison to moderate intensity classes (Rokka et al. 2010).

Using the background research

Consider how you could use the background research to support answers to the following questions. See exam guidance on Component 3 Section B questions on page 8.

(a) Using the key research by Lewis *et al.* (2014), explain the benefits of exercise to mental health. **[10]**

(b) Evaluate the validity of research into the benefits of exercise to mental health. **[15]**

(c) James is a head of PE who wants to improve the mental health of his pupils.

Outline advice you would give James to help his pupils' mental health. **[10]**

| Mental health and exercise | Mental health describes how we feel about ourselves, our ability to make and keep friends and our ability to learn from others and develop psychologically and emotionally.

The link between mental health and exercise can be explained in terms of both biological (physiological) and psychological factors. |

Biological explanations of the benefits of exercise

Brain-derived neurotrophic factor (BDNF) This is a protein that promotes the growth and survival of neurons. Research suggests that exercise increases BDNF activity in the brain, reducing stress and thereby increasing well-being (Erickson *et al.* 2012).

Endorphin hypothesis Endorphins released during exercise reduce the sensation of pain and bring about a state of euphoria that leads to psychological well-being and positive mental health, e.g. 'a runner's high'.

Endocannabinoids (eCB) These are neurotransmitters that act as messengers to control pain and reward perceptions in the brain. Research shows increased eCB levels following exercise on a treadmill (Raichlen *et al.* 2012). In other words, we get a neurobiological reward for aerobic exercise and this may explain why we are motivated to run 'through the pain barrier'.

Psychological explanations of the benefits of exercise

Health-related quality of life Improved life satisfaction is associated with physical activity, physical self-worth and self-efficacy (belief in your own competence) (Elavsky *et al.* 2005).

Mood A more general set of feelings than emotion, and is not linked to one specific event (e.g. irritability, vigour). One meta-analysis showed that aerobic fitness training has a strong positive relationship with vigour and reduced negative mood.

Enjoyment People enjoy exercise, which might be explained by the concept of 'flow', a state of extreme enjoyment achieved when task difficulty is matched by an individual's skills (Csikszentmihalyi 1975). 'Flow' is the extreme pleasure experienced when engaging with a task.

Self-esteem (feelings a person has about their self-concept) Sonstroem (1997) suggests two approaches to self-esteem and exercise:

- Personal development hypothesis – exercise helps maintain or enhance self-worth.
- Skill development hypothesis – self-esteem can change due to experiences while exercising.

Benefits of exercise Links to the mental health topic. Exercise has been shown to benefit depression (Rethorst *et al.* 2009), anxiety (Wipfli *et al.* 2008) and mood (Lewis *et al.* 2014).

Application 1

Dance aerobics

Different types of dance may prove to be beneficial for positive mental health depending on personal goals, physical condition and health history.

A warm-up This prepares the body for aerobic activity (e.g. raised heart rate). This should involve stretching the large muscle groups used during the dance session.

The main session At least 30–50 minutes, twice a week for the most beneficial effects. The programme need be no longer than 16 weeks for maximum benefits to mental health.

Cooling down Continue the workout session for five minutes or so, but at a slower pace and reduced intensity.

Do dance aerobics work?

Usefulness Aerobic dance routines successfully improve mental health providing a cheaper, healthier alternative to drug therapy for those with a psychological disorder.

Effectiveness Dance interventions improve mood states but this may depend on the type, duration and intensity of the dance (Rokka *et al.* 2010).

Practicalities Dance routines need to consider the personal health history of the participants and their existing physical condition. Different types of exercise may benefit different types of mental health issues.

Application 2

Rowing exercise

Workouts on an indoor rower vary from long steady workouts to interval exercise with rest periods between bouts of rowing.

Interval workouts Warm up for five minutes using stretches and light paddling, then do short or long intervals:

- **Short intervals** For example, you might have two-minute intervals between each set of rowing.
- **Long intervals** For example, you might have four-minute intervals between each set of rowing.

At the end of the session there is a warm down for five minutes doing stretches and light paddling.

Does rowing exercise work?

Usefulness If psychologists know endorphins provide a painkilling effect, they can prescribe rowing as part of a treatment programme to improve mood and well-being for patients.

Effectiveness Research shows that the painkilling effects of endorphins are increased when people row together (Cohen *et al.* 2009).

Practicalities Rowing can be carried out indoors so it is a good way for people to improve their mental health from the comfort of their own homes or at their local sports centre.

As an intense form of aerobic exercise, rowing is likely to produce low negative mood states and high vigour in performers.

Although there is a biological/physiological focus to this topic, do not forget that there are social benefits to dance which are especially important to elderly people who often live alone.

How psychology contributes to the success of the economy and society ... If a society is mentally healthier this will have a positive impact on the economy.

Key research

Lewis *et al.* (2014) on *Social dance*

Background

Dance increases mood in all individuals but may be especially beneficial for the elderly and those with Parkinson's disease (PD) because both groups often experience anxiety and depression.

Aims

To investigate:

- The effect of dance on mood in the elderly, specifically a group of people with PD.
- The effects of a long-duration programme of 12 weeks and a short-duration programme of one hour.

Method

Design

Matched participants (repeated measures).

IV1: Elderly PD or control (age-matched to PD participants).

IV2: Long cycle (scores compared over 12 weeks) or short cycle (scores compared before and after one session).

DV: Participants' mood scores

Sample

37 participants, aged between 50 and 80 years (mean = 65.5 years). PD group with mild to moderate PD: 22 participants (12 men, 10 women). Control group: 15 participants (7 men, 8 women).

Materials/apparatus

Profile of mood states (POMS) measured mood changes, including Tension (T), Vigour (V), Confused (C) and Total Mood Disturbance (TMD).

Brunel University mood scale (BRUMS) measured mood changes.

Mini mental state examination (MMSE) measured cognitive impairment.

Procedure

1. Participants gave informed consent and completed the POMS.
2. Before the week 1 dance class, participants completed the MMSE.
3. A qualified dance instructor ran ten weekly dance classes (weeks 2-11).
4. Sessions consisted of Bollywood, tango, cheerleading, Old Time Music Hall and party dancing (based on the Charleston and Saturday Night Fever).
5. Style of dancing changed every two weeks.
6. Dance classes lasted 50 minutes: a ten-minute warm-up, 30 minutes' dancing, and a five-minute cool-down. There was a five-minute break midway. Participants could sit down if they wished.
7. In week 9, BRUMS was used to measure mood before and after the dance class.
8. A few days after completion of the dance classes, participants were given the POMS again for long cycle data.

Results

Demographic and normative data comparisons

1. No significant differences between the PD and control groups for age, MMSE scores or baseline mood scores.
2. Both PD and control groups showed higher TMD scores than the norm, and the PD group had higher scores for T, V and C than the norms.
3. No significant differences from the norms were found for the control group.

Long cycle time

4. TMD was lower after dance sessions but no significant differences were found between PD and control group.
5. Anger was the only subscale to show reduced levels.
6. The depressed group had higher TMD scores. The PD group showed a higher TMD score than the control group.

Short cycle time

7. BRUMS showed a reduction in TMD score over the short-term cycle but no significant difference between PD and control groups.
8. There were no significant subscale improvements over the short cycle time.

Dance benefits memory, learning and spatial awareness due to the mental challenges of moving in time with the music.

Conclusions

Dance provides physical and psychological benefits over both a long and a short cycle time, for the elderly and especially those with PD.

Dance improves mood states (e.g. anger) in elderly people, especially those with PD.

Exercise, including dance aerobics, can improve levels of vigour, TMD score and fatigue.

How the key research explains ... exercise and mental health	**Psychological benefits** Dance has a beneficial effect on mental health for all populations (there were improvements in TMD scores for both PD and control groups). Anger reduced significantly and fatigue reduced in participants with pre-existing high levels of depression.
	Sociability Dance is an enjoyable social activity and counteracts the lack of social contact seen in people with depression. Dance also provides opportunities for improved self-esteem through personal and skill development.
	Well-being The improvement in fatigue as well as mood can be attributed to the endorphins released during exercise.

Dancing can make you mentally fit and exercise is good for body and mind.

Links between the topic and the methodological issues

Validity	⊕ Extraneous variables were controlled (high internal validity) in the Lewis *et al.* study, e.g. participants' PD symptoms were of a limited range.
	⊝ Participants may have given socially desirable answers when answering questionnaires to measure mood (e.g. reported positive moods), thus reducing validity.
Reliability	⊕ Lewis *et al.*'s procedure was standardised, increasing reliability (e.g. there was always 30 minutes of dancing).
	⊕ POMS is an established mood measurement tool with good internal and external reliability.
Sampling bias	⊕ The PD sample between 50 and 80 years is representative as PD typically develops in people over the age of 50 years.
	⊝ It was a self-selected sample (local advertisements and PD support groups), therefore participants may have been more motivated to take part in dancing than other people with PD.
Ethnocentrism	⊝ Individualist cultures focus on the needs of the individual. In line with this, Lewis *et al.* focused on how dance could benefit an individual. In contrast, collectivist cultures focus on the group, so dance may be seen more as a collective experience meaning these results may not generalise to other cultures.

Revision booster

It is better, when answering exam questions, to polarise a debate so you can make clear comparisons. However, in reality, debates are more of a continuum.

Methodological issues are discussed in Chapter 1 and also on pages 95-96.

Don't forget that you need to be ready for questions on all eight debates

Links between the topic and the debates

Reductionism/ holism	It is a reductionist argument to say that our mental health is only related to the release of neurotransmitters in our brain (as suggested by the BDNF explanation).
	Increase in self-esteem through skill development is a more holistic explanation of the benefits of exercise on mental health.
Individual/ situational explanations	Individual dispositions may determine the extent to which exercise actually affects mental health, e.g. 'runner's high' may differ from person to person.
	Lewis *et al.*'s results could be attributed to the social (situational) aspect of dancing (as opposed to biological benefits).
Ethical considerations	Informed consent was gained from participants who had PD.
	Potential psychological harm was considered (e.g. participants could sit down).
	Two participants took up the right to withdraw.

Exam-style question examples

Component 3 Section B part (a):

(a) Using the key research by Lewis *et al.* (2014), explain how exercise is beneficial to mental health. **[10]**

Component 3 Section B part (b):

(b) Evaluate research into exercise and mental health. **[15]**

(b) Assess the extent to which research into exercise and mental health is reductionist. **[15]**

Background
Self-efficacy and sports confidence, including imagery and sports orientation

Goal-oriented athletes tend to have high perceived ability. Any failure is seen as a challenge to improve.

Research using the SOQ on American college physical activity students shows that men score higher for competitiveness and win-orientation than women but women score higher for goal-orientation.

Overall results show that athletes see goal-orientation as more important than win-orientation.

Using the background research

Consider how you could use the background research to support answers to the following questions. See exam guidance on Component 3 Section B questions on page 8.

(a) Using the key research by Munroe-Chandler *et al.* (2008) explain how imagery can improve motivation in sport. **[10]**

(b) Discuss the validity of research into motivation and sport. **[15]**

(c) Bhavna is the coach for her daughter's hockey team. They have lost their first six matches and some of the girls have lost interest in the sport.

What advice might a sports psychologist give Bhavna to motivate the players in her daughter's hockey team? **[10]**

Motivation in sport	*Motivation* refers to the direction and intensity of one's effort.
	Intrinsic orientation To participate in sport for its own sake.
	Extrinsic orientation To participate in sport for social or material rewards.
	Achievement motivation The need to achieve something, e.g. to gain satisfaction or avoid failure.

Self-efficacy	*Self-efficacy* refers to your belief in your own competence. It stems from four sources (Bandura 1994):
	1. **Performance accomplishments** Personal mastery experiences affect efficacy - raised by success and lowered by failure.
	2. **Vicarious experience** Created by observing or imagining others engaging in a task that performers themselves have never performed. This enhances personal efficacy expectations.
	3. **Verbal persuasion** Widely used by coaches and teammates in an attempt to influence the personal efficacy of the performer.
	4. **Physiological arousal** Physical indicators (e.g. arousal levels) help gauge how ready a person is to perform an activity.

Sport confidence	*Sport confidence* is the belief in one's ability to be successful in sport (Vealey 1986).
	Trait sport confidence (SC-trait) Perceptions about one's general ability to be successful in sport.
	State sport confidence (SC-state) Perceptions at any particular moment about one's ability to be successful in sport.

Imagery	**Types of imagery**
	• Mental imagery - mental practice techniques used to create an athletic performance.
	• Internal imagery - imagining yourself performing a task.
	• External imagery - seeing yourself performing the task, e.g. on film.
	Using imagery Elite players imagine a perfect performance, injured or resting players can practise. Mental practice is a skill improved through practice.

Sport orientation questionnaire (SOQ)	The SOQ (Gill and Deeter 1988) measures sport-specific motivation across three orientations:
	• Competitiveness - how performers enjoy competition and strive to succeed.
	• Win orientation - the satisfaction athletes feel when they compare themselves with others.
	• Goal orientation - the interest athletes have in developing their own technical standards.

Application 1

Imagery – PETTLEP

PETTLEP is an acronym representing a seven-point checklist of guidelines to be followed when devising an imagery intervention.

P - Physical Imagery should be seen as a physical process with measurable physiological outcomes.

E - Environment The place where imagery is performed should be similar to the performance environment.

T - Task Imagery content should be appropriate to the performers' skill level and the skill to be improved.

T - Timing Performers create the imagery in 'real time'.

L - Learning As a performer becomes more skilled, imagery content is adapted in response to learning.

E - Emotion Imagery needs to be an emotional experience to be realistic.

P - Perspective Can take an internal perspective (the performers' viewpoint) or external (another person's perspective).

Does imagery work?

Usefulness Coaches find imagery to be most useful when they provide innovative imagery interventions that involve the performer.

Effectiveness PETTLEP method has been found to be effective with novices and experts, children and adults alike. The more motivated the performer is to use PETTLEP, the more effective it will be at increasing self-confidence and motivation (Wakefield and Smith 2012).

Practicalities Introduce PETTLEP progressively to limit overload and to assess which aspects are useful for the athlete. PETTLEP imagery can be used at least three times per week to maximise the effect on performance (Wakefield and Smith 2012).

Application 2

Positive self-talk

Positive self-talk is what athletes say to themselves to concentrate, to control their anxiety and judge their performance. Mikes (1987) suggested five strategies for self-talk:

1. **Short and special statement** Can help to focus attention.

2. **A positive word** (e.g. 'relax') Can control arousal levels.

3. **Instructional self-talk** (e.g. 'wrist, centre' for basketball shooting).

4. **Talking friendly** Affirmative statements, e.g. 'I can' helps performer as motivational cues can build confidence.

5. **Repeating statements** Aids learning the message as a performance improvement tool.

Does positive self-talk work?

Usefulness Creates confidence, motivation, effort and controls anxiety and arousal. If coaches understand the different types of self-talk they can personalise the intervention.

Effectiveness Varies from sport to sport. Activities that need timing and accuracy (e.g. somersault) benefit from instructional self-talk, but soccer players find motivational self-talk is better (Ramlanc and Adzhar 2015).

Practicalities Self-talk can be used at any time by both novices and experts to influence their motivation and self-confidence.

Instructional self-talk can help performers of all ages by triggering desired actions through proper attentional focus and technical information.

Revision booster

When answering Component 3 Section B part (c) questions such as those below, remember to describe how to carry out the strategy you suggest, not just simply identify it.

Exam-style question examples

Component 3 Section B part (c):

(c) Kerry is the coach for a netball team. One of the girls in the team needs to improve her goal shooting but does not want to practise.

What advice might a sports psychologist give Kerry to help motivate her goal shooter to practise? **[10]**

(c) Carlos is a sport psychologist who has been asked to work with young tennis players at a training academy.

Outline **one** strategy that Carlos might use to improve the motivation of his tennis players. **[10]**

Key research

Munroe-Chandler *et al.* (2008) on *Imagery use*

Background

Self-efficacy plays a significant role in influencing sport performance.

Motivational-specific (MS) imagery involves seeing yourself winning an event.

Motivational general-mastery (MG-M) imagery is based on seeing yourself coping in difficult circumstances.

Aims

To examine the relationship between MG-M imagery use and self-confidence and self-efficacy in soccer players aged 11–14 years.

The specific hypotheses were:

- H1: MG-M imagery is a predictor of both self-confidence and self-efficacy in young athletes.
- H2: The relationship between MG-M imagery use and self-confidence and self-efficacy is stronger in competitive than recreational athletes.

Method

Design

Correlational design.

Sample

An opportunity sample of 122 soccer players from Canada, boys and girls aged 11–14. Of these, 72 participated in 'house' recreational soccer and 50 participated in 'travel' (elite) soccer. Mean of 6.11 years of soccer-playing experience.

Materials/apparatus

SIQ-C – Sport imagery questionnaire for children.

CTAI-2C – Competitive trait anxiety inventory-2 for children.

SEQ-S – Self-efficacy questionnaire for soccer.

Procedure

1. Parental and player informed consent obtained.
2. Coaches sent details of the research.
3. Data collected over a two-week period in mid-soccer season.
4. Players completed questionnaires before practice.
5. Players asked their age, gender, level of expertise and the number of years they had played soccer.
6. Participants completed the SIQ-C, CTAI-2C and SEQ-S.
7. Data collection took about 15 minutes.

Results

H1

1. MG-M imagery is a predictor of both self-efficacy and self-confidence in youth soccer players.
2. There were no significant differences between level of play, gender or the number of years playing.
3. All imagery subscales correlated significantly with self-efficacy and self-confidence, supporting the first hypothesis.

H2

In competitive athletes (rather than recreational athletes):

4. The MG-M subscale from the SIQ-C correlated more significantly with the SEQ-S for self-efficacy.
5. The MG-M subscale from the SIQ-C correlated more significantly with the CTAI-2C scores for self-confidence.

If you don't use imagery for complex movements that require precision you could be in for the high jump.

Conclusions

Imagery can be used at both elite and recreational levels to improve self-confidence and self-efficacy.

Imagery is effective at increasing self-confidence and self-efficacy in boys and girls regardless of playing experience.

Encouraging young athletes to use more MG-M imagery is an effective way of enhancing their self-confidence and self-efficacy.

How the key research explains ... motivation	Sports confidence correlated significantly with the imagery subscales. This suggests that the use of imagery by sports performers is related to increased expectancy of success and therefore improved motivation to compete.
	Self-efficacy specific to soccer correlated significantly with the use of imagery. This supports the role of self-efficacy (past accomplishments) in motivating athletes to perform and be successful.
	Players seeing themselves coping in difficult circumstances and mastering challenging situations will have improved motivation.

Links between the topic and the methodological issues

Validity	✛ Munroe-Chandler *et al.* used questionnaires that have good construct validity, e.g. CTAI-2 measures trait self-confidence for children.
	⊝ A correlational design means cause and effect cannot be established between the use of imagery and self-confidence and self-efficacy. This reduces the validity of the study.
Reliability	✛ Questionnaires used by Munroe-Chandler *et al.* have a standardised format, increasing reliability. Measures of test-retest reliability confirm this (Stadulis *et al.* 2002).
Sampling bias	⊝ Munroe-Chandler *et al.* used a very specific sample of 11-14-year-old soccer players, so the results are only representative of that group of sports performers.
Ethnocentrism	⊝ Canadian youth soccer players may have quite high levels of self-confidence. This means it may be difficult to generalise Munroe-Chandler *et al.*'s results to other sports in other countries/cultures.

Links between the topic and the debates

Nature/nurture	Vealey's model of sport confidence (see page 198) explains self-confidence based on SC-trait and SC-state, supporting an interaction between nature and nurture as factors explaining motivation in sport. Nature (the person's natural ability) is influenced by nurture (how perceptions of their ability have been influenced by ways in which they have learned to develop self-confidence).
Free will/ determinism	Improved motivation in sport can be internally determined (a person's biology enables them to be good at particular sports) or externally determined (by the use of imagery).
	However, in reality people can choose to use imagery or not to help their motivation, which is a position of free will.
Usefulness of research	Munroe-Chandler *et al.* showed that self-efficacy and self-confidence in footballers increases with greater use of MG-M imagery. Therefore, coaches should use imagery techniques such as PETTLEP to increase the motivation of their players.

People with goal-orientation believe the effort they put into a task is likely to be rewarded with success.

Revision booster

'Peer motivation' refers to making an effort to both encourage and challenge your friends in what they do – including revision. This is a good way to improve your friend's confidence because they will feel they must have improved by getting this help and this alone increases self-efficacy (their belief in their own competence).

Exam-style question examples

Component 3 Section B part (a):

(a) Use the key research by Munroe-Chandler *et al.* (2008) to explain how imagery can improve motivation in sport. **[10]**

Component 3 Section B part (b):

(b) Discuss the validity of research into motivation and sport. **[15]**

(b) Discuss research into motivation in sport in relation to the nature/nurture debate. **[15]**

How psychology contributes to the success of the economy and society ...
The motivation to succeed underpins a successful economy.

Background
Personality, its measurement and its relationship to sport

Freud used cathartic release to explain the venting of negative emotions such as aggression. Channelling negative emotions can be done acceptably by playing aggressive sports (e.g. ice hockey).

Revision booster

The mnemonic **OCEAN** helps recall Costa and McCrae's big five personality dimensions.

Using the background research

Consider how you could use the background research to support answers to the following questions. See exam guidance on Component 3 Section B questions on page 8.

(a) Use the research by Kroll and Crenshaw (1970) to explain personality in sport. **[10]**

(b) Discuss the validity of research into personality and sport. **[15]**

(c) Fred is a hockey coach who wants to find out if certain personality characteristics match different attack patterns in his team.

Using his knowledge of personality, outline **one** strategy Fred could use to improve hockey performance in his team. **[10]**

Personality	*Personality* refers to individual differences in characteristic patterns of thinking, feeling and behaving (American Psychological Association).
Psychoanalytic theory of personality	**Freud's theory of personality** (see page 82) suggests personality has three parts: • Id – governed by instincts (e.g. aggression) needing immediate gratification. • Ego – seeks to find socially acceptable ways to satisfy the id. • Superego – judges whether the ego is behaving properly or not.
Trait theories of personality	**Eysenck's dimensions of personality** • Extravert–introvert: extraversion means how outgoing we are, whereas introversion explains how inward-focused we are. • Stable–neurotic: stable personalities are calm but neurotics tend to be anxious. • Psychoticism is where a person shows aggression or a lack of empathy. **Cattell's personality factors** Cattell (1965) analysed 4,500 personality adjectives and identified 16 personality factors (PF), e.g. warmth, liveliness, dominance. **Costa and McCrae's big five personality dimensions** **O - Openness** Tendency to seek new experiences. **C - Conscientiousness** Level of organisation and goal-directed behaviour. **E - Extraversion** Quantity and intensity of interpersonal interactions. **A - Agreeableness** Concern for cooperation and social harmony. **N - Neuroticism** Proneness to psychological distress such as anxiety and hostility.
Measuring personality	**Eysenck's EPQ** The revised version (EPQ-R) contains 106 questions, answered with yes or no, measuring six scales: extraversion, neuroticism, psychoticism, a lie scale, addiction and criminality. **Cattell's 16PF** This has 185 multiple-choice questions providing a profile of his 16 personality factors. Each factor is expressed on a continuum, e.g. a person's 'warmth' is scored somewhere between 'reserved' and 'outgoing'. **NEO PI-R** This measures the 'Big five' using 240 descriptions of behaviour. A person is ranked for each factor on a five-point Likert scale.

Application 1

Improving interpersonal relationships

Performer-performer relationships Personality assessments (e.g. NEO PI-R) can identify performers' preferences for interaction and communication with other team members. This provides greater awareness of the effect of individual personalities in team settings, helping performers to share ideas effectively with their teammates.

Coach-performer relationships Coaches and athletes who are outgoing (extraverts) and engaged with the task are usually more committed to improving performance in their sport. A performer is more likely to learn from a coach who is perceived to be dedicated to improving their performance.

Does improving interpersonal relationships work?

Usefulness Knowledge of personality scores means a coach can identify team members who are having a destructive or a constructive influence on the team's performance (Allen *et al.* 2013).

Effectiveness Coaches can identify players with different personalities but, to improve the team's relationships, the coach must also be an effective communicator to engage players with their ideas (Allen *et al.* 2013).

Practicalities Coaches need to give time during training to explain the benefits of taking personality assessments and the importance of completing them truthfully so that interventions to improve interpersonal relationships become meaningful.

Application 2

Support for team selection

Team cohesiveness Performers' behaviour can be predicted from personality assessments, e.g. NEO PI-R. This can help coaches and sport psychologists to select players to fit the teams' needs, e.g. high levels of conscientiousness and agreeableness are associated with high levels of task cohesion.

Player positions Personality differences exist between playing positions as they require different personality characteristics, e.g. players in attacking positions seem to have better anxiety control and are more extraverted than those in defensive positions. A coach should use personality assessments to confirm their selections and decisions about tactical formations.

Does support for team selection work?

Usefulness Personality assessments often provide only quantitative data. A more qualitative approach would let coaches engage in one-to-one meetings with players to find out more about their positional preferences and how they perceive their role in the team.

Effectiveness It is most effective to use personality assessments as part of a whole package of information about player performance that also includes skill level, fitness and tactics.

Practicalities Sport psychologists must understand the performer's personal and sporting background in order to establish rapport. They should adapt the way they communicate with players if they are to use personality assessments for team selection.

Attackers are more likely to be extraverts and have more responsibility and anxiety control than defenders.

Some personality types cope better than others with negative emotion, e.g. fear of failure. So, a coach who understands the personality of his or her players can personalise strategies to optimise the player's performance.

Exam-style question examples

Component 3 Section B part (c):

(c) Lucie is a sport psychologist who has been asked by the team coach to help in the selection of a netball team.

Outline **one** strategy Lucie might use to support the choice of netball players. **[10]**

(c) Sameena is a cricket coach who wants to use personality assessments to improve the performance of her team.

Outline the advice you would give Sameena to help the performance of her cricket team. **[10]**

Don't forget to read all the exam advice on pages 4–15.

Key research

Kroll and Crenshaw (1970) on *Personality profiles*

Background

The relationship between personality and sport performance has been investigated by comparing personality test scores of athletes competing at different performance levels and in different types of sport, such as individual or team sports.

Kroll and Crenshaw believed previous research used inadequate statistical analysis and lacked representative samples.

Aims

To use a standardised psychometric test of personality (Cattell's 16PF) to assess personality factors and only use national or regional level performers.

Method

Design

Quasi-experiment, independent measures design.

IV: The sport played.

DV: Athletes' personality characteristics, measured by Cattell's 16PF.

Sample

387 sport performers (regional or national level). 81 American football players (college), 141 gymnasts (college and university), 94 wrestlers (Olympic, national, university and college level), 71 karate participants (amateur).

Materials/apparatus

Minnesota multiphasic personality inventory (MMPI), Cattell's 16PF.

Procedure

1. Cattell's 16PF questionnaire was administered to all participants.
2. Participants completed the MMPI 15-item lie scale (to assess truthfulness).
3. Participants who scored seven or above on the lie scale had their data discarded.
4. Comparisons were made between six pairs of sports:
   - American football and wrestling.
   - American football and gymnastics.
   - American football and karate.
   - Wrestling and gymnastics.
   - Wresting and karate.
   - Gymnastics and karate.

Results

Differences and one similarity

1. Significant differences were shown to exist across the personality profiles of all four groups: American footballers, wrestlers, gymnasts and karate players.
2. Differences were found for: social boldness, self-reliance, liveliness, vigilance, rule consciousness, privateness, reasoning, warmth, emotional stability, openness to change and tension.
3. Wrestling and American football players had similar personalities.

16PF personality characteristics

4. Tension – Gymnasts scored lowest and karate players highest.
5. Rule consciousness – Gymnasts scored lowest and karate players highest.
6. Self-reliance – American footballers and wrestlers scored highest on group dependence in contrast to the gymnasts or karate players. This was a significant difference ($p < 0.01$).
7. Liveliness and reasoning – Gymnasts scored the lowest on the liveliness factor but highest on the reasoning factor.

Probability of group membership being highest

8. Of the 81 footballers tested, 32 were predicted (on the basis of their personality profile) to actually be footballers. The remaining 49 footballers were placed as follows: 22 in gymnastics, 18 in wrestling and 9 in karate.

Chicken or egg? A genetic personality characteristic may lead participants to choose karate as their sport. Or participation in karate may have influenced their personality.

Conclusions

At regional and national level there is no single personality for sport.

High scorers on group dependence do better in team sports than in individual sports but the opposite is true for high scorers on self-reliance.

It may benefit players to select the right sport for their personality as success is related to personality.

| How the key research explains ... personality | **Nature of the four sports** Personality may be related to aspects of the sport, e.g. American football and wrestling are both physical contact sports. This could explain why there were no significant differences in the players' personality factors in these two sports. |
| | **Self-reliance personality factor** The individual players of karate and gymnasts are likely to be more self-reliant compared to the team players of American football. The football players would be more group dependent than karate players or gymnasts due to the interaction needed between football players. |

Gymnastics coaches should focus on developing creative skills in their trainees as gymnasts scored lowest for rule consciousness.

Links between the topic and the methodological issues

Validity	✛ Questionnaires (e.g. Eysenck's EPQ-R) contain a lie scale. Therefore, participants giving socially desirable answers may have their responses discarded, increasing validity.
	✛ An advantage of using Cattell's 16PF to measure personality is that its scales have good construct validity.
Reliability	✛ Cattell's 16PF questionnaire has good external reliability (+.70), meaning that their results are consistent when assessed again.
	✛ NEO PI-R has been assessed using the split-half method and has good internal reliability (+.86).
Sampling bias	▭ Kroll and Crenshaw used a range of different sports, however, within individual categories, the sample was limited. For example, team sports was represented by American footballers and the results might not generalise to all team sports (e.g. rugby).
Ethnocentrism	▭ Kroll and Crenshaw used sports that represent sport participation in an individualist culture (America). Collectivist cultures may participate in different sports and for different reasons.
	▭ Psychometric measures of personality may use language to describe personality traits (e.g. self-reliance) that would be less likely to make sense in collectivist cultures.

Revision booster

Find an answer you have previously written to a practice exam question, and highlight each of your points, examples and conclusions in a different colour.

This helps you monitor how much you have included of these different elements.

Links between the topic and the debates

Nature/nurture	Genetic influences may contribute about 50% to personality (Allen *et al.* 2013). Personality factors influence sporting success, so nature is likely to have an important influence on sporting ability.
	However, personality characteristics also develop due to social experience linking to sporting experience, supporting nurture.
Reductionism/ holism	Simplifying a complex behaviour (e.g. participation in sport) to a score on a personality test (e.g. 16PF) is reductionist.
	The genetic aspect of personality is only a partial explanation. Social influences (e.g. the coach) also mould personality and participation in sport. This is a more holistic analysis.
Individual/ situational explanations	Individual explanations show that people who participate in team sports have different personality characteristics (e.g. extraversion) from those who engage in individual sports.
	Situational explanations suggest that personality might be affected by the sport in which people participate (e.g. playing a team sport teaches you to be more willing to compromise).

Exam-style question examples

Component 3 Section B part (a):

(a) Outline how the key research by Kroll and Crenshaw (1970) explains personality in sport. **[10]**

Component 3 Section B part (b):

(b) Discuss the reliability of research into personality in sport. **[15]**

(b) Discuss the usefulness of research into personality in sport. **[15]**

The debates on the left are examples of how you might link the eight debates to the background and key research. In the exam be prepared to think on your feet if you can't recall how a particular debate links to the key research.

Background
Teams, coaching and leadership

Divers show task cohesion and collaboration to perform their moves at exactly the right time.

Using the background research

Consider how you could use the background research to support answers to the following questions. See exam guidance on Component 3 Section B questions on page 8.

(a) Use the research by Smith *et al.* (1979) to explain coaching effectiveness in sport. **[10]**

(b) Discuss problems conducting research into performing with others in sport. **[15]**

(c) Marc coaches a basketball team that has lost its last five matches. He wants to find a way to improve their performance.

Suggest **one** strategy Marc could use to improve the performance of his team. **[10]**

Teams	Teams have a collective identity between players who depend upon each other to achieve the group's shared objectives.
	Cohesion The tendency for a group to stick together in pursuit of its goals (Carron *et al.* 1998).
	Task cohesion Players' attraction to team objectives and their work towards those goals.
	Social cohesion Players' attraction to group social activities.
A framework for cohesion (Carron *et al.* 1985)	**Group integration-task (GI-T)** How a team works together in order to win the game.
	Group integration-social (GI-S) How likely the team is to socialise together away from sport.
	Attractions to the group-task (ATG-T) A performer's motivation towards team performance.
	Attractions to the group-social (ATG-S) How motivated a team member is to spend time with others on the team.
Group formation - a stage theory (Tuckman 1965)	**Forming stage** Team members meet one another and adjust themselves to the task and team context.
	Storming stage Teams undergo a period of interpersonal conflict, e.g. challenging for positions.
	Norming stage Team members accept each other, and establish roles and norms within the team.
	Performing stage Players fulfil their roles and team energy is channelled towards task performance.
Coaching	**Roles of the coach** Coaches are advisors to players, they need to influence players' learning and performances, build team cohesion and set players' performance goals.
	Coaching efficacy Coaches have a wide range of skills (e.g. motivation and game strategy) that affect their performers and the situation. High impact coaching is characterised by high perceived ability, high self-esteem, and enjoyment of coaching.
Leadership	**Early research** Stogdill (1948) found that decisiveness in judgement, speech fluency and interpersonal skills were important as stable leader qualities.

Interactionist theories

- Situational influences moderate the effects of specific traits (e.g. motivation) on leadership.
- Contingency models suggest personal traits match situational needs in effective leaders.

Chelladurai's (1990) multi-dimensional model Based on three types of leadership: prescribed (behaviour required by a particular team), preferred (team member preferences) and actual (largely a function of the leader's own characteristics).

The interaction between leader behaviours predicts outcome:

- If all three are congruent, then team performance and satisfaction should be high.
- If there is an interaction between prescribed and actual, then there is high team performance but not high satisfaction.
- If all three are incongruent, there is no leadership and laissez-faire occurs.

Application 1

Improving team cohesion

Improving social cohesion Coaches and athletes work together in small groups. The aim is to establish an agreed team code of behaviour regarding how teammates should react to hypothetical yet realistic situations (e.g. arriving on time for training).

Improving task cohesion Ensure that players are satisfied with their position in the team. To ensure this, coach and player can write down what they think is the player's ideal position on the team (e.g. guard in basketball), then both coach and player have clear expectations of the player's role in team success.

Does improving team cohesion work?

Usefulness It is useful for coaches to know that successful teams are more cohesive but the value of cohesiveness will vary depending on the levels or type of interaction for different sports.

Effectiveness Sports leaders must adapt their strategies. For example, developing cohesion for children is different than for adults as children view relationships and group processes as less complicated than adults (Martin *et al.* 2013).

Practicalities Team building is a longitudinal process, therefore strategies are best assessed over the long term, e.g. a whole season. Coaches need qualities (e.g. listening skills) to create an environment of support to stimulate processes of team cohesion.

Application 2

Goal setting

Locke and Latham's (2002) goal setting theory suggests if performers achieve their individual goals, the combined effect is to help the team achieve its overall goals.

Goals are directional Each player's individual goals must be directed towards the team's goals.

Goals have an energising function Goals that are challenging lead to greater effort than goals that are achieved easily.

Goals affect persistence Breaking long-term goals into shorter-term goals maintains player motivation towards the team's goals.

Goals are adaptable Sport performers use or adapt their knowledge, skills and tactics to meet their goals.

Does goal setting work?

Usefulness Goal setting increases both individual players' performance and the collective performance of the team. Goals need to be specific, measurable, agreed upon, relevant, time-based (SMART).

Effectiveness Performers need feedback that reveals progress in relation to their goals. Effectiveness of goal setting also depends on the complexity of the task, e.g. complex tasks (such as triple somersaults) need short-term learning goals to achieve effectiveness.

Practicalities There are time implications for coaches and players in meeting to discuss and agree SMART targets but this is a normal part of the coaching process. Coaches need to find mechanisms to measure the impact of goal setting on team performance.

Having clear, measurable and attainable goals helps performance. You could also apply this to your psychology revision.

How psychology contributes to the success of the economy and society ... Good teamwork and leadership produces high quality interactions and a good economy.

Exam-style question examples

Component 3 Section B part (c):

(c) Vickie is the new coach of a girls' basketball team and has noticed players seem to give up quickly when they are losing.

Outline the advice you would give to Vickie to improve her team's performance. **[10]**

(c) Hannah is a netball coach who always likes to challenge her players to improve their netball skills.

Describe **one** strategy Hannah could use to improve the performance of her netball team. **[10]**

The exam questions above are just representative examples. Read the guidance for Component 3 exam questions on page 8.

Key research

Smith *et al.* (1979) on *Coach effectiveness training*

Background

Youth enrichment in sports (YESports)

This project led to a programme called *Coach effectiveness training* (CET) that fosters mutual respect amongst coaches and players.

Aims

To make coaches develop positive interactions between themselves and their players.

Specifically, it was expected that:

- CET would promote positive changes in coaching behaviours.
- Differences in attitudes toward trained versus untrained coaches would be most pronounced for low self-esteem children.

Method

Design

Field experiment, independent measures.

IV: Coach did CET (experimental group) or no training (control).

DV: Coaches' behaviour during matches, players' perceptions of the coaches' behaviours, and attitudes towards the coach, teammates and baseball. Players' levels of self-esteem.

Sample

Thirty-one Little League Baseball coaches from Seattle, all men, mean age = 36 years, mean of 8.37 years' coaching experience.

Materials/apparatus

Coaching behaviour assessment system (CBAS) and Coopersmith self-esteem inventory (SEI).

Procedure

1. Experimental group (18 coaches) were taught guidelines to increase positive interactions between coach and players, e.g. told that increasing children's liking of a coach is not associated with greater success.
2. Behavioural feedback was given during the first two weeks using CBAS.
3. Coaches monitored their own behaviour after the first ten games of the season.
4. Coaches encouraged to give positive reinforcement to players for one in four of their behaviours.

Measurement of variables

5. Behaviours were recorded by 16 trained observers (undergraduate research assistants) who had four weeks' training on using CBAS.
6. Players' perceptions and attitudes to coaches' behaviours were evaluated using structured interviews with 325 boys.
7. Player self-esteem was measured using the SEI.

Results

Observed behavioural differences

1. Reinforcement was the only significant discriminator between the experimental and control coaches ($p < 0.05$).

Player perceptions and attitudes

Experimental group coaches were rated as giving:

2. More verbal or nonverbal rewards.
3. More encouragement following a mistake.
4. More spontaneous instruction in technique.
5. Less lack of response to a good performance.
6. Less negative verbal or nonverbal reactions after a mistake.
7. Less technical instruction in a punitive manner after a mistake.

Player self-esteem

8. Pre- and post-season analysis showed a significantly higher level of self-esteem for children with experimental group coaches ($p < 0.01$).

Team records

9. Experimental group coaches won 54.5% of their games whereas the control group won 44.7% of games.

Players said they enjoyed playing for trained coaches, had a greater desire to play for the same coach the next year, rated their coach's ability to teach baseball more highly and had a more positive relationship with their teammates.

Conclusions

CET has a significant positive influence on children's attitudes toward their coach, their teammates and to baseball.

CET has a significant positive influence on coaching behaviours of the experimental group (the trained coaches).

Trained coaches have a positive influence on the self-esteem of Little League Baseball players.

| How the key research explains ... performing with others | **Developing positive interactions and self-esteem** Coaches who developed a positive approach helped younger performers improve their self-esteem. In addition the Little League Baseball players wanted to maintain their participation. There were also more positive attitudes towards teammates and coaches. |
| | **Training leadership style** Smith *et al.*'s use of CET and CBAS showed that leaders can be trained to develop their coaching styles to suit different situations and ages of performer. |

Links between the topic and the methodological issues

Validity	✚ CBAS uses a standardised coding frame to record coaching behaviour accurately and in clear categories, e.g. general technical instruction. This increases the internal validity of the observations.
	▬ Structured interviews (predetermined questions) were used to measure players' perceptions and attitudes, therefore players could not expand on their responses. This limits validity.
Reliability	✚ The structured interviews (with a fixed set of closed response questions) means that each participant was tested in exactly the same way, i.e. the method was reliable.
	✚ The use of 16 trained observers to assess coaching behaviours in the CET means inter-rater reliability is likely to be high.
Sampling bias	✚ Smith *et al.*'s results have been replicated in other sports, e.g. basketball. This reduces sampling bias.
	▬ The number of baseball coaches was small (18 of them) and the group came only from Seattle. This is a limited sample and means it is difficult to generalise the effectiveness of the CET to other groups, e.g. women coaches.
Ethnocentrism	▬ Smith *et al.*'s results only represent an individualist culture where sport is more concerned with personal needs rather than the needs of others. Players in a collectivist culture might show greater willingness to contribute to positive relationships in the team.

Links between the topic and the debates

Nature/nurture	Trait theorists suggest a leader's innate characteristics are central to their effectiveness as a leader. This supports nature and suggests that leaders are born.
	Smith *et al.* showed that learning leadership skills using CET improved coach effectiveness (improved the interaction with and self-esteem of Little League Baseball players). This supports the nurture side of the debate.
Reductionism/ holism	Early theories of leadership were more reductionist, reducing successful leadership to, for example, physical size.
	Interactionist theories are more holistic (Chelladurai 1990). Such theories take account of the interaction between actual leadership of the coach and the prescribed behaviour demanded by the situation.
Individual/ situational explanations	Smith *et al.* provided a situational explanation, that it is the coach (rather than the individual players) who influences self-esteem and the interactions between players.
	Trait theories of leadership support the individual explanation, e.g. speech fluency and interpersonal skills are stable leader qualities that leaders can use in any situation.

Coaches have to develop a wide range of skills in order to have a positive impact on their performers, e.g. develop motivation, game strategy, technique and character.

Methodological issues are discussed in Chapter 1 and also on pages 95–96.

Revision booster

It is good to understand that CBAS categorises coaching behaviours as either reactive (e.g. positive reinforcement) or spontaneous (e.g. general encouragement).

Exam-style question examples

Component 3 Section B part (a):

(a) Outline how the key research by Smith *et al.* (1979) explains coaching in sport. **[10]**

Component 3 Section B part (b):

(b) Discuss the reliability of research into performing with others in sport. **[15]**

(b) Discuss nature/nurture in relation to research into performing with others in sport. **[15]**

Background

How an audience can facilitate or inhibit sports performance; home advantage

Triplett (1898) noticed a 'co-action effect' when cyclists raced with other cyclists – their times were faster than when racing alone. Allport called this 'social facilitation'.

Revision booster

Remember that social facilitation makes the task of winning easier because a supportive audience increases expectations of success.

Using the background research

Consider how you could use the background research to support answers to the following questions. See exam guidance on Component 3 Section B questions on page 8.

(a) Using the research by Zajonc *et al.* (1969), explain the effects of an audience in sport. **[10]**

(b) Discuss the extent to which research into audience effects in sport can be considered valid. **[15]**

(c) Mike has been selected to play rugby in front of a large crowd for the first time.

Outline **one** strategy the coach might give Mike about how to prepare for this match. **[10]**

Audience effects

Psychologists categorise the term *audience* in different ways:

Audience People watching as spectators at the event or through media at home, e.g. TV.

Co-actors Another player performing the same task but not in direct competition, e.g. rowers in the same boat.

Competitive co-actors Players doing the same task competing with each other, e.g. rowers in different boats.

Social reinforcers Others with direct influence, e.g. a coach.

Explaining social facilitation and inhibition

Social facilitation The positive influence of the presence of others on performance.

Social inhibition The impairment of performance in the presence of others.

Task complexity The mere presence of an audience tends to enhance performance when a task is either simple or well-learned. But performance decreases as the task becomes either more complex or novel.

Drive theory (Hull 1943) As arousal increases, the likelihood of producing a dominant response on the task increases. (A 'dominant response' is the reaction elicited most quickly and easily by a given stimulus.)

Alternative explanations Cottrell *et al.* (1968) suggested that social inhibition occurs when performing in front of an audience because the performer feels evaluation apprehension. It is not simply the presence of the audience that creates the anxiety but the fear of being judged.

Baron's (1986) distraction-conflict theory proposed that a performer's attentional limitations explain the effect of an audience.

Home advantage

Home advantage Occurs when the home-winning percentage minus the away-winning percentage is greater than 5% (Bray 1999).

Home advantage is attributed to the effects of the home crowd, the familiarity with the playing surface and stadium-related factors, as well as travel-related factors.

Explaining home advantage Schwartz and Barsky (1977) found that the greatest home advantage is seen in ice hockey and basketball (compared to baseball and American football) and that it is the *proximity* of the audience to the play rather than the *size* of the audience that is the crucial factor.

Other explanations include the level of noise and supportiveness generated by the density of the crowd (Nevill *et al.* 2002).

Home disadvantage Occurs when the home team wins fewer games at home than away often due to higher personal expectations of players and home supporters.

Application 1

Mental imagery and rehearsal

Mackenzie (1997) identified five categories of imagery:

1. **Motivational-specific** Visualisation of a specific event, e.g. winning a tennis match.
2. **Motivational general-mastery** Imagery of coping in difficult situations, e.g. playing in front of a large audience.
3. **Motivational general-arousal** Imagery that reflects feelings, e.g. relaxation, stress, arousal.
4. **Cognitive-specific** Visualisation of specific skills, e.g. a tennis serve.
5. **Cognitive-general** Imagery of strategy and tactics, e.g. basketball fast break.

How to carry out successful imagery Performers should be relaxed and visualise detailed, colour images of their movements. Imagery should be positive and result in a successful performance to increase self-confidence and self-efficacy. Imagery training typically lasts between three and five minutes to be most effective.

Does mental imagery and rehearsal work?

Usefulness Performers use imagery during practice and performance. Imagery is especially useful for injured players as neurons continue to fire during mental rehearsal even with no physical movement (Roure *et al.* 1998).

Effectiveness Depends on a performer's level of imagery skill and motivation. Experts regularly practise this skill and find imagery most effective because they often have to play in front of large, distracting audiences.

Practicalities Coaches should be aware of the different forms of imagery, e.g. internal versus external. Coaches should tailor mental rehearsal to suit each of their players.

During a basketball match mental imagery might involve rehearsing a successful free-throw shot. This is particularly beneficial for elite performers who are regularly exposed to the audience effects of large crowds.

Application 2

Selective attention training

Selective attention Sift through all the stimuli presented to a performer so that only the relevant information for the task is processed.

Learn to attend to relevant information Practise with distractions and with crowd noise playing in the background.

Coaches analyse videos of performance to identify cues that help performance, e.g. position of the ball toss in tennis. These cues can then be learned and better recognised during actual performance.

Does selective attention training work?

Usefulness Used in all stages of learning but most useful for experienced performers as they know what to look for when facing an opponent, e.g. table tennis players might focus on the different grips used by opponents.

Effectiveness Arousal levels affect alertness and the ability to select appropriate cues. Overarousal can lead to processing too many stimuli, slowing down the selective attention process.

Practicalities The quality of coaching is very important for beginners, so coaches should be suitably qualified. Improving selective attention is especially important for elite players.

Exam-style question examples

Component 3 Section B part (c):

(c) Laura is a novice golfer who is always anxious about her tee shot at the first hole with lots of people watching.

Outline **one** strategy Laura could use to help her hit a good tee shot.   **[10]**

(c) Emma is a county-level basketballer, who finds that the audience distracts her when taking free throws.

Outline the advice you would give to Emma to improve her focus when taking free throws.   **[10]**

Key research

Zajonc *et al.* (1969) on *Audience effects*

Background

Gates and Allee (1933) suggested that poor performance in group situations is due to distraction caused by others but also just due to their presence.

However, the presence of others may lead to *improvements* in performance.

Aims

- To test the drive theory of social facilitation.
- To determine if the mere presence of other cockroaches facilitates or inhibits performance times for a simple and complex task.

Method

Design

Laboratory experiments, independent measures.

IVs:

Experiment 1 Cockroaches: 1. Alone or in pairs, no audience. 2. Alone or in pairs, with an audience. 3. In a maze (complex task) or a straight runway (simple task).

Experiment 2 All cockroaches ran alone: 1. Mirrors on the walls. 2. Odour of other cockroaches present. 3. No distractions (control condition).
[In each group half were in a maze and half were in a straight runway.]

DV: Time taken to reach the goal box.

Sample

Experiment 1: 72 female cockroaches. Experiment 2: 180 female cockroaches.

Materials/apparatus

20 × 20 × 20-inch clear Plexiglas cube that formed either a runway or a maze. A 150-watt floodlight.

Procedure

Experiment 1

1. Cockroaches' dominant response was to run when the light turned on (fear of light).

2. Time recorded for cockroaches to get from the starting box to the goal box.

3. Cockroaches were either alone or in a co-action condition (in pairs), with or without an audience, doing simple or complex task.

4. Cockroaches were given ten consecutive trials, separated by one-minute intervals.

Experiment 2

5. Condition 1: 60 cockroaches ran with mirrors along runway walls.

6. Condition 2: 60 cockroaches were exposed to the smell of other cockroaches.

7. Condition 3 (alone): 60 cockroaches had neither mirrors nor odour as a distraction.

8. Timings were taken as in Experiment 1.

Results

Experiment 1

1. The complex (maze) co-action condition was slowest for those running with an audience.

2. The simple (runway) co-action condition was fastest with or without an audience.

Experiment 2

3. Total running times for the mirror and odour conditions were both significantly different from the alone condition ($p < 0.05$).

4. Total running times for the complex (maze) and simple (runway) were significantly different from the alone condition ($p < 0.001$).

Summary

5. Maze performance was impaired for both co-action and audience conditions, but runway performance was facilitated by co-action/audience compared to solitary performance.

6. Cockroaches in mirror and odour conditions took longer on the runway than the alone condition.

7. Cockroaches in maze mirror condition were quicker than alone condition but slower for odour condition.

Sprinters' dominant response is to run as fast as possible after the gun and the cockroaches are similar in trying to escape from light.

Conclusions

Mere presence of others for co-action and audience conditions leads to dominant response enhancement.

Performance on simple tasks is improved and performance in complex tasks is impaired.

Data supports the drive theory of social facilitation.

| How the key research explains ... audience effects | Zajonc *et al.*'s research supports the theory that arousal from the presence of others leads to social facilitation or social inhibition. |

Drive theory High arousal will have different effects depending on whether a sports performer is an expert or not:

- Expert sport performers perform well in high arousal conditions because their dominant response is likely to be the correct one, demonstrating social facilitation.
- Novice performers are less likely to perform well in high arousal conditions because their dominant response is likely to be weak, demonstrating social inhibition.

High arousal creates social facilitation for simple, gross motor skills, e.g. throwing a cricket ball overarm. Lower arousal is necessary for social facilitation when fine motor skills are required, e.g. throwing darts.

Links between the topic and the methodological issues

Validity	✛ Zajonc *et al.* carried out research under laboratory conditions providing a high control of variables. This increases validity as other extraneous variables (e.g. light intensity) were controlled.
Reliability	✛ High control of variables enables the procedure to be standardised, e.g. always a one-minute inter-trial interval. This increases reliability.
	✛ Schwartz and Barsky (1977) collected quantitative data on home advantage, which enabled the research to be easily replicated, so reliability (and validity) could be demonstrated.
Sampling bias	▭ Zajonc *et al.*'s use of cockroaches is problematic when trying to generalise the results because the arousal experienced by an Olympic 100m sprinter will be different from that induced by the light phobia of the cockroach.
Ethnocentrism	▭ Audiences' support for teams and homefield advantage is seen from an individualist perspective of competitiveness. Non-individualist audiences may be more reserved and home advantage less pronounced.

Links between the topic and the debates

Reductionism/ holism	Research oversimplifies the factors at work in sport, e.g. the home advantage may not be due to arousal but due to the away team's hostility (e.g. committing more fouls) leading the referee to favour the home team. This is a more holistic approach.
Individual/ situational explanations	Zajonc *et al.* used the same cockroach species to control individual factors, and concluded that differences in performance were due to the situational factors (the presence of other cockroaches).
	Schwartz and Barsky provide a situational explanation as game location can influence whether teams win or lose.
Psychology as a science	Highly controlled, objective conditions in Zajonc *et al.*'s study meant that cause and effect could be inferred between the independent and dependent variables, e.g. maze or straight runway caused running times.

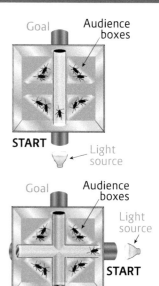

Zajonc et al.*'s apparatus. The simple 'runway' task is on the top and the complex 'maze' task is on the bottom.*

Revision booster

Students very often forget to link the Zajonc *et al.* results to sport and just write about cockroaches. Always remember to show application of your knowledge by including sport examples.

Debates are explained on pages 90–94.

Exam-style question examples

Component 3 Section B part (a):

(a) Outline how the key research by Zajonc *et al.* (1969) explains the effects of an audience in sport. **[10]**

Component 3 Section B part (b):

(b) Discuss the reliability of research into audience effects in sport. **[15]**

(b) Evaluate research into audience effects in sport, in relation to psychology as a science. **[15]**

overt observation Participant is aware of being observed. **23**

participant observation Observer is also a participant in the behaviour being observed. **23, 100**

positive correlation A relationship between two co-variables such that as the value of one co-variable increases, this is accompanied by a corresponding increase in the other co-variable. **12, 28, 48, 78, 86, 138**

qualitative data Data in words or pictures, non-numerical. **18, 31, 42, 45, 47, 53, 63, 67, 73, 75, 77, 79, 80, 83, 85, 89, 184, 203**

quantitative data Data in numbers, i.e. quantities. **13, 15, 18, 31, 42, 43, 45, 47, 49, 53, 55, 57, 59, 63, 65, 67, 69, 75, 77, 79, 80, 85, 89, 203, 213**

quasi-experiment Experimenter does not manipulate the independent variable. The dependent variable may be measured in a laboratory. **14, 27, 48, 49, 66, 68, 72, 73, 74, 75, 78, 79, 84, 88, 104, 118, 124, 144, 145, 168, 172, 173, 204**

questionnaire Respondents record their own answers to predetermined questions. **6, 12, 14, 16, 18, 19, 20, 21, 29, 39, 52, 53, 64, 65, 96, 100, 120, 148, 168, 169, 172, 173, 176, 177, 180, 181, 189, 197, 198, 200, 201, 204, 205**

random sampling Produced by using a random technique such that every member of the target population has an equal chance of being selected. **17, 84**

rating scale Respondents are asked to give an assessment of their views using a set of ascending numbers, e.g. from 1 to 5 where 5 represents very positive and 1 represents very negative. **6, 18, 24, 25, 63, 68, 156, 176, 177**

reliability A measure of consistency both within a set of scores or items (internal reliability) and also over time such that it is possible to obtain the same results on subsequent occasions when the measure is used (external reliability). **20, 21, 22, 23, 45, 47, 49, 51, 53, 57, 59, 65, 67, 69, 71, 73, 75, 77, 79, 85, 87, 95, 96, 101, 107, 115, 119, 121, 125, 129, 133, 137, 138, 141, 145, 149, 153, 157, 161, 165, 168, 169, 173, 177, 181, 185, 189, 193, 197, 201, 205, 209, 213**

repeated measures design Each participant takes part in every condition under test. **25, 35, 37, 39, 52, 56, 57, 64, 65, 68, 78, 128, 184, 196**

replicable/replication The opportunity to repeat an investigation under exactly the same conditions in order to test the method used (reliability) or results (validity). **27, 38, 39, 50, 57, 69, 79, 95, 96, 129, 153, 209, 213**

sample A selection of participants taken from the target population being studied and intended to be representative of that population. **6, 7, 9, 10, 12, 15, 16, 17, 19, 34, 36, 39, 42, 43, 44, 45, 46, 47, 48, 49, 52, 53, 54, 55, 56, 57, 58, 59, 60, 62, 63, 64, 65, 66, 67, 69, 70, 72, 73, 74, 75, 76, 78, 79, 82, 84, 85, 86, 87, 88, 89, 93, 96, 100, 106, 107, 115, 120, 124, 125, 128, 132, 133, 136, 137, 140, 141, 144, 148, 149, 153, 156, 157, 164, 165, 168, 169, 172, 173, 176, 177, 180, 184, 188, 189, 193, 196, 197, 200, 201, 204, 205, 208, 209, 212**

self-report Data collection techniques where a participant describes their behaviour, for example questionnaires, interviews or diary studies. **18, 19, 20, 21, 22, 26, 42, 65, 82, 95, 100, 116, 145, 169, 177, 188**

self-selected sampling Produced by asking for volunteers. **6, 12, 15, 17, 44, 58, 59, 84, 88, 125, 132, 148, 197**

semi-structured interview Some questions are predetermined but also new questions are developed as the interview proceeds. **12, 19, 66, 88, 89**

snowball sampling Relies on referrals from initial participants to generate additional participants. **6, 17**

standard deviation (SD) A measure of dispersion that assesses the spread of data around the mean. The SD is the square root of the variance, which means that it is expressed in the same units as the data points themselves. **30, 31, 33, 58, 120**

standardisation/standardised procedures Ensuring that all procedures are the same for every participant so that their performances are comparable. **20, 38, 39, 45, 47, 49, 50, 54, 57, 59, 69, 79, 84, 96, 101, 120, 121, 125, 129, 133, 137, 141, 145, 149, 152, 153, 157, 177, 181, 185, 193, 197, 201, 204, 209, 213**

structured interview Predetermined questions delivered by an interviewer who does not probe beyond the answers received but may answer straightforward questions from the interviewee. **19, 123, 152, 188, 208, 209**

structured observation The researcher uses various 'systems' to organise observations, such as a sampling technique and behavioural categories. **22, 23**

target population The group of people that the researcher is interested in. The group of people from whom a sample is drawn. The group of people about whom generalisations can be made. **16, 17, 27, 34, 43, 47, 59, 87, 96, 107, 181**

time sampling Recording behaviours at regular intervals (such as every 5 seconds or 8 minutes), or taking a sample at different times of the day or month. **6, 22**

unstructured interview No questions are decided in advance. **19**

unstructured observation Using no system to record behaviours. **23**

validity/validated Refers to whether an observed effect is a genuine one. This includes the extent to which a researcher has measured what he/she intended to measure (internal validity) and the extent to which the results can be applied beyond the research setting (external validity). **8, 11, 18, 21, 22, 23, 26, 27, 31, 43, 45, 49, 50, 53, 55, 57, 59, 63, 65, 67, 69, 70, 73, 77, 83, 87, 89, 95, 96, 97, 101, 107, 115, 118, 119, 121, 122, 125, 126, 128, 129, 133, 137, 141, 145, 149, 150, 153, 157, 161, 165, 169, 173, 174, 177, 181, 185, 186, 189, 190, 192, 193, 194, 197, 198, 201, 202, 205, 209, 213**

variance A measure of dispersion that assesses the spread of data around the mean. **30, 35, 156**

Cover photo: © Shutterstock: topseller

© Shutterstock: p4 Standard Studio; p5 BarboS, NAR studio; p9 SNeG17, Petr Toman, Stmool; p10 Valentina Kalashnikova, Number1411; p11 cammep, ImageFlow; p16 jan kranendonk; p17 Elaine Barker; p18 abimages; p19 Per Grunditz; p20 iQoncept, kirbyedy; p21 Aha-Soft; p22 mvc_stock; p23 polygraphus; p24 Trutta; p25 RedKoala, glyph; p26 Jacob Lund, p27 Prazis Images; p28 WAYHOME studio; p29 FGC; p30 tanuha2001, p31 fyv6561, BarboS; p32 Rena Schild; p33 f11photo; p34 Gearstd; p35 Natashka-mamashka; p36 iamtui7; p37 dencg, Monkey Business Images; p38 Ellerslie; p39 delcarmat; p40 Elnur; p41 Rawpixel.com; p43 ploy2907; p44 Maridav; p45 Lightspring; p47 Clari Massimiliano; p48 Krakenimages.com, p49 Andrey_Popov; p50 Lightspring; p51 Andrey_Popov; p52 Monkey Business Images; p53 CC7; p55 Stokkete; p56 Chendongshan; p57 G-Stock Studio; p58 Reinhold Leitner; p59 Standret; p60 aastock; p61 Proxima Studio; p62 Just dance; p63 wongstock; p64 bubutu; p65 JivkoM; p66 Victoria Denisova; p67 Rob Wilson; p68 MIA Studio; p69 Krakenimages.com; p70 sciencepics; p71 Sanja Karin Music; p73 Fabio Berti; p74 Daisy Daisy; p75 Orawan Pattarawimonchai; p79 Chris Jenner; p80 kwest; p81 WAYHOME studio; p82 Gr8t Shots; p83 Michelle D. Milliman; p85 Ann Haritonenko; p86 melissamn; p87 Everett Collection; p88 Martial Red; p89 J.K2507; p90 Soify; p91 kdshutterman; p92 Inked Pixels; p93 desdemona72; p94 antibydni; p95 Fesus Robert; p96 m.mphoto; p97 Michael Stokes; p98 Malatilar; p99 Stokkete; p100 gorkem demir; p101 Monkey Business Images; p102 zhu difeng, Photographee.eu; p103 Eric Isselee; p104 Pikovit, Shen max; p106 wavebreakmedia; p107 nobeastsofierce; p108 Ravital; p109 Maridav; p110 Kurit afshen; p111 Nubefy; p112 Febrina noor prihandini, Soffi Sk; p113 Everett Collection; p114 Eric Isselee; p115 HowLettery; p116 Linda Bestwick; p117 Yuganov Konstantin; p118 Levranii; p120 szefei; p121 Anatoly Vartanov; p122 Lopolo; p123 Karramba Production; p125 fotosparrow; p127 chomplearn; p129 bezikus; p130 Monkey Business Images; p131 Alexandra Lande; p132 Vladimir Prusakov; p133 Somnuek saelim; p134 Prostock-studio; p135 Robert Kneschke; p136 Halfpoint; p138 Brenda Rocha - Blossom; p139 ayelet-keshet; p140 DRN Studio; p141 Prostock-studio; p142 3Dstock; p143 Bamboo Gold Studio; p144 ShotPrime Studio; p145 Lightspring; p146 Alexander Supertramp; p147 PRESSLAB; p148 New Africa; p149 Irina Levitskaya; p150 Photographee.eu; p151 ninefotostudio; p152 Kzenon; p153 Ann Kosolapova; p154 Khakimullin Aleksandr; p155 Yayayoyo; p156 AndriiKoval; p157 F8 studio; p158 Jakub Kramny; p159 Marcin Mazurkiewicz; p160 Simone Hogan; p161 Stephane Bidouze; p162 Rebekah Zemansky; p163 artellia; p164 Ilija Erceg; p165 Volodymyr Herasymchuk; p166 Alexander Sorokopud; p167 puhhha; p168 Arseniy Shemyakin Photo; p169 Sam72; p171 Wirestock Creators; p172 xyfen; p173 Prostock-studio; p174 HitToon; p175 Hryshchyshen Serhii; p176 photka; p177 photka; p178 ucchie79; p179 Pressmaster; p180 sfam_photo; p181 Friends Stock; p182 Tungphoto; p183 romakoma; p184 Derya Cakirsoy; p185 Artorn Thongtukit; p186 Ozgur Coskun; p187 Light Bulb Studio; p188 Krailath; p189 Shift Drive; p190 mooinblack; p191 Microgen; p192 Jimmie48 Photography; p193 Philip Bird LRPS CPAGB; p194 Sonya illustration; p195 Corepics VOF; p196 ivanfolio; p197 Featureflash Photo Agency; p198 LiveMedia; p199 Anatoliy Karlyuk; p200 sportpoint; p201 Greg Epperson; p202 Agris Krusts; p203 Cosmin Iftode; p204 Sararoom Design; p205 Salty View; p206 Paolo Bona; p207 Dmitry Argunov; p208 Steve Bower; p209 muzsy; p210 Gaie Uchel; p211 Nadir Keklik; p212 dotshock

All other illustrations © Illuminate Publishing